One Voice Raised

A Triumph Over Rape

One Voice Raised

A TRIUMPH OVER RAPE

JENNIFER WHEATLEY-WOLF

with

CHIEF INVESTIGATOR DAVID H. CORDLE, SR.

CURRENT TOME PUBLISHING
Arlington, Virginia

For information about permission to reproduce selections from this book, write to: Current Tome Publishing, 3519 13th Street, North, Arlington, VA 22201

"Angel From Montgomery" words and music by John Prine, Copyright © 1971 (Renewed) WALDEN MUSIC, INC. and SOUR GRAPES MUSIC, All Rights Administered by WB MUSIC CORP. All Rights Reserved. Used by Permission.

All quotes from *The Capital* and *The Capital: HometownAnnapolis.com.* All Rights Reserved. Used by Permission.

"How the Legs Reveal What the Mind Wants to Do," *http://westsidetoastmasters.com.* All Rights Reserved. Used by Permission.

Quote from Disney's *Pooh's Grand Adventure: The Search for Christopher Robin.* All Rights Reserved. Used by Permission.

First Edition

ISBN 978-0-615-56247-6

Manufacturing by Create Space • Amazon.com
Book design by Sherry Audette Morrow/Creative Endeavors
Front cover photograph by Jennifer Wheatley-Wolf, January 17, 2010, Annapolis, MD.
Back cover photographs by Jennifer Wheatley-Wolf and William Johns.
Evidence photographs from Annapolis Police Department case files, Chief Investigator David H. Cordle, Sr., Investigator William Johns, and Jennifer Wheatley-Wolf. All photos Used by Permission.

Current Tome Publishing
3519 13th Street, North
Arlington, VA 22201

DEDICATION

For Marcus, my husband, who was the last to know.
Thanks for being by my side to see me through this
and for always believing in me.

To my family and friends: I appreciate that you walked this
long road with me and supported me all the way.

~ J. W. W.

First and last is Jennifer Anne Wheatley.
Her courage, perseverance, understanding, and tolerance
of the years she spent enduring the emotional rollercoaster
of this investigation is a tribute to all victims of violent
crime, for those cases solved and unsolved.

May this book be a help to all who read these pages.

~ D. H. C.

CONTENTS

THE TRIAL

ILLUSTRATIONS

Truth is stranger than fiction, but it is because
Fiction is obliged to stick to possibilities; Truth isn't.

~ Mark Twain ~

THE CRIME

*"Your life is so much more than the events of one night,
And it is more than the days since. Your story is one of hope and justice.
It's friendships and finding love and creating a life with Marcus.
It's your family and friends and your beautiful art and the beauty you
find in the everyday things. Your spirit is beautiful."*

~Jackie ~

1

The Beginning

Early in the morning of August 21, 1988, an unknown assailant climbed onto the balcony to the open door of my home, crept down the stairs, entered my first floor bedroom, and waited for me in the dark. As he grabbed me and pulled something tight around my throat, I was sure my life was over.

I call this my story, but it really isn't just mine. Much of this story started long before I was sexually assaulted and raped. However, it took twenty-one years for me to see the connections. It is usually only in retrospect, I think, that we are finally made aware of how deliberately ordered the events of our lives can truly be.

Our lives often appear to be a seemingly random group of occurrences that take us through one journey after another. We often do not understand how an event one day or an encounter with a stranger the next becomes a more significant meeting down the road in our future. It is rare to see how a simple decision and the timing of that decision can tie experiences together. For me to be able to witness the coming together of what appeared to be random choices, it took a terrifying encounter with a stranger and advances in technology to complete a puzzle left undone for so many years. This was nothing short of a miracle.

For twenty years, I believed the man who raped me would remain a mystery. I never saw his face. There was not much evidence. I reconciled myself with the events of that night although I never really stopped wondering who the person was. Even though my case had been revisited several times by Chief

Investigator for the State's Attorney's Office in Annapolis, David H. Cordle, Sr., over the years, no one was arrested or charged with committing the crime. It didn't take long for me to believe that no one would ever be arrested.

Years passed, and I began to think of the events of that horrible night and the subsequent piles of investigative paperwork as "The Case." It no longer really involved me at all. I had moved beyond that night and gone on with my life. I never imagined I would sit in a courtroom surrounded by friends and family and tell of the events as they had occurred.

I was asked recently what I want to gain from writing my story and what I hoped someone would take away from its reading. I am taking advantage of the opportunity, while the events are still fresh in my mind, to purge myself of the last remnants of this crime. My writing is cathartic. It is also a challenge, and I like to challenge myself. However, I also believe it is much more.

I am writing this story for all rape victims in the hope that the importance of reporting the crime is made clear. I hope those who have a similar story, but have lost faith, will once again believe that good does eventually triumph over evil and not give up hope. This book is for those who have lost the ability to believe in themselves and the kindness of others, who doubt they are strong enough to re-assemble their lives after a horrible encounter, and for those who have forgotten it's okay to stumble, forgive yourself, and get back to living.

The Bureau of Justice Statistics reports that the majority of rapes and sexual assaults perpetrated against women and girls in the United States between 1992 and 2000 were not reported to the police. Only thirty-six percent of rapes, thirty-four percent of attempted rapes, and twenty-six percent of sexual assaults were reported.

Unfortunately, this all but gives the sexual predator permission to strike again. Because a rapist knows he stands a good chance of getting away with his crimes, he will continue to terrorize, sexually assault, and rape women. The odds of winning in Vegas are not this good.

It is important to report these crimes because by doing so we send the message to all rapists that they will eventually be caught. It never occurred to me not to report my attack. My assailant had to be stopped and I intended to do my part in apprehending him. Even though catching the man who was responsible for my rape was delayed and the process of getting to court was frustrating, knowing he was finally off the street and unable to hurt anyone else was worth the wait.

I went though a period of darkness following my rape. I believed I did not have anything left for a heartless God to take from me. I do not think of myself as being particularly religious. Failing to find a reason to get up in the morning is my idea of losing all faith and hope.

As I prepared to enter the courtroom to testify against my rapist, I realized how the prosecution of this crime from so long ago, and seeing my assailant for the first time, were only part of a bigger picture. It wasn't until I was in the courtroom surrounded by friends and family that I knew how empowering the experience of testifying against my rapist would be. By testifying in court against him, I was able to take charge of *me* again.

As I was telling my story to the court, I understood I was giving a voice to countless women who would not or could not speak for themselves against this man and other men like him.

I suppose a big piece of this puzzle is the very fact that I have written this book. Although I have attempted to write a short story or two over the years, I do not call myself a writer. I am a visual artist, a painter, a quilter, and a photographer. Maybe it is because of my eye for detail that I am telling this story. I can clearly see now how the puzzle pieces are interconnected. It has only been through writing this story that I realize just how bound to my attacker the words in this book really are. I believe it was not only his selfish attack twenty-one years ago, but also the way *he* chose to end the story, that made it possible for me to write these words at all.

When we find ourselves in the middle of a jumbled collection of details, it is impossible to make sense of the total picture. It is only when we stand back far enough that each piece of the puzzle comes together to make the whole image clear. In many ways, all of us involved could see how our own piece fit into the whole picture, but none of us guessed just what the last piece — the one that completed the image — would be.

The links between people and the seemingly random events that led to solving "The Case" had to unfold just the way they did to reach its conclusion. To remove any piece of the puzzle anywhere along the way, to change the timing of anything, would have, I believe, drastically changed the outcome.

The elements of this puzzle consisted of the crime, advances in science and technology, and the disbursement of funds that had recently become available for retesting cold-case evidence. Most importantly, its solution depended on the dedication of a few to a job that extends far beyond the walls of an office. Its outcome was about friendships both old and new. As I stepped into the courtroom on January 13, 2010, I had yet to realize that elements of the story that was about to unfold had woven their way through my life, reaching all of the way back to my childhood.

2

For Starters

$\mathcal{A}$nnapolis, Maryland, an historic city on the Chesapeake Bay, was in the late '50s and '60s a small city where everyone knew everyone. A weekly street sweeper came by year-round. The mosquito-sprayer truck came around every week during the humid summer months to blow huge plumes of insecticide through the neighborhood. We loved when "Bug Man," as we liked to call him, drove down the street in his huge gray truck, and we would run behind, chasing him through the neighborhood. In the winter, we went sledding down a very steep road all the kids called Dog Hill. In summer, we broke out the strap-on skates to speed down this paved road. Dog Hill was aptly named for the gazillion dogs of questionable breed that chased everything that dared to move. To approach this street required ten percent determination and ninety percent sheer stupidity. The dogs owned that hill. They stood guard and on alert for intruders. Occasionally, and only after sending a scout out ahead, were we able to take full advantage of its paved slope.

At the bottom of Dog Hill sat an abandoned house that I always thought was haunted. A huge house, it looked like a dilapidated version of Tara from *Gone with the Wind*. I imagine it was beautiful at one point in history, but I had never seen it in its prime. I was never brave enough to go inside and I don't know of anyone who did. However, I certainly had no trouble conjuring up tall tales of what one might discover once they stepped over the threshold of that place. Eventually, the old wreck of a house was torn down and upscale condominiums were built on the land. I would live in one of those condominiums with my mother when I was twenty-eight and twenty-nine years old.

When I was a kid, the neighbors looked out for each other, and houses were rarely locked unless the owners were going away for a stretch. I did not get a key to my childhood home until high school, and that only after a suspected prowler tripped over our grill in what Mom and Dad supposed was an attempted break-in gone sour. This incident prompted the duplication and distribution of house keys. Honestly, I do not remember ever using mine. It was not until after I'd graduated from college that locking doors became habit. Annapolis had grown over the years and the incidences of crime had grown as well.

I have two brothers and two sisters. All are older than me except for my brother Greg. Greg and I were pretty close growing up. Many of my friends were his friends and vice versa. Greg introduced me to mini bikes, fishing, and cigarettes. My older brother, Todd, took to the yacht yards in our neighborhood and learned sailing and boat rigging at an early age. Although I learned to swim as soon as I could walk and I was considered a "water-rat," I never caught the sailing bug. I enjoyed the fine art of being a deck ornament rather than the hard work of actually propelling the vehicle.

My sister Mollie is a few years older than I, and we had just enough of an age difference that she preferred hanging out with her girlfriends instead of me. I didn't know my sister Deborah at all while I was growing up. She babysat for us when Mom and Dad went out. Except for showing up to the dinner table every night, and being first in line for the shower/bath rotation, I never saw her. She had moved out by the time I got interesting enough to talk to. It wasn't until years later that I got to know my older siblings.

I had a couple of friends when I was young, but I wasn't what anyone would call popular or pretty. Elementary school was seven years at St. Mary's — actually eight years, if you count a repeat of the second grade. I lost my hearing for several years during my childhood, and although I compensated for the loss by reading lips like a pro, that didn't get me through the *Dick and Jane* stories. Learning to read was really a bear when I couldn't hear the sounds my mouth was making. I eventually did learn to read, but I had to be kept back a grade since I was so far behind everyone else in my class. It was a sad time for me. All of the friends I'd made in first and second grade went on without me and I had to start over with a new group of strange kids. I did have corrective surgery for my hearing loss and got most of it back. However, because of the surgery, I was the only kid in my class who was allowed to — no, *instructed* — to chew gum in school. After my ear surgery, chewing gum kept the Eustachian tubes clear. That was great!

During the summer of 1972, my sister Mollie got a babysitting job for a week in Ocean City for three kids she watched on a regular basis. She asked me if I wanted to come along and help her out.

"Sure," I said. Who wouldn't want to spend a week at the beach? The kids were little. One was an infant and the other two were toddlers. "Okay, no problem, I would love to go." There would be lots of beach time and long naps for the kids. The parents had mentioned that we would be able to spend some time on our own in the evenings. It sounded like fun.

It was the worst trip to the beach of my life.

Hurricane Agnes picked that week to wreak havoc on the east coast. From June 19th through June 25th, it pummeled every coastline city with torrential rain and wind. By the time it reached the Ocean City area, it had merged with a non-tropical low and the combined storms raged all the way up to New York. The day we arrived at Ocean City was sunny, breezy and perfect. By the next morning, gray skies had taken over and rain had begun to fall. I think it was that day when I got my second-ever menstrual period. I was fortunate to have my sister there to instruct me on how to survive my "monthly visitor" by taking Midol for cramps and using the "modern convenience" of Tampax. The whole week, all I could focus on was my unbelievably bad luck.

Mollie did most of the babysitting. I tried to help her, but I went nuts from the combination of menstrual cramping, screaming bored kids, and rainwater turning streets into rivers and parking lots into lakes. We were supposed to have had some free time in the evenings, but we never got a break from the kids. When the parents came home around dinnertime, it was too dangerous to go outside. We had no option but to stay put.

Our last day at the beach dawned with brilliant blue skies and warm breezes. The mother offered us the day off. Finally, we could go to the boardwalk. The streets and parking lots were still covered in water, but it was no longer being blown around to create its own rip tide. We could make it to the beach and cruise the shops. That was all we cared about.

Mollie and I headed to Boardwalk Fries, the Salt Water Taffy candy store, and the souvenir shops. We had fun and, most importantly, we regained some sanity walking along the beach and going in and out of the packed stores. I had some spending money with me, money I had earned from previous babysitting jobs. I bought a box of taffy, a box of tampons, and then I splurged and bought myself a T-shirt. Since we had been cooped up the entire miserable week, I was ready to treat myself.

I had never purchased an article of clothing before, so this was a momentous occasion. With the tens of thousands of shirts to choose from, I settled on a plain green shirt. It was nothing fancy. There was no printed design on the front or back. The price was right. I could afford to buy it. This T-shirt would be a favorite of mine for about fifteen years. After it developed a small hole, instead of tossing it out, I used it in my car as a rag for the windshield and a sun-shield for the steering wheel.

We made it home with our sanity intact. I am not positive, but I think it was during this babysitting experience that the idea of never having kids might have started to formulate in the back of my mind. Being cooped up all week with three little ones was more than I could handle. Funny that

I had those thoughts, as I had just become "A Woman." What I didn't realize was the role the T-shirt I had bought would play in my adult life.

I believe I was born to be an artist. Going back to school after summers off as an elementary student meant getting a new box of crayons and pencils with good erasers. I remember being given math problems in elementary school. My teachers would tell us to fold our papers into six or eight squares. Then we wrote, with our oversized pencils, a simple math equation in the top of each square. We were asked to draw out the equation with our crayons using apples, squares, stars, etc. I would spend an endless amount of time getting my small drawings just right, but I did not do as well when it came to getting the actual answers correct.

After spending eight years in grammar school with the same classmates and friends, my parents made the decision to move me and some of my siblings from private to public school. Eighth grade in Annapolis Junior High School was divided into split sessions. I, thank heavens, got to attend the afternoon session. It was probably the easiest school year of my life. The classes I had to take were essentially a repeat of seventh grade. School was finally easy for me.

The eighth grade was my first real experience with changing rooms for classes. During seventh grade at St. Mary's, we'd spent one half of the days in one classroom and the other half in another. Annapolis Junior High seemed huge, and getting lost was easy. Our homeroom class was for taking attendance. Everyone with a last name that started with the letters W, X, Y, and Z met in my homeroom in the morning. We answered "here" when our names were called, and then scattered to various classrooms. I did not know it then, but my husband-to-be was among the kids in this homeroom class.

All of my experience with crayons paid off. By the time I got to high school, I was pretty good at drawing and loved all the art classes.

I graduated with honors in Fine Art from Annapolis Senior High School in 1977, and a Bachelor of Fine Arts from Virginia Commonwealth University in 1983, with a major in painting and printmaking.

After I graduated from VCU in the mid-1980s, I worked as a pressman for a stationery gift shop in Annapolis. The shop was owned by a married couple, Carl and Nancy. Carl had been a regional manager with the Chart House and often worked at their Annapolis restaurant. Nancy's attic stationery business was growing and she wanted to expand. Since she needed a manager and Carl had experience, they opened a store on Maryland Avenue. I was hired to run an A.B. Dick Offset Press. I found learning how to use a printing press fun, but once I had the "how-tos" down pat, it didn't take long for me to get bored with the job. It was not very challenging work and the pay was not great. Occasionally a special order would come in for artwork that the owner could not do, and Nancy would turn the assignment over to me. However, that didn't happen often enough to keep me happy.

After a little over a year, I quit my job as a pressman and went to work in the kitchen of a local restaurant. In addition to working in the restaurant, I continued to draw detailed pen and ink sketches and pencil or pastel portraits. Often, I would do commissioned portraits for people from photographs of their loved ones. This would put a little extra money in my pocket, but I made most of my money from my full time job.

An old family friend owns McGarvey's Saloon in Annapolis. At the time, Mike was an airline pilot who, for years, had dreamed of owning his own pub. After construction was completed, my sister Deborah worked there as one of the bookkeepers and my younger brother Greg and cousin J. worked in the kitchen during their junior high and high school years. I worked at McGarvey's on two separate occasions. I was a cook in their kitchen just after graduating high school in 1977 and again in 1985, after I quit working as a pressman.

In 1985, I started working in the prep kitchen and, after a few months, I was offered a position on the floor in the seafood raw bar. It was here that I learned how to shuck oysters and clams and prepare some simple seafood dishes such as Oysters Rockefeller, Clams Casino, and Shrimp Scampi. Although the job was smelly and dirty and I would be covered in oyster, shrimp, mussel, and clam juices by the end of the night, the pay was good and I made lots of tips. Working a regular schedule meant getting to know many of the other employees and becoming friends with some of them.

Weekend nights behind the raw bar were "ladies' nights." I worked with another girl who was a student at St. John's College. Heidi was always on time and I loved working with her. She was lots of fun and together, the two of us could usually garner quite a few tips. Our shift started at four o'clock in the afternoon and overlapped the morning's opening crew by about half an hour. I got worried one night when she had not shown up by 4:30 and I could not reach her by phone. We ran a Friday night oyster special from 4:00-7:00pm when oysters were a dollar a dozen. I was swamped because the day crew had already taken off for the night, leaving me alone to fill the growing stack of orders.

Around five o'clock, Heidi ran in, full of apologies. As she picked up an oyster knife and joined me in shucking, she told me her live-in boyfriend would not allow her to bring her work shoes into the apartment they shared. "They look terrible and they stink!" she said. Heidi would leave them on the porch by the front door. That afternoon, when she was heading out for work, she could only find one of her shoes. She searched all over until finally she saw two cats playing in an alley down the block. Upon closer observation, she realized they had carried off her tennis shoe and were attacking it as if it were a live tuna.

There were a couple of guys who worked the day shift at the raw bar. I hardly ever worked during the day, but occasionally someone would need to change his or her schedule and I would fill in. One of the guys working behind the raw bar, George, became an acquaintance. We didn't date or anything; our relationship was confined to work. The only time we spent together outside of work was when George helped me move some things out of my parents' house when they put it on the market.

My parents sold the house I grew up in around Christmas of 1985 after living there for twenty-six years. In the early part of 1986, they moved into a four-story condominium at Horn Point at the foot of Dog Hill. Shortly after moving in, they divorced and Dad eventually moved to California. Mom stayed in the condo, but didn't want to be there alone. After a few months by herself, she asked me to move in with her. I took her up on the offer.

Chesapeake Landing was a nice upper-class development in a gated community. I set up my bedroom on the ground floor. It was great. I had a huge bedroom with my own bathroom. A sliding glass door opened to a patio where I could sit and enjoy the sun in the summer. During the warm months, I often sat outside on the patio amongst my large assortment of plants and worked on pen and ink drawings. In addition, these doors let in lots of light in the winter so my plants were happy year round.

I also had a studio on the fourth floor. A skinny spiral staircase led up to a large open room. Mom stored needlework yarn up there, but there was not much else in the room. It was wonderful for painting because two large skylights let in bright natural light.

The living room, kitchen, and dining room were on the second floor and my mom's bedroom was on the third. The living room had sliding glass doors that opened to a balcony. The second floor balcony was just above the carport in the back where I would park my twelve-year-old Datsun B-210. Mom always parked in the garage just to the left of my car.

When I moved in with Mom, one of the neighbors complained to her about her teenage daughter making so much noise and leaving beer cans all over Horn Point beach. Mom laughed and said, "She's twenty-eight and she doesn't have to sneak beers. I think you have her confused with someone else." I was probably one of the youngest people living in the development. That was a little weird. However, it was quiet and safe.

After living at Chesapeake Landing for several months, I saw an ad in the local paper that was placed by the Chart House restaurant on Severn Avenue. The restaurant, a popular place for tourists and locals alike, and just a few blocks away from where I lived, was hiring cocktail waitresses. I applied for and got the job along with several other girls. The gal who trained us, Ellen, was the same gal who had been a bookkeeper at the print shop where I had worked just after graduation from VCU. She had been hired by the Chart House as a cocktail waitress in Connecticut and had become part of their traveling training program. She was in Annapolis training new cocktail girls as needed.

Ellen trained the group of us for two weeks by having us follow her around the dining room while we learned abbreviations for mixed drinks and a long list of beers, table numbers, and the names of the other hundred plus employees. I worked with these folks five days a week for nearly two years. They were my friends and we enjoyed hanging out together on days off and after our shifts were over.

Even now, twenty-two years later, I consider waitressing at the Chart House one of my favorite jobs. I became friends with many of the bartenders, waiters, and waitresses and thought of them as my extended family. There was a huge amount of talent among us in the form of fine artists, musicians, and actors. I believe it was the creative energy that connected us and made friendships so easy.

While working at the Chart House, it didn't take long for me to develop a routine that included listening to music at the local bars and attending local theater with other employees after work and on my nights off. My group of friends expanded to include many talented friends of friends. We visited Reynolds Tavern on Thursday night, Harry Browne's on Sunday, The Drummer's Lot at the Maryland Inn, Middleton's Tavern, Marmaduke's, and Ram's Head Tavern. There was always a familiar face or two among the crowd.

Summer time and the living was easy.

Indeed, and it was fun!

Once you had established yourself as a reliable employee for the bar or restauant where you worked, and you had gained a bit of seniority, you would get a fairly regular schedule of shifts. Working as a bartender, waiter, or waitress means you don't keep "regular" hours. The high-paying shifts are on the weekends and work hours are late afternoon until 2:00am. Getting home before 3:00am was an "early" night. As a group of night owls, we slept until noon, or later, and were up until the wee hours of the morning. Our lunch hour was a 9-5er's dinnertime and our dinner hour was the crack of dawn or not at all. It didn't take long to figure out who was working where or what hours, so the network of restaurant and bar employees who frequented other establishments quickly grew as we all added to our expanded family of friends.

One of my Chart House friends, Tim King, was a talented musician and actor. He played guitar and sang in a couple of the restaurants. He had a following of fans who came to listen to him perform every weekend. Many of these fans were also musicians or singers and it was not uncommon for them to sit in on a song or two. Even I would get up and sing from time to time.

Tim introduced me to a friend of his, Patrick, who was in search of a fine artist. He was looking for artwork to hang in the lobby of the Colonial Players Theater during the run of the play *Amadeus*. Patrick and I instantly became friends, and at the end of the play's run, he asked me to ride with him across country. He was meeting some friends in LA at the same time I planned to fly out to the west coast with my sister Mollie. She would be attending a convention in San Diego, and then we were heading up to Long Beach to spend a few days with my father, who had moved there after the sale of our house.

The next day the power was back on and we were back to business as usual. Except now, we had quite a few extra candles out around the restaurant. This time the manager asked us to repack the extras into the boxes. Oops, we hadn't kept all of the boxes and did not have a place to put all the extras. After filling the few small storage areas, there were several of the new candles left over. I asked the manager on duty if I could take one home, and he responded, "Okay, but don't let me see you do it."

A new candle was a treat. I was a smoker in those days and always had a candle lit in my bedroom during the day when I was in there reading or sitting on my bed drawing. I would also light a candle every night before I went to bed. The candles from the Chart House were poured wax in a tall cylinder of frosted white glass. Awesome! Little did I know that taking a candle that night, or moving in with my mom, or buying a T-shirt, or so many other insignificant choices I'd made were pieces of a puzzle and would play crucial roles in my future.

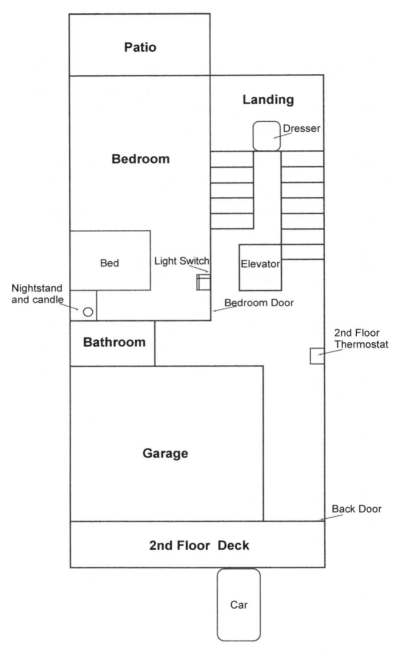

Patio

Landing

Dresser

Bedroom

Bed   Light Switch

Elevator

Nightstand
and candle

Bedroom Door

2nd Floor
Thermostat

Bathroom

Garage

Back Door

2nd Floor Deck

Car

*Chesapeake Landing floor plan showing
ground floor, second floor and carport area.*

August 21, 1988

$\mathcal{T}$he first time I heard the song *Fast Car* by Tracy Chapman was in March, 1988 on my cross-country trip with Patrick. We were driving through Texas when it came on the car radio, and it seemed as if the song had been written for us. We had been driving on the interstate for several days in our own fast car. Before the end of the last verse, we were singing along. I had never heard of Tracy Chapman before and headed into a local record and tape store when we returned home to see if I could buy a cassette of her music. I think it was several months before her music made its way to the east coast. After I was able to get a cassette, it wasn't long before I learned the lyrics to this song as well as the others from the album. *Fast Car* was the song that had been stuck in my head all day. And I was still humming it to myself on my way home from work in the early morning hours.

I had worked the 4:00pm-2:00am closing shift. I drank a couple of beers with the bartender on duty while I was doing my closing chores. By the time I cleaned the lounge, did my paperwork, divided tips, changed into my jeans, and punched out, it was close to 2:20am. By the time I approached the condominium's security gate, pushed the security code into the phone at the entrance to Chesapeake Landing, and drove around the block of condos to my parking space in the carport, it was about 2:30am. I left my glasses on the dashboard as I only wore them when I was driving. I didn't bother to lock my car when I came home. Wasn't a gated community enough of a lock?

Two overhead light bulbs mounted on the bottom of the second floor deck lighted the carport and back door area. The lights automatically came on at night. This rear entrance door opened into a long corridor with another door to the garage about halfway down its length on the left. Straight ahead, at the end of the corridor, was an elevator enclosed by a gate that ran up to the third floor. My bathroom was to the left of the elevator, as was my bedroom. An open staircase to the right of the elevator led up to the landing and the foyer by the front door. Up a few more steps lay the dining room and kitchen to the right and the living room straight ahead and down two steps. The gate to the elevator shaft and the stairway to the upper levels were to the left. Mom always used the elevator at night, so the carrier was docked on the third floor.

I walked into my bedroom, turned on the overhead light, and kicked off my shoes. I flipped the switch that turned on my stereo as I walked to the sliding-glass door at the far end of my room and cracked it open as far as the safety bar would allow. The curtains caught the wind and began to blow into the room. I changed into my new red, short-sleeved nightshirt. It had blue and yellow piping on the sleeves and down the button inset. Sitting on my bed, I lit the candle I'd brought home from work, then counted my tips for the night. I separated out about $25-$30 for spending money for the next few days and dropped it into my purse, which sat next to me on the bed.

I realized I was hungry and decided to get myself something to eat. On my way up to the kitchen, I dropped the rest of my tips into a ceramic pot sitting on the bookshelf. I would store the majority of my money in this clay pot until I had a chance to get it to the bank. *Time to make a bank-run,* I thought as I walked out of the room. I had about $400 in tip money in the pot.

Sometime during the evening it had stopped raining and a cool breeze now blew in off the water. Gone was the sticky, oppressive humidity that usually hung around after these storms. In the storm's place was a refreshing breeze. Before she'd gone to bed, Mom had turned the central air conditioning off and opened the sliding glass door in the living room a few inches. This door opened to a balcony over the carport where my car was parked below. A window in the kitchen was also open, and a pretty stiff wind was blowing through the house. I went into the kitchen to get myself some food and a beer, and I cranked the window shut. It was really cold!

When we were kids, Mom concocted a pasta casserole that we dubbed "German Spaghetti." There was nothing German about the dish, but Mom named it after we bugged her, asking, "What's it called?" and the name stuck. It was easy to make and cheap, and I had made some for dinner the night before. I usually only ate a baked potato and salad at the Chart House before my work shift to get me through the evening, but I would get hungry by the end of the night and would often get a bite to eat before going to bed. I scooped some of the leftovers into a bowl and popped it into the microwave.

Fast Car started running through my head again. I kept time with the song in my head, tapping my leg and softly humming while the food was heating. It was a good night.

Back downstairs with my dinner and beer, I picked up my paperback book, ate my food, and started to read *The Drawing of the Three*. It was the second book in *The Dark Tower* series of novels by Stephen King. He had started publishing these books in 1970. I'd read the first one in the series, *The Dark Tower: The Gunslinger*, during my senior year of high school. There had been an extended wait between each of the seven novels and I relished having the new paperback.

I was not going to be able to read for long because I was scheduled to work the Sunday brunch shift in the morning. This was unusual. Typically, I worked the closing shift on Sunday. One of the other girls must have been on vacation or was sick or something and I was filling in for her. I would have to get up in a few hours, but needed to unwind a bit before I tried to go to sleep. My stereo was playing softly in the background and my belly was full of food. A steady breeze blew the curtains on my sliding glass doors. After reading a few pages, I started to get drowsy. It was 3:00am.

My phone rang, piercing the quiet with its shrill sound. I grabbed it quickly thinking to myself the caller must be someone from work. I must have forgotten to do something before I left.

"Jennifer, you have a beautiful body."

What? Are you kidding me? When the phone rings at 3:00am it had better be important; someone from work or an emergency. This was a prank-call in the middle of the night. I hung up the phone.

A few seconds, maybe a minute after I'd hung up, the phone rang again. I didn't want to answer it; I was annoyed. But, I didn't want the noise to wake my mother.

"You were born to live in 1958."

Okay, I admit, this one threw me. How many prank callers would have this kind of information about me?

"Who is this?" I asked. I do not remember what, if anything, was said at this point. I hung up the phone again. I was feeling anxious and nervous, not from the call so much as from what was said. Who could it have been? I did not recognize the voice. It was a guy for sure, and from the sound of his voice, a smoker. However, that wasn't much to go on. It could be anyone.

I started thinking back on the night at work and even my recent nights out. I could not remember anyone who might have shown any interest in me overtly or covertly. The phone rang again. This time I did not listen to it. Instead, I laid the receiver face down on the mattress next to me.

Who could this be? Where was he calling from? Cell phones had not been invented yet, so whoever this was had to be calling from a residence or pay phone. He could be nearby, or for all I knew, he could be in Timbuktu, Africa. Doubtful, though. How would he know what year I was born if he did not know me? But, if he did know me, why all the crazy phone calls in the middle of the night?

I was getting tired of the recorded voice telling me, "If you'd like to make a call, please hang up and try again. If you need help, hang up and then dial your operator," so I hung up the receiver. Almost immediately the phone rang for a fourth time. This time I put the phone under my pillow so I wouldn't have to hear the operator. I was irritated by all of this and now I was feeling pretty nervous. But, what else can you do when you get a prank call in the middle of the night?

I'd had a prank caller in college who called himself Robert. He would call from time to time and try to get whoever answered the phone to talk dirty to him. (I wonder if he went on to invent the 900 phone-sex industry.) At first, I had been taken aback by his calls, but soon he became a joke. He was harmless, as far as I knew. When I told him I couldn't talk, he would hang up and try another girl.

He figured out that the phone numbers in the New Residence Center dorm at VCU were sequential. Each apartment-like dorm had three bedrooms with a jack in each. Each jack was assigned a phone number different by one digit in sequence. The dorm apartments alternated boy-girl, boy-girl. Once he figured out the system, he was in heaven.

But this caller wasn't going away, and I didn't know how to make him stop.

Feeling shaky, I continued to read my book with the phone under my pillow. I figured he would give up on me and move on to the next number in the phone book. Still, that 1958 birthdate thing did bug me. It wasn't as if it was secret information about me. But whoever was on the phone would have to have access to personal information. Birth record, social security, driver's license, or employee files all would have a birthdate listed. None of these documents would be too difficult to obtain. Heck, it was common in the restaurant business for customers to ask about employees. I could think of countless times when a customer would inquire about someone's schedule or innocently ask for even more detailed information like name, age, or availability. It was rare that we *didn't* answer these questions, trusting that there was no malice intended by the inquirer.

However, I didn't know of anyone who had recently shown any interest in me. And, if there had been someone asking questions, chances are they would just stop in at the Chart House and say "Hi." Calling me in the middle of the night was creepy.

After about ten or fifteen minutes, the prerecorded operator voice stopped. I hung the receiver back in the cradle. I kept my hand close to it for a few seconds, fully expecting to have to pick it up again when it rang. It stayed quiet. Good. I began to calm down and focused on my book.

Around 3:15, I heard the central air conditioning turn on. Crap, it was cold! Why had Mom turned the air on? The machine housing for the air conditioning was in the garage and when it was running, I could not hear my stereo unless I turned it up much louder than I had it playing now. I would have to turn it off because to turn up the volume meant it would be too loud when the air cycled off. I got up, flipped my stereo off, and got a pair of socks out of the drawer. Since I was up, I took the opportunity to use the bathroom. While in the bathroom, I began thinking about how Mom would never have turned the air on with the doors and windows open. And there wasn't any reason for it to be on, anyway. I think the house was well below seventy degrees. I considered, for a minute, going up and turning it off. The toilet seat was freezing. But I didn't go upstairs. I rationalized that maybe it was warmer on the third floor. Still, it didn't make sense.

I made my way back to my bedroom and sat on the bed reading. My stereo was now off, and because it was so cold in the house already, it did not take long for the air conditioner to cycle off. It was very quiet downstairs.

I heard the CRACK of a step upstairs.

A blast of adrenaline shot through my heart. That stair only made noise when someone actually stepped on it. I froze and strained to listen for any other noise. All was quiet. I lit a cigarette and sat on the edge of my bed for a few puffs. I couldn't relax. My nerves were raw and I was tired. I was spooking myself. I was going to bed. I had to get up to go to work early, anyway.

It was close to 3:30am.

I went to the bathroom again to get ready for bed. I finished my cigarette while in there, put in a fresh tampon, peed, and brushed my teeth. This routine helped to relax me and I began to berate myself for feeling so nervous before. I flipped off the bathroom light, turned left into the hall and turned left again to face my bedroom door.

The adrenaline shot through me again.

Did I turn off the overhead light before I went to the bathroom?

The only light in my room was the golden light from the candle on my nightstand. The rest of the room was totally black.

I must be really tired 'cause I don't remember turning the light off, I thought. *But I must have.*

I hesitated outside my bedroom for just a second.

4

Intuition

1. Direct perception of truth, fact, etc., independent of any reasoning process; immediate apprehension.
2. A fact, truth, etc., perceived in this way.
3. A keen and quick insight.
4. The quality or ability of having such direct perception or quick insight.

I have always been intuitive. I suppose we are all intuitive to some degree. But maybe my feeling of "something isn't right here" was a bit keener than even I believed. I have been asked, if I'd felt something was wrong, "Why didn't you do something?"

Indeed, why didn't I? Hindsight is always twenty-twenty. However, even if I had followed my instincts, to what outcome? Who knows? In truth, the answer to "why not?" isn't, "I was tired and overreacting," or even "I had spooked myself by reading Stephen King at 3:00am." It is much simpler:

I'm home, getting ready for bed; I'm in my pajamas.

I am home. Isn't this the place where we feel the most invincible, the safest? Don't we all feel like the weight of the day begins to fall off once we come into our homes and kick off our shoes? We turn on the TV or stereo, grab a beer or glass of wine, get ourselves something to eat, and begin to relax. We naturally put our guard down. Getting ready for bed, dressed in my pajamas, and unwinding after a busy night at work is so far opposite from running out of the house screaming for help like a maniac. I didn't believe I was in danger because I was *home*. I didn't listen to my intuition. All the warnings were there and I got them all loud and clear.

I did not react to any of the intuitive signals I was picking up on because I wanted to continue to believe my home was a safe haven.

I am home. I'm safe.

Forget all the advice you have heard like, "When you are in *this* situation you do *such-and-such*." There is no way for you to know how you will react when you *are* in *this* situation. Nothing in life really prepares you for this. You can read a thousand books and hear a thousand victims tell a thousand different stories and still you are not prepared. Forget conventional thinking entirely. What is about to take place is beyond convention. Being attacked while in your pajamas getting ready for bed is unreal; surreal. Nothing you have read or heard about even enters your mind. What came to my mind were two thoughts:

I'm going to die today.

And,

I'll be damned if I'm going to die today.

Unless you can somehow practice defensive moves all the time and make them instinctual, prepare to count on your survival instincts. Self-preservation is a strong motivator and I was about to have mine tested.

It was just after 3:30am.

With my eyes focused on the candlelight, I took one step into my bedroom.

I didn't see the man who was in my room, but sensed him move in from my right and grab me. Instantly, I screamed and struggled to break free of his grip. He moved behind me and locked me in a tight bear-hug grip.

I was immediately bombarded by a blur of racing thoughts that were jumbled up with panic and terror. What's my advice? If you are lucky, you will get a chance to scream, so make it a good one. If you are really lucky and quick, maybe you can land a punch or wiggle free. Most of us are not skilled in martial arts and we have to rely on our willpower to get through what is in store for us.

"Why did you hang up on me? I told you if you hung up on me again I would kill you."

What? My thoughts came in a tumble, one over the other: This doesn't just happen in the movies. Kill me? Why? Who is this? Let go of me. What did I do to piss you off?

Something was being wrapped around my neck and I felt panic well up in me.

He was going to strangle me. Who was this? Why was he doing this? How did he get in the house? How long had he been in the house? Where was my mother?

"Scream again and I'll kill you."

As if in slow motion, I watched his right hand move up in front of my mouth. Poised, he waited for me to scream again. He knew I would scream again.

I couldn't help myself. I screamed.

As soon as I opened my mouth to scream a second time, he forced a wad of cloth into my mouth and down my throat. I wasn't even able to get the sound out before it was forced back down into me. Everything was happening so fast my mind could barely comprehend what was going on. I tried to slip down and out from his arms. No luck. He gripped me tighter in the bear hug and forced my head back onto his chest. My mouth was all the way open. His right arm was wrapped around my face holding the gag in place and forcing my lower jaw out of alignment. The pain was horrible. I had to close my mouth or my jaw would break. Every time I tried to struggle away from him, he jerked my head back further and held on tighter.

"Touch me and I'll kill you."

My mouth was open too far. His arm was clamped around my face and he was forcing my lower jaw to move down to the right and onto my chest. He pulled my head back so far I was afraid my neck would snap.

The gag was pushing up on the roof of my mouth and the pressure was closing my nasal passage. I could not breathe. Why was he doing this? What did he mean by *I told you if you hung up on me I would kill you?*

No one had said this to me...

Crap! Fuck! This was the guy on the phone.

What I had mistaken for annoying prank calls had escalated into a fight for my life.

Really? Where had he come from? Where did he call from? Who was he? What had I done to make him want to kill me?

I began to realize he must have been on my back patio when I got home. He must have watched me through the blowing curtain on the sliding glass door as I changed into my pajamas.

He'd seen me naked. I felt sick.

How did he get into the house? My mind was racing.

The door upstairs. Mom had left it open.

He had turned on the air conditioner.

Oh my God! I thought.

He had been in the house for at least fifteen minutes. *He* had turned on the air conditioner knowing the sound would mask his footsteps overhead.

How had he known where the thermostat was? Had he been in the house before?

He was the one who had made the step crack.

He'd been waiting on the landing, watching me.

How long had he been planning this? Who the fuck was this guy?

All of these thoughts and realizations bombarded me in just seconds. No matter how much I wracked my brain, I could not figure out who he was and I had no idea what I had done that made him so mad he wanted me dead.

I was feeling the panic beginning to win. I couldn't breathe. I couldn't swallow. I could make noises, but that was it.

This was not good. I needed to get a breath. I reached up to move his hand.

"Touch me and I'll kill you."

I tried to move my head forward, but he had the back of my head clamped tightly to his chest. I thought if I could move my head forward just a bit, I could get some air through my nose. I reached up again and this time I tried to grab my own hair. I wanted to pull my head forward.

"Touch me and I'll kill you."

I had to do something quickly. I was beginning to feel woozy. I tried to use my tongue to move the gag out of my throat. That didn't work. I tried twisting my tongue. My mouth was so dry. I wanted to swallow, but every time I tried, I began to choke. I worked my tongue some more. I was able to make a small opening in the cloth on the left side of my mouth and I could suck a little air in through the hole I'd created, but it was not enough. My jaw was close to breaking. I reached up again to grab my head to pull it forward in order to relieve the pain.

"Touch me and I'll kill you."

I tried to make some noises that sounded like, "I can't breathe," and I continued to try to turn my head so that it aligned with my jaw. I was losing my mind. The pain in my neck was overwhelming. I tried to close my mouth a bit. That didn't work. His arm was gripping too tightly over my face and my jaw felt stuck.

"Touch me or look at me and I'll kill you!"

Again, I made some noises like *I can't breathe.*

"Do you have any money?"

"Do you have any drugs?"

I shook my head, "No."

"Are you here alone?"

Again, I shook my head, "No."

"Oh yes, you are!"

He had killed my mother.

Why else didn't she come when I screamed? If she were alive she would have to have heard me scream and she would have, at least, called downstairs to find out what was going on. He'd killed her and he was going to kill me as well.

I had to get free of this guy. I had to get the gag out of my mouth. I had to breathe. My upper arms were pinned against me, but I could move my arms from the elbows down. I continued to try to move my head forward to relieve the pain in my neck and jaw.

"I can't breathe." The noises I was making were not exactly words, but he clearly understood what I was saying. He pinched my nose shut and held my nostrils closed for several seconds, sneering.

"This is what it's like not to be able to breathe."

I felt myself giving up. I was convinced whoever this was had killed my mother and now he was going to suffocate me. I was light-headed, and fighting him was using up the little bit of air I was able to suck in through my gag. Believing he intended to kill me, I gave up my struggle and went slack.

Again he asked me:

"Do you have any money?"

"Do you have any drugs?"

I shook my head, "No."

I did have money, but I wasn't going to give it to him. If I had had any drugs, I would have given them to him. I didn't. I occasionally did do cocaine in those days, but not often. Even if I did have some drugs, it probably would not have been enough to make him happy and leave.

He started to bargain with me. I guess since he was not getting money or drugs he decided he wasn't leaving without something. I'm sure that's what made him say:

"I'll take the gag out if you promise not to scream again."

I nodded my head, "Yes." I would be able to breathe again and maybe he would not kill me. It took some persuasion on my part through vigorous nodding, but he did finally remove the gag from my mouth and unwind the cloth from my neck. My mouth was stuck open. My jaw had become dislocated and I had to use my hands to push it back into place. I almost did scream, it hurt so badly.

"Take off your panties."

I realized the price of air was not going to be cheap. He intended to rape me. He still might kill me, but now he was focused on rape. Maybe if I did what he said he would not kill me. Using my left hand, I slid my underpants down my left leg as far as I could. Wiggling, I was able to get them to fall to the floor.

"Touch yourself."

Maybe he would not rape me. Maybe he would leave me alone if I did this. I touched my genitals. I felt one of his hands move down and his fingers entered my vagina. His fingers encountered the tampon string.

"It's too bad we've met and you're on the rag."

He removed his hand and said, *"Take this off."*

He wanted me to take off my nightshirt. I didn't want to but I knew he would get mad if I refused. If he got mad again, he might kill me. I asked him if I could take it off over my head. He did not want to let go of me.

"No. It will come off this way. Try harder."

I reached up with my left hand and tried to pull my nightshirt off my left shoulder. It wouldn't come off. He was starting to get mad.

"Rip it."

I tugged and did hear a tear.

"That's right. Rip it more, baby. Just get it off!"

He was getting excited.

Once I got the left shoulder of the nightshirt off, the whole thing fell to the floor. I have never felt more naked. I hated his hands on me. I hated that he could see my body. I cried silently.

He took both of his hands and cupped my breasts.

"I love baby-sized tits."

He maneuvered me over to the side of the bed.

He was always behind me and always had at least one arm tight around me.

"If you look at me I'll kill you."

He told me to lie across the bed face down. I did. Then he immediately told me to stand up. I was standing facing away from him. With one hand pushing the top of my head down so my face was angled toward the floor, he turned me around and told me to sit on the edge of the bed. He was now standing in front of me.

"Get rid of that thing."

He gestured toward the tampon string. I took the dry tampon out and dropped it into the empty bowl on the floor.

"Get hot for me, baby."

He wanted me to touch myself again. I did, but he wasn't satisfied with that.

He had been standing at arm's length from me with his hand on my head pushing it down toward the floor. He took a step toward me.

All I could see of him was from the hips down.

He was naked.

White shorts or a bathing suit of a nylon-type fabric lay at his bare feet.

With one hand on the top of my head and the other on the back of my head, he pulled my face toward his belly.

"Take me. Take all of me," he said as he jammed his erect penis into my mouth. I was gagging. There was a hair in the back of my throat. I tried to tell him I had a hair in my mouth and that I was gagging. He didn't care.

"Forget about the hair."

He sounded angry.

He thrust himself into my throat a few more times.

It occurred to me at this point that I could take the advantage. I could, in fact, take total control of what was happening. However, I could not bring myself to bite off his penis.

Again, hindsight is twenty-twenty. It is exactly what I would do if, God forbid, I ever found myself in this situation again. Even if I could not bite it off completely, I would do what I could to disable an attacker. He would not have made it out of the house without handcuffs on and bleeding badly if I could have chomped down.

I threw up my dinner. I threw up on his penis and pelvis and then vomited in my hand. I motioned to the empty bowl on the floor near me and he gestured to get rid of the puke. He seemed concerned. Perhaps he was just grossed out, but when I asked him if it was okay to drop the vomit into the bowl he said, *"Yes, yes,"* as if he was saying, *"Clean yourself up and let's get on with this."*

He then turned me around and had me lie face down on the bed again.

"Move your butt to the edge."

I scooted my knees to the edge of the bed.

"Get up on you knees."

He raped me as I cried into my bedspread. He was rough and it was painful. I was conscious of what he was doing, but I tried not to think about what was happening to me. I tried not to make any noise at all because I was afraid if he knew I was crying he would get mad again. I focused on anything except what he was doing. I could see both of his forearms and hands. I tried to find anything that might help me identify this person. If he let me live after this was over, I wanted to be able to identify him. He was white, the hair on his arms looked blond in the candlelight, and the base of his fingernails were round. He had something, a small mole, a cut, a birthmark, or dirt smudge on the back of his right hand. I knew when he first grabbed me that he was at least between 6' and 6'2" because he was talking down into my ear. Not much information at all to help identify who this was.

He ejaculated into my vagina and then pulled out of me.

He kept one hand on my shoulder. I sensed him taking a step back from the edge of the bed.

"Lay down flat," he said as he rustled with something behind me.

I lay flat across the bed and he stood straddling my legs. My feet were sticking straight out behind me and I did not want my feet or legs touching him. I extended my feet so my toes could reach the floor and my upper body was lying flat on the bed.

He pushed on the small of my back with his hand and I went stiff. Were the rustling noises I was hearing him searching for a weapon? I realized I was holding my breath. I waited for a knife to be stuck into my back. For just a second I imagined a gun. My breath sucked in and I braced myself, expecting to feel the pain. Instead, he asked again, *"Do you have any drugs?"*

"No. See for yourself."

He picked up the candle from the nightstand and moved it over me from left to right toward my purse to get a better look inside. He looked at the hand mirror on the bed next to my purse and asked me what was on the mirror. I didn't know what he thought he was seeing. Drugs? The UPC code sticker was still on the glass front. He must have thought, in the dim light of the candle, that the sticker was something else.

"What have you been doing?"

"Reading," I answered.

"Do you have any money?"

"No."

"That's a lie, I saw you counting it."

Christ, how long had he had been spying on me from the patio?

How long had he been watching me? Obviously, he watched me change into my pajamas. He must have been there when I got home. He must have been waiting for me. But he only saw me counting my tips and didn't see me put the majority of my money in the clay pot or he would have taken it already. He must have gone to a phone when I put money in the pot on my bookshelf. I risked lying to him rather than tell him where all of my money was. If he knew, I figured he would have taken it and left. I believed he was going to kill me anyway, so risking a lie didn't seem like such a big deal.

I told him I had some money in my purse. I reached into the purse, grabbed the money, and handed it over my shoulder to him.

"Just what I have in my purse, twenty or thirty dollars. You can have it."

"Is this all you have?"

"Yes," I lied. He hesitated, indecisive for several seconds.

"I can't take that; it will make this look like a robbery."

Really? He thought a robbery was bad? He honestly believed that raping me wasn't as bad as taking a few dollars? I started to cry again.

He put the candle back on the nightstand and he asked me, *"Are you here alone?"*

Believing that my mother must be dead, this time I answered, "Yes."

"Do you want to know how I know you?"

"Yes."

"I'm your DMV man. It's on your pillow."

At this, he reached over my head to the left and laid something on the pillow.

"You can look at it after I'm gone. Stay flat on the bed until after I leave or I will kill you. If you get up, I will kill you. If you look at me, I'll kill you."

He walked out of my room into the dark hallway.

I tried to catch a glimpse of him from the crook of my arm. However, because he was walking away into the darkness and I had no glasses on, it was no use. All I saw was a small flip of his hair on his neck as he turned to go down the corridor.

I heard the Venetian blind rattle on the back door. I started to get up, but then I heard him running back down the hall toward me. I pressed my body back onto the bed while I tried to get a look at him through squinting eyes.

"That's a good girl," he said as he jogged up the steps. I couldn't see anything in the dark hallway.

I lay on the bed for just a minute straining to hear any noise from upstairs. It was really quiet. Was he gone? Was it safe to get up? Slowly, I sat up, expecting at any minute that he would rush back into the room again. I reached for the paper he left on my pillow. It was my driver's license renewal form. I was confused. Was this a clue? Did he work for the DMV? No. This form had been in the envelope I had left on the front seat of my car as a reminder to go to the DMV on my day off. It wasn't a clue to his identity at all, but rather it told me how he knew my name and year of birth. He had gone into my car to find out who I was. I laid the paper back on the pillow. I shook my head to try and clear it.

I lit a cigarette, not really sure what to do next. My neck was sore and my jaw hurt like hell, but it wasn't broken. I was in a fog. I didn't know what I was supposed to do. I wondered what other women who had been raped had done after the attacker had left. I wanted to feel safe. I wanted to feel normal again. I wanted everything to be like it had been just a few minutes before.

I felt split, as if I were two people. I seemed to have stepped out of time and I didn't know what to do next. Everything I had believed true about the world had been changed. I felt like a stranger to myself, and I suddenly didn't know, couldn't figure out, what to do or even how to *do* anything.

I had been on my way to bed before he grabbed me. So, that's what I'd do.

I guess I'll go to bed, I thought.

I put my nightshirt back on and collected my underpants from the floor. I picked up the bowl with the discarded tampon and vomit in it and took it into the bathroom with me. I dumped it into the toilet and then sat down and peed. I put in another tampon and finished smoking my cigarette while sitting on the john. When I stood up to brush my teeth, I caught a glimpse of myself in the bathroom mirror. I did not recognize myself.

My face was white. There were bright blotches on my cheeks and several pimples stood out bright red around my face. I began to feel panic again. Where was my mother? Was she upstairs, dead? Was he gone? I had to do something. I couldn't just go to bed if Mom was upstairs dead. I was too afraid to go up to find out.

I went back into my bedroom, turned on the light, and picked up the phone.

I called my sister Mollie, forgetting that she was away at the beach with a friend of hers. I listened to her answering machine message hoping she would pick up the receiver. Eventually, I hung up the phone and lit another cigarette. I did not find out until twenty-one years later that I had indeed left a message on her machine. I had no recollection of doing this.

I wasn't sure who I should call next. It was about ten minutes after 4:00am. I was unable to think clearly. I picked up my address book and opened it to my sister Deborah's number. As I dialed her number I thought, *I should not call her. It's the middle of the night.* She answered the phone.

"I was just raped," I said.

Deborah jolted awake.

"Where are you? Are you hurt?"

"My neck is sore and my jaw hurts, but I'm okay. But I screamed and Mom didn't come downstairs. I think she might be dead."

"Can you go upstairs or is he still in the house?"

"I don't know if he's gone or not. I don't want to go upstairs to find out."

"Hang up and call 911."

Hang up? Was she kidding me? Deborah was my link to everything that was safe, everything that was normal. To hang up meant I was back in a room alone and that was terrifying to me.

"How do you do that?" I couldn't remember how to do anything.

"Just hang up and then push 9-1-1. I'm on my way over."

Breaking that contact with my sister was one of the hardest things I've ever had to do.

Her voice was soon replaced by another woman's voice.

"911. What's your emergency?"

"I was just raped and I think my mother might be dead because she didn't come downstairs when I screamed. I'm afraid to go upstairs to find out."

"Stay where you are, I've called the police and they are on the way. Do you know if the guy is still in the house?"

"I don't know. I don't hear anything. I can't tell if he got out or not."

"I've got your sister on the other line. Let me tell her it's okay for her to hang up.

"Are you hurt?"

"I wasn't stabbed or shot or anything, but my jaw was dislocated and it hurts. I'm more afraid for my mother."

The operator continued to ask me questions, and she told me to stay on the phone and not to go upstairs until she heard from the police to confirm that they were at the front door. It seemed to take forever for them to get to the house.

Finally, she said, "Okay, go let them in. The police officer is at your front door. It's okay to hang up now."

I thanked the operator, hung up, and ran up the steps.

My sister Deborah and a police officer stood at the door. Right away, I told the policeman that I had been raped, and that I did not know if my mother was alive or not.

Just then, my mother came down the steps from the third floor.

"What the hell is going on?" she demanded.

I was instantly relieved and angry.

"I was just raped! Where the hell were you?"

I watched her crumble and sit down on the step as she realized the screams she'd heard had been mine.

"I thought it was outside on the beach," she said.

5

Aftermath

Soon policemen were filling the house and firing questions at me from all angles. They all wanted to know what and where everything had happened. An officer followed me down to my bedroom and I told him what I could figure out. I was exhausted and confused. Everything became a blur. I answered his questions, but it didn't seem like I was able to finish one answer before the next question was fired at me.

"Do you know who it was?"

"No, I never saw his face."

"How did he get into the house?"

"I believe he climbed onto my car and up to the balcony and came in the sliding glass door."

"Was the door unlocked?

"Yes, it was opened a few inches to let in some air."

"Did he hurt you?"

"He tried to strangle and suffocate me by wrapping something around my neck and gagging me.

"He dislocated my jaw."

"What did he try to strangle you with?"

"I don't know."

I looked around my bed to see if any of the clothes lying there looked like they had been used to gag me. None of the clothes there were the right texture.

"What were you wearing?"

I pointed out the jeans and flannel shirt I had been wearing to and from work and my nightshirt.

I heard my mother scream from my bathroom.

"Did he hurt you? Are you cut?" my mother asked.

"No," I told her. "He didn't cut me."

"The toilet is full of blood. Are you sure he didn't hurt you?"

"No, I have my period." Apparently, I had forgotten to flush the toilet when I'd gone in earlier.

"Is there anything else you can tell us?" the police officer asked me.

"He called me four times."

"Do you know where he called you from?"

"No."

Eventually the officer said he had to take me to the hospital to have me checked out and collect whatever evidence could be found.

Around 5:00am, Deborah helped me get dressed. I rode to the hospital with one of the police officers. My mother was in the hospital waiting room waiting for the doctor to finish with me. I didn't know how she got there. A doctor and at least one nurse plus a rape crisis counselor named Lynn were in the examining room with me. Also present was a police officer from the sexual assault and domestic violence division, Detective Zora Lykken. She was there to observe the collection of evidence, including hair and semen.

Detective Lykken talked me through everything the doctor was doing, the examination, and the evidence collection. She tried to make the experience as easy for me as possible. She asked me questions about what had happened, but the details of my conversation with her quickly became fuzzy. I was grateful for her gentle hand on my shoulder.

Before she started, I told the doctor that I was on my period and asked her if she wanted the tampon I was using. I withdrew the tampon and dropped it into a clear plastic bag. A vaginal swab was then done and I used a comb on my pubic hair to collect any hairs that might have transferred from the rapist to me. Lynn, the Rape Crisis Center advocate, and Zora told me what to expect emotionally over the next few days.

"You should write down everything you remember about the night. Everything, no matter how small. Every detail, because you never know what will be important," Zora said.

I nodded, "Okay."

"You never know how long it will take for us to catch the guy and even though it doesn't seem like it now, you will begin to forget some of the details."

I nodded again. "I'll start it tomorrow after I get some sleep."

I didn't have them x-ray my jaw or neck. I was able to open and close my mouth, so I didn't see any need for x-rays. And I was tired. More exams meant more time in the ER, and I wanted to get out of there and go home. I was given a "date rape" or "morning after" pill and two huge shots of penicillin, one in each butt cheek. The nurse who was to give me the shot told me to bend over the end of the bed in my curtained room while she went in search of another nurse available to give me the other.

"I want to give you both of these at the same time because if I do them one after the other, you won't want me to give you the second one," she said.

I bent over the edge of the bed with my butt exposed, dozing off as I waited for the nurses to return. My mother sat in a chair across the room. When had she come into the room?

The doctor who'd examined me decided not to give me any kind of sedative or tranquillizer because, she said, "We want you to be able to tell the police everything you remember. If we give you a sedative, you may forget something."

Later that night, I wondered if there could have been a more foolish lack of compassion from a medical professional in this particular circumstance. Certainly giving me a pill to take later, when I was back home in bed, would only help. I was not given anything to help me sleep.

I had never known anyone who had been raped. I wasn't sure what good the "evidence" was going to be. How could you find a criminal with a used tampon or hair? I had no idea who he was and never saw his face. How could the police find a suspect if I could not identify him? None of this made any sense to me. It was not until years later that I realized just what an important role the collection of DNA evidence would be in solving this crime.

When I was finished at the hospital I thought I would be able to go home with my mother. That wasn't the case. A new detective, Detective Leo, was waiting for me in a hallway outside the emergency room.

"I want you to come downtown and give a statement," he said. "But first, I want to go back to your house to see where the crime was committed."

I was mad. All I wanted to do was to go home and sleep. It had to be close to 8:00am, and I was about to drop from exhaustion. The last thing I felt like doing was telling the events of the night before all over again. It seemed I had told half a dozen people already.

Detective Leo drove me back home and pulled up behind my car in the carport. Detectives were still at the house collecting evidence. A female detective told me, "I have good news and bad news. Which do you want first?"

Are you kidding? I didn't know if I could even tell the difference at that point, but I answered, "How 'bout the good news first?"

"I was able to get a great print from the hood of your car."

"What's the bad news?" I asked.

"I took a lot of paint off with it."

I chuckled. "Don't worry," I said. "Ida's old, it's okay."

I had named my car Ida Ratherhava. It was a Datsun B-210 and I had been driving the car for almost thirteen years by then. It was a dependable car, but nothing fancy. I looked inside the passenger door and saw that some of the papers I had left on the front seat were still there. I explained to Detective Leo that the guy had said he was *"your DMV man,"* and that he must have taken some papers out of my car. Something else seemed to be missing, but I could not figure out what it was just then.

I walked into the house to show Detective Leo where the rape had occurred. I told him most of what had happened and some of the things I'd figured out after the fact. We walked to my bedroom doorway. My sister Deborah was in the bedroom with a couple of evidence collectors. The evidence collectors had bags of my things in their hands and were getting ready to head out. Before they left, one of them asked me, "Is there anything in here you think he may have touched or picked up?"

I remembered that he'd turned the light off when he came into the room. Then I looked across the room at my nightstand and saw the candle I had taken from the Chart House just a few nights before still sitting there.

"That candle," I said. "He picked it up."

I have wondered a million times just how fleeting a moment this was and yet how important it became in solving this case. A few minutes longer in the examining room or stuck in traffic on the way home and these investigators would have been gone. I doubt I would have mentioned the candle to anyone if they had not been there to prompt my memory. I might have assumed they had already dusted its surface for prints. Combined with the circumstances under which I obtained the candle in the first place, it remains one of the *Oh, Wow!* elements of my story and the key to bringing all the pieces of the puzzle together to ultimately find a suspect.

After the evidence collectors left, I went upstairs to find a few more police officers in the living room. I sat on the step leading up to the third floor. My mother's dog, Susie Wong, was sniffing around nervously in the sea of feet, looking for me. One of the police officers asked me if the dog had barked when the guy was in the house. I laughed again. He has to be kidding. Susie was pretty old, couldn't see much at all, was almost deaf, and couldn't walk up and down the steps because of her arthritis. But her nose still worked. She sniffed out my extended hand and sat next to me on the step as I reached to pet her on the head.

Detective Leo was talking with some of the officers in the room. I looked over at the screen door and noticed a footprint on the floor just inside the room near the door. I mumbled, "There's a footprint on the floor over there."

I don't know if anyone heard me. I didn't care. I sat there remembering he wasn't wearing any shoes when he was in my room. *I guess he left them on the balcony and that's why he decided not to go out the back door,* I thought, shaking my head. Damn, he was slick. Too slick for this to have been his first time. I wanted these people out of my house. I wanted to sleep. When Detective Leo was finished talking to the investigators, he told me we had to go down to the station so he could get a statement. He also wanted my mother and sister to come and give fingerprints so their prints could be matched against any prints that had been lifted.

I told my mother to call the Chart House and tell them I would not be in to work.

"Ask to speak to Kate."

Kate was the only female manager working at the Chart House. I figured, not only would it be easier for Mom to tell her why I wouldn't be in to work, Kate would be better at letting the rest of the girls I worked with know what was up. Unfortunately, Mom didn't remember who to ask for and just told the person who answered the phone.

Whoever it was told Mom to tell me to take a couple of weeks off and to "*Come back when she is ready. We'll fill in for her.*" The news traveled like a wildfire from the Chart House through Eastport, and had made its way into all the bars and restaurants in downtown Annapolis before they'd opened for brunch that morning.

6

Ripple Effects

So when you sent out the message yesterday asking if anyone had any thoughts...to contribute, I began to replay everything from 1988. We had lost touch for so much of that time, but the events of that night in August always stuck with me.

I remember going into [the] Chart House for the 1/4 till meeting, and the management telling us that you had been assaulted. I remember being unable to process it. (I was 19 and had NEVER come close to any sort of experience close to yours.) And for someone I knew and worked with almost every day to be the victim of rape — it was just unfathomable. From that day forward, none of the female staff ever walked out to their car alone after their shift — they were accompanied by a waiter, a busboy, a manager, but they never went alone.

I remember being at your house. Was your mother out of town? And I remember it being a beautiful home, and how hard it was to comprehend that something so horrific had happened in such a tranquil place. You never shared many specifics, and frankly, I thank you for that. What little I knew truly did stay with me even when you and I weren't in contact.

I will tell you that never, no matter how beautiful and peaceful the night, [I question:] Are my windows left open when we go to bed? My doors are always locked. That I feel safe and secure in my home does not mean that I am safe and secure in my home. There have been times when my air conditioner or furnace comes on as I'm drifting off to sleep, and the thought has popped into my head that it really didn't seem warm or cold enough for it to come on. There were bits and pieces of your story that stuck with me.

I thought about you from time to time, and I wondered how your life turned out. Were you happy, were you okay?
~ Jackie

7

Evidence Found

Once Detective Leo and I arrived at the police station, Mom and Debbie went in to give their fingerprints. I stood outside in the bright sun with my brother-in-law Mike. *When did he arrive?* I wondered. *Did he come with Deborah to Mom's?* I honestly didn't know when he arrived on the scene, but I was happy to have him there waiting with me. He asked me if I was okay. We didn't talk much. It didn't matter. I felt safe with him there. After Detective Leo finished with Mom and my sister Debbie, Mike drove them home.

"I'll bring her back. You don't have to wait," Detective Leo said.

We were sitting in a small room painted blue-gray. He sat on one side of the table, I sat on the other. There was a small tape recorder in front of me. I began to tell him the story as the recorder captured my words.

"He's done this before and he's going to do it again," I said.

"What makes you say this?" Detective Leo asked.

"He was too careful and controlling. He had it all planned out. He stood in the dark on my patio and watched me as I changed into my pajamas. He went to my car and found some papers with my name and address on them. He turned on the air conditioner to block any noise he made. He stood at the top of the stairs watching and waiting for me to leave my bedroom. He hid in the shadows, and when he grabbed me, he had something wrapped around my neck and stuffed into my throat in seconds. He always had a hold of me and made sure I never saw his face. You don't do this for the first time and get it so right. It took practice. He enjoyed it. He's going to do this again."

I started to again tell the events of the night. I was able to fill in some of the gaps at this point, but there were still a few missing pieces.

The detective asked two questions repeatedly: "Where do you think he was calling you from?" and "What do you think he had wrapped around your neck and down your throat."

My answer was always the same: "I don't know."

I knew whatever he had around my throat was soft fabric, but I didn't think it was anything he'd found in my bedroom.

 About halfway through telling my story I asked if I could use the bathroom and go outside for a smoke break. Just my luck, a law had passed in 1988 that banned smoking in hospitals and police stations. I needed a cigarette. Or ten. Detective Leo showed me to the bathroom. After I peed, I splashed some water on my face, and as I dried my cheeks, I looked at myself in the mirror. I didn't look any better than I had at 4:00am. In some ways, I looked worse because now my eyes were bloodshot from lack of sleep and crying. Any makeup I may have had on my face earlier had been wiped or cried off.

Detective Leo let me smoke my cigarette in the room where I was giving my statement. He did not want me to go outside and he didn't want me to be caught smoking in the bathroom. He reasoned that no one would bother us during the time we were in the small interview room.

After a couple of hours, it was finally time to go home and get some sleep.

The detective made small talk with me as we drove from downtown toward the Spa Creek Bridge. As we drove along Compromise Street, about fifty yards from the foot of the bridge, he said something like, "If you think of anything else, you can call me and let me know."

I wasn't really listening. My eyes were glued to something lying in the middle of the bridge about a hundred yards away. Under normal circumstances, seeing this and knowing what it was would have been impossible. It was barely visible. However, nothing about the past eight hours had been normal. I knew instantly what I was seeing in the road. It was the same thing that was missing from my car — the T-shirt I had bought years ago in Ocean City.

Detective Leo looked at me and asked, "Are you alright?"

I nodded my head, "yes."

"I know what he tried to strangle and gag me with," I said. "I think that's my T-shirt lying in the middle of the bridge." I nodded with my head as a way of pointing to the spot where I was looking. He followed my gaze and slowed his car as we drove closer. To my surprise, Detective Leo decided to drop me off at home first and then return to pick up the shirt.

"I'll stop and pick it up on my way back and then call you when I get back to the station," he said.

Maybe he did not believe that it could be my T-shirt. It did seem unlikely — even unreal. Detective Leo dropped me off at my back door and then returned to the bridge to retrieve the shirt. While I waited for him to call, I walked down the hall and went into my bedroom. It was a mess. A bigger mess than I would have normally left it.

My sister Deborah was there trying to clean. Who knew all of this went on behind the scenes after an assault? It was awful. There was fingerprint powder on everything. My white iron footboard and headboard looked black. She discovered that wiping the black powder off the frame was not enough to remove the dust.

I later learned that black fingerprint powder is made of a pigment and gum arabic that allows it to stick to the oils on a surface. Graphite is popular to use for color because it can be ground to an extremely fine dust. This allows for greater detail when dusted onto a light surface that contains a print. When mixed with gum arabic, it in effect becomes "glued" to the surface to which it is applied. This gum keeps the dust in place and prevents distortion from bumping or wind. Graphite by itself is not so difficult to remove. However, add the gum arabic to the graphite and it's a bitch to clean.

The fingerprint powder oxidized the white paint of my bed frame and everything it touched turned yellow. The light switch, doors, and nightstand were all covered in the blackish-gray powder. It seemed like everything was gone from my bed. The clothes I had left on the bed were gone. *Damn,* I thought, *They took my new flannel shirt and my new nightgown! Crap. That was a new shirt, the first time I ever wore it.* I was too tired to figure out everything that had disappeared in the name of evidence that day.

I walked upstairs and found Mom doing the same thing upstairs that Deborah was doing downstairs. The sliding glass door, screen door, and the thermostat were covered in black smudges. I think this day might have been the day I started to get to know my oldest sister. Although the circumstances stunk, I love that we did finally discover each other.

I was so tired. I went to sit in the kitchen to wait for Detective Leo's call.

The phone rang.

"Okay, I have it. Can you identify it for me?"

"Yeah, it's an ugly light green shirt, kind of speckled dark flecks on light. It has a dark green band around the sleeve and neck. It's the first T-shirt I ever bought. I got it in Ocean City years ago. It does not have any designs on it or anything. I think it's a size "Large." I used to wear it all the time, but it got a small hole in it and I put it in my car to use as a rag. I wipe the windshield with it and cover the steering wheel with it to keep the sun off. I guess that's about it."

"Yup, that's it. Only you cannot wear it anymore because it is torn in half. And it's got your name in it."

"My name?" Of course it had my name in it. I'd taken the shirt to college with me. I'd written my name on the tags of all of my clothes so if any got mixed in with anyone else's laundry, I would still find them. "I guess he's back on your side of town now," I said.

After I hung up the phone, I took a shower — a long, hot shower — dressed, and lay down on my stripped bed, falling instantly asleep.

The phone seemed to be ringing non-stop. Occasionally, Mom would call down to me to pick it up.

I talked to every one of my friends that day, and do not remember a word I said to any of them. As soon as I hung up the phone, I was asleep again. By late afternoon, I woke up feeling a little hungry. I couldn't bring myself to eat the leftover German Spaghetti — and wouldn't eat it again for more than ten years. Mom fixed me some toast.

As the sun started to go down, Mom stood outside talking with a few of the neighbors.

I went out to join them, afraid to be alone in the house with the growing shadows. As we stood talking about what had happened, what was known and what was not known, we noticed the automatic lights over the carport did not turn on.

I realized that was why he'd taken the T-shirt out of the car. He wanted to unscrew the lights so he wouldn't be seen getting into the house, and the bulbs must have been hot.

He'd used the T-shirt as protection from the heat. It then came in handy as a sort of glove to keep him from leaving prints all over the house. And, of course, ripped in half from bottom to the collar, it was plenty long enough to use as a gag.

8

The Night After

Once the sun was fully down, I went back into the house to the kitchen where the overhead light blew out all the shadows. I was really shaky. I watched TV with Mom and drank a couple of beers to try to calm my nerves. It didn't work. A tranquilizer would sure have come in handy right about now. Mom changed the sheets in the guest room on the third floor and I slept there for the first few nights.

That first night was horrible.

I had never been afraid to be alone or to be in the dark. I am a night owl by nature and loved to sleep in a pitch-black room. However, that night I felt physical terror at every noise inside and outside of the house. I could hear every sound as if it were right in the room with me. I was in the bedroom just a couple of doors down from where my mother slept, now armed with a baseball bat under her bed. The window in the room was open and a slight, cool breeze was drifting in. Under normal circumstances I would have considered this to be perfect sleeping weather. However, this wasn't a normal night and there was no sleep for me.

Even though there were no strong winds blowing, I could hear every sound from miles away. Even the river failed me. The water was calm. There weren't any waves on the river to drown out the sounds of the house, the neighborhood. The breeze that barely lifted the curtains carried with it every noise from miles around. I lay there alert, hearing everything — every car horn, every burst of laughter, every dog bark, every yell, every motorcycle rev, every police car siren downtown, every nightingale chirp, and every leaf rustle.

Every sound sent a shot of adrenaline through my heart. I was terrified that each noise I heard was the monster coming back. A few times, I dozed off from exhaustion and then awakened with a start, panicked.

The sound of my heartbeat was like a freight train in my ears. I could see my heart beating in my chest. I lay in bed with my hand over my heart, trying to slow its beat. As soon as it would calm to a fast-racing pace, I would doze off. Then, as I realized I had fallen asleep, the adrenaline would shoot through me with a loud rush in my ears. I wondered many times that night why a tranquilizer was supposed to be a bad thing.

Morning couldn't come fast enough. As the sun came up, I heard the new Naval Academy plebes out early doing their morning exercises, and the *"pop-pop-pop"* of a group practicing on the rifle range miles away. I did not fall fully asleep until the sun had risen completely in the sky and the shadows in the room had disappeared. I think I aged ten years that night.

It was on this night that I decided that drinking myself to sleep was much better than lying awake with this terror.

9

Missing Pieces

$\mathcal{M}$y brother Greg stopped by on Monday. His birthday was August 26, which was just a couple of days away. I remember some of the neighbors getting nervous when he showed up. They had heard a description of the rapist from the police and several of them were sure Greg was the perpetrator returning to the scene of the crime. It seemed unlikely that the rapist would return in broad daylight. However, no one was thinking very clearly. Poor Greg didn't know what was going on when a few of the neighbors started giving him the third degree.

When Greg arrived, he dialed our two-digit gate-code number. He needed the four digit number that would open the drive-through security gate. It was during this call that I realized that although only the kitchen phone controls the gate, all the phones in the house ring when the two digit number is entered into the gate phone. I then realized how close the perpetrator had been when he'd made the calls.

We asked Greg to re-screw the light bulbs into place over the carport. He didn't have a very good birthday that year.

During the two weeks I took off work, I went through a whole range of emotions and behavior changes. It was while attending therapy sessions at the Rape Crisis Center that I realized everything I was experiencing was "normal" behavior for a rape victim. I spent a few nights sleeping on the third floor. I would only go down to my first floor bedroom to shower and get clean clothes. I do not remember really *doing* much of anything for the first week except sleeping during the day and lying awake all night. Once I did start to sleep on my bed again, I slept fully clothed and with the lights on. Somehow, I ended up with a set of sheets and a blanket to replace the ones the police had taken, but I didn't have any idea where they'd come from. I was really in a fog. I did not recognize myself when I caught a glimpse of myself in the mirror. My face was pale and my eyes were puffy. I hated answering the phone because I was always afraid it would be him.

In addition to noticing the unscrewed light bulbs in the carport, I discovered a rather large wet area at the foot of my bed where my attacker had grabbed me. My first thought was maybe I had been so afraid that I'd lost control of my bladder, and I was responsible for the wet rug. However, I would have known if I'd wet myself. I remembered the shorts I'd seen him wearing and realized they could have been a white bathing suit. The fabric seemed right. Maybe he had been in the pool?

My mother was cleaning the last traces of the fingerprint dust off the inside of the front door and the dry-sink that sat on the landing. On the marble top of the dry sink sat an ornately carved ivory urn. The top portion of the urn has some areas that are carved all the way through so you could put a flower stem in each hole. Mom called to me to come up.

"Come look at this," she said. The bottom of the urn, which was usually empty, had about an inch of water in it. I decided we should call Detective Leo to tell him about these things. They might be important somehow, so I dialed the number printed on the card he'd given me.

"He's on vacation and won't be back for two weeks," the woman who answered told me.

I thought, *You're kidding? Two weeks? That's a lifetime.*

"Is it possible to get someone else to come out and take a look, make some notes to give him or something?"

"Okay, we will send someone out," she said.

The woman I spoke to did send an officer to the house. However, it wasn't anyone who was familiar to the case. In frustration, I had to tell this guy that Detective Leo had the case, was out of town, and the things we discovered might be important. I also had to tell him pretty much the whole story all over again. I told this officer I thought that maybe the guy had been in the pool and had seen me when I was in the kitchen getting my food — more recently, I realized he'd probably hopped over the bulkhead to get back out to the phone at the gate once he'd taken the driver's license renewal form out of my car. With the winds blowing so strongly that night, the tide at Horn Point would have been very high. He got wet each time he went back and forth over the bulkhead. No matter how it had occurred, my attacker had been wet.

I showed the police officer the large wet spot on the carpet and then showed him the water that had collected in the urn. After I'd heard the *"crack"* of the step, he must have stood on the landing, leaning over the top of the chest of drawers and his hair dripped into the top of the urn. He had to have been on that landing for approximately fifteen minutes.

I gave the officer Detective Leo's phone number and asked him to give Detective Leo the notes he had taken. I don't know if Detective Leo ever got this information. In fact, I only spoke to Dectective Leo on one other occasion over the course of the next several weeks. It seemed that whenever I called he was not in the office, on vacation, or "would return my call as soon as he can."

He did call me back one time. I asked him if there had been any developments in the case. He told me about a pool party that allegedly had taken place that night.

"I'm looking into who was at this party," he said.

I told him there had been no one in the pool when I came home. In fact, I didn't know anything about any party. If there had been a party, everyone was gone by 2:30am. I'd looked right into the pool as I'd leaned out to close the kitchen window. If anyone had been in the pool then, they weren't supposed to be. And I didn't see them.

Detective Leo then told me the officers going door-to-door in Chesapeake Landing the morning after I was attacked had been met in the parking lot by an elderly woman. She lived in the row of condominiums directly across from the main gate. He said he was sure my attacker had used the gate phone to call me because the woman said she had received a few phone calls in the middle of the night.

Apparently it had taken my assailant a few tries to figure out the gate's phone system. Thinking he was calling my house, he must have called her first and said something suggestive to her. He knew my house number and pushed those two numbers when he saw them on the panel. However, the two-digit number in front of the last name did not correspond to the house number.

When the elderly woman answered the phone, he realized he needed to know my last name to dial the phone in my house. He must have walked onto the beach at Horn Point and hopped over the bulkhead. He knew where I lived, saw my car parked in the carport, and saw the car was unlocked. He found my registration renewal form on the front seat and took it with him. Unfortunately, I'd made it very easy for him to get all the information he needed. With the form in hand, he must have hopped back over the bulkhead, headed to the gate phone, and dialed.

"Jennifer, you have a beautiful body."

In his anger at my hanging up on him, he misdialed at least one more time. Enraged he called the elderly woman by mistake. She picked up the phone.

"If you hang up on me again, I'll kill you."

She had looked out her window toward the gate and could see someone standing there, but could not tell who it was. She was scared and confused. She knew he didn't know who he was talking to; that the call was meant for someone else. She hung up the phone, shaken. The woman broke into tears when she heard what had happened just minutes later. She blamed herself for not calling the police.

10

What Friends Are For

$\mathcal{A}$ few of my friends from Chart House really helped me get myself back on my feet and moving again. Jackie, Jen, and Karen either called or came by every day. We did not talk much about what had happened. They did not ask for details. They didn't know what to say to me. And, sensing their discomfort, I didn't discuss what had happened unless someone asked.

I felt different. My whole world felt different. Everything was off balance, strangely and uncomfortably new. I longed for the day when I would wake up and get dressed without thinking about the consequences of wearing one outfit over another. I wanted to be able to walk in front of a window without being afraid of seeing a face looking back at me. I wanted to be able to be alone inside or outside of my house and feel comfortable again.

Everyone was treating me differently. When I came within earshot of people talking in hushed voices, they would stop. I couldn't blame them; none of us had ever been through anything like this before. This was one of those life experiences that did not come with a manual, and consequently, none of us knew what helpful or healing behavior was.

However, even then, it seemed to me that my therapist from the Rape Crisis Center should have had a manual. The therapists at the center were supposed to be the ones who had the answers, weren't they? This is what I believed when I went there for help. However, I didn't find what I needed.

My therapist had difficulty discussing the details of my rape and was unhelpful in offering practical ways for me to get through a day. Instead, she wanted to focus attention on what I was going to do "down the road," when I got back to work or even during the next year.

I wanted to know how I could survive the next few minutes and hours without feeling the panic boil up into my throat again.

I was jumpy during the daytime and terrified at night. The hours of darkness in the middle of the night were the worst. Because I was not getting the help I need from my therapist, I only went to see her a few times. Instead, I stuck with my friends who wanted to do all they could to help.

I suppose everyone — my family, friends, and I — believed our lives would get back to "normal" if we avoided discussing the elephant in the room. Jackie, Jen, and Karen wanted to help their friend find her footing on what had become some very unsteady ground. Since I did not know then the value and healing in discussing my fears and anxieties, we turned to activities that made us laugh. Laughter helped us to forget the pain…for a while.

We got together just to hang out and try to restore a bit of "normal" to an abnormal situation. We would play cards or I'd get out my Ouija board. I remember one night Jackie got scared to death because the planchette started moving freely around after she asked a question. That might have been her last encounter with an Ouija board.

They didn't push me. They would continue to chat amongst themselves, seeming not to notice when, for no apparent reason, I would begin to cry. They were there for me and this kindness saved me from falling into an emotional abyss. It was the love from these friends and support from my family that stayed with me even when, down the road a bit, my life did begin to fall apart. With the help of these friends, I found the courage I needed to get through the rough spots. It would not be the only occasion I leaned on these friends for support. After many years apart, we would find that our lives would intertwine again.

Occasionally they would ask me if there were any new developments in the case, any leads.

"No," I would answer.

After the first week, I returned to sleeping in my pajamas again and was able to turn the bedroom light off at night. However, the hall light had to be on all night or I did not sleep at all. It lit not only the long corridor that leads out to the carport, but also the landing upstairs and the elevator. I could drift off to sleep knowing that, when I awoke any time during the night, there were no shadows in any corners.

I still hated to hear the air conditioner turn on. It made so much noise, it drowned out everything else in the house. I fought with my mother for quite a while, begging her to turn off the air conditioning. When we were growing up, we didn't have air conditioning and we'd survived. "Couldn't we do without for just a few months?" I didn't win this argument. At first when the air would turn on and I was in my bedroom, I found myself making excuses to go into the hallway to listen for any strange sounds coming from upstairs. Thankfully, this defensive behavior did not last long.

I returned to work after the second week. Being back there was challenging. I discovered I was cautious of everyone I did not know. This made my job as a cocktail waitress difficult. However, I pushed through the shaky start and did the best I could to put on a happy face for the customers. My friends were there, keeping an eye on me and watching for anything or anyone who looked suspicious. Since we had no way of knowing who had attacked me and how he knew me, everyone was on edge.

My friend, the musician Tim King, was one of the headwaiters, and he was responsible for closing the restaurant and locking up at the end of the night. For the first week I was back at work, he insisted on not only walking me to my car, but also following me home. He wasn't satisfied with just watching me make it into the house safely. He went in the house ahead of me, checking all of the rooms except for my mother's.

"She sleeps with a bat nowadays," I told him. "She's likely to swing first and ask questions later."

Once Tim was satisfied the coast was clear, he would let me come in. I had to tell my mom he was doing this after the first time, because I didn't want to scare the crap out of her. Tim was about the same height as my assailant and she would have freaked if she saw him scoping out the place. She was cool with the idea. Actually, I think it helped her sleep better, too.

After about five or six nights of this, I told Tim I wanted to go into the house on my own. I would not have him around to do this for the rest of my life and I had to be able to do it by myself. He wasn't ready to relinquish his role as my protector just yet, so we compromised. For a few more days, we walked in together, and then when we both were satisfied everything was okay, he would leave. Eventually I told him I was ready to do it on my own. I recall the look on his face when I told him. It was concern. *He* wasn't ready to stop being my protector. I am not sure if I ever properly thanked him for his kindness, but I hope he knows how much his nightly vigil meant to me.

11

Moving Out, Moving On

I moved out of Chesapeake Landing right around my thirtieth birthday in mid-November, 1988. I rented a house in a community a few miles away. I had a few different roommates over the course of time, but none more fun than Marnie. She and I briefly lived with another gal who also worked at the Chart House. Shannon, Marnie, and I were three individuals who, on the surface, could not have seemed more mismatched. However, we all liked music, laughter, and fun. Marnie and I became as close as sisters, maybe closer. The time we spent living together was high-energy and very spiritually connected. I believe we have been friends forever, through the ages, and we find each other in each new lifetime.

Soon after Shannon moved out to do her thing and Marnie moved out to live with her boyfriend, Jim, I started dating Stephen. He was a brother of a friend of mine. Rita set up a dinner at her house where we could meet and Stephen and I were instantly attracted to each other. I was beginning to feel like I might just get back to normal again. Work was easier because the awkwardness that existed when I'd returned had begun to fade. My friends were finding it easier to talk to me. Conversation was flowing again. We were returning to our after hours and days off routines of listening to music downtown. However, I no longer got up to sing. I was afraid the man who raped me might have been hanging out in one of the bars I frequented. I wasn't comfortable with the idea of being in the spotlight. Girls at work were still leaving in pairs or groups at the end of the night. Even though none of us knew who my attacker was, we all began to relax a little. Life was getting better.

Mom called me one day in early December, 1988 to say, "Someone tried to break in last night. They jimmied the lock on the door downstairs."

She was talking about the sliding glass door — the door to my old bedroom. I felt the familiar chill run through me.

"Call Detective Leo and tell him about it. He can send someone out to dust for prints."

"I called the police. They are here now."

"Call him," I repeated. "Call Leo. His card is by the phone in the kitchen. He can have the door dusted for prints and they can be compared to the ones they got from the candle."

I don't believe Mom did call Detective Leo. If she did, he did not send anyone to dust for prints. I did not think this break-in attempt was random, a coincidence. I believed it was my attacker returning to the scene of his crime. I would discover, years later, he had made another woman a victim of his horrible ways on December 11, 1988.

I had moved out of my mother's house. If it was my attacker coming back looking for me there, then he did not know I wasn't living there anymore. I felt relief realizing he did not know my whereabouts.

Meanwhile, Stephen and I saw each other several times a week and on the weekends. He and his sister were friends of one of the bartenders at the Chart House. We would meet there when I got off work. He lived just a few blocks from me, so we easily alternated between houses. We went out to dinner, to the circus, to ballgames, and we spent quite a bit of time just hanging out at home. Stephen even included me on a family trip to the beach. I was happy and I felt safe. After a few months of dating, Stephen asked me if I would consider moving in with him. I told him I would consider it, but I thought we should wait before taking such a big step. I felt we needed to date a bit longer to be sure if our relationship would last. Life was looking good again!

Sometime in early spring of 1989, my friend Tim and his roommate John, also a waiter at the Chart House, asked me how the investigation was going.

"What investigation? Is there still an investigation?" I asked, sarcasm dripping from my words. "You wouldn't know it.

"Detective Leo doesn't return my calls, and when he does, all he can talk about is some alleged pool party that took place that night at Chesapeake Landing that he's "looking into." I don't know anything about a pool party. There was no party going on when I got home. I don't think he ever did much to try to find the guy." I was frustrated with the lack of interest being shown by Detective Leo. I had to admit there wasn't much to go on, but to give up altogether didn't make sense to me.

"Our next door neighbor works for the State's Attorney's Office," John said. "Let me talk to him. I'll let him know what's going on and see if he can help."

12

A New Investigator Takes Over

On May 4, 1989, I received a call from David H. Cordle, Sr. He was an investigator for the Annapolis State's Attorney's Office. Dave was investigating a rape-murder case where the victim had been strangled with something wrapped around her neck. Dave had a suspect in mind and wanted to see if I could identify anyone in a photo lineup.

"I don't know how I'm going to be able to help. The only time I really saw him at all was when he was walking out the door and I only saw the flip of his hair."

"You never know," he said. "You might remember something."

Dave set up a photo ID. Although I had not seen my attacker's face, he thought maybe some memory might be triggered when I looked at the pictures. I may have seen more than I would allow myself to remember and seeing a photo might retrieve those details. At the same time, he also set up a voice ID. He had his suspect and several other police officers read a line out of my journal. I was unable to pick anyone from the voice ID or the photo line-up. I felt useless. I did not have any idea who the man was who had attacked me, and the longer he went free, the greater the chance he would strike again.

Sometime at the end of spring in 1989, the manager of the Chart House called me upstairs to his office.

"I think it would be in your best interest to work in the bookkeeping office," he said.

"Why?" I asked.

"We are worried because no one was ever charged in your assault. We are afraid you might be in danger."

Did he really think I wouldn't see through this? Was he kidding? I knew what he was afraid of. He thought this guy might be stalking me. He didn't want to risk anyone else being attacked, so he wanted me out of the way. I felt like I had been punched in the gut. I had considered the Chart House my home-away-from-home. I had developed great friendships during my time working there. The management had always talked about how we were all "family" and how working together led to great things. *Yeah, I guess that was only true until the Big Bad Wolf got too close. Then you threw one of your own out the front door. Good riddance.*

"There is a position opening upstairs in accounting and it's yours if you want it."

I didn't wait to hear what else he had to say. I needed a job. I had rent to pay. Rather than choosing to be fired, which I am sure would have been my other option had I turned down the bookkeeping job, I said, "Okay, I'll try it out."

I worked in the office for a couple of weeks and hated it. Ellen, who had also been my trainer when I was hired as a cocktail waitress, was still the bookkeeper. She trained me to do the job, but I found working with numbers tedious and boring. I heard that Davis Pub was hiring, so I applied there. I was hired to wait tables in the small restaurant right away.

"Anyone who's waited tables at the Chart House can handle this job," Richard said as he handed me the paperwork to fill out.

After I started at Davis Pub, eight months after the attack, Dave Cordle called me again. Dave apparently had another suspect in mind and wanted to see if anyone in the bar crowds stood out to me. He and Detective Zora Lykken took me downtown to several restaurants.

At Middleton's Tavern, Dave suggested we sit at the bar. As I slid onto the stool, I noticed the bartender had hands similar to the guy who'd raped me. His fingernails were rounded at the base and he had a small mark on the back of his right hand. I started to tremble. I wanted to get out of there. My breath came in quick gasps.

Dave noticed I was upset.

My reaction gave him "probable cause" to get a warrant for a DNA sample. He would have it tested and compared to the sample collected at the hospital as part of my rape kit evidence. After about six weeks, we would have our answer as to whether or not the bartender was my rapist.

"Crime Scenes" — Annapolis, Maryland — 1988

Often called the gem of a city on the world-renowned Chesapeake Bay, Annapolis is known as a sailing town with a population of approximately 37,000 locals. Annapolis is also the seat of government for the City of Annapolis, Anne Arundel County, and the Maryland State government, as well as the home of the United States Naval Academy and St. John's College, a liberal arts school. Throw in the accompanying tourist industry, marine industry, multimillion dollar waterfront homes, and the largest per-capita public housing inventory in Maryland, and you have quite a policing challenge.

In the late 1980s, the Annapolis Police Department's Criminal Investigation Division (CID) consisted of four detectives and a supervisor. Depending on staffing issues, sometimes there were more employees, sometimes there were fewer. The unit was a generic investigation unit. There were no divisions between crimes against property, such as breaking and entering, and crimes against persons, such as murder, rape, and assault. As an investigator, I had a good working relationship with all of the detectives and command staff.

Converging Lives

Elizabeth

Annapolis has sponsored a spectacular 4th of July fireworks show for its hometown crowd and tens of thousands of visitors. This is a tradition from as far back as I can remember. The July 4th weekend of 1988 would prove to be the start of an investigative puzzle that included the death of Elizabeth Greenberg, the rape of Jennifer Wheatley, and a Peeping Tom incident involving victim Susan Johnson. I believed the Peeping Tom may be what connected all three crimes. As of the time of this writing, two of these crimes remain unsolved.

Stanley Morgan was an employee of the Annapolis Sailing School, located on Back Creek, just off the mouth of the Severn River and Spa Creek, and adjoining the Chesapeake Bay. He arrived at work on the morning of July 5, 1988 with a new challenge. The manager of the school had decided to leave the gates open for the previous night's fireworks festivities. The sailing school's location was a prime viewing point for the annual fireworks show. In past years, many people would converge there and set up blankets and chairs to party and watch the show. My wife Michele and I, along with a group of friends, were there the night of July 4, 1988 enjoying the fireworks.

On the morning of July 5th, Morgan began a walking survey to determine the extent of damage to the property. He wondered if, with the open access to the sailing school's premises, the damages would be more or less than in past years. As he walked the property, he came to the long rock jetty which parallels Back Creek and reaches out into the bay. Trash and debris were everywhere. As he walked the jetty, something caught his eye. A mid-sized cabin cruiser had run aground near the end of the jetty and was caught up on the rocks.

As he walked closer, Morgan saw an object floating next to the jetty on the Back Creek. To his horror, he discovered the body of what appeared to be a woman floating face down in the water. He immediately thought she must have been thrown from the grounded boat. Morgan quickly returned to the office and dialed 911. Annapolis Police responded by both land and water. The body was, in fact, that of a white female. She was nude from the waist down and appeared to have head trauma. Had she fallen off the boat or had she been thrown from the boat? Her purse was found in the water, as well. All I knew about the woman in the water was that her name was Elizabeth Greenberg.

My subsequent investigation of Elizabeth's death led me to developed three potential suspects:

Suspect #1: A civilian U. S. Customs electronic surveillance expert who placed himself near the Greenberg body recovery site at the approximate time of the murder. He was a member of the United States Coast Guard Auxiliary who had noticed the grounded boat and, although off duty, had walked out on the jetty to get a closer look.

Suspects #2 and #3: The two male companions last known to be with Elizabeth Greenberg on the night of her murder.

My theory hinged on the latter and I ran with it.

Jennifer

In the early morning hours of August 21, 1988, the Annapolis Police Department received a 911 call from Jennifer Wheatley. She reported having been raped in the gated, waterfront condominium community of "Chesapeake Landing" at the end of Chesapeake Avenue. This upscale part of Eastport was not known as a problem area for crime other than the occasional loud party or vandalism.

At the time, this was what law enforcement called a "Whodunit." No witnesses, no probable victim ID, but maybe some forensic possibilities. Only a few characteristics of the attacker were observed by Jennifer. He was white, his fingernails were very rounded in shape, and he had a small scar, mole, or healing wound on the back of his right hand. Could we develop and identify someone on as little evidence as this?

Susan

Susan Johnson owned a house in Eastport on Chesapeake Avenue. Susan had two roommates, Beth and Jo Ann. All of them were young, attractive professional women. On the evening of October 22, 1988, Jo Ann heard something on the back deck area of her house. Looking out to see if anyone was there, the young women saw nothing, but noticed the outdoor porch light had been turned off. They suspected a prowler or Peeping Tom had been outside. They called the police to report their suspicions and a report was taken. The investigation conducted by the reporting officer revealed the light bulb on the porch had been unscrewed.

Several days later, Susan was approached in a local grocery store by a white male. He was tall, with curly hair. He leaned down and licked her neck, smiled, and walked away. Susan instinctively felt this person may have been the one who had been on the back deck several days earlier, and was stalking her.

At the time of Susan's unusual encounter with the stranger in the grocery store, my wife Michele and Jo Ann were coworkers. Jo Ann told my wife about the porch light being unscrewed, possibly by a Peeping Tom, and about Susan's experience in the grocery store. Michele knew about my work in the Greenberg case and thought I would want to know about these incidents.

Also around this time, I was approached by a neighbor who was a coworker of Jennifer Wheatley. Jennifer had expressed to him some frustration involving the investigation, or seeming lack of investigation, of her rape case. My neighbor had read in the Annapolis newspaper about the story of Elizabeth Greenberg's murder and thought there were some similarities with Jennifer's attack. Elizabeth had suffered some head trauma and apparently she had been raped.

My boss at the time, State's Attorney Warren Duckett, knew of my involvement in the Greenberg case and he agreed to my joining with the Annapolis Police on all three of these cases and others thought to be related.

The three separate incidents took place in a relatively short span of time, in a small geographic area, and appeared to be connected. All of the victims were young, attractive women and the crimes indicated a sexual predator. But, were they related?

14

My Pieces of the Puzzle: Diverging Cases

On May 4, 1989, I met with Detective Paul Leo and Detective SGT Zora Lykken, the Annapolis Police detectives who were assigned to Jennifer Wheatley's rape case, and I began to officially assist in the investigation.

Detective Leo left the Criminal Investigation Department shortly after I became involved in the Wheatley case. Sergeant Lykken and I continued working on the three cases, developing leads and possible suspects.

Our primary suspect, developed through my work on the Greenberg case, was cleared relatively early in our investigation. However, another suspect in that case, Mark Gorman (name changed), could not be eliminated without closer scrutiny. He fit the description of the person in Susan Johnson's supermarket incident case, and I believed he may also have been involved in the rape of Jennifer Wheatley. Sergeant Lykken and I needed Jennifer Wheatley's help.

On May 11, 1989, Detective SGT Lykken introduced me to Jennifer Wheatley. Although it was nine months after she had been raped, my first impression of Jennifer was that of a frightened victim. I could tell from the look in her eyes that she was still emotionally traumatized by the events of the night she was raped.

Through my training and extensive on-the-job criminal investigation experience, I instinctively observe everything about the person I am talking with — the expression in their eyes, facial movements, body language, and speech patterns. Jennifer's gaze bore into me and I immediately felt connected to her anguish and pain. From that moment, I knew I would exhaust all avenues to apprehend her attacker. I had no idea it would take twenty years to do it.

After hearing Jennifer tell the details of her rape, I believed her attacker had watched her for an undetermined amount of time and then methodically made his way into her home. These stalking actions showed an organized, coherent plan to achieve his ultimate objective — the sexual assault of Jennifer.

I listened as Jennifer relayed details of what occurred on the night of August 21, 1988, and I was particularly alarmed by the methodical actions of her attacker. He apparently took a T-shirt and identification papers out of her car, he unscrewed the light bulbs in the carport, and once inside the home, he turned on the air conditioner to mask the sounds of his intrusion. Then he waited in the shadows until his victim was completely vulnerable and struck without warning. Of particular note were the boldness, deliberateness, and confidence of this intruder. Had he done this before? I believed he had.

Detective SGT Lykken was a skilled, veteran sex offense detective and was known throughout the region as an expert on rape/sexual assault cases. As this was my first direct involvement in a rape case, I looked to Detective SGT Lykken to lead the way.

We discussed a few possible ways for Jennifer to make a positive identification of our remaining suspect. Jennifer never saw the face of the man who raped her, however she did notice he had rounded fingernails, and a small mark on the back of his right hand. She had also noticed an odd smell, possibly that of chlorine, about him.

Detective SGT Lykken and I decided to arrange for Jennifer to "observe" Gorman at his job at Middleton's Tavern, located on the City Dock in downtown Annapolis. As part of my investigation I had become familiar with the route Gorman took to work. Knowing he lived around the corner on Prince George Street and regularly walked to work, we decided to arrange for Jennifer to unknowingly be in proximity of our suspect in order to "observe" him.

In order for us to be sure Jennifer would not know our intended target we started by taking her to a different restaurant for a bite to eat. Detective SGT Lykken and I were really clock watching waiting for our suspect to arrive at his job at Middleton's Tavern.

Once we were certain Gorman was at work, we took Jennifer into Middleton's and took a seat at a table near the bar where Gorman was a bartender. I noticed that Jennifer was unable to get a close look at his hands from this vantage point so I casually suggested we move to a seat at the bar.

It wasn't too long after we took our seats at the bar that Jennifer was able to see our suspects hands. She was sitting just a few feet away from a man who might have been her attacker and possibly the murderer of Liz Greenberg. I felt Jennifer's apprehension and fear — it was palpable and she was trembling.

She indicated to me that she saw a small mark on the back of Gorman's hand. Was it dirt or the same spot she had seen months ago? The fingernails looked similar, however she just wasn't sure.

Based on the mark Jennifer identified on Gorman's hand and the possible connection to the Greenberg murder case, I applied for a search warrant of Gorman's residence. The warrant also allowed me to transport Gorman to the Anne Arundel General Hospital to obtain a blood sample and collect head and pubic hairs. The Annapolis Police Department wired me in case Gorman made any incriminating statements during the search, recovery, and collection of evidence.

Detective SGT Lykken and I conducted the search with a backup team outside monitoring the events from an undercover surveillance van. The specific item I was searching for was not located. (I do not identify the item here because, as of this writing, the Greenberg case is still an active cold case).

After the search of the residence, I asked Gorman if he wanted to provide the hair samples in private. He said he did want privacy. We entered a cramped bedroom and, as I closed the door, an ironing board fell from behind the door, unfolding and creating quite a racket. Detective SGT Lykken began yelling to see if I was okay. The backup team in the van started scrambling, not really knowing what was going on or what to do. After the commotion, a panicked Gorman literally ripped his head and pubic hairs out in one pull providing the minimum twenty hairs needed for laboratory analysis. I cringed involuntarily as I imagined how much that must have hurt. After I carefully collected the hairs into evidence bags we proceeded to the local hospital for the blood draw. This evidence was delivered to the Maryland State Police Crime Lab in Pikesville, Maryland for analysis and comparison to the DNA evidence from the Greenberg and Wheatley cases.

Several months later, I was notified that Gorman's DNA profile did not match the evidence from either the Greenberg or Wheatley evidence. In addition, there were no new leads in the Susan Johnson Peeping Tom-Grocery Store case, and no forensic evidence available to be tested. Consequently, that case went cold. It was time to move on to other cases…for now.

15

A Year Later

I found the whole process of trying to figure out who had raped me very stressful. In my mind, it was simple (probably this was illogically simplified thinking): find the guy. I didn't have a clue how this was supposed to happen. However, the investigators did this kind of thing all the time. I just wanted the guy who'd attacked me locked up. The reality was there was not much to go on, and finding the guy would have been difficult even with great evidence. Finding him would be nearly impossible with almost no evidence. My inability to provide a description wasn't helpful to the police at all. Still, waiting to find out if this or that suspect was the guy was unnerving.

While we were waiting for the results of the bartender's DNA results, Stephen decided we should take a trip down to Nags Head and go fishing with his family.

The weather was very changeable during the days at the beach. During the afternoons, the sun heated up the atmosphere, and by evening, the storms would roll in. It was a great trip of barbecues, tropical drinks, fresh fish, swimming in the ocean, and walking on the beach. I had brought along a kite and we had it flying from the balcony of our beach rental for the entire trip...rain and shine!

For a while I forgot about the DNA testing going on back home. Even as I was unwinding, Stephen seemed a bit on edge. This was not what I expected from him on vacation. Stephen's sister, Rita, told me he was having a problem dealing with my involvement in the investigation with the State's Attorney's Office. He couldn't stand to see me so upset and wanted me to drop it. I asked her where all of this was coming from. How could he not want to find the guy who'd attacked me and put him in jail? She told me a story about how she believed a person named Jeff had set her up to be assaulted because of some drugs or money she owed him.

Rita said Stephen had a difficult time getting over her attack and he was not ready to go through it again. I knew the Jeff she was talking about. He was a regular customer at the Chart House. He was a truck driver who delivered boats all over the country. He was also a huge drug dealer who was known to carry a concealed weapon and large quantities of cocaine most of the time. I got chills when she told me her story. Her account of drugs not being delivered sounded eerily familiar.

In 1986, after George, my coworker from the raw bar at McGarvey's, helped me with the move from my house in Eastport, he offered to share some cocaine with me. I found out later he was supposed to have delivered this cocaine to Jeff, this same Jeff who may have arranged Rita's assault. I wondered if Jeff had arranged a similar fate for me in the name of payback for not being paid for the cocaine George shared with me.

I tried to put Rita's words in the back of my mind while we were at the beach. However, I couldn't forget something Jeff had asked me about three weeks after my attack: "How is the investigation going? Do they have a suspect yet?"

Although I had seen Jeff a number of times since I had returned to work, this was the first time he had asked me anything about the assault. I'd told him as far as I knew, no one was ever going to be caught because I never saw the guy's face and could not give a useful description.

He then asked me, "Have you seen George lately?"

"No," I said, "not since I quit working at McGarvey's." I felt uneasy. I had not given George much thought in almost two years. Had Jeff been intimating that he was behind the assault? Did George have something to do with it? Rita's words gave me chills.

One year and one day after I was attacked, I got a call from Dave Cordle concerning the DNA profile he was testing from the bartender at Middleton's Tavern.

"Not a match."

Dave promised me he would keep my case in mind. "Don't worry," he said, "I'll get him."

Because his call had come at the first anniversary of the day I was raped, I really believed I would have an answer. I wanted to believe the creep would be caught and I would not have to look over my shoulder anymore. I was disheartened when Dave told me the news. I knew finding the guy had been a long shot, but I hoped maybe my prayers would be answered. I had slept that night of the first anniversary with the hall light on. After the depressing news, I started drinking pretty heavily, especially at night when I was alone in the house.

I didn't know which was worse: the search for a suspect, the waiting for results, or knowing the man who attacked me was still out there. I fell into a depression that I could not shake. It started to undermine my relationship with Stephen.

One night, a short time after the news from Dave Cordle, Stephen pulled into my driveway to drop me off after dinner out. He asked, "Want me to come in?"

"I think I need to be alone for a while," I said.

I did not mean for our relationship to end with this phrase, but it did.

I wanted to be alone that night. I ended up alone for a few nights, and I used the time to sort out my thoughts. By the time I got myself into a routine of work that kept my mind off my disappointment, a couple of weeks had passed. I called Stephen a few times, but when he was not home, I didn't leave messages.

I was struggling with what Rita had said: *"He wants you to drop it."*

I absolutely wanted to find the man who was responsible for assaulting me, but Stephen thought it would be better for me to let it all go. I loved him, but I could not agree that it was worth putting other women at risk by "dropping it." I knew in my heart this man would rape again if he were not caught. I also knew I would do whatever was necessary to find him.

I let Stephen go without properly ending the relationship. Rita tried to get Stephen and me together again — she hoped to create a situation where we could talk. I had left a shirt in her car when we came back from our trip to the beach. She planned to call me to come and pick it up one day when Stephen was home. She never got the chance.

I remember hearing the ambulance the morning it sped down the street. Somehow, I knew Stephen was dead. Edie, my housemate at the time, answered the phone when the call came. She told me the news as I walked out the front door heading to work.

"Stephen died of a heart attack this morning," she said.

"I know," I said. I was profoundly saddened by the news.

I went to Stephen's viewing. I hated that. Seeing him laid out in that box was horrible. I hated myself for not going to him to tell him how I felt. Even if our relationship hadn't been re-kindled, at least we wouldn't have ended it with everything between us unresolved. I was inconsolable. I didn't care about anything anymore. I drank. I drank a lot. Drinking was the only thing that helped to dull the pain inside.

16

The Christmas Miracle

Stephen died right around Thanksgiving of 1989, on "Black Friday," the busiest Christmas shopping day of the year. Knowing how much he loved Christmas, I took two rolls of quarters to a Christmas tree lot a few blocks away and picked out a tree. I stuffed it in my car and drove home. I wasn't feeling at all like celebrating the holidays, but I wanted Stephen close to me. Having a tree and decorating it while thinking of him was all I had; it would have to do.

I avoided all of the parties my friends were having. My friendship with Edie was becoming strained. She didn't know what to do to help me. Truth was, she couldn't do anything. I set up the tree in the living room. Edie told me she would be moving out in January. I was depressed.

I put lights and sparkling glass bulbs on the tree. Christmas came and went. A new year dawned and I didn't notice. I would go to work and then come home, and then I would start drinking beer. If I had the day off, I would go out to listen to music with friends and drink beer. All the while, the tree stood tall, green, and as supple as the day I'd brought it home.

Eventually, I withdrew from everyone and stopped going with my friends to listen to the music at Reynolds Tavern on Thursday nights. I stopped going to listen to Tim play at Harry Browne's on Sunday nights. I stopped doing almost everything I used to love, except for drawing. I continued to draw even through the round-the-clock beer haze. I drew portraits and detailed pen and ink drawings. I even did a painting or two. It was the only thing that gave me any enjoyment at all. Nothing else I did seemed to give me any pleasure and even drinking stopped numbing my pain.

It took more and more beer to quiet the voices in my head and dull the ache in my heart. Sometime in late winter, I took the lights and glass balls off of the tree, and stopped giving it water. Unbelievably, the tree was still full of sap. With the decorations taken off, the tree looked more like a very large potted plant. Only it wasn't in dirt. It didn't have roots. But somehow it thrived. Visitors were amazed to see a Christmas tree in my living room in middle of the summer. They would ask where I was planning to plant it, believing it was a growing tree. It looked like it had just come off the Christmas tree lot.

Sometime in mid-July, I finally dragged the tree out to the back porch. It was still green and fresh and had not had a drink of water in over five months. It was the hot, humid summer days that finally sucked the life out of the tree. Within a week or so of sitting on the porch, Stephen's Christmas tree had turned brown, and the needles fell off everywhere. I still wonder how long it might have lasted had I not moved it out into the heat. I believe Stephen was with me during those days after he died. I believe he was the guardian angel I needed to help me through the long and lonely nights. Stephen's tree was a real Christmas miracle that continues to remind me that anything, even the unbelievable, is possible in life as long as we allow ourselves to see.

17

Lasting Effects, New Habits

*A*fter my roommate Edie moved out and before I got a new roommate, I was afraid to be alone in the house. I would drink myself to sleep every night because I didn't want to be able to hear any noises inside or outside of my house. I hated being home alone. I was scared. But I was usually not in any mood or condition to go out. My family members and a few friends made attempts to get me out into the world again. They believed it would help snap me out of my depression to be among the living. I had lost almost everything. I felt like my spirit had been broken and couldn't see the point. It seemed to me that as soon as I thought the circumstances in my life were improving, something else went horribly wrong. I didn't want the price of re-joining the living to be followed by yet another devastating blow. Being alone felt safer; I didn't have anything left and I was tired of being a target for a heartless God.

There were so many things that reminded me of either Stephen or the night I was raped. So many things triggered memories that made my fear bubble to the surface again. Some of the reminders were fleeting and barely noticed. But others were hard to overlook. Within weeks after I was raped, a thick, skunk-like stripe of gray showed up in my hair. I am sure it was the result of sheer terror. It was a constant reminder of the events of August 21, 1988. I hated it. Permanent hair dyes didn't cover it. I couldn't stand looking in the mirror and seeing that stripe of hair and being reminded of the jerk who'd raped me. I began lightening the color of my hair to try and get the stripe to blend in better. Many people over the years thought it looked "great" or "distinguished." Some just thought it was "really cool." I didn't think so and avoided looking at myself in mirrors and having my picture taken.

The gray hair wasn't the only reminder. I'm pretty sure my battle with weight gain over the years has its roots in the assault. I remember thinking if I hadn't been so slender — if I didn't look so good — maybe none of this would have happened. Stupid and illogical, I know. But that didn't keep me from believing this on some level. So my weight went up and down and up again.

For the first couple of years, loud or unexpected noises were the worst. All it took was a noise that didn't fit in with the normal "house sounds" and adrenaline would shoot through me. It took years to get to the point where I wouldn't jump at every sound, where my heart would not race out of control. Even now, unusual sounds during the night make me hold my breath and listen for anything out of the ordinary.

I became a really light sleeper and sleep didn't come easily. If I couldn't fall asleep, I would drink until I was able to pass out. Sleep was never as comforting or rejuvenating as before the attack. I started to have bad dreams and reoccurring nightmares of being pursued by a faceless monster. These dreams continued off and on for twenty years. Whenever my life was stressful or chaotic, the bad dreams would be more frequent. All of my life's trials and tribulations would manifest at night as this monster that springs from the shadows. In twenty years, I never completely stopped worrying that there could be someone out there, ready to grab me unawares.

To alleviate some of my fear of the dark, I made sure to have nightlights on around the house and porch lights on outside to greet me when I returned home after dark. I never entered a room without turning on a light first. Shower curtains were always pushed all the way to one side and doors were swung open wide so I could be assured no one was hiding behind them. I adopted these small habits, many of them unconsciously, the very first night after I was raped, to help me feel safer when I was alone in my home. These practices became second nature to me. Now, I don't even give them a thought unless something is out of place. When something startles me, looks or feels wrong, or is out of sync somehow, I am instantly reminded of that night and I feel traces of the fear again. Although I still do not like being home alone, it isn't as scary as it was during those first few years. I may never get to the point where I feel completely comfortable being in my home by myself. As my friend Jackie said so well: *That I feel safe and secure in my home does not mean that I* am *safe and secure in my home.*

Indeed.

After about a month or two of living alone, I got a new roommate. Ray worked for the cable company. He was very nice and easy to talk to. I gave him an abbreviated version of what had been going on with me for the past year or so. We quickly became friends.

He began to help me pull out of my depression. He made sure I ate something every day, and would sit and watch TV with me. If he had to be away for a few days for business, he would call and check up on me. He always called me when he was on his way home so he wouldn't scare me coming in late at night.

Ray planned a fishing trip to Nags Head and invited me to go with him. It was difficult at first for me to be there because, around every turn, I was reminded of Stephen. But Ray kept an eye on me. He managed to keep my spirits up and had me laughing as he helped me get past the first emotional day. I went out fishing with him and "the guys" and caught a ten pound black tuna. I needed help getting it reeled in, but eventually I did land it in the boat.

The seas were terribly rough and it rained half the time we were out fishing. If I went down below the boat's deck, I would start to feel queasy, so I had to stay out on deck with the fresh air and torrential rains. I was soaked to the skin and shivering by the time we got back to the pier, but I didn't puke. I was the only girl on the boat and the only one in the group who didn't get sick.

Even though Ray was successful in helping me out of my depression, I continued to drink. I no longer felt the need to drink myself to sleep, but I was unable to stop. What had started as a way to numb myself from the pain I felt inside had become a full-blown addiction. And it was really getting out of control.

18

Taking Charge of Me Again

I didn't ever really work through the fear that gripped me after I was raped. When I started seeing Stephen, I managed to push the feelings from that night pretty deep inside. I was happy when I was with him, but I had not released the anxieties. When Stephen died, I was not in any shape to take on any more emotional trauma. With his death, I stored even more hurt and despair on top of the lump I had created inside. No amount of alcohol was going to be able to melt away these internalized emotions. It was going to take some kind of divine intervention and soul-searching.

I quit my job at Davis Pub, hoping that being away from the bar atmosphere would help me stop drinking or at least get myself under control. It didn't work. Without a job and no money coming in, things didn't take long to go from bad to worse. Pretty soon, I was having trouble paying my bills. I had to get help.

I had spent too many days and nights feeling terrible. I had already lost most of the people in my life I really cared about. All of my old Chart House friends were gone. I knew if I didn't stop drinking I was going to die. It was a few words from my friend Patrick that made me realize that my life was worth living. I don't remember exactly what he said to me that day; I am sure it was something he said all the time. However this time his words hit home and I realized he believed in me even though I no longer knew who I was. His words stirred a realization in me: I had given too many days to the monster who'd raped me, and it was time I take charge of *"Me"* again.

In the summer of 1990, I checked into rehab at the Charter Hospital in California for twenty-eight days. This hospital was close to where my father and brother lived, and it was as far away as I could get from all physical links to my troubles. I felt I would be more successful in working through my emotional distress and starting anew if I removed myself from constant reminders of the rape and Stephen's death. The Charter Hospital had a good reputation for helping addicts recover. I knew when I went in that I was going to be the one in thirteen who would succeed in reclaiming my life by kicking my alcohol addiction.

Rehab is all about discovering what your strengths are while shedding your weaknesses. The hardest part about rehab for me wasn't about kicking my alcohol addiction. It was trying to figure out what I was going to do with the rest of my life. I wasn't skilled in anything. I hadn't been a great student. The only thing I had was my art. What could I do with that? Could someone really make a living as an artist? I wanted to try. My drawing was the only constant in my life. It was the one thing that had gotten me through so many difficult times. Drawing was a therapy for me, but it was also a source of enjoyment. I was pretty good, even though I had not found my niche yet.

Most of my time in rehab was spent in group counseling, one-on-one counseling, and learning how to face my hurts and fears by working through them in practical ways. Developing positive solutions to problems and conflicts that arose without wanting to reach for a drink became easier as I got better at facing the hurt I had bottled up inside. This allowed me to focus on anything other than being afraid and sad, and made it possible for me to focus on my strengths.

After I had been out of the hospital for a while, my father sent me a letter that upset me. He had been told by one of my sisters that I hadn't learned anything during my time in rehab and that I was right back in the bars again. It wasn't true. I did go back to the bars where I had worked, but I wasn't drinking. Part of the process of reclaiming my life involved finding out who my true friends were and discovering how much exposure to alcohol I could allow before I was too tempted to drink again. I was starting my life over and I had to know who was going to stick with the "new" me. At the time, my sister didn't understand this. I wasn't sure if she ever really would. Picking yourself up after a horrible sexual assault and rape, losing someone you loved, falling apart, and then starting all over again was thankfully not something she had had to do. No one who has had the good fortune not to have to experience this roller coaster can ever really know the struggle of starting over completely. Finding the ability to rebuild a foundation for my life was only possible after I could see what was left to work with.

Even though some things about the letter annoyed me, I realized Dad was reaching out to me. He included the inspirational words he'd found that had sustained him while he and my mother were divorcing.

I made my dad's letter my mantra:

Until one makes the "commitment" there is certain hesitancy, a desire to hold back and generally a lack of accomplishment. With all acts of initiative and change there is one basic truth, the ignorance of which can kill most ideas and plans and that is the moment one commits: "Providence" moves also. All sorts of things begin to happen that would never have otherwise occurred. A whole stream of events comes out of that decision to commit, raising in one's favor all kinds of unforeseen incidents and assistance which no one could ever dream would happen. One of Johann Goethe's couplets puts this clearly in perspective: "Whatever you can dream, you can do, begin it immediately; boldness has genius, power, and magic in it."

19

The Making of an Artist

While I was in California, my sisters stopped by my house and cleaned it for me. After I returned home, my mother helped me by paying my bills until I could find a job. I wasn't sure exactly what I was going to do, but I wanted to use my artistic talent in one way or another. So I went in search of a job. In the window of a "Deck the Walls" frame shop in the local mall, I saw a small handwritten sign that said, "Artist Wanted."

Hey, I was an artist! It was as if a light bulb had gone off in my head. Maybe making a living at being an artist could be possible. Up till that moment, I thought that making a living as an artist meant painting all the time. That certainly didn't hurt, but maybe it was not the way to go about realizing the goal. Seeing the "Artist Wanted" sign in the frame shop showed me that sometimes reaching a goal means you have to allow yourself to take a different path, to be flexible in *how* you get what you have your heart set on.

I got the job as a sales clerk and worked my way into a full-time framing position. Now that I had a full-time job, I decided to get myself a pet to keep me company. I saw an announcement in the classified ads for free kittens. I called and the woman who answered said she had one left. She lived just a couple miles from my home. I drove over and instantly fell in love with the skinny gray kitten with gold eyes and huge ears. Knucklehead was a Russian Blue mix. He was probably the smartest cat I ever had. The first time I heard him meow he said:

"Ma, Ma."

I thought that was pretty wild, but he was just getting started. He never stopped amazing me.

Knucklehead wasn't exactly an attack cat. He wouldn't have been much good at protecting me. But he was really good at letting me know when someone was approaching the house. He greeted everyone indiscriminately by running to the door. It was up to me to figure out if the person was someone I wanted to let in. "Knuck," as I came to call him, was more dog-like in behavior. When it came to agility and hunting, though, his skills were lacking. But throw a small puff ball or fat rubber band across the room and he'd fetch it for you. I knew I was in for a lifetime full of laughs with that cat when, on his first adventure outside, he followed me across the yard by doing some crazy balancing act on top of the garden hose. Turns out he was afraid of grass. Thankfully, that fear didn't last long.

I had Knucklehead for fourteen years, and he provided me with a new story to tell every day.

For years, I paid my bills by working as a picture framer in various frame shops and galleries around Annapolis and doing commissioned artwork. Picture framing is a precise skill that works in fractions, and fractions require sharp math skills. As I've mentioned before, math was not a subject I was good at. I can do basic addition and subtraction, but that's about as far I go. My understanding of numbers had not improved much since those early school days.

When I took my SATs in high school, I answered the first math problem without trouble. I read the second question and didn't even understand what was being asked of me. I scanned through a few more of the questions and realized I was in trouble. I made the decision at that point to put my artistic talents to work since my math skills were severely lacking. I decided to fill in the tiny circles designated for answering the questions in a pretty pattern rather than leave all but the first circle blank. I managed to get sixty percent of the answers correct.

The art of framing required training. While I tried to find a way of bypassing the need to learn too much math, I surprisingly managed to work out a way to do the precise equations needed for measuring frames and matting without actually having to do any fractions or division problems. Picture framing was a skill I took to very easily. I have an eye for detail and color and learning the mechanics of conservation framing for nearly everything that could be put into a frame came easily to me. Eventually, one of my employers had me take the Professional Picture Framers Association (PPFA) exam. I passed the test with flying colors and could then call myself a "Professional" picture framer.

I was trained by an older man who knew just about everything there was to know about framing. Butch had been working as a framer for thirty years or more, and he was also an artist. One day, he told me he was trying to challenge himself by doing a small watercolor painting every night. I thought this was a great idea and decided I would try watercolor painting, too. There was a craft store close to my house that had all kinds of art supplies. The only watercolor paints I was familiar with were little dry cakes that took forever to get wet, didn't offer much color and cracked to bits when they dried. I was pretty sure this is not what I wanted to use. Instead I bought a small set of watercolor paints in tubes for $5.00. Wet watercolor paints were something new to me, but I used my experience with oils and acrylics to get me started.

As a picture framer, I had access to lots of scrap conservation matting. Archival mats are made of a colored layer and an acid-free cotton, four-ply, smooth white surface that was perfect for painting on. Grabbing an old dinner plate from the kitchen, I laid out a palette of paints to work with and sat down with a couple of scrap archival mats. At first, I just played with the paint and got used to what it could do. After a few days of this, I tried a "real" painting. I was hooked. I could use the watercolor as thick as oils or as thin as a wash of water. I was able to get as much or as little detail as

I wanted. The paints on my palette would dry out every night, but with just a little water, they were moist and vibrant again. I loved it!

At first, I had difficulty figuring out what to paint. I took my Instamatic camera around town and photographed many of the houses and gardens in the historic district. I would then paint from these photographs. Everywhere I went, I had my camera with me. I would see "paintings" in every garden I happened across. Over time, I got familiar enough with my camera to use the viewfinder to map out my paintings for me. After I got the film developed, I would put the pictures I liked into a photo album. When I was ready to start a painting, I would just flip through until I found the picture I wanted to paint.

For fourteen years, I painted every night. As I was always eager to see the finished product, I would usually finish a painting in two or three sittings, or about ten to fifteen hours. After a few years of this steady practice, one of my friends asked me how much I wanted for a particular picture.

Hmmmm, I hadn't given much thought to selling them. I wasn't even sure if they were much good at that point. But my friend liked the painting enough to pay me for it, so I said, "$50." That started a twelve-year painting avocation. What had started as a challenge to me turned into something I loved to do and could make money from. I was beginning to see a natural progression in my work from beginner to skilled artist. I had pushed myself, and now I was ready to really pursue painting as a lucrative hobby.

One day, my friend Marnie suggested that I sell my paintings through local galleries. I thought that was a great idea. It was scary as crap, but it was a great idea. As I had regularly framed my favorite paintings, I already had a body of work to show the gallery owners. I went to a couple of places on Main Street and they all said no. I went to the galleries on Maryland Avenue and showed them my paintings.

"No."

Marnie took a handful of paintings to a couple of places. Even with her gung-ho attitude, they said no. I felt defeated. All my friends loved my paintings, bought them regularly, and were very encouraging, but it seemed the gallery owners didn't love them as much as we did. I had a hard time believing I would ever see my dream of being a "real" artist take shape. I was having a difficult time keeping my hopes alive in the face of so much discouragement.

Although at first, I wasn't successful in persuading the galleries to take a chance on me by showing my work, I did not stop. I continued to photograph every garden and inspiring doorway and window I came across. My paintings were getting better and better. Often I was recruited to do commissioned paintings for people. Many wanted their homes, gardens, or pets painted. When the Annapolis courthouse was being renovated, I was asked to do a painting of the old facade. This painting hung for years in the wedding chapel inside the courthouse until it was moved to one of the judge's chambers. As the word spread and more and more people saw what I could do, the requests for special paintings came to me fairly steadily. Watching the expressions of people when they get the first look at an artwork I have done for them has always been a delight for me.

After two years of "no"s from local galleries, I finally got a break in 1995. A gallery on West Street was looking for a picture framer. I wanted out of the high volume framing place where I was working at the time, so I applied for the job. Not only did I get the position, but the owner took five of my paintings to hang in the gallery. All of them sold within a couple of weeks. The magic had started and I couldn't be stopped. Working at this gallery was less stressful than my previous job, paid more, and enabled me to work regular hours. I had lots of time each night to paint.

In 1996, the gallery hosted my first one-woman show. I had thirty to forty watercolor paintings hanging in the gallery and nearly all of them sold on the night of the opening. By the close of the show, all of them had new homes. Doing something I loved and having my talents validated through the appreciation of others was an amazing feeling. I was seeing the beginning of a long and rewarding career take shape.

20

Success and Isolation

*A*lthough painting every chance I could was very rewarding, it was also very isolating. So if anyone were to ask me is there were anything I regret during this time of my life, I would say, "Yes, losing touch with my friends." The very thing that I loved to do took a lot of time. Painting every night after I got home from work at the frame shop made it easy for me to lose touch with almost everyone. I remained close friends with Marnie and saw her whenever our schedules worked out. But I didn't go out very much to socialize. I wasn't going out to listen to music or to the local theaters. Since I wasn't getting out to meet new people, I wasn't dating anyone. I reasoned that a lasting and profitable career was more important for me and that my friends would be around when I got my life in order. And they probably were, but by the time I did get my life in order, I didn't see them much at all. I would occasionally run into a familiar face, but it was always in passing: *"Hi, how are you? Good! Take care."* Just a minute of chit-chat and then we were off on our separate ways.

Although one reason for my isolation was my new passion for watercolors, another reason was shame. Although I missed my friends, I didn't know if they would feel comfortable being around me. If they knew I had let my life fall apart, maybe they would treat me differently. None of them really knew how bad I had let things get before I went into rehab. I was embarrassed. Even in the middle of building a new life and making a name for myself, I couldn't forgive myself for my human frailty.

It wasn't until after several years of holding a steady job, paying my bills, and throwing myself into painting that I was able to feel really good about myself and my life again. By then, my friends had moved on. Finding them again seemed a daunting task.

In retrospect, I believe my true friends would have said I had nothing to be ashamed or embarrassed about. But I never gave them the chance. I stayed away from the music and theater and people I cared most about, choosing instead to work at becoming a respected artist. While I was having art shows, developing my picture-framing skills, and painting nightly, my friends were getting married and having families and getting on with their lives without me.

21

20th High School Reunion

*I*n 1997, I was working on West Street in Annapolis, framing during the day, selling my work, and painting every night. Life was good. I was still single. I hated being the only one who never had a date to any function. I attended family get-togethers solo. Being single was, unfortunately, normal for me. But on the other hand, I was developing quite a following of collectors and a bit of notoriety in the art world, and that was a good thing.

My twentieth high school reunion was scheduled for September. I decided to go. I sent my money in to the reunion committee for a ticket for one. Just a few days before the night of the reunion, I sprained my ankle running down the steps at work. The doctor in the emergency room gave me an air cast. Great! No date and now a silly looking air cast on my ankle. I started thinking maybe I shouldn't go. Maybe this was a sign.

But, I reasoned, I hadn't seen many of these people for ten years, since the last reunion, and probably wouldn't see them again for another ten years, so what would it hurt? It would be fun to do the "reunion comparison" thing: *He looked great in high school, but look at him now; she looked frumpy in high school, but now she looks great.*

Also, there were a couple of people I had remained friends with I wanted to see, but whom I didn't get to see very often. One of my friends, Janis, had kept in touch with another mutual friend, Gena, and we arranged to meet and hang out together for the weekend functions.

The three-night affair included an informal cocktail hour at the Chart House — the same restaurant I had worked at years ago — on Friday night, the actual reunion on Saturday night, and then a family picnic on

Sunday. I figured I had paid my money and had my ticket in hand, so if nothing else, sprained ankle and solo, I would have fun catching up with Janis and Gena. I went.

At the Chart House cocktail party, I sat with my friends, having fun reminiscing. We told stories about when the three of us would go out together to the dances at the Naval Academy on Friday night. It was a wicked and yet unintentional twist of fate that gave us such similar names and then made us good friends during school. How confused the unsuspecting midshipmen were once they approached our table and asked to join us! Just getting through introductions was enough to send us into fits of laughter.

"Hi, I'm Gena."

"I'm Janis."

"I'm Jenny."

We visited with quite a few old friends that night, catching up on each other's lives, when I spied Marcus Wolf across the room. He was standing alone. I remembered him from way back in my eighth grade homeroom, but didn't recall actually having any classes with him in high school. I think he knew who I was right away, but I introduced myself anyway.

"Hi. You're Marcus, aren't you? I'm Jennifer."

We exchanged pleasantries and I thought, *Damn, he looks good!* And I was pretty sure, based on the answers to my three questions, he might just turn out to be the "Mr. Right" who had been missing from my life.

I worked my important questions into what turned out to be a very short conversation.

"What do you do?" I asked

"I work for the FCC..." Marcus told me just a little about what he did for the FCC.

"Are you married?" I asked.

"I was married. But I just recently separated," he said.

"Oh, that's too bad," I said thinking, *Bingo!*

"Where are you living these days?"

"I live in Arlington, Virginia," he answered.

Crap. Might as well be Alaska. Who wants to deal with a "long-distance" relationship? I had to give the idea of dating someone almost an hour away some more thought. I said the usual, "Okay, good to see you again." He did the same. Then I rejoined my group. Both Janis and Gena started grilling me.

"So? How did it go? Is he married? What's going on?" I answered all their questions and said I would have to mull over the whole Virginia part of this.

"If it's meant to happen, it will happen."

The next night, Saturday, I was sitting at the table with Janis and Gena and a few other old friends and we saw Marcus walk in. Janis immediately invited him to join our table.

"Thanks. But I am sitting with my friends Scott and Sherry Morrow. You remember them?"

We said we did and that we would stop by their table later to chat.

The dinner was predictably bland and overcooked, but the night was fun. Three old friends talking and laughing just like we did twenty years ago at the Naval Academy dances. Only I wasn't doing too much dancing that night. I was wearing a tiger-striped gauzy dress and a blue plastic air cast. Not the chic fashion statement I was hoping for. At one point during the evening, a slow song was playing and it seemed like everyone was dancing except for Marcus and me. He was standing in front of the bar drinking a beer and looking really sharp in his dark silk suit. I made my way over to him and asked him to dance. We danced a few more songs during the remainder of the evening. Before the night was over, I gave him a matchbook with my phone number scribbled in it. (He still has it. I saw it not too long ago when I was cleaning.) As we were walking to our cars, another friend invited the two of us back to his house for the "after-hours" party. We went together in his new Z-3.

Marcus didn't come to the Sunday family picnic. But Janis and Gena were there and so were Scott and Sherry. Scott had brought his guitar and we all joined in singing with him. It was a great weekend with friends, and I had reunited with an old eighth grade homeroom friend and fellow high school classmate who would eventually become my husband.

Marcus called on the Wednesday following the reunion to ask if I was interested in having dinner with him. He drove to Annapolis that evening and we went to McGarvey's. It didn't take long for us to fall into a routine of him coming to my house or me going to his on the weekends.

During the six years we dated, I continued to paint and work in the framing industry. I also continued to have an annual show of my paintings and they continued to sell. In April of 2003, I moved away from Annapolis and in with Marcus, and a year later we invited his best friend Jon and my sister Mollie to join us in Vegas. We were eloping! Mollie could not get the time off of work, but Jon happily took on the role of our chauffeur, photographer, and best man at our wedding. After a twenty-four hour engagement, we were married on June 26, 2004. The three of us went to Hoover Dam and a Penn & Teller show. It was a terrific and lucky wedding week.

In 2007, we attended our thirtieth high school reunion and we were all the buzz. Before the evening was over, most people were talking about how Marcus and I had danced at our twentieth reunion and how we'd been together since.

Over our years together, our circle of friends has grown to include the people Marcus was close to and my friends. It amazes me how easily we all fell into place with each other. I was accepted as part of the family by his relatives and he fits right in with mine. We have an annual party that includes all our family and friends. Our barbecue has grown to be quite the anticipated event. It's the one time during each year when we try to get everyone together and just have fun. The barbecue is like a literal version of the annual Christmas card where you insert the letter about what has happened to your family over the past year. Only this is better because we all get together and enjoy a day or two of music, food, and laughs.

Marcus' friendship with Scott and Sherry started in the fourth grade. Scott and Marcus were buddies growing up and have remained friends over the years. Sherry and Scott were fulfilling the grand plan of destiny when Scott jockeyed into position right next to Sherry for the fifth grade class photo. We get together with Scott and Sherry and their girls as often as life permits. I have had the good fortune of getting to know them over the past dozen years and consider them part of my family. Marcus and Scott also had another friend from the neighborhood, Bill, who was also a classmate in the fourth grade. You could call the boys the three musketeers.

A Break In The Case

*"Don't ever lose sight of what a strong woman you are!
As I'm sure you have discovered over the years, there are lessons from
the universe in every experience, no matter how painful."*
~ Shirli ~

22

Forensic DNA

$\mathcal{T}$he collection of DNA evidence was first begun in the late 1980s. During my visit to the emergency room in 1988, two sources of DNA were collected: a vaginal swab and a tampon. This DNA information could only be checked against actual suspects after obtaining a court order to collect a DNA sample. Although Dave Cordle had a couple of opportunities over the years to check the evidence from my case against suspects for similar crimes, unfortunately there was never a match. In 1988, the DNA national database was in its infancy and there were only a limited number of DNA profiles on record that had been assigned an identification.

The use of DNA evidence has become one of the most powerful forensic tools used in the courtroom today. DNA is easily extracted from any human (or animal) cell and can be matched to DNA extracted from another cell so accurately that it is ordinarily considered conclusive. In this way, cellular material found at a crime scene can be compared to cellular material taken from any person to determine if that person was there.

Almost all human tissue contains DNA. Most bodily fluids and excretions will also contain cells from which DNA can be retrieved. Skin, hair, and even dandruff contain DNA. All of the cells of a given person contain the same DNA, so the type of tissue it is extracted from does not matter — the DNA extracted from any tissue identifies a specific individual. DNA is such a complex molecule that (with the exception of identical twins) the odds of two individual having identical DNA are 350 million to one. Thus, DNA matches are conclusive.

One example of how this could be used would be to extract DNA from a murder victim and match it with DNA extracted from blood found on the clothing of another person. If the DNA matches, then there is no question as to whose blood it is, only, perhaps, how it got there. Another example would be the case of a rape victim. Semen extracted from the victim could be conclusively matched to a specific man through DNA. DNA can also be used to prove that two people are related. This is particularly useful in determining paternity. The similarities in the DNA of a child to a parent can be used almost as conclusively as direct matching. Similarly, DNA can be used to prove that there is not a match between samples. By this method, a number of wrongly convicted people have been exonerated.

In recent years, a number of important pieces of federal legislation have been enacted to facilitate the use of DNA in crime solving. Notable among them is the DNA Identification Act of 1994 (Public Law 103-322 [HR 3355]) which regulates federal funding of DNA analysis laboratories and authorizes the collection of a national index of DNA records and samples, all of which are designed to enhance quality assurance. This law improves the ability of various law enforcement agencies to cooperate and coordinate their efforts.

A DNA profile can help to prove either innocence or guilt in a crime and it can determine if the DNA tested was from one person, several people, or even from an animal. Being able to determine DNA profiles from saliva, blood, and skin cells and then ultimately linking a profile to an identity has changed the way felony crimes are investigated today.

23

DNA Initiative

*I*n the spring of 2003, President Bush instituted the DNA Initiative. This program offered police agencies all over the country more than one billion dollars over a five year period for testing DNA from cold case rapes, homicides, and kidnappings. Since technology in forensic testing of DNA had advanced so much over the years, evidence that was once thought to be unusable to help solve a crime was now considered viable. Once tested, profiles garnered from the DNA samples were uploaded to a national database that compared these new samples with profiles already entered into the system.

In May 2005, the Annapolis Police Department applied for and received $600,624 to cover the cost of reprocessing evidence from cold cases on file. By 2008, several arrests and convictions had been made. Some of the cases were just a year or two old and some went back as far as twenty years. Among the cold cases being revisited was mine.

24

Time Marches On

In 1995, the State's Attorney's Office joined with the Annapolis Police Department to form the first cold case review unit in Annapolis, and as far as we knew, the State of Maryland. I retained the two cold cases I had worked on — the Wheatley rape and the Greenberg homicide. I followed leads and showcased the old unsolved cases in the media on date-appropriate occasions such as the anniversary dates of the crimes, but with no luck. I hit a lot of dead ends.

Unfortunately, with no new leads or case clearances, our cold case team was disbanded. Over the years, I would continue to periodically review the files and compare new cases that bore a resemblance to the two cold cases. After our concerted, yet unsuccessful, efforts to include or exclude possible suspects in Jennifer's assault in 1988, her case went cold again.

The cold case phenomenon, which "officially" became recognized by Sergeant David Rivers of the Metro-Dade, Florida Police Department in the early 1980s, was now a viable branch of many police departments around the country. Investigative methodologies were developed and refined over time. The most important of these scientific advances was that of DNA testing. Advances in technology in the collection, identification, and record-keeping of DNA evidence, while in its infancy in the 1980s, had become a sophisticated and routine forensic practice by the turn of the century.

As the years passed, I became more involved in cold case investigations, gaining more experience and knowledge of the advancing technologies. Periodic reviews of my cold cases began to show more results of closures and convictions.

New technologies were introduced every several years, it seemed, and the law enforcement community was moving forward in entering DNA profiles into a national database known as "CODIS," or Combined DNA Index System. This storage system grows with every conviction, and has the ability to link or match new and old DNA evidence profiles to any profile entered into the system, no matter what state entered the profile.

In February of 2004, I again reviewed Jennifer's file. Over the years, nagging questions rose from the depths of the initial investigation.

In addition to some missing reports, there was missing evidence. Jennifer's T-shirt, the one the suspect used to gag her and that was later recovered after she spotted it lying on the Spa Creek Bridge, was gone. Also missing from evidence was her recorded statement to Detective Leo. As in many cold cases, evidence gets moved around in the storage rooms, and unfortunately, occasionally gets completely lost. Missing key pieces of evidence in Jennifer's rape case added another challenge to an already difficult case.

On February 23, 2004, I resubmitted the DNA evidence collected from Jennifer's rape kit to the Maryland State Police Lab for retesting. Because of the advances in technology, old cases with any DNA evidence had a good chance of finding a match in the CODIS system because labs were now able to do more with less.

On May 5, 2005, I was once again contacted by the lab with results. This time I was informed by DNA scientist Melissa Stangroom that the Wheatley case evidence matched another cold case rape that had taken place in Anne Arundel County on December 11, 1988.

This is what is known as a "cold hit" — evidence that matches a perpetrator who is unknown to the CODIS database, but matched to another victim forensically.

I immediately contacted the current Anne Arundel County Police cold case rape investigator, Detective Tracy Morgan, to compare thoughts and notes. We did a detailed analysis of each case, looking at victimology issues, geographical relationships, and anything we could think of in order to find a commonality that would pinpoint a likely suspect. Leads were developed and followed, but we weren't hitting pay dirt yet.

I began to review previous suspects and attempted to re-locate those suspects who had not had a DNA sample taken during my initial investigation in 1989. Additionally, I sent a letter to Jennifer asking her to give me a call. She did. I told her I had some questions about her case and asked her if she could come to my office to speak with me. Jennifer asked me if I would be interested in looking through the journal she had written in 1988 about the incident. She hoped it might provide new clues.

25

DNA Links

On June 13, 2005, I received a letter from Dave Cordle.

Dear Jennifer,

It has been quite some time since we last spoke. I hope you remember me from when you lived here in Annapolis. I need to speak with you at your earliest convenience.

Looking forward to hearing from you.

Very truly yours,
Dave Cordle, Sr.
Chief Investigator

It was as if someone struck a match inside me. I could not remember the last time I had actually seen Dave or spoken to him. It really had been years. But I had not forgotten him. Even though it had been a long time since we'd talked, I knew he had not given up on finding my attacker. After all, he had promised: *"I'll find him."*

I picked up the phone and called him right away. Dave did not tell me in detail what he wanted to see me about, but he mentioned he had some questions for me and wanted me to meet with him in his office. The meeting was scheduled for a few days away. During the interim, I was really anxious.

What could he possibly need to ask me that he couldn't ask over the phone? I spent the next few days asking myself a million different questions, then providing myself with that many more answers. The biggest question, though, was undoubtedly, did he finally get the guy? I didn't dare to hope.

The day came for me to make the drive to Annapolis. It was one of those awfully hot and extremely humid summer days that would be typical for August, but this was late June. By the time I arrived at the courthouse, I was soaked with sweat. I was eager to find out what Dave had called me in for, but I was a drippy, sweaty mess. I stopped off in the bathroom to wash my face and cool off for a minute before seeing him. Realizing how really nervous I was, I took a minute to calm down.

Dave escorted me to his office and told me we were waiting for another investigator. Detective Tracy Morgan had been delayed with something and was going to need some time to prepare for our meeting. After Detective Morgan arrived, she and Dave went into the hall outside his office to discuss something. I gathered from what I could overhear that they were waiting for some news about a few other victims, but the information they were expecting was not ready yet. So Dave sent me back out into the sweltering heat, asking me if I could go have lunch and then return in about an hour.

After my lunch, I had a hot walk back to his office. I was introduced to Detective Morgan, and the three of us talked briefly about my case until Dave received the expected phone call. Right away, I could see the disappointment on his face. Shaking his head "no," I overheard him say quietly to Detective Morgan, "It wasn't him."

And, that was it. Our meeting was over and Dave escorted me to the hallway. I was pretty puzzled and not too happy. I had been stuck in traffic for almost two hours in the heat getting to Annapolis. Then I'd no sooner gotten to his office and he'd asked me come back in an hour. And now, when I'd only just begun to cool off, I was being shown the door again.

We made small talk on the way out to the corridor. I don't remember what about. But I did ask him, "Okay, what now?"

"Well, I keep working your case," Dave said.

Three years later, I learned what the meeting had been about from Dave and Detective Tracy's perspective. On May 5, 2005, Dave had received notification of a "cold hit" when DNA from my rape kit was entered into the Index System (CODIS) database. This meant that the man who had raped me had raped again.

At the time of our meeting, Dave and Tracy had a suspect in mind and were waiting for the DNA results, hoping all of the cases would be linked to the same suspect. However, the DNA profiles did not match.

They knew there was another victim linked to my DNA evidence because the sample collected when she reported her rape and entered into the automated system matched the profile that CODIS had developed from my evidence. However, because they had no name to connect to the DNA, it was impossible to know who had committed the crimes.

It is hard to accept that sometimes evidence provides a DNA profile, but no suspect information. DNA alone is not always enough to solve a crime. Unidentified profiles can remain anonymous indefinitely or until the perpetrator of the crime is caught and DNA is compared.

Not knowing any of this when I left Dave at the State's Attorney's Office, I felt puzzled and irritated.

Crap, I wondered, *Why didn't he wait until he had something to tell me before calling me in to his office?*

It occurred to me as we said our goodbyes to ask about the fingerprints recovered from the candle, but I immediately dismissed the question, reasoning that maybe no fingerprints had actually been pulled. Or, if they had been recovered, wouldn't he have already checked them out? They probably hadn't led to anyone.

I drove home in the heat, with no air conditioner in my car. I was really irritated. There was a police roadblock set up at one point along my drive. Yellow police tape was strung across two lanes of traffic and several blocks were cordoned off. I had to take a detour. This added an additional half hour to the trip. It was rush hour by the time I was just a few miles from home and the traffic had thickened to a crawl. The traffic jam added another hour to my trip. What normally takes an hour to drive took me two and a half hours. *Great*, I thought. *Next time, Dave, just tell me your news on the phone.*

It took me a few months to put the meeting in Annapolis behind me. Getting into my routine without being preoccupied with thoughts of, *What if?* and *If ever...* was tough. The visit to Annapolis had given me hope that maybe something was actually happening — someone was going to be caught. No matter what news Dave had or didn't have for me during that meeting, he had stirred up a lot of thoughts. Was it ever going to be possible to catch the guy? Was the creep even still alive? I often hoped for the sake of other women that he was not. Or, if he wasn't dead, maybe he was already serving time in jail. Maybe someone else had managed to identify him during another crime and maybe he was locked up for life. Even if my case was never to be solved, convincing myself that this monster was already in jail gave me some peace of mind.

Leaving the State's Attorney's Office after such a bizarre meeting was frustrating. I realized Dave would not have called me all the way into his office for nothing. I'm sure he believed he had great news. But, in the end, we'd ended up with nothing. Now, it looked as if I had to bundle up all my hope and wishful thinking, tie the emotional pack tightly, tuck it away, and get back to living, again. Swallowing all of this again was hard. I wanted to believe Dave would "get the guy" as he had promised so many years ago. But without anything to go on, almost seventeen years since the attack took place, finding the creep seemed unlikely. It wasn't the first time I had trouble remaining optimistic.

I remembered the 1998 night of the tenth anniversary of my rape. I'd felt really depressed. I'd figured if my attacker had not been caught after ten years, he would never be caught. I'd cried that night. I'd given up hope.

I guess you really did get away with it.

That thought made me really angry. Knowing he had eluded police all these years and was free to continue to prey on other women made me sick. I should have done more to stop him.

It really wasn't until the odd 2005 meeting in Annapolis with Dave, seven years after the tenth anniversary date, that I realized I had been wrong. There was no statute of limitations for the state of Maryland for felony crimes. If it were possible to find the perpetrator, it would also be possible to prosecute him. I knew as long as justice was still possible, Dave would not give up, even if I had.

26

Automated Fingerprint Identification System

$\mathcal{T}$he widespread use of the Automated Fingerprint Identification System (AFIS) starting in 1991 allowed fingerprint technicians to scan fingerprint images into a database for easy storage, retrieval, and comparison. Automated fingerprint identification is the process of automatically matching one or many unknown fingerprints against a database of known and unknown prints. AFIS is primarily used for criminal identification initiatives, the most important of which include identifying a person suspected of committing a crime or linking a suspect to other unsolved crimes. AFIS gives crime investigators the capability of real-time identification of a suspect in investigations, based on fingerprints found at the scene of a crime.

27

Another Perspective

During the June, 2005, meeting with Jennifer, I introduced Detective Morgan and explained that we were working on an investigation of a possible suspect. We talked for a short time, and I asked if I could hold onto her journal. I believed it might prove to be valuable.

Cold case investigators sometimes become so immersed in details and theories and following leads, they get to the point where they can't see the forest for the trees. Our office had a National Institute of Justice Cold Case grant with the Maryland State Police. By 2008, I had become immersed in DNA evidence from fourteen different cases and my office was becoming a jungle. After re-reading Jennifer's file and not finding anything new to get me closer to a suspect, I needed someone else to take a look. I was fortunate to have an astute Annapolis City Police detective detailed to our office to work with me.

Detective Bill Johns was a veteran of the Annapolis Police Department (APD) Criminal Investigation Division, who, like me, had a passion for cold cases. He had been involved in several homicide cases, but luckily, he was now available to work more closely with me. Having him look at several of the cases from the stack offered the "new pair of eyes" I needed.

I brought him up to speed by telling him about the investigative efforts Tracy and I had made since the cold hit notification in 2005, then left him alone to go over the numerous notes that had been collected over the years. Because Bill was reading through the file fresh, he was able to find the missing puzzle piece that had been hiding in plain sight. We were about to hit pay dirt.

At the time, Bill's office was two doors down from mine with an interview room in between. No one else shared our secured wing of the office, so communication was held largely by yelling back and forth. As Bill was reviewing the file, he called out, "Did you know there were latent prints recovered?" Latent prints are those fingerprints left on a surface at a crime scene that can be "lifted" and preserved for comparison with a suspect's fingerprints. In Jennifer's case, the prints had been recovered from a candle on the table next to the bed. Early on in my investigation of her case, I knew prints had been lifted. Several suspects had been developed whose fingerprints were compared and ultimately excluded. Recently, though, I had been so focused on the DNA evidence of this case, certain we would find a match in CODIS, that I had completely forgotten about the fingerprints.

Then Bill asked the $64,000 question: "Have the prints been entered into MAFIS?" MAFIS is the Maryland Automated Fingerprint Identification System. Remembering it had been quite a few years since I'd last checked the prints against a possible suspect, I wasn't sure.

My first step was to determine what date the Anne Arundel County Police Department (AACPD) began utilizing the system. The AACPD was the "entry point" for fingerprint submissions for Annapolis Police Department cases. I called AACPD Fingerprint Technician Ernie Lowman and asked him when the department had begun to utilize MAFIS. Ernie said he would get back to me. Two days later, Ernie had an answer — approximately 1992.

It was before 1992 that I had last compared the latent prints, so this meant the recovered fingerprints had not yet been entered into MAFIS. On July 9, 2008, I requested and obtained the latent prints from the Annapolis Police Department, and on July 14th, I delivered them personally to the AACPD Crime Lab. Now, all I could do was hurry up and wait. Anticipation abounded. On July 29th, I finally received an answer. The latent prints recovered from the candle on Jennifer's nightstand matched those of William Joseph Trice. Now we had a name and the DNA evidence to possibly tie him to Jennifer's rape and another rape.

There were, however, several problems. Where did the candle come from? Were the latent prints those of Jennifer's attacker, or were they from someone else who had handled the candle? It was possible the prints belonged to someone unrelated to the rape. At the time of this discovery, I had forgotten about the journal entry that mentioned Jennifer had acquired the candle from the restaurant where she worked. And, more importantly, I had forgotten her entry about the suspect handling the candle. However, the candle was listed on the original evidence inventory and had been safely packed away for twenty years.

With these questions in mind, it was time to talk to Jennifer once again. Detective Morgan and I made arrangements to personally visit her under the guise of wanting to discuss her case, when in reality we were eager to share the news of the fingerprint match discovered by Detective Johns.

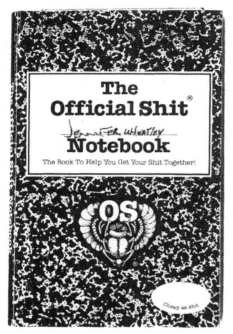

The OSN notebook in which
I wrote everything down that happened
that night.
The title, compliments of the
notebook company,
was particularly appropriate.

The OSN entry where I describe how the candle was picked up by my attacker. The fingerprints left behind would, 20 years later, link William Joseph Trice to this crime.

28

Jennifer's Journal

In early August, 2008, we drove to Jennifer's home. I asked her if she knew a man by the name of William Joseph Trice. I could tell by her face she didn't know the name. I went on to explain that his prints were identified as those recovered from the crime scene.

"From the candle," she said.

I asked her how she knew the prints had been lifted from the candle. Did she mention anything about the candle in her journal?

Jennifer said she was sure she had mentioned the candle in *The Official Shit Notebook,* as she called it. I remembered I had her case file in the car with me and I went out to retrieve the file to see if the journal was among the other papers.

Actually, there were two copies, the original and a photocopy. Detective Morgan took the copy as Jennifer flipped through the original journal she had written all those years ago. I waited with great anticipation as the two took what seemed like an enormous amount of time to find the right page. Jennifer recalled when her attacker had picked up the candle; all she had to do was find the passage. After we determined that her attacker *had* picked up the candle, we talked for a few more minutes about the implications of matching a name to the prints in evidence.

We said our goodbyes a short time later, and I promised I would give Jennifer a call as soon as I had anything new to report. Both Tracy and I got through all of this without showing too much emotion, but it was all we could do to contain ourselves.

As I turned the first corner, Tracy and I just looked at each other and shook our heads, smiled, then laughed and began rattling on about the significance of this revelation and discovery. The impact of having a diary entry memorializing the events of the attack was monumental — and I vowed to review the journal one more time.

For Jennifer to have written a journal detailing the events of that night was, in itself, incredible. Though we didn't have this information recorded in a police statement, we had the next best thing — the events in her handwriting, in a personal journal. This was just as good as a written statement, and in some regards better, because we had her words, not directed questions and answers by law enforcement agents.

For this journal to have survived all these years was phenomenal. This was just one of those few-and-far-between investigative breaks we crave in the field of cold case investigation.

29

Latent Fingerprints

*I*n August, 2008, three years after my last odd meeting at the Maryland State's Attorney's Office, Dave Cordle called my house and left a message on the answering machine. Marcus listened to the message then told me about the call with a puzzled look on his face.

"You have a message from some policeman; some guy from the State's Attorney's Office," he said. "He wants you to call him."

I had not told Marcus about being raped.

What would be the point? Telling him and then having it hanging between us unresolved for the rest of our lives didn't make sense. I opted to keep this past trauma to myself and deal with it privately, as I had been doing for twenty years. I had given up long ago on believing the day would come when someone would be caught. I decided I'd tell him just enough to satisfy his curiosity without giving details.

"Years ago I was involved in a crime and it looks like there might be some new information," I said. "Don't worry. I didn't do anything wrong. The crime was committed against me."

This seemed to satisfy him. I decided I would tell Marcus about the assault if and when he needed to know. I wasn't sure this call from Dave would be any more fruitful than the last. There was no sense in opening that can of worms if I didn't have to. Marcus didn't ask, so I didn't tell.

I returned Dave's call. He asked if he could meet with me to discuss some details of my case. *Okay, here we go again,* I thought. Of course, I said I would meet with him. Silently I was praying he would not ask me to drive to Annapolis this time. All I could think about was the last trip I'd made to meet him three years previously. I had spent almost five hours in the sweltering car for a fifteen minute discussion that left me feeling bewildered, angry, confused, and depressed. I didn't want to do that again.

This time he wanted to meet at my house (*yeah!*), and he was bringing the other detective, Tracy Morgan, with him.

Holy crap! What was going on?

The two showed up at my house in the early afternoon. We talked a bit about my flower and vegetable gardens, and quilting. I showed them into the kitchen, and as the three of us sat down at the kitchen table, Dave asked me, "Do you know someone by the name of William Joseph Trice?"

"No," I said. "Where would I know him from?"

"I didn't think you would know him. Maybe your mother knew him when she lived at Chesapeake Landing?"

I shrugged my shoulders and said, "I don't know for sure. I suppose it's possible. How would she have known him?"

"He was a courier in the area when you were living there. Maybe she had something delivered by him."

I didn't know. Deliveries arrived at the house for Mom from time to time, but for the most part they were brought by UPS or the mailman.

"Who is this....What was his name?" I asked.

"Trice," Dave said.

"Who is he? Why do you ask?" *Was this the guy?* I wondered.

Dave told me that President Bush had made money available so that police departments could retest evidence from cold cases, including fingerprints. He had, in fact, had the fingerprint on the candle compared to those in the national database.

"We got a hit from a fingerprint..." Dave started.

"...from the candle," I finished.

Dave was genuinely surprised that I knew where the latent print had come from.

"What makes you say the print came from the candle?" he asked me.

"Because it was the only mistake he had made," I said. "When Detective Leo brought me home that day, there were a couple of investigators getting ready to leave with bags of my stuff. One of them asked me if there was anything they had missed. I was the one who told them to take the candle because I knew he had picked it up. I was going to ask you about the prints the last time I was in your office, but I figured, either there weren't any left behind, or you had already checked them and didn't get a match."

"Actually, we got two prints from the candle. Did you mention him picking up the candle in your journal?" Dave asked.

"I'm sure I did," I answered.

"I have a copy of your journal in my car."

Dave hopped up and went out to retrieve the journal for me. Tracy stayed behind. She told me there was another victim whose attacker's DNA matched the DNA recovered the night I was raped. The other woman had worked in downtown Annapolis at a yacht yard at the time that crime was committed. She had been out with friends, and when she returned home Trice grabbed her just outside her condo. "He got her wallet, found her phone number, and called her on the phone the following night."

Damn him, sick son of a bitch.

Tracy said that Trice was a truck driver now and had been a delivery person back in the late '80s. Then Dave came back into the kitchen with my journal. When Tracy mentioned that Trice was a truck driver, I remembered the story Stephen's sister had told me involving drugs and George and Jeff and rape. I had told Dave about this in 2005, and now I filled Tracy in. I was pretty sure it was nothing.

"Jeff was a drug dealer and a truck driver. He used to deliver boats. It's probably nothing." I told them I had wondered if it was possible that Jeff had arranged to extract revenge on me as a "pay back" for George's misdeed from 1986. I also told them that a few weeks after I was attacked, Jeff asked me if I thought George had anything to do with my rape or if I had heard from George. I had not seen or spoken to George in years, but he did fit the vague description I had of the attacker. I thought perhaps Tracy's victim might have also had a connection to Jeff.

Dave handed me a photocopy of my journal, *The Official Shit Notebook*. I flipped through it for a few minutes and then found the passage concerning the candle in my journal:

> *"After he was done he asked me about coke again. I told him I didn't have any and he could check if he wanted to. He asked me again as he picked up the candle — what I had been doing? "Reading." Now he's convinced that I have no drugs and is asking for money. "I don't have any." "Oh yes, you do. I saw you counting it." I handed him about $20 that I left in my purse. He asked me "Is this all you have?" I said 'Yes' knowing I was lying and hoped he didn't know that..."*

Dave was ecstatic.

"It's a good thing I didn't read that last night," he said. "I wouldn't have been able to sleep and I would have been here at sunrise!"

I'd discovered the *Crime and Investigation* network years ago and I started watching, thinking that maybe, just maybe, they would have a show about a crime that had been solved, and it would be about the guy who'd raped me. I guess I was praying the creep had been thrown in jail somewhere along the way. Over the years, as new shows were created, I added them to my regular viewing list. These true crime programs detail rapes and murders. Most have been solved and the perpetrator put behind bars, but some remain a mystery.

Occasionally, a show would detail a crime with some similar characteristics to mine, but nothing definitive. Many episodes focused on rapists, and I noticed these criminals followed a particular pattern in the execution and progression of the severity of their crimes. The element of surprise was one of their favorite tactics, because it enabled them to quickly overpower their victims. Quite often, the perpetrator became unsatisfied with just raping his victims, and often he would amp up his level of criminal behavior to include murder. I couldn't help but wonder if my assailant had made this change. I prayed he had not, although I believed he certainly was capable of it.

I find the cold case investigation shows fascinating. I am constantly amazed at how the tiniest, seemingly insignificant thing becomes the one clue that helps to solve the case. I have watched lots of episodes showing how rapes and murders were solved through DNA collected from a tiny piece of evidence. I saw episodes where fingerprints, palm prints, footprints, and shoe impressions helped to solve a crime. I often wondered if the fingerprints lifted from the candle would be the thing that could crack my case.

For years, I knew there was a DNA profile of my attacker, but this profile had remained anonymous. Dave Cordle had compared the DNA from evidence collected in the rape kit against at least two possible suspects back in 1989, but there had been no match. I realized from watching these shows and from experience with my own case that it took more than just DNA to solve a crime. The only other clue we would have had to work with was the fingerprints. And for years, I wasn't even sure any prints had been found.

Dave seemed to feel we were on the right track, but I remained cautious. Although I was not entirely surprised to learn the fingerprints played a big role in finding a suspect, I didn't let myself get too excited about the match. Although advances in technology have improved imaging of prints, and computer storage of this information makes it possible to locate a match no matter where in the country a criminal was processed, fingerprint identification is still not an exact science.

I knew the candle had been out on the table at the Chart House and could have been picked up by anyone. It was possible a customer or fellow employee could have picked it up. Maybe they had been in jail and had had their prints entered into AFIS. Hell, the prints could have been put on there by someone packing the case of candles. I told Dave and Tracy the story of how I'd obtained the candle and how it was possible any number of people could have picked it up before I brought it home.

I didn't want to let myself believe that, after all these years, Dave had finally found the guy. I didn't want to have my hopes raised only to be replaced with disappointment again. I wasn't sure I was going to be able to handle any more dead ends.

Still, be it my spirit guides or intuition, something was whispering soft and low in the back of my mind, *"Got him!"*

Dave and Tracy explained that their suspect lived in upstate New York. They would be working with the police department there to obtain something from him that could be tested for a DNA match. Once they had the results from the test they would be back in touch with me. I saw the two of them to the door. Before they left Dave gave me a hug and said, "Keep your fingers crossed." I tried to ignore the twinkle of hope in his eyes. As soon as I closed the door behind them, the voices in my head got louder:

"What if?"

"Nah, it can't be him."

"It could be him..."

"No, it's not."

"But it could be..."

"What if? What if? What if?"

I was going to go nuts! These voices in my head had only just begun to pester me.

30

Limbo

After a few days of this mental ping-pong, I had to tell someone. I couldn't keep it to myself any longer. The day after our annual barbecue, I was sitting with Hope, my sister-in-law, and told her about the fingerprint. (Actually, Hope is Marcus' cousin Art's wife. Marcus is very close to Art — like a brother — so I have always thought of Hope as my sister-in-law.) I think she immediately believed Dave had caught the guy and was very excited. I cautioned her about getting her hopes up and then I asked her to keep the news a secret. I thought she was going to clobber me. She wanted to tell Art. But we both knew if she told Art, he would want to tell Marcus or it might slip out in conversation, and I wasn't ready for Marcus to know. The fingerprint match might turn out to be nothing. We had to wait for the DNA sample results.

It was the longest few months of my life.

Waiting for Dave to call me with news was endless. During the days, I could keep myself occupied so I wouldn't think about it all the time, but once I lay down in bed at night, my mind wouldn't stop. Over and over again, I would play out every possible scenario until I eventually fell into a fitful sleep, trying not to get my hopes up.

Weeks passed with no news. Finally, in late September, Dave called to check in with me. He told me the New York Police were having trouble obtaining a DNA sample from Trice. They needed the DNA to run a comparison test against the DNA recovered the night I was raped. Apparently, Trice lived in a very rural area. The New York police had not been able to obtain Trice's DNA the usual ways, from a napkin, a hair, a Kleenex™, or cigarette butt. Dave promised me he would keep in touch. "They have some ideas they are working on," he said.

Before I hung up the phone, I had to know what his gut reaction was. I could trust that. Maybe hearing his answer would quiet the battle going on in my head. I asked Dave what he thought.

"Oh, I think we've got him. He fits the profile," he told me.

Crap! That really didn't help me at all. If Dave believed he had the guy, I should, too, but I was still reluctant. I was trying so hard to adopt a "wait and see" attitude. Now he had me full of hope, and I had nothing but time ahead to hurry up and wait.

At first, I didn't tell either of my sisters about my conversation with Dave because I didn't want my mom to find out that anything was in the works. I didn't want to get her hopes up, and then possibly have to disappoint her if things didn't work out. I was afraid if either of my sisters knew, they might accidentally let something slip about the latest developments. Eventually, I told Mollie, and I made her promise not to tell Mom. I told my friend Marnie knowing she wouldn't say anything to anyone who would let it slip to my mother.

Every now and then Mollie, Hope, or Marnie would e-mail me to find out if I had heard anything. The suspense was getting to them, as well. My answer was always the same: "Not yet."

During these wait-and-see months, if I did let myself believe this guy could be the one who'd assaulted me, then all I could think about was seeing his face for the first time. This both frightened and intrigued me. Who was he? What did he look like? If the DNA sample obtained by the New York police did match the evidence collected the night I was raped, I would finally know who he was. I knew he was a monster who had terrified women. And although I knew he could never live up to being the larger-than-life monster I had made him out to be in my dreams, the thought of seeing him for the first time was just plain scary.

What kid really wants to peek under the bed or open the closet door to face the very creature that haunts their dreams? I felt like that kid. I felt like I had to know, but I wasn't sure at all if I would be able to be in the same room with him. Wasn't knowing what you are afraid of supposed to be better than a fear of the unknown? I don't know. Both were pretty frightening.

Marnie asked me, "Jen, what if it turns out to be someone you know? What if it was someone you worked with at the Chart House? How will that make you feel?"

I thought about her questions carefully. I had not recognized the name Dave and Tracy had given me, and I was pretty certain I didn't know the person who'd assaulted me. Although it was possible he could have been someone from the Chart House, I knew none of the people I had come to know as friends had attacked me. But it was possible the attacker was someone working at the Chart House whom I didn't know. There were over a hundred people working there in 1988. Who better to have known my comings and goings?

With confidence, I answered, "It's possible he could have been someone from there. But it would have to have been someone who did prep work during the day or worked in the kitchen at night. I didn't know any of the kitchen staff. But, I know who he wasn't. No way was it anybody I hung out with. So I can live with finding out it was someone from there because I know who it's not."

When I talked myself into believing he was not the right guy, that the fingerprint was left behind innocently enough by just a random stranger, then I felt extreme disappointment and anger. No way, after all these years, could we get this close and then find out it was all another dead end. I truly believed this was the last chance to find the guy. Modern advancements in DNA testing and fingerprint analysis had brought us this far. These technical advancements had to see us to the end. Once Dave retired, the case would be tucked in a drawer and forgotten. I could not allow myself to think that the creep had gotten away with his crimes and would never be punished for them.

During all of this waiting, I sent these thoughts to Marnie and Hope in e-mails and discussed my jumble of emotions with them whenever I could. The two of them were great at trying to keep me optimistic. I'm pretty sure as time went on they both felt Dave had the right guy, even if I wasn't certain. They were just waiting for confirmation.

Hope was afraid to say out loud what she felt. She didn't want to jinx anything by declaring one way or the other. But she did say she thought the whole thing was pretty incredible. She was dying for an answer so she could tell her husband all the details. I had put her in a tough spot indeed.

Marnie was sure; no doubts: "They got him, Jen. Don't you think so? Don't you feel it, Jen? You know he's the guy."

I had to hear it from Dave. I would believe it only when he called and said, "We got him." I needed an answer, one way or another, if just to quiet the tug-of-war going on with my thoughts.

31

A Viable Suspect

William Joseph Trice was an attractive young man in 1988, not one whom people would have suspected would resort to rape for sexual satisfaction.

However, Trice had a dark side. In 1983, he was arrested in Prince Georges County, Maryland, for indecent exposure. This case was later dropped for unknown reasons. After committing the two sexual assaults in 1988, Trice was arrested by Annapolis Police as a Peeping Tom after being located and identified by two women who saw him looking into their bathroom window on Academy Street in downtown Annapolis.

In 1994, Trice was again arrested for indecent exposure to a young girl who was walking to her school past his residence. Trice was convicted this time and sentenced to three years in jail. He served eighteen months in prison, and was given three years of supervised probation. Then he had another arrest in 1997 in Calvert County for a telephone misuse charge. Lastly, he was charged with the burglary of a woman's home, also in Calvert County in 1997. He was a true sexual predator.

On December 11, 1988, just four months after Jennifer's attack, Trice's next known victim, a 42 year-old woman, was returning home from a night out with friends. She was "blitzed" — she was brutally attacked by Trice as she walked from the parking lot to her townhouse. He placed her in a choke hold and dragged her between two rows of townhouses. Trice then threatened to kill her if she screamed, forced her to her knees, and sexually assaulted her from behind.

Besides assaulting her, Trice stole the victim's wallet, which contained her identification. He had the audacity to call her the following night to see if he could meet with her again. This victim's rape kit DNA evidence matched Trice, linking this case to Jennifer's. It was this case that brought Detective Morgan and me together to apprehend this rapist.

32

Showtime in New York

Unbeknownst to Jennifer, I had begun researching the whereabouts of Mr. Trice immediately following the identification of his prints. Was he alive or dead? Was he incarcerated? Utilizing currently standard investigative tools — also known as the Internet — I easily located a William Trice in Eagle Bridge, New York. All the vital statistics, including date of birth, matched. But to be sure I had the right man, I enlisted the support of the FBI Violent Criminal Apprehension Program (VICAP) Unit. Analyst Kristin Nelson quickly produced a comprehensive report on Trice which included an "Off-line" or "Hand-Researched" report detailing all law enforcement contacts with him.

Upon receipt of the report, I contacted Senior Investigator David Madden of the Albany Barracks of the New York State Police (NYSP). SGT Madden commanded the homicide unit and assigned several of his investigators to assist us in the investigation. Since the only identification of Trice had been from the fingerprint on the candle, we needed to obtain a sample of his DNA to see if the fingerprint we identified from the candle would also match the DNA evidence recovered from our two victims.

Madden and I discussed various possibilities and we agreed that a preliminary surveillance should take place to determine Trice's work and personal habits, to see where he lived and with whom, and to determine how we could obtain a sample of his DNA without his knowing of our investigation.

New York State Police agreed to the plan since they were familiar with this rural area outside of Albany. Surveillance took place for three days, but actual recovery of any items we could use to test his DNA was difficult. Trice lived with his wife in a rural area of upstate New York with little vehicular traffic. In addition, adding to our frustration, Trice worked in the City of Albany as a tow truck driver and was all over the region on a daily basis. The troopers did make one important observation during the surveillance, though — Trice smoked.

After several frustrating days, Madden and I consulted again and we devised a new plan. He suggested his men have their Commercial Vehicle Enforcement Unit set up what would look like a "routine" traffic stop on Trice to do a valid NY State Commercial Vehicle Inspection. It sounded good to me.

On October 21, 2008 at 7:00am, troopers began a stationary surveillance of Pearlman's Towing, Trice's employer, awaiting his anticipated arrival to pick up his work vehicle. The official surveillance log of the NYSP reported as follows:

7:00am. Stationary surveillance established at Pearlman's Towing, North Manning Blvd., Albany, NY. As Trice begins his workday, troopers follow Trice and eventually [effect] a traffic stop and begin the inspection. Coincidentally…another trooper, ([Mike] Student) in an unmarked patrol car pulls up and engages Trice in a conversation. During this time Trice pulls out a cigarette and begins to smoke. Trooper Mike Student engages Trice in small talk while the inspection is conducted. When Trice is done, he flips the butt to the roadside… The inspection is completed and Trice was free to go.

And Trice did go, leaving the very evidence behind that we needed to compare with evidence he left behind in Maryland over twenty years ago.

Because, at that time, the Anne Arundel County Police Laboratory turnaround time was much faster than that of the Maryland State Police

Lab, and because we had the Anne Arundel County Police working with us on the related county case, the New York State Police sent the recovered cigarette butt overnight directly to the AACP lab.

Knowing that every day that the DNA sample was held up in testing was giving Trice another day to strike again was frustrating. "Hot cases" get all the attention; others, especially cold cases, are done when the DNA scientist gets around to it. Who is to say that any offender left to his own means is not still committing crimes? Time spent waiting for test results is the accomplice of undetected serial rapists and serial killers. Waiting in anticipation for the DNA tests comparing the cigarette butt to the two pieces of evidence we had was excruciating.

We were able to get our case "bumped up" to a higher priority list, and on November 4, 2008, I got the call I was hoping to get — the DNA was a match.

33

Sharing the Results

Once again, I called Jennifer. This time I asked her to come to Annapolis on the pretense of having to take photographs of the exterior areas of the crime scene. I was making a legitimate request, knowing we were going to eventually make an arrest and go to trial.

Jennifer came the following day, and we drove out to Chesapeake Landing. It was a relatively cold and overcast day. The wind was blowing in off the Chesapeake. I could tell Jennifer was uncomfortable being at her former home, but as always, she overcame her anxiety and walked me through the complex, allowing me to snap the pictures I needed. Then it began to drizzle. Rain is not very friendly for photography — at least not with my office's digital camera.

It was time. I had played this scene in my mind hundreds of times. How do I tell her? Should I have a victim's advocate from our office with me? Should I have a family member present? I think I always knew the answer. I was remembering our first meeting and the look she had in her eyes all those years ago. Jennifer had been so traumatized on that August night and I was so worried about her. But, as we got into my car, I knew this was the moment that I would tell Jennifer about the DNA match. I didn't need to have a victim's advocate or a family member present. I knew she would want to hear this news from me alone. We could handle it together.

As we sat in the car, only yards away from where she had been brutally attacked, I looked over to her and said, "We have a match, we have a name, and we're going to go get him."

Jennifer was silent for a moment — it seemed like forever, and she took my hand and began to cry. No words, just tears. I vowed to remain silent until she was ready to talk.

Jennifer hugged me and finally said, "This is the first time I've cried about this since that night." All I could do was smile and hold back my emotions. We weren't done yet.

34

Another Day, Another Meeting

*D*ave finally called a few months after he told me about the fingerprint match.

"Could you come to Annapolis and go with me so I can take a few photographs at Chesapeake Landing?"

Dave wanted to get photos of the correct carport and back patio/pool area. Damn, another goose chase that would take me forever to get to and leave me with nothing. "Yeah, I can meet you, no problem."

November 5th was gray, cold, and rainy. The wind was blowing a stinging rain that bit into my face. It was nasty. I parked my car at the library on West Street and went with Dave in his car to Eastport.

It was weird being at the old house again. I wasn't afraid, but I was uncomfortable. We got out of his car and I led him down to the patio that was outside of what used to be my bedroom. I did feel a rush of emotions being there, looking into my old bedroom window. I felt for a second like my assailant was there, too, peeking in through the break of the curtain. After showing Dave the patio and sliding glass door, we walked around to the side of the house that faced the water, and I pointed out the carport where I used to park my car. By then, the rain had picked up and it was too drizzly for him to take pictures.

"I'll have to come back again when it isn't raining," Dave said. "Let's go back to the car."

Great, I thought, *I came here for nothing. Here we go again.*

Dave asked me how I felt being there. "You don't have to be afraid. It's okay, I'm here, and he can't hurt you."

"I'm not afraid," I said, "But it is weird. This is the same kind of weather we were having during that week: cold and rainy."

Dave saw me shiver and led me back to the car.

Once we were inside the car, Dave put his right hand over my left and said, "We got a hit."

"On the fingerprint?" I asked.

"No, we got a hit on the DNA. We got him."

I couldn't talk. It was suddenly very quiet and time seemed to stop. Twenty years rushed past me. Doubt, anxiety, anger, and defeat disappeared and were replaced by this moment of silence. I heard the little voice in my head say, *"I told you he got him!"* I smiled and tears welled up in my eyes.

"Holy Crap!" I said shaking my head to clear it. Did he mean what I thought he meant? The creep was finally in jail?

"How long will he be in jail?"

"Oh, he could get life," Dave said.

Some kind of coughing sob escaped from me and the tears fell from my eyes.

"You know I've never cried about that night," I said. "I've been scared to death, but I never cried because of what happened to me."

"You will," Dave assured me. "Don't worry, you will."

I should have known Dave was up to something. I mean, really, why would he want pictures of Chesapeake Landing if he didn't have a good reason for them? On the way back to the library, I felt like I was full of butterflies. I couldn't think straight. I knew then I should have listened to my intuition...again!

Dave explained a bit about how the New York Police had been following Trice and knew his routine. They knew he would drive by the spot they'd chosen for a traffic stop and they knew what time to look for him. Dave said the stop was set up to look routine and that a few other cars were also pulled over to be inspected. Apparently all of the other staged cars were manned by plainclothes policemen. One of the officers there was a smoker. Knowing the suspect was also a smoker, he invited Trice to join him behind his truck for a cigarette while another police officer "searched" his car. Trice never suspected a thing. Once the officers finished the security search and told Trice he was free to go, the suspect dropped his cigarette on the ground and drove away. The butt was scooped up, bagged, and then sent for DNA testing.

"I had the test pushed through so we wouldn't have to wait another few weeks for results. Just found out yesterday," Dave said.

I got out of his car at the library and gave him a hug.

"I don't even know how to begin to thank you." I was crying and smiling at the same time.

I had to keep shaking my head in an effort to clear it. "Unbelievable. Amazing!" kept going through my head. After twenty years, the son of a bitch had actually been caught.

Before I got in my car and started making phone calls on my cell phone, I asked him, "What happens now?"

"You go on living your life."

"Of course," I said. "I know. I mean is there going to be a trial or anything? Will I ever get to see who this guy is? For twenty years, I've wanted to put a face to this guy."

"Detective Morgan and I will be making arrangements to go to New York, and with the help of the police there, we will arrest him. Kathleen Rogers and Cindy Haworth are who I will be giving your case to. They are the best. I can have Cindy call you so you can ask her your questions. Kathleen is your lawyer; I'm just your investigator."

35

Sharing the News

I drove home in a fog of disbelief. I was amazed, relieved, stunned, and nervous all at the same time. I couldn't believe what Dave had said to me: *"We got him."* I was speechless. After all these years, a fingerprint made it possible to find the guy. This was astounding. I was in shock. I had a difficult time wrapping my head around everything that had happened over the past few years. For so long, I did not allow myself to believe this day would or could come. I never let myself imagine how it would play out. Now that it had happened, it felt like a dream. Unbelievable!

I called my sister Deborah.

"I have some news. It's big. Are you sitting down? You might want to sit down," I said. "They found the guy who raped me."

"Holy shit!" she cried, "No! Really? How? When? Really? Kick-ass! Really? How? This is unbelievable! What? No, Really? Never in a million years did I think those were words I would hear you say. Never. Really?"

This was the reaction I got from everyone. No one could believe the news and everyone wanted to know how he was caught, and then they wanted to share it with someone else.

After a dozen phone calls where I relayed as much of the story as I could, I realized how tired I felt. It had been hours since Dave had said, "We got a hit." And yet his words were only beginning to sink in. No more looking over my shoulder. No more wondering who the creep was. He had a face and he had a name. He was a real person and not just some phantom that haunted my dreams. It is impossible to really put into words just how I felt. I have used the words "incredible," "amazing," "wonderful," and "astounding," but none of these really comes close to describing the feelings. Somewhere in my head, where I had stored away all the questions about my attacker, there was always a sort of low-volume buzz. As soon as I heard the words, *"We got him,"* this buzzing was replaced with a silence; a calm. The puzzle pieces had come together and given a face to the man who had raped me.

I called my mother last to tell her the news. She was thrilled. "Oh, I'm so excited. The SOB is finally going to get what he deserves. I can't wait to tell your Uncle Jim, Darby, and Babs. You be sure to thank the detective for me!" she said.

After we hung up I found myself thinking about how entwined each element of this puzzle appeared to be, how one thing seemed to rely on another, all the way down the line and over the years, to reach this end.

During the second week of August 1988, a storm had knocked out the power to the Chart House, causing a blackout. The blackout prompted the use of extra candles to light the dining room. Having extra candles around the restaurant when the lights came back on (with no place to store them), made it possible for me to take one home. My rape was committed just after the time DNA collection of samples were included as part of rape kits.

Detective Leo brought me home before he took me to the police station to give my statement. I got home just in time to tell the evidence collectors to take the candle, the only thing I knew my assailant had touched. Without the candle in evidence, there would be no fingerprints.

If I had not voiced my dissatisfaction about Detective Leo's lack of interest in my case to John and Tim from the Chart House, they would not have spoken on my behalf to their neighbor from the State's Attorney's Office, Dave Cordle. And Dave would not have taken over my case in 1989.

If Investigator Johns had not found the latent fingerprint in the file and realized it had not been submitted to the national database, we would never have made a connection to the suspect.

Without the DNA initiative in 2003, where President Bush made money available to retest cold case evidence, there would have been no resubmission of the DNA evidence collected from my case. Without the Combined DNA Index System that automatically cross-checks and compares DNA evidence submitted, Trice's profile from a 1994 arrest and conviction would not have been known.

The development and widespread use of the Automated Fingerprint Identification System (AFIS) starting in 1991 made it possible for the Annapolis police to enter Trice's known fingerprints into the system following his arrest in 1994. Without AFIS, the latent print retrieved from the candle the night I was raped and entered into the database system in 2008 would never have been matched to Trice.

Without the database to compare the prints, there would be no suspect.

Without a suspect, there could be no arrest.

Remove one link from the chain and it all falls apart. "Amazing" doesn't even come close to how I felt. This puzzle took twenty years to put together. Now that it was complete, I could easily see, in all its complexity, this puzzle could not have been resolved any other way.

36

Telling Marcus

By the time I'd finished with the phone calls, it was just about time for my husband, Marcus, to come home from work. I spent some time trying to figure out just exactly how I was going to tell him the news. This was big, really big, and I began to feel as if I should not have kept the rape from him. Maybe I should have filled him in back when Dave and Tracy told me about the fingerprint. It might have been easier for him to understand why I had been such a mess for so long. He didn't understand my mood swings. He didn't know why I was so preoccupied and depressed one day, and then manic and nervous the next. I guess he assumed I was menopausal, which I was. And throwing the symptoms of menopause in on top of everything else made me a nut case. I decided to tell Marcus as soon as he sat down to watch TV after he got home.

"I have some news. It's big," I said.

He turned the TV off, sensing from my voice that what I was getting ready to say was serious.

"Twenty years ago, when I was working at the Chart House and living with my mother, a man broke in and raped me," I said. "I didn't know who he was and I never saw his face." Marcus got very quiet and attentive.

"I didn't tell you before because I never expected he would ever get caught. A few months ago, I found out there was another victim. That woman was raped just a few months after me. I went to Annapolis today to meet with Dave Cordle, the detective who has had my case for almost the entire time. He told me that a DNA sample collected from a suspect in New York matched evidence from my case."

Marcus took my hand, kissed me, and said "A serial rapist? Good, I'm glad they figured out who the bastard is and he'll be going to jail for the rest of his life, where he belongs."

He asked me a few questions about how my assailant had been tracked down and what we could expect in the upcoming months.

"The detectives are going to go to New York the day after my birthday to arrest the guy."

"Okay, good. Well, I guess you will eventually have to go to court?" he asked.

"Yeah, I'll probably have to testify, but not for a while. I'll find out about all that stuff after the guy is arrested. If I'm lucky, maybe he will admit he did it and I won't have to go to court. But I do want to see who he is."

"I know who he is," Marcus said. "A scumbag, that's who he is."

37

The Arrest

On November 14th, 2008, I applied for and received a warrant charging Trice with 1st degree rape and the various lesser charges associated with the rape: rape, 2nd degree; sex offense, 1st degree; sex offense, 2nd degree; battery; assault. I coordinated with SGT Madden, and it was agreed that Tracy and I would come to Albany on November 20th, when we would attempt to apprehend him.

With great anticipation, we left Baltimore Washington International Airport and headed to Albany. On the short flight, I played various scenarios through my mind. Would we find him? Would he run? Would he resist? So many possibilities...Tracy snored.

I rented a car and we headed to our hotel, checked in quickly, and headed to Troop G of the New York State Police. SGT Madden greeted us and took us back into the Criminal Investigation Unit where we met Trooper Mike Student, who would take us to William Trice's place of employment to arrest him for the rape of Jennifer Wheatley.

Trooper Student had obtained a New York State fugitive warrant based on my Maryland warrant. The local police would use this warrant to arrest Trice. SGT Madden had also contacted the Albany Police Department and informed them that we expected to take Trice into custody at his place of employment, Pearlman's Towing, on North Manning Road in Albany. We decided to arrest Trice at his work place for a number of reasons, the most important being officer safety. Albany was a much better choice as a place to arrest Trice than his isolated, rural home in Eagle Bridge.

SGT Madden had organized a surveillance/arrest team which included his troopers, as well as a federal marshal and an Albany Police Department detective from the Federal Marshal's Fugitive Apprehension Task Force. Based on surveillance, we knew that Trice normally returned his tow truck to Pearlman's Towing between 4:30 and 5:00pm. He would then drive home in his personal vehicle.

Detective Student, Tracy, and I left Troop G about 3:40pm to join the surveillance team. It was about a ten minute ride. We had radio and telephone contact with the surveillance team and quickly learned that Trice had returned his tow truck to Pearlman Towing earlier than expected — just after we'd gotten on the road. Detective Student stepped up the speed of the car as we traveled towards Albany. Five minutes into the ride, we were advised that Trice was exiting the office and appeared to be heading towards his car in the parking lot.

God love the locals. They know the back roads, shortcuts, and all the means necessary to get from point A to point B very quickly. With Trooper Student at the wheel, we sped along the back roads headed to Pearlman's. I really didn't want to miss this arrest. Neither did Tracy. We both were tense with anticipation. The surveillance team saw us arrive and said, "GO!" We all jumped out of the unmarked Ford Crown Victoria. The Fugitive Apprehension Task Force officers surrounded Trice as he opened his car door.

Trice seemed to panic. As the arrest team attempted to place him in handcuffs, he began to resist. But he was no match for the Fugitive Apprehension Task Force officers. Trice initially seemed to think he was being "busted" for the small amount of marijuana he had in his car. He was told there was a warrant for his arrest, although at this time we did not tell him why he was being arrested. He would learn that soon enough.

Trooper Student and Tracy Morgan transported Trice back to Troop G. I rode back to Troop G with another trooper. Upon arrival, Trice was led to the small, cramped polygraph room on the second floor of the barrack. We had arranged the chairs around a folding table with Trice sitting at the end of of the table, facing Tracy. Trice kept asking what this was all about, especially after we told him we were from Maryland.

Tracy read Trice his Miranda warning and Trice agreed to speak with us without an attorney. The interview began at 4:05pm. A New York State trooper stood outside. Tracy began the questioning by asking Trice if he had any idea why we were there. He had not yet been given his copy of the charging document listing 1st degree rape as the primary charge. Trice appeared puzzled and said he had no idea.

Before leaving for New York, Jennifer gave me pictures of herself that had been taken around the time of her rape. Tracy showed the pictures of Jennifer to Trice and asked him if he recognized the woman in the two photographs. Trice studied the pictures carefully and said he had never seen her before, and if he had seen Jennifer, he would remember her.

I next produced pictures I had taken of the Chesapeake Landing sign outside the gates of the community, as well as several shots of the complex, including where the attack had taken place. Tracy showed these photographs to Trice and he said he had no idea where that was. On a roll, I produced pictures of the Chart House restaurant taken from downtown at the City Dock across Spa Creek. Tracy asked Trice if he recognized the place and whether he had ever been there. As before, Trice denied having ever been there, stating that was not the kind of place he would go.

The purpose of showing him the photographs was, of course, to negate a consensual sexual encounter as well as negate the possibility that the fingerprints identified as Trice's could have been left on the candle during a visit or a delivery to the restaurant.

My research on Trice prior to our New York trip had revealed that he had been a courier in and around the Washington, D.C. area around the time of

Jennifer's assault. However, during our interrogation Trice denied ever being in the Annapolis area. Trice said the closest he came to the Annapolis area was Davidsonville, a rural area approximately ten miles outside of Annapolis, where his father resided at the time.

Tracy pressed Trice on why he thought we were there questioning him. Trice offered that we might be there related to an earlier allegation by his step-sister. A Maryland State Trooper had spoken to him about his step-sister's allegations, but that was all he could think of. Trice then admitted he had served eighteen months for indecent exposure and that he had "had issues" back then, acting out and feeling inadequate.

Trice went on to say he had sought mental health counseling for anger issues and a "sexual misconduct thing." He was referring to his arrest for indecent exposure involving the twelve-year-old girl who had passed by his window on her way to school.

Tracy next told Trice about his fingerprints recovered from a candle found at a crime scene. Trice said he had no explanation as to how his fingerprints ended up on the candle. I showed him the Chesapeake Landing pictures again, and Trice said, "That's a money place," and that he would never "hang out" there; that he would stay in the D.C. area.

Tracy and I had previously discussed our strategy. If Trice wouldn't admit his connections to Annapolis, the Chart House restaurant, Chesapeake Landing, Jennifer, or the candle, she would move straight into the DNA profile match. Since Trice admitted to nothing, Tracy explained the generalities of DNA evidence and how the CODIS system worked. Then she moved in for the kill.

"Mr. Trice, your DNA, which was obtained by the New York State Police, matched that of not only the evidence recovered from the Wheatley rape, but that of a second victim in Arnold, Maryland. Trice was then advised he was being arrested for raping two women.

Startled, Trice said, "Oh my God, no way."

There was a moment of silence, then he said, "I'm worse than I thought I was."

It was 4:25pm. Trice placed his head in his hands on the table and began to cry, invoking his right to an attorney. A moment later, he abruptly sat up saying, "I need to go to the bathroom; I need to go right now!" I summoned the trooper from the hall and he escorted Trice to the men's room. A distinct, foul-smelling odor was left behind in the small room.

After taking care of personal business, Trice was taken to the booking area to be photographed and fingerprinted. This would normally take only half an hour, but technology malfunction kicked in and we waited quite a while before Trice was brought out to the transport unit to appear in court for his initial appearance.

Albany County Court operates a night court, but we had arrived too late for initial appearances, so Trice was placed in lock-up. Finally, the prosecutor was able to convey to the judge the special nature of our case due to the crimes committed and because the case involved out-of-state investigators. Trice appeared in the courtroom represented initially by the local public defender, who requested a reasonable bond for release, as Trice was a law abiding resident of the area, was employed full time, and had a wife and home. The State rightfully objected, citing the serious nature of the allegations brought by our warrants. The judge ordered Trice to be held in a "no bond" status, pending extradition proceedings to the State of Maryland.

Tracy and I had been riding on adrenalin since the start of our day around 5:30am. I knew I couldn't relax until I made one phone call. As we left the court complex, I dialed Jennifer's cell phone. It was 7:30pm on November 20, 2008. I took a deep breath and said, "We've got him. He's in jail with no bond. We're coming home."

After that, I was in a fog. Twenty years later...We were closer to seeing justice done and putting an end to this twenty-year-old case.

But we were not done yet.

After a late and quick celebratory dinner at the hotel, Tracy and I called it a night. The next morning we headed back to Maryland to prepare our reports and begin the process to obtain a court ordered DNA sample from Trice for use as evidence when the case went to trial.

Additionally, we waited to hear if Trice would waive extradition. He could either voluntarily come back to Maryland in custody to face the charges we had brought, or fight extradition, demanding a court hearing in New York. If he chose to fight extradition, the State of Maryland would then have to prove there was probable cause for Trice to be brought back to face trial.

Trice took a few days to think over his options, but eventually he waived extradition proceedings. Under custody, Trice was flown back to Maryland by the Anne Arundel County Police Fugitive Squad on December 5, 2008. He was ordered held without bond in the Anne Arundel County Detention Center on Jennifer Road in Annapolis on the charge of the first degree rape of Jennifer Wheatley on August 20, 1988.

With Trice back in Annapolis, the necessary court order for Trice's evidentiary DNA sample was directed to Tracy to serve and collect, which she did on January 16, 2009. Once again, we waited for the Anne Arundel County Police Department lab to confirm that the known evidentiary DNA sample matched the DNA from Jennifer's rape case and also the second victim. We now moved into the trial preparation phase.

38

November, 2008
"He never saw it coming."

*O*n my fiftieth birthday, after Marcus and I had finished dinner, the phone rang. It was Dave Cordle. He was organizing his information and getting the questions ready to ask the suspect. Dave was pumped up and running on pure adrenaline. I shared his excitement and told him it was one of the best birthday presents I'd had in years. He promised to call me after they had the guy in custody. He wished me a happy birthday and hung up. I doubt he slept much that night. I know I didn't.

Late in the afternoon of November 20th, my stomach was starting to feel bad. In anticipation of what was going to be happening that day, I had forgotten to eat anything. "Too much coffee to drink," I thought as I went into the kitchen and got a wedge of cheese. Marnie called me while I was sitting and nibbling on my cheese.

"Anything yet?"

"No, not yet. They were planning to meet the creep at work when he returned with the truck. I have no idea when I'll hear from Dave. I'll call you as soon as I find out anything."

I hung up feeling shaky.

Damn, what was wrong with me? I went back to the kitchen got a half a bagel and returned to the sofa. I started to read through e-mails and work on some computer drawings for my mother-in-law. I really felt like crap. My heart was racing a mile a minute and I was getting short of breath. This wasn't too much coffee. This was something else. Great. They'd finally catch the creep and I'd drop dead of a heart attack. Wouldn't that be ironic?

What the hell was going on? Maybe if I got up and walked around I'd feel better. I went into the kitchen to see what else I could eat to help settle my stomach. I couldn't sit still. Adrenaline was pumping and I couldn't figure out why. Was I having an anxiety attack? I'd never had one before and I wasn't entirely sure what the symptoms were, but something was wrong. If it wasn't an anxiety attack it could really be a heart attack. I liked the idea of an anxiety attack better.

I started to hyperventilate. Holy crap! This really was bad. Why in the world was I hyperventilating? What next?

Maybe I was allergic to the cheese.

Not likely.

I started to feel scared. I had never had this kind of thing happen out of the blue before.

Maybe I should let Marcus know what's going on with me, I thought. He was in his office playing an online computer game with some of his friends. I took a couple of deep breaths and decided to sit for a second. Maybe if I concentrated on my heartbeat I could slow everything down a bit. If this didn't work, then I would tell Marcus. I started counting slowly in my head and took several more deep breaths, letting them out slowly. The deliberate breathing seemed to help; I could feel my heartbeat beginning to slow down.

And then, as abruptly as they had started, all the weird symptoms stopped. I was fine. I sat in the living room for a minute waiting to see if the disturbing symptoms would start up again.

That was weird, I thought. *Really weird*. Was the attack or whatever it was really over, or just taking a break? I felt okay. No shortness of breath or heart palpitations. My stomach still felt a bit like I had swallowed a fistful of bumblebees, but even that feeling was beginning to fade.

I walked into the kitchen to get something to drink and glanced at the clock on the microwave. It was 4:00pm.

Wow! It came to me. I couldn't prove it, but I suspected Dave and Tracy had just apprehended the guy. The odd progression of my symptoms may have been some of what Dave was feeling as the whole thing went down. Dave had told me they were going to meet the guy when he got off work. That had to be it. I began to relax when I realized I probably wasn't going to die that day, after all.

Many months later, I had the opportunity to tell Dave about my crazy experience, the odd combination of symptoms, and that I believed there was some connection between what I was going through and what he was doing at the time.

"Oh, you were definitely with me," he said. "It was all over by four o'clock."

39

"We Got Him!"

$\mathcal{A}$round 7:00pm my cell phone rang. I didn't even have to look to see who was calling. Dave couldn't wait to tell me the news.

"Hi Dave," I said before he could speak.

"He's in jail, he's not getting out, and he can't hurt anyone else," Dave said.

Apparently the suspect had no idea he had been under surveillance for so long. He was completely surprised when Dave, Tracy, and a few of the New York State Police showed up at his workplace and told him he was under arrest. When a police officer grabbed him as he started to get into his car, Trice began to put up a struggle. He was told to calm down, but still he tried to get free. When the officer asked him why he was putting up such a fight, he said, "I have some weed in the truck." The policeman told him they were not interested in his weed and that he had much bigger problems to worry about. He was taken in to the police station and questioned by Dave and Tracy.

"We couldn't get him to confess, but he said some things we can use," Dave said.

"Thanks, Dave." I was crying.

"He didn't waive extradition. We will have to get a court order to have him brought back. But, he's in jail. You can sleep peacefully again."

I had million questions: What did he look like? What did he say? Where did he come from? Did he know me? But I couldn't form any words. This was a huge day for both of us. I imagine calling me to share the news of the arrest was probably a career highlight for Dave. All previous cold cases that Dave Cordle had solved over the years were resolved in a bittersweet fashion. Even though he'd locked up the bad guys, he could not celebrate as he might have wanted to because the victims of those crimes had died during their attacks. I had the distinction of being his first surviving victim. Although he couldn't wait to share the news with me, the events of the day had taken their toll. Now that the excitement of the arrest was over, Dave sounded exhausted.

"Get some rest, and then when you get back, go out and celebrate," I said.

"I think I will," Dave said. "I'll be in touch."

After Dave hung up, I immediately dialed Marnie's number. I started to cry as soon as she picked up the phone. I could hardly talk.

"They got him, Marnie. The fucker's in jail." I could hardly speak the words through my tears.

"Holy crap, Jen," Marnie said. "Unbelievable!"

We talked and cried together for about a half an hour. It was unreal; it was such a relief. It was so incredible to be saying those words to my best friend. Marnie realized more than anyone how much having this guy in jail meant to me. She had known me before I was raped and had been with me all along the way. She had stood by me when I'd sunk to the bottom, and she had helped me get back up again. She never judged and was always there to offer an ear. To be able to share that moment with her was just miraculous.

I made the round of calls to my sisters, mother, and father to give them the news. Marcus came in the room wondering what all the phone calls were about. With tears streaming down my cheeks, I said, "They caught him. He's in jail."

Then I sent e-mails out to everyone else letting them know the creep was in jail.

And he never saw it coming!

40

Press Conferences

$\mathcal{A}$ couple of days after the suspect was arrested, Dave and Tracy spoke to the press about him. Newspapers and television stations from all over the east coast carried the story: *William Joseph Trice, 47, of Eagle Bridge, New York, is being held in the Albany County jail, awaiting extradition on first-degree rape and assault charges that could send him behind bars for life.*

On November 25, 2008, Scott Daugherty of *The Capital* — the Annapolis paper — reported:

> *"We are currently reviewing over twenty cold cases,"* Dave Cordle said in a press release in 2008. *"We have resubmitted evidence from eight to nine sexual assaults to crime labs for new analysis. We hope to have some positive results. We knew we had related cases, but we did not have a name."*

I spent nearly the entire day of Dave and Tracy's press conference in the emergency room. Marcus and I were planning to travel to Pennsylvania to visit Art and Hope for Thanksgiving, but I was concerned I wouldn't be able to make the trip. I had been feeling really terrible for days. Thinking it was just the stress of the arrest, I ignored the symptoms I was having. I had tightness in my chest and a nauseous stomach. These symptoms were similar to the symptoms I'd had on the day the suspect was arrested.

When I told Marcus I didn't think I was going to be able to go to Pennsylvania for Thanksgiving, he decided it was time to do something.

He drove me to the hospital and told the woman at the emergency room desk I was having symptoms of a heart attack.

"I've been feeling like crap for days. Don't you think if it was a heart attack I would be dead by now?" I asked.

The nurse said it was best not to take any chances. She attached a heart monitor to me and rushed me through to the doctor. He checked my heart and had me do a stress test. Except for needing exercise, my heart was fine. I told the doctor I had been diagnosed with a hiatal hernia and acid reflux a few years previous, and I had been taking Prilosec™ for the symptoms. When I'd gone shopping the previous week, I'd noticed a less expensive version of the same drug. I had been taking the new heartburn medicine for a few days and it didn't seem to be working as well. Once the doctor pumped me full of acid reducers, my symptoms subsided and I was released with instructions to get back on the Prilosec™ and get more exercise.

Marcus and I were in the parking lot of the Giant grocery store, having just bought more Prilosec™, when Dave called my cell phone. Apparently my lawyer, Kathleen, was concerned because someone in the press wanted to release the arrest photo of the suspect in their evening televised story.

"Is there any way you can recognize the suspect?" Dave asked me. "You didn't see his face, right? Kathleen is concerned you might recognize the suspect after you see a photo of him."

"Not to worry, Dave. I didn't see his face and his name means nothing to me. You could release a photo of Elmer Fudd, tell me he was the guy, and I would have to take you on your word."

"Watch the evening news tonight. It should be on Channel 4," he said.

"Okay, thanks Dave. Have a great Thanksgiving!"

"You, too. I'll be in touch."

In December, 2008, Trice was extradited to Maryland and moved to the Anne Arundel County Detention Center on Jennifer Road in Annapolis.

41

Finding Old Friends

I, too, am so thankful for the opportunity to reconnect with old friends. I get to be reminded of what drew me to these people in the first place, and they all make me smile to this day! Your note just made me smile... Thank you for sharing your thoughts and story with us — just amazing... And after all of these years, to find you on Facebook! And then to discover that they had found your rapist. How unbelievable. And I know we've all had conversations about how things don't just happen — that there seems to be a bigger plan and that we were meant to find each other again. I'm literally getting goose bumps again just thinking of it.
~Jackie

Facebook is great!

Okay, I get why people are leery of Facebook. There is a huge amount of concern about identity theft and privacy concerns such as people you don't know finding out all kinds of information about you. But, the truth is, they don't need Facebook to do that. We're in the "Information Age." Anything you want to know is right at your fingertips. What's the catch-phrase? "Google it!"

Keeping my identity hidden is impossible. I have an online business — www.ArtGiftsEtc.com — and I advertise my business. Many of my quilts have won awards and prizes, have been shown all over the country, and have been published with my bio in magazines and books. I have sold hundreds of paintings in this country and Europe. Some people are more exposed on the web than others, and I am one of them. Trying to locate old friends the old fashioned way can still be a challenge. Facebook made what was almost impossible very easy.

I discovered this cyber world by accident early in December, 2008. I had received an e-mail from VCU School of the Arts, my Alma Mater, that mentioned "Contacting old friends" and "Keeping in Touch." I clicked on the link, curious. I was hoping to locate a few of my old roommates from school. I discovered, in order to "Keep in Touch," I had to sign up for a Facebook account. So, I did.

I didn't have any luck finding any of my old roommates from college at first, but once I had my Facebook profile setup, I learned that quite a few family members and friends already had accounts. It took me just a couple of days to figure out how to find my way around the site, and once I figured out the basics, I was able to reconnect with a lot of people.

After I discovered I could flip through everyone's list of friends, I started finding people — friends-of-friends I had not seen in quite a while. Finding one person quickly led me to others, and before I knew it, I had reconnected with many of my long-lost schoolmates and Chart House coworkers. In addition to seeing what they had been up to during that time we had been out of touch, I got to see photos of their families. Although I realized I had missed so much of what had gone on in their lives, in many ways it was as if we had not missed a beat.

I sent a collective e-mail to the Chart House crew letting them know the latest developments about my case. I also let them know I would welcome their support when it came time to go to trial. I was so happy to be back in the fold. Although I had been concerned that maybe too many years had gone by and our lives had drifted too far apart to renew old friendships, I was reassured by the responses I got to my request:

Gosh Jen, this brought back so many memories. You were so brave and I know that's something I picked up and have carried with me since.
~Jen

Everything happens for a reason. I would love to be there to support you. Please let me know.
~Andrea

It felt right that all of the girls who'd helped me get back up on my feet so long ago were back in my life in time to see justice prevail. I was reminded that, just because we lose touch with friends, it doesn't make the impact of the friendship less important.

42

January, 2009
"Hurry up and wait."

$\mathcal{A}$s fascinating as solving murder and cold cases appears to be, there is an equally frustrating side. No part of catching the bad guys and seeing justice done moves very quickly. Even when evidence has been collected and technology has caught up with the crime itself, progress can be slowed by unforeseen delays. The discovery and processing of possible evidence can get tied up in so much legal red tape and budget limitations that it's a wonder anyone is ever convicted of any crime. This aspect of the job would truly make me nuts. Even though I have an eye for detail and a mind that can solve some tough puzzles, I don't know if I would have the patience the job requires. It takes a special person to solve a crime and see it through until justice is achieved.

Even though a suspect may have been caught and the case makes it as far as trial preparation, this does not mean there will be smooth sailing from then on. Our justice system is really a tangle of legalese that at any given time can cause a case to implode. Getting a case as far as that moment when the plaintiff and the defendant walk into a courtroom involves months of "two steps forward and three steps back." I was soon to experience this firsthand.

In January, 2009, just a couple of months after Trice was arrested and extradited to Maryland, I arranged a meeting at the State's Attorney's Office in Annapolis to talk with Kathleen Rogers, my lawyer, and Cindy Haworth, my court advocate. Apparently asking to meet them this early in the process was highly unusual. I was told that they didn't usually meet with the victim involved with the crime until close to the trial. I wanted to find out what I might expect, from the legal standpoint, over the next few months, and I knew they would be the ones who could answer my questions.

I knew there had been a couple of hearings in front of the judge, but I was amazed that, although they knew the crimes Trice was charged with, Kathleen and Cindy didn't seem to know any of the details of the crime itself. I was beginning to get the first inkling of just how crazy and convoluted our justice system really is. How could they recommend to a judge that someone should not get bail when they didn't even know the circumstances that had led to his arrest?* True, my attorney had worked directly with Dave Cordle for a long time and knew he would not pursue a case for twenty years if he didn't believe the person who had committed the crime needed to be caught and thrown in jail. Essentially they were taking Dave at his word. Not knowing the particulars of the crime at the beginning of their involvement with pursuing justice really seemed nuts to me.

"How can you represent someone in a courtroom if you don't know anything about them?" I asked.

"We haven't read about your case yet," Kathleen told me. "Right now we are letting the judge know that the defendant is a bad guy who needs to stay in jail."

I learned there are many court proceedings that have more to do with serving and protecting the defendant's rights and making sure he or she gets to enlist all available legal options and processes available to him or her than they do with obtaining justice for the victim. Obviously, determining guilt or innocence is the goal of our judicial system. Convicting the guilty and setting the innocent free is the ultimate goal. Many of the proceedings leading to that goal must have been born from oversights or

---

I later learned that Kathleen was very familiar with the case. She had been working on the case for months and had made many of the arrangements with the New York police and prosecutors. She also coordinated the arrest and questioning to make sure all laws were complied with. Everything that Dave and Tracy did, including the way the defendant would be questioned, were gone over with her ahead of time.

mistakes made throughout the years. Might not some of these procedures be avoided if details of a crime were more familiar to lawyers before they approached a judge? When you combine the endless procedures and a backlog of cases waiting to go before a judge, it's no wonder it can take years to get to trial.

I didn't want to wait years. Getting this far had taken four years already, from the first unsuccessful meeting with Dave Cordle in 2005, and twenty from the date of my rape. Now that there was a suspect and he was in jail and there was evidence against him, I couldn't see what would take so long in getting a trial underway. I wanted to be done with all of this. I wanted it over and I wanted it over quickly.

As the saying goes: *If wishes were horses then beggars would ride.*
I didn't get my wish.

On the afternoon I met with Kathleen and Cindy, I gave them a quick account of what had happened to me the night I was attacked, and I asked them some questions.

"If this ends up going to trial, how long from now do you think it will be, six months? Eight months? A year?"

"Oh, it won't be a year. But six to eight months sounds about right," Kathleen said. "There is a lot to do between now and the time we go to court."

Cindy added that cold cases like these were complicated. "Witnesses have died or are difficult to locate, and evidence can be lost."

My case would have been more difficult, if not downright impossible, to prove in a court of law twenty years ago. True, some of the witnesses may have died or evidence might have been lost in all those years and this could cause some problems, but the really important evidence in my case, the DNA samples and the fingerprints, were still available. Advances in science and technology should make trying this case easier. DNA testing had been in its infancy in 1988, and although DNA evidence collection had just begun in the '80s when I was raped, advances in the testing itself had improved over the years. AFIS, the fingerprint database, was not in existence at all back then. Without the fingerprint database, there would be no suspect at all. The fingerprints in evidence in my case were checked in the 1980s against the ink and paper cards on file and nothing had come of that. From my perspective, the passing of time should make this case easier, not more difficult for them. I kept my mouth shut about these observations, but I did ask, "Will I be allowed to have family and friends in the courtroom with me?"

"Yes, it is open court." Kathleen said it was her experience that rape victim witnesses were usually alone in the courtroom, and those who did have family with them did better if their spouses or boyfriends were not in the courtroom during the victim's testimony. She found it was easier for them to tell their stories if they did not have to worry about how a husband or boyfriend might react to hearing the details. I explained there were a lot of people who wanted to support me by being there when I took the stand. I said Marcus also wanted to be there with me because, as he'd said, "That's what a husband is supposed to do, support his wife." Kathleen told me it wouldn't be like it is on TV. She and Cindy would be there, the defendant and his counsel, the jury, and the judge. There would also be a few others, including the bailiff, police guards, and reporters.

"It's not like you see on CSI with a crowd of people on the benches. But, yes, it is open court. It's your decision. It's up to you who you want in there with you and if you want anyone in there when you testify," she said.

You might just be surprised, I thought. *It could be quite a crowd this time.*

I knew Marcus was not going to be happy if he wouldn't be able to be there with me. But I had time to make my decision about this and knew we could work something out. I had already decided I wanted any women friends and family members there who wanted to come. I was going to need all the support I could get.

I had been thinking about the defendant and how his incarceration must be affecting his family and friends. It should not have come as a surprise to them that he was in trouble again. He'd had many run-ins with the law during his lifetime, from moving violations and parking tickets to burglary and indecent exposure. On one of my visits to his office, Dave showed me the printed list of traffic violations. It looked like he was unfurling Santa's "Naughty or Nice" list. In addition, there were other crimes he had been convicted of that were more serious than the hundreds of speeding tickets. But being held without bond and having been charged with two separate felony crimes had to have an effect on his family. Learning that he had committed this crime twenty years ago and managed to keep it secret for so long must have been shocking to them.

"Is he married?" I asked Kathleen and Cindy. "Does he have kids?"

"Yes, he is married," Kathleen said. "I don't know if he has any children, but he is married."

"The repercussions of his actions are only beginning to be realized," I mumbled.

Before I left, Cindy said I would probably receive a subpoena for a trial date in a couple of months.

"Ignore it. We never make it to trial on the first date, never."

I left the State's Attorney's Office feeling relieved about the trial. I could forget about it for several months. In the beginning of February, we were heading to California to surprise my father on his eightieth birthday, and at the end of the month, we were going on a cruise to the Bahamas with some family members. I was happy to get away and spend time with family — especially in warmer climates. I needed a break from all of this.

43

Summer, 2009

*A*s promised, the first scheduled date for the trial was postponed. No problem. When I got a second notice from the State's Attorney's Office telling me the trial was scheduled for August 24, 2009, I thought there was a certain poetic ring to this date. It would have been just twenty-one years after the assault had occurred. What a perfect time for a conviction.

I sent an e-mail to my friends letting them know about the trial date. I knew I could face my assailant if I had family and friends there with me.

No matter how much support I was going to have in the courtroom, it seemed there was nothing that could prepare me for the mix of emotions I would go through during the months before the trial. This was another one of those times in my life when I wished there was a manual to which I could refer. I had no previous life experiences that could help me through this time. No one I knew had been through anything like this. I suppose therapy might have helped.

Dave Cordle told me counseling was available if I wanted it. However, I hesitated to take him up on the offer for what I considered a good reason. My counseling directly following the rape had not been helpful. And once the creep was in jail, I believed the hard part was behind me. The twenty years of wondering was over — the rest of this process should be a real breeze. Who needed therapy?

Unfortunately, the timing of the trial date interrupted several of our usual summer activities. Our annual barbecue had to be canceled because we couldn't work out a date that fit well with everyone's schedules. Marcus, the "Grill Master," was not happy about it, but he was willing to wait and have a big get-together at our annual pumpkin carving party around Halloween.

I spent the summer months before August in a horrible manic-depressive state. Neither my hobbies of gardening or photography, nor my passion for creating art quilts could pull me out of it. For the most part, I felt depressed and nervous. It was difficult to concentrate for more than a few minutes at a time. When I did start a quilting project, I found my thoughts going over and over what was ahead of me.

In addition to my anxiety at seeing this guy for the first time, I couldn't keep myself from thinking about how the news of this man's arrest must be affecting his family. How much of the truth, if any, had he told his wife? I doubted he'd told her much. Perhaps he gave her a twisted version of the story. He may have told her some tale he might have come to believe was true. Maybe he told her a fantasy spun together in which he looked like the victim and not the bad guy. Maybe he didn't tell her anything, pretending instead not to know why he had been arrested, because, according to him, *"I didn't do anything wrong!"*

I believe I knew what Trice's wife was going to go through to some extent. Her life was being turned completely upside down, as mine had been so long ago. I hoped, for her sake, she didn't ever blame herself for not seeing what he had kept hidden. She could not have known. It was his nature to ambush his prey. How terrible for her to realize her entire life with this person had been a lie. She might stand by him for a while — convincing herself he had not done these horrible things. But I could not imagine she would be able to see this to the end once the truth was made clear to her. Her life would never be the same because of this man's selfish and violent behavior. The results of his actions were now beginning to ripple through his family.

No matter what anyone said to me, I felt some degree of responsibility for what his wife was going through. I realized I was not responsible for this man's behavior, but my good fortune in having him finally locked up was her misfortune. His wife might even blame me in part for the mess her life had become. Her husband was in prison awaiting trial and she was alone with her thoughts. I knew she would eventually have to face a harsh truth about a man she thought she loved.

At times, I imagined maybe their relationship was not good and the arrest would be the best opportunity for her to get away from a bad or abusive situation. I hoped she was strong enough to rebuild her life. I hoped she would come to know she was better off without this man.

I was sure Trice must have parents somewhere, too. I could not imagine what a mother must feel to hear the words, "Your son has been arrested in connection with two rapes."

It might not have been a surprise to his mother that her son was a bad seed. But facing the reality to this degree under the scrutiny of everyone in her life and the public's eye was unimaginable to me.

Did he have any friends? What would they think? Had he kept company all these years with people who would understand and relate to the kind of crimes he committed? Maybe he shared details of his brutality with some of his buddies. I could imagine them patting each other on the back in celebration of his viciousness. Did he tell his friends about all of his attacks? Or, did his friends have no clue who he really was? Would they stand by him, even when his family could not? Or would they scatter, feeling disgusted? Would others abandon him, believing it was best to lay low in case a suspicious eye were cast their way?

What was a victory for me had to have become a raw truth for his family. Everyone he was close to, to some degree or another, would be affected by his crimes. The truths he had kept hidden for so many years were being revealed. The circle was coming to a close.

While I waited for the trial, all of these thoughts, plus my own fears and anxieties about facing this monster in the courtroom, continued to bubble to the surface. It was enough to drive me mad. Being so adversely preoccupied was not like me. I could usually work through anything. I did get a few small projects completed, but I had no luck starting anything too involved or time consuming.

The art quilts I make require anywhere from six months to a year to complete. With my attention span so short, I couldn't "get into it," as it were. Much of the time in my creative process is spent rearranging bits of fabric until I get a design I am happy with. While I'm working on getting the image just the way I want it, I have lots of time to think. I didn't like the direction my thoughts headed each time I started to work. My solution to quiet my thoughts was to avoid involving myself in anything that gave me time to think.

Anything I started that required more than a couple of days to finish became a chore and got put on the back burner. I quickly ran out of back burners. Eventually, I quit starting new projects altogether. It was an unproductive summer for me and completely uncharacteristic. I wanted the trial to be over so I could get back into my life and what I love to do. August 24th couldn't get here soon enough.

"We'll be there sister! I can't imagine looking at him, couldn't pretend to know how that feels for you. Try to have July be yours, put aside what will begin in August, it'll be enough to deal with it then. Not sure how exactly to do that..."
~ Marnie

I did try to distract myself by taking lots of photographs and keeping busy with my online business. However, I measure the success or worth of each day by how much I have accomplished. Not being creative, for me, is intolerable. If I don't *do* something every day, I feel I have wasted that time. There were many wasted days for me between the arrest and the trial.

My brother-in-law David is a professional photographer. He was planning a photography cruise to Mexico for September and asked Marcus and me if we would like to join Mollie and him. *Yes!* This would be the perfect escape for after the trial. My father and step-mother decided they would join all of us. This was perfect. I began to think of it as the "Thank God the Trial is Over Cruise." It was to be a reward of sorts. Knowing I had something really exciting to look forward to after the trial was over made the waiting easier.

44

Pre-Trial Preparations

Assistant State's Attorney Kathleen Rogers, a veteran sex crimes prosecutor, would be prosecuting Jennifer Wheatley's rape case in court. Witness Advocate Cindy Haworth, another veteran and part of the Sex Crimes Trial Team, would act as Jennifer's advocate. Prosecutions of major crimes normally involve several postponements, and this case was no different. Several trial dates came and went. It was up to Cindy to keep Jennifer's spirits up after each letdown she felt after each postponement. Jennifer had waited so long for her "day in court."

Our journey through the court system officially began on December 19, 2008. After I testified to the events which lead to Trice's arrest, Trice was indicted for first degree rape by a Grand Jury. Assistant Public Defender Heather Tierney was initially to be Trice's attorney and had entered her appearance in the case.

After the indictment, the State's team provided discovery to the defense team. Discovery is the presentation of the State's evidence against the defendant which will be used in the trial to the defense team. This evidence includes physical evidence, statements, and witness lists.

Next, the defense filed a "Motion to Dismiss" with the court for "Pre-Indictment Delay." The defense accused the State of not filing timely charges, which allegedly enhanced the State's case, and the resultant passage of time caused the inability for Trice to locate witnesses favorable to his defense. This motion was denied by Judge Paul A. Hackner, who would hear the case. The defense also filed a "Motion to Suppress"

Trice's brief statements to Tracy and me during the questioning of him after his arrest in New York. This motion was also denied.

One more roadblock to get past was a "Motion to Suppress Tangible Evidence," filed by the defense team on December 15, 2009. This was a last- ditch effort by the defense to have our New York State Police Commercial Vehicle Enforcement Unit's truck-stop/inspection to surreptitiously gather the cigarette butt evidence thrown out based on the premise that this was an illegal stop. Judge Hackner denied the motion.

The defense decided to opt for a jury trial instead of a trial before a judge. However, there would be one more change in the defense team. Ms Tierney cited a conflict of interest and Judge Hackner concurred that if she were to represent Trice, he could have a conviction overturned. Trice was to be represented by Andrew Szekely.

45

Postponement

*I*n early August, Cindy called. I sensed something was off. Even before I heard her voice on the phone, I knew it was bad news.

"Hi, Jennifer, this is Cindy Haworth of the State's Attorney's Office. I have some bad news. The trial has to be rescheduled because the key DNA witness is scheduled to have a baby the day the trial is supposed to start."

"You have got to be kidding me." I felt like the wind had been knocked out of me and I started to cry.

"I'm really sorry about this," she said. "I will let you know what the new dates are as soon as I know them. Kathleen is in with the judge right now."

I thought I would go insane. It was just a few weeks till the trial was supposed to begin. I had made it this far, feeling like crap every day, but getting closer to having the waiting game over. And now I had to steel myself for more of the same. Unbelievable.

I was really angry when I hung up the phone. How could someone forget they were going to have a baby? Didn't it occur to this DNA specialist to pass this bit of information on to Cindy? There had been plenty of time between the first subpoena and subsequent rescheduling to let someone know the DNA expert was already six months pregnant. This was an incredibly stupid and completely avoidable screw-up as far as I could see. Had this woman passed this information on to Cindy after the first subpoena, the trial could have been scheduled for a later, or earlier, date. Instead, I had to wait who knew how much longer.

Marcus was happy about the news. He started making calls right away to get our annual barbecue planned. August was the best month for the majority of our family and friends, and now August was completely open. He didn't have any problem bringing it all together. I wasn't in the mood for a party, especially a party for more than fifty people, as well as house guests. Getting the food ready and the house cleaned was an impossible chore. However, it was also a welcome distraction from my emotional upheaval. Even though I didn't want to have to pretend with all of our guests that life was great, spending a week in the kitchen after hours in the grocery store gave me something productive to do and it kept my mind off the trial.

I don't remember much about the day of the party. It was ungodly hot. A few of the people who came knew the trial had been delayed, but most of our friends didn't know anything about any of this. I was an emotional wreck and on the verge of tears at any given minute. I felt like I needed to scream and throw a tantrum. But I didn't. I had to maintain an air of composure. What I really needed and wanted was to talk about how all of this waiting was making me a nut case. I suppressed my feelings and smiled when I was around our guests. When I could slip away, I would let the tears flow. I don't remember talking to anyone. If I did, I can't remember anything I said.

After the sun went down, we had torrential rains and a wicked thunder and lightning storm. The rain brought relief from the heat. I remember sitting on a metal chair out in the rain welcoming a bolt of lightning that would put an end to all of this crap. Mother Nature succeeded in drenching the hamburger rolls and I got soaked to the skin in the chilling downpour.

Marcus told me it was the best barbecue we've ever had.

46

More Waiting

*T*he trial was rescheduled for October 26, 2009 and was expected to last five days. Telling Marcus the Halloween pumpkin carving party would have to be canceled wasn't any fun. Carving pumpkins together was an annual tradition we'd started in 1997. Marcus began planning his pumpkin party as soon as the grill got stored away for winter. At first, it had been just the two of us, but over the years, it had grown to more than a dozen friends and family members. This would be the first year we wouldn't be able to carve pumpkins and hand out candy to the kids on Halloween.

"Well, at least you got to have the annual barbecue, and, you could still carve pumpkins if you want to. You could bring them to Annapolis and carve them there. Not much of a party, but it's something," I said.

He was disappointed.

I got a call from Cindy before we went on our cruise to Mexico in September.

"Could you drive to Annapolis and meet with Kathleen and me?" she asked.

When I got to the State's Attorney's Office, I learned that Kathleen and Cindy wanted to talk over the possibility of a plea bargain. They hadn't wanted to discuss this over the phone and they didn't want to make a deal without my input.

In light of the fact that there was another victim, plus Trice had a pretty extensive criminal record, they were not willing to go too low with the offer and neither was I.

They asked me what I thought was fair.

"I want him to serve as many years in jail as he walked free after raping me," I said.

We decided that we would offer him forty-five years. He would have to serve sixty percent of the sentence before he was eligible for parole. He would be in his seventies when he got out. I agreed to the offer, but did not expect him to take it. To accept the offer would mean admitting guilt, and he would not be able to file an appeal. If he took his chances in the courtroom, he might get forty-five years, but then be able to file an appeal asking for a lighter sentence. Kathleen was going to write up the deal and submit it to his lawyer. They were hoping to have an answer by the time I got back from my cruise.

The cruise to Mexico was great. I had never been to this country before. It was really hot and humid and I hated that part. But it was great to hang out with family and discover new places together. We visited two Mayan temples. Both, I believe, were located about a mile from Hades, based on the temperature during the days we were there.

The trip was a wonderful distraction from the impending trial. I welcomed the opportunity to throw myself into documenting our adventures. I took hundreds of photographs. It was not the "Thank God the Trial is Over" cruise I had hoped it would be, but I had a great time sightseeing and relaxing. Occasionally, when I was alone and had a chance to think, I found myself getting teary because the trial was still ahead of me. I was hoping against hope that while we were away, the creep would accept the deal we offered him and the whole thing would go away.

That didn't happen.

When I got back home, I received a call from Cindy. She told me Trice's lawyer had not yet shown him the deal we'd offered. Apparently, his lawyer did not believe I was alive, ready, willing, and able to testify. I guess she thought Kathleen was trying to trick her or something. Who knows?

"Could you call his lawyer and tell her who you are and that you are, in fact, ready to testify?" Cindy asked. "You don't have to if you don't feel comfortable doing it. You can say as much as you want, but we would like you to let her know you are going to testify."

"What? Are you kidding me?" I couldn't believe this.

"That's all you have to say. For some reason she does not believe we have secured you as a witness."

I had hoped Cindy's call would be, "He took the deal." Never in my dreams did I think I would come home to this crap.

I had a feeling Trice's lawyer suspected something was up since it was we who had proposed the deal to him. Usually it works the other way around. But she was off the mark. Good thing, too.

The truth was, Kathleen was having trouble getting the first in the chain of command with the DNA evidence secured as a witness. This woman was out of the country working with the Defense Department and might have difficulty returning for the trial. Without her, none of the DNA evidence could be introduced in court. Without the DNA evidence, our case was weak at best. But Trice's lawyer's suspicions were, thankfully, not in the right place. She thought I was missing from the roster of witnesses. My guess was that she didn't want to accept the proposed offer, only to discover the key witness had been missing from the line-up.

Cindy gave me the attorney's phone number. I called her, got her voice mail, and immediately hung up. I was thrown by the fact that she did not identify herself in her message. I couldn't even be sure I was dialing the right number. I was reluctant to leave such a cryptic message on a phone's answering device. I called two or three more times and still she did not pick up. Realizing the attorney was not going to answer the phone, I eventually did leave a message: "My name is Jennifer Wheatley. I wanted you to know I am alive and well and ready to testify."

Cindy had asked me to call her back after I'd contacted the woman and let her know how it went. I told her I'd had to leave a message and hoped it was the right number.

"It was very unprofessional behavior on the attorney's part," I said. "She does not even identify herself in her greeting. I didn't like that. I'm not entirely sure I called the right person. I hope so, though, because it's an odd message to receive if you don't know what it's about."

Before I hung up, I asked Cindy if it would be possible to get a copy of my journal to read. I was feeling like I might not be as ready and "great" in court as they assumed I would be.

"It has been a long time since I've read through it. I'm sure there are things I don't remember very well. I might feel better, more relaxed about everything, if I can refresh my memory."

But Cindy turned me down. "No," she said, "I don't think that's a good idea. Kathleen and I don't want your testimony to sound rehearsed. You'll be great, don't worry."

I hung up, shaking my head in disbelief.

Rehearsed? Seriously? They were talking about something that happened almost twenty-one years ago. Although there were parts of the crime I will never forget, there were a few details, including things he had said, that I could not remember very clearly. Unreal! I had not read the journal for at least eleven years. I'd last read it the night of the tenth anniversary of my rape. I was planning to read it and throw it away. In fact, I did read through the pages that night, and when I got to the last page, I tossed it into the trash. A few hours later, I listened to the voice in my head that was saying, "*Are you nuts? Get it out of there! You might need that one day.*" I retrieved it from the trashcan and stuck it on a shelf where it sat until I moved. I didn't believe I would need it, ever, but it wasn't taking up much room. And, what the hell? I packed the journal when I moved to my new home. There it had sat on a new shelf for years, undisturbed.

But not being allowed to read it because I would sound "rehearsed" was ludicrous. Was Cindy serious? In my head, ever since I had been told I would have to testify, I could not stop going over every detail of that night. I'd relived the event over and over in my waking hours and in my dreams for the past year. Rehearsed? Never. No amount of reading was going to get me to the point where I felt like I was performing a play or acting a part.

The closer the trial got, the more exposed and raw all of this became for me. Even though I had been raped so many years ago, there were often times during the past few months when it seemed like it had happened just yesterday. Although I had been able to tuck my emotions away for all of those years, that night felt like it was getting closer and closer instead of further and further away. Every day nearer to trial brought me closer to my assailant, and every day closer to seeing him for the first time brought me closer to the crime. Sure, I knew everything I was going to say in that courtroom was absolutely the truth, but to sound rehearsed implied either a confidence or disconnection I did not feel.

In mid June I'd sent an e-mail to my friends letting them know the deal had been proposed to Trice's lawyer and asking them to keep their fingers crossed:

September 16, 2009:
Hi All!
I just wanted you all to know that so far the plea bargain submitted by my lawyer has not been accepted nor has it been rejected. Since there will be witnesses from out of state [who] will be testifying, and my lawyer does not want to bring them into town unnecessarily, there will be a date submitted to the defense attorney for the final answer. But, I don't know when that will be.

This being said, we will be moving ahead with preparations for trial. This should start in a couple of weeks. I'll let you know when I'm in town and maybe we can plan a get-together downtown.

The trial dates are still the same (Oct.26-30) and unless the plea is accepted, they are not likely to change. I'll let you know if anything develops during the next couple of weeks. I have been getting whispers from spirit guides to brace myself for a trial, but I am hoping they are wrong this time!

Can't begin to tell you how crazy this is making me...thanks for all the support & good wishes!

~ Jen

I received this thoughtful response from my brother-in-law:

September 30, 2009:

Jen,

If you go to trial, no matter how hard it will be, it will give you a chance to get what you deserved all along; justice. You'll be putting an end to the brutality and despicable acts that one person has inflicted on so many others.

You will find, and have the strength, to finally face the prick and play a major part in negatively affecting the rest of his life, as he so deserves. You'll be the saving grace of so many other women [who] could have fallen prey to him. You will represent strength, justice, and get some finality to all of this.

So many women could not do what you're doing, and because of that, they need you more then they know. They need you more than you know.

I applaud your strength and what you stand for. So does every potential victim.

~ Dave B.

47

Birthday Plans

*O*nce October rolled around I started thinking, *My fifty-first birthday is coming up.* I wanted to plan something fun. Marcus suggested I have a party and invite my friends. That didn't sound like such a great idea to me. First, I would have to clean the house. Then I would have to prepare all the food. Then I would have to clean up after everyone left. Nope, that's not a birthday present at all.

I started thinking of Vegas, but couldn't find any good deals on flights. So I headed to the Royal Caribbean site to check out cruises for November. There was one leaving from Baltimore and the price was great. Four nights for two with taxes and tips included was less than $450. No airfare was needed since we could drive to the port. This sounded like just the thing! I could hang in there as long as the reward was time away from this craziness. I got the okay from Marcus and booked the trip. Again, I had a getaway planned for after the trial. This Bermuda cruise would be my "Thank God the Trial is Finally Over" cruise for sure.

That didn't happen.

48

Here We Go Again

*T*en days before the October 26th trial was to start, Trice's public defender met with the judge to cite a conflict of interest. The judge listened to her conflict in his chambers and agreed that if the trial were to proceed with this public defender representing the defendant in court, Trice would be able to get any conviction overturned because of the conflict. The judge would be appointing a new attorney to Trice's case. The trial was postponed again.

Cindy called to tell me about this latest development. I was sick. This was beyond unbelievable to me. His lawyer had been assigned to the case in December of 2008. It was now October, 2009. And she'd just discovered this conflict of interest? I couldn't take any more. I really thought I was going to go nuts. I asked Cindy to let me know when there were new dates for the trial and hung up.

For days, every time I thought about the delay I cried. I hated this. The waiting had consumed me for too long. It was time to have this guy extracted from my life. Every day the trial was delayed was another day spent with restless anticipation. I felt powerless, defeated, angry.

This postponement flabbergasted me. I would have understood if the postponement were due to an injury or illness. It was unbelievable to me that Trice's public defender had just started looking into the details of this case. What had she been doing for the past ten months? I would have to deal with the constant mental ping-pong for at least a couple more months.

Again, I sent out an e-mail to my friends to let them all know of the schedule change:

October 14, 2009 at 1:40pm

"Here we go again!"

No trial in October and he turned down the offer.

Apparently the defense lawyer discovered that she had a "conflict of interest" and could not represent the creep. Although the judge had said last time, "No more delays," after speaking with her, he agreed if she were to represent the creep, he could appeal his conviction and it would be overturned. He's getting a new lawyer. (Just feels right to call the defendant "the creep"...I hate saying his name.)

I just got a call from Cindy, my advocate, and they are trying for a start date of January 11th. But all the witnesses have to be re-confirmed. If any of them is not available for that week, the date will change. I should know soon if this date works.

I can't blame any of you who were planning to attend for bailing. I would too.

Only the judge knows what the conflict was. It was an "in my chambers" discussion with the defense attorney. I'm pissed because if she had actually been preparing for court 1, 2, 3, 4, 5, 6, 10, 11 months ago like she should have been, this conflict probably would have been discovered. A new attorney could have been appointed and it wouldn't have affected the trial date.

Last week my lawyer was in court with the same public defender (different creep, but an old case, too). They made it all the way to jury selection (meaning all the witnesses had been flown into town & put up in a hotel). The (now) 79 year old victim was "ready" for trial, and they accepted the plea during jury selection! Unbelievably incompetent lawyer!

Cindy said the new lawyer asked to keep the offer on the table, but I doubt the creep will take it. If he accepts the offer he has to serve 23-25 years before becoming eligible for parole. He'd be 73 or 74 by then. If he goes to court, he may get a life sentence, but he will appeal it and the sentence may be reduced. He can't appeal if he accepts a plea. It's a life sentence for sure if he accepts the plea (doubtful he'd live too far into his 70s in jail). He's probably going to take his chances in court. Neither I nor my lawyer is willing to reduce the number of years offered in the plea just to get him to accept it. They probably will not be going through the other trial if he gets a life sentence in this one. So, really his time in jail would effectively be for both rapes.

~ Jen

I felt completely exhausted and drained. I couldn't imagine getting through the holidays with the trial hanging over my head. I really considered telling Cindy I couldn't do this anymore. I couldn't testify. We were going to be looking at a year of delays by the time my birthday rolled around. My friend Andrea responded:

Jen, don't worry about anyone else. You need to hang in there and keep the faith that this will come around and he will get his karma served to him. January it is if it needs to be!!!

Hang in there! I am sending positive energy your way. Please, please, please keep me posted.

~ Andrea

I sent yet another e-mail to my friends and family.

November 2, 2009 at 3:23pm:

OK, these are the dates I was just given by my advocate and it should actually happen this time, but I've said that before!

Wednesday January 13th, 14, 15, (weekend & holiday on Monday) 19th & 20.

They believe I [will] be on the stand Wednesday or Thursday. Although it may not take all five days, they have those days blocked off.

I'll be in Annapolis from the evening of January 12th-20th. I hope to see you in court or downtown!

Thanks,

Jennifer

Right around Christmas, I got an e-mail from Cindy asking if we could arrange a meeting after the holidays. Kathleen wanted me to come to Annapolis before the trial so she could go over my testimony with me. She had her list of questions ready and she wanted me to answer them just as I would if I were in the courtroom.

They were ready to go to trial. I wasn't.

The reality of it all unnerved me. I felt like every fiber was tingling with tension and would snap at the least provocation. I wasn't sleeping and many days I forgot to eat until dinnertime. We arranged to meet on January 7th at 10:00am.

I decided to make the most of the day. I knew the meeting at the State's Attorney's Office wouldn't take all day, but it could last until mid afternoon. Since I was going to be around for happy hour, I figured a fun night of laughter and music would do my spirit good. I got in touch with my Annapolis friends and a few of them said they would be able to join me downtown.

49

Pre-Trial Meeting

I left home the morning of January 7th at 8:30am figuring this would give me plenty of time to get to Annapolis by 10:00am. I was wrong. At 9:30 I had only gone eight miles of an almost forty mile trip. At a red light, I called Cindy and left her a message. "There is no way I am going to get to your office by 10:00. I'll do the best I can to be there by 10:30."

The traffic jam broke up just after I left the message. I flew down the road and was in the State's Attorney's Office by 10:15.

Cindy greeted me with a copy of my journal.

"Kathleen and I have both read this," she said, "It's great; reads like a novel. Instead of the usual way of preparing for trial where Kathleen asks you questions and you wrack your brain trying to remember, we want you to sit and read this first."

Really? I thought. *Now it's okay? Now it's a great idea that I read my journal?* A few months ago, when it was my idea, reading it was vetoed. I kept my mouth shut and followed Cindy into an office, sat down, and began to read. After I finished reading, I joined Cindy and Kathleen in Kathleen's office.

"Well, he didn't take the offer." Kathleen said. "We kept it on the table until last week when we had a hearing with the judge and his lawyer. We were able to enter statements from witnesses as stipulations so there was no problem with the DNA witness like we had before."

Apparently working with the new lawyer was a lot better because he had more experience with this kind of case. He knew who was important to have on the stand and who could submit their testimony and not have to be in the courtroom. This meant there would be fewer witnesses to call and the whole proceeding should not take as long.

"But, our fingerprint expert will not be able to testify until after the holiday, on Tuesday. He is on a cruise and will not be back until Sunday. But he will be our only witness on Tuesday. After that, we will do our closing arguments, and it should be in the hands of the jury by lunchtime," Kathleen said.

"I didn't think he would take the offer," I said. "I guess he figures he'll take his chances in court. But isn't he likely to get from the judge what we offered him as a minimum, anyway?" I didn't get it. If he was going to be in jail for the rest of his life, why go through all of this? I figured he just wanted to see me squirm.

"If we get the conviction, and I'm sure we will..." Kathleen knocked on her wooden desk to ward off any bad karma. "It's hard to say what Judge Hackner will give him. But we like this judge for this kind of case. He's handed out two life sentences on the last two cases we tried with him. We are recommending a life sentence. He will weigh all of Trice's criminal history in making his decision. And that's why sentencing will be about eight weeks from the conviction."

Again she knocked on her desk, not willing to risk upsetting any bad-luck gremlins that might be lurking near. "The judge will announce the date of the sentencing after the verdict is read."

"This is a "Made for TV" case. And with a "Made for TV" case, we will probably get the "Made for TV" ending of a life sentence," added Cindy.

Seriously? Now you are calling it a "Made for TV" case? I couldn't remember how many times Kathleen mentioned how, *"This isn't going to be like you see on TV with the benches full of spectators and everyone carrying on."* How many times had she said the courtroom was usually empty except for the "key" players? I remembered her saying words to this effect at least a half-dozen times. And now they were referring to my "Made for TV" case. How ironic. I just smiled and laughed, shaking my head a bit.

"I'm going to start out with the easy questions, and then I want you to tell the story about what happened on August 21, 1988."

I wasn't at all sure I would be able to get through the telling of the events without Kathleen asking me questions along the way.

"I get horrible stage fright and I'm going to be nervous," I said. "It could get so bad that I can't speak at all and I might hyperventilate."

"You're going to do great."

I didn't believe I was going to be good at all. I stutter and lose my way so easily when I am talking. I get sidetracked and lose my train of thought.

Kathleen started asking me a few simple questions to get me started:

"Where were you born?"

"Annapolis"

"How many brothers and sisters do you have?"

"Four. Two brothers and two sisters; all older except for one brother."

"How old were you in August, 1988?"

"Twenty-nine."

"Where did you work in 1988?"

"The Chart House"

"How old are you now?"

"Fifty-one."

"Was there anything special about the week proceeding August 21, 1988?"

"Yes, it had been really rainy and unseasonably cold..."

I proceeded to tell her about how I acquired the candle.

I told her how one of the managers had reluctantly given me permission to take one of the extra candles home.

"I stole it."

"Hmm, since the manager said it was okay, you didn't really steal the candle right?

"That's true. But he didn't really want me to take one."

"That might be true, but he did say it was okay."

"Right."

"When you talk about how you got the candle, remember to talk about the conversation with with the manager."

"Okay."

I went on to tell her the events of that night. I was getting confused, and I felt myself having trouble breathing. I didn't want that to happen while I was in the courtroom. It was one thing to be upset and cry. It was something altogether different to be unable to speak because I was completely overwhelmed with stage fright. Or worse, my fear of the creep. I had no idea if I could control this, or how.

"Just focus on me. You will feel nervous at first, but if you look at me and tell your story, you will be fine. You're going to be great!"

Damn, I wished she would stop saying that. Even in this trial run, I kept forgetting things Trice said and got the order of things he did mixed up.

"It's not so important to get the order of when things happened right as long as you tell us everything he did," Kathleen said.

I got through the story, then said, "I don't think I made it very clear that at no time during this whole thing did I feel like my life was *not* in danger. I was in fear for my life the whole time. It wasn't until I let the police in the house and I was sure he was gone that I knew I was safe. This is the most important part of the whole night and I didn't even mention how terrified I was."

"It is very important for you to relate this information. But don't worry. If you forget to say something, I will have questions ready to ask," Kathleen assured me. "I'll make sure I have answers to all my questions before I let you go. That's my job."

While I was telling the story, either Kathleen or Cindy would interject a comment or question. But for the most part, I did all the talking.

"When you went with Detective Leo to the police station, did you make a statement?"

"Yeah, a tape-recorded statement."

Apparently there was no statement. It was lost. It was impossible to know when the tape disappeared. It could have been days, weeks, months, or years afterward. Whatever had happened, it didn't exist anymore.

"Detective Leo has no recollection of this case," Kathleen said, "None. He doesn't remember you, the T-shirt, none of it. There will be a few problems with him in court. But you don't have to worry about this. It's my problem. No matter how sloppy he was regarding this case, it doesn't affect the evidence."

"Yeah, he didn't collect the evidence," I said. "Unbelievable that he lost the statement. I knew he was worthless. I guess I can be glad my instincts about him were spot-on or else I might not have had Dave take over the case." *No way would Detective Leo have seen this through to this end,* I thought.

"Is it possible that two different things were used on you? One was wrapped around your neck and something else stuffed into your mouth?" Cindy asked.

At first, I said I thought it was possible since I had not seen what had been used, but later, I realized this was not true. "No, I'm sure it was the T-shirt. The texture is right and it got tighter around my neck as he stuffed it into my mouth. I know it was the shirt because Detective Leo told me on the phone it was torn. Tearing it would definitely have made it long enough."

"The T-shirt is missing from evidence," Cindy said.

"Yeah, and I know why. Well, not why, but I can tell you the last time I saw it."

I told them that after I moved out of Mom's house in November and the weather got really cold, I called Detective Leo to ask him if I could get one of my blankets back that had been taken as evidence.

I had made it in college. I didn't have any other blankets and couldn't afford to buy another.

"Now that I think about it, he should have said, 'No. We may need it as evidence once we catch the guy.' But I suppose he already believed there was no chance of that ever happening. He told me I could have it back."

"I went to the police station evidence room to get the blanket and there was a young kid working there. He didn't really seem like he was a policeman. Who knows? Maybe he was a janitor or something. Anyway I told him I was there to pick up one of my blankets from the evidence room. He left and returned waving the T-shirt around in the air, and asked me 'Do you want this back, too?' I told him, 'No, that's what the guy tried to strangle me with.' He sort of danced off and that was the last time I saw the shirt."

Both Cindy and Kathleen were stunned.

"What did the nightgown you were wearing that night look like?" Cindy asked me.

"It was red with yellow and blue piping around the cuffs and button inset on the front."

"Is it possible it was not collected as evidence? Maybe it was still there when you got home? Do you have any memory of sewing up a tear in a nightgown after all of this?" Cindy asked.

"I didn't see anyone bag it up and take it as evidence. When Detective Leo brought me back home before taking my statement, all the stuff the detectives were taking was already in bags. But I never saw the nightgown again. It wasn't on my bed when I got home from the police department." I explained that pretty much everything that had been on my bed, including sheets and blankets, was gone when I got home. All the clothes I was wearing that day were gone.

"They took my socks, underwear, and the blue and green checked flannel shirt I had worn that day. It was the first time I had ever worn it."

"That we have, but, we can't find the nightgown," Kathleen said.

After going over my testimony with them, I told Kathleen and Cindy I had made the decision that I didn't want any men in the courtroom with me when I testified. That meant Marcus, Art, and Scott could sit in on the opening statements, but then would leave while I was called to the stand. They could listen to any or all of the other witnesses they wanted to after I was finished.

"I'll be fine with my sisters there and all my girlfriends, but I don't think I'll be able to get through telling the story if the guys are there. It's one thing for them to know what happened; it's something else altogether different to hear me tell the story."

After I finished going over the details of that night and Kathleen was satisfied she had all the questions and answers she needed, I asked if I could see the courtroom. Except for TV shows, I had never seen the inside of a courtroom and I was feeling really nervous about it.

I am so glad I asked. The layout of the room was similar to those you see on TV with one huge exception. The witness chair faced the jury booth and was directly in front of the defendant and his counsel. They would be only about six feet away to my left. Talk about being thrown to the lions! I couldn't believe that not only would I be seeing him for the first time, I would also be sitting just a few feet away. I wondered who had thought this design was a good one. All of my supporters would be way in the back of the room in the four benches on the right. They might as well be in another county.

There was an officer in the courtroom when we walked in to look around. He said to me, "Don't worry; there will be at least one and probably two officers standing directly behind him the whole time. He isn't going to be able to hurt you."

"Okay, that's good," I said, still not feeling at all better. Why couldn't I sit up by the judge like the people on TV do? That seemed so much better to me than this crap. I asked Kathleen where she would be standing.

"Right here at the corner of my table." Kathleen walked over to where she would be standing during her questioning of me so I could get a better idea. "Everyone who comes with you will sit behind me, and the defendant's family and friends, as well as court reporters, will be sitting in the benches behind the defendant's table," she said.

Her table stood diagonal to the witness stand about fifteen feet away. I stood in front of the witness stand and looked over to where Kathleen stood.

"Like the bride and groom seating at a wedding," Cindy said. "Don't be surprised to see lots of people sitting behind the defendant taking notes. In addition to the reporters that Kathleen mentioned, other attorneys often sit in during trials to watch Kathleen at work. She's one of the best at presenting sexual assault trials, and often other lawyers come to observe and learn."

"I see," I said, not liking the situation at all. Even though I was looking directly at her, I could clearly see the officer standing where the defendant was going to be sitting. My peripheral vision is excellent. Wonderful. The whole time I would be testifying, I would be able to see the creep, too. This was horrible.

"Don't worry; you're going to do great."

There it was again. Crap. How was I going to talk about what this guy did to me when I could see his face the whole time? I was feeling less confident than when I'd started — if that were possible.

I stopped in Dave Cordle's office before I left the courthouse.

"I wish I felt as confident as Kathleen and Cindy are about all of this," I said to him.

"Do you want me to tell you how I think you are going to do?" he asked.

I nodded, "Sure."

"You're ready. You may not believe it yet, but you're ready to have this done. You'll be great," Dave said.

Oh no, not you, too, I thought. He did get part of it right, though. I was ready to have this over with. It had been an endless year; fifteen months, really.

I asked him if he had any idea what kind of a defense his lawyer was going to launch.

Dave told me that at the motions hearing the defense attorney tried to claim the evidence — the cigarette butt — collected by the New York Police was obtained illegally and should not be admissible. The judge threw the motion out. Dave assumed the defense attorney would probably try to attack the DNA evidence by claiming sloppy police work on Detective Leo's part.

"I knew he was no good; worthless. But, I guess that's turned out to be a good thing," I said, smiling. "Otherwise you would never have taken over my case."

"He's not allowed to attack you, the defense attorney. He doesn't have anything to work with. The DNA and fingerprint, along with your testimony, makes it a solid case," Dave said.

I handed Dave a small package wrapped in Christmas paper and said, "This isn't really a Christmas present; it's the only paper I had. It's a thank- you gift."

"I'll open this if we get...*after* we get a guilty verdict. If we don't get a guilty verdict, I'll give it back," Dave said.

What was the appropriate gift for someone who has played such a role in my life? Dave had now been involved with this case for almost twenty-two years, practically the whole time he has been with the State's Attorney's Office. I had selected one of my miniature watercolor paintings of the Annapolis State House. It was my way of giving Dave Cordle the "Key to the City" for all he had done. He had devoted countless hours to solving cold cases and putting bad guys behind bars. My gift seemed woefully inadequate for all of his years of hard work and determination.

50

Twelve Strong Women

$\mathcal{F}$or the most part, the days just before the trial started were long. I wasn't able to keep my mind off what was coming up. My nerves were raw, my stomach upset. Restless, sleepless nights of tossing and turning were keeping me awake. I was wide awake long before the sun rose. I felt like a zombie all day. I couldn't wait until all of this was behind me.

My friend Andrea sent me an e-mail chain letter on January 9th. I don't usually pay any attention to the e-mails that tell you to pass this on to 'X' number of people and then wait to see what happens. But I read it and the words struck me as very appropriate to my situation.

I don't believe in coincidence. I think things happen when they happen for a reason. I might be the first to say "this is crap" when I find myself right in the thick of something inexplicable. But, once I get the chance to step back and put some distance between me and "it," the "why" is usually pretty clear. I believe this e-mail made its way to me because I needed to really know the message it spoke. This message was sent by a friend I had recently reconnected with after a twenty year absence — and that was no coincidence either:

I am supposed to pick twelve women who have touched my life and whom I think might participate.

I think that if this group of women were ever to be in a room together, there is nothing that would be impossible. I hope I chose the right twelve. May my hugs, love, gestures, and communications remind you how special you are.

Just send this to twelve women and let me know what happens on the
fourth day.

Quotation: "May today there be peace within. May you trust that you
are exactly where you are meant to be. May you not forget the infinite
possibilities that are born of faith in yourself and others. May you use
the gifts that you have received, and pass on the love that has been given
to you. May you be content with yourself just the way you are. Let this
knowledge settle into your bones, and allow your soul the freedom to
sing, dance, praise and love. It is there for each and every one of us.

This e-mail arrived in my "in" box on the 9th and I was scheduled
to testify after lunch on the 13th — four days later. I didn't think I even
knew twelve women, but I gave it my best. I sent it to as many women as
I could; being sure I included all those who planned to be sitting in the
courtroom with me when I testified. One of my friends, Sherry, realized
the e-mail's importance right away and she passed it on to all the women
she knew. But Sherry also went a step further.

51

You're Never Alone

*D*ear friends,
I was sent this e-mail by a friend of mine. This week she faces in court the man who raped her more than twenty years ago.

Whether or not you pass this e-mail on, please be thinking of her and send her strength as she goes through this difficult time.

You are all very special people to me, just as this friend is. I want to believe we are creating a network of power that will cradle her and protect her as she is called on to recall this very difficult past.

I love you all. You are the wonderful, caring, special women I have known. I think, as the following message says: that if this group of women were ever to be in a room together, there is nothing that would be impossible.

Thank you in advance for your prayers, for your thoughts, and for anything else you do to send that strength and sense of right out into the universe. Lots of love,
Sherry

Sherry then sent me an e-mail letting me know she had forwarded the message with an additional message:

Dear Jennifer,
I have sent this message on to many, many of my women friends.

Strength and joy are coming your way.
Lots of love,
Sherry

At first I thought okay, probably won't hurt, but I doubted a chain e-mail was going to do much good.

I was wrong.

An incredible display of love and warmth was elicited from this simple gesture. I was overwhelmed by the responses. Sherry let me know she was receiving many notes from her friends and then she started to forward the responses to me. The effect of this networking of collective prayer and strength was nothing short of a miracle. Even after just a few of the women's thoughts and prayers were passed on to me, I began to feel the tension and stress start to leave me. The tight ball behind my sternum was loosening. The fear and anxiety that had been building for months was beginning to slip away. I was starting to relax!

I was stunned by the effect this response had on me. I believe the power of positive thoughts and energy from these women helped me to realize I could do this thing. I could face the monster of my nightmares and come away a much stronger person because I was not alone in this undertaking.

Hi Jennifer,
I have forwarded some responses I've gotten back from my friends for you.

I just want to let you know that I told them what was going on, but did not include your name. I wasn't sure who or how many people you wanted to know that it was you specifically who is going through this ordeal.

I love you so much and it hurts my heart to know you are going through this. I hope this week goes exactly as it is supposed to. I'll see you on Wednesday. Hugs and hugs to you!
~ Sherry

I hope all goes well, my friend. Justice is not abstract. It has a face.
~ Olga

Dear Sherry,
Thanks for including me in this list. I am so sorry for your friend and will definitely uphold her in my prayers this week.

How difficult a trial she is facing, but I hope it will result in her healing.
~ Loris

I'll be sending positive thoughts and prayers for your friend, Sherry. What an ordeal!

I wish her the best and lots of inner strength.
:) Joya

Hi Sherry,
I will hold your friend in the light.

Thank you for sending this. I don't usually read through a chain letter email, but this is not simply a chain email.

You have an actual need for a friend.

Wishing you well, happy, healthy always,
~ Mary

Wow. Thanks for sending this my way. I will hold her in prayer. I wish I knew what day.
~ Marian

I will most definitely keep her in my thoughts and prayers Sherry — I wish for her strength in adversity, peace, and a sense of justice.
~ Kay

52

Calm

*T*his unexpected outpouring from women I did not know was indescribable. Call it the strength of prayer or the power of positive thinking. Call it a "bond," "karma," "God," or "justice." Call the effect these words had on me whatever you feel most comfortable with. I'm not sure what to call it. But I will say the power and strength wrapped up in these sentiments was like being clad in an enlightened, calming light. Not only did I begin to feel the knot of tension I had been carrying around in my chest begin to break down, I was also able to sleep. Sleep was something I had not had much of for months; maybe years, really. The healing power of sleep itself fortified me. With my body rested, my mind and spirit were able to fall right into step. I knew that seeing my assailant for the first time was going to be hard. It, however, was not going to be paralyzing. I sent Sherry a couple of notes to pass along to her friends for me:

Thanks, Sherry,
I did get the messages & thank you so much. I think they may be working already because I feel surprisingly calm today.

That might have something to do with finally getting some much needed sleep, but not entirely.

Although I have used my artwork as a kind of therapy for years, Wednesday is the therapy I have needed all along.

I can't tell you how much it means to me to have you (and yours!) there

with me on Wednesday. You're a true friend and I love you a lot.
Bring Kleenex!
~ Jen

As the messages worked their magic on me, I also sent Sherry a note to pass on to all the women she had sent the e-mail message to:

I'm overwhelmed. This is amazing. Wednesday afternoon will be made easier for me because of the love from family and friends and in the strength to be harvested from the bonds that bring us and keep us together. I believe I will finally return the demon that has been locked inside me all of these years and who knows, maybe I'll join in the Karaoke fun! Thank you all!

53

Purpose

*I*f the trial had proceeded in either August or October as it had been previously scheduled, I would not have been ready. Although I would have testified and gotten through the ordeal, I believe I would not have been able to comprehend how important my part in this was. I may not have been able to really purge myself of the darkness that had been left behind that night so many years ago. Also, I would not have understood that there are many women who need to believe that good does eventually triumph over evil. One in four women is a victim of this crime. Not all of these women have had the opportunity to see justice done. Not all of them are able to stand in front of the accused and say, "What you did to me was *not okay*."

How a rape victim has been treated in the court room has changed since the mid-'70s. Unfortunately, the legal reform rape shield statutes which limit the admissibility of a rape victim's prior sexual history in court has been slow to be put into practice. In her book, *Rape On Trial*, Asst. Prof. Lisa Cuklanz notes that until the 1970s, rape victims had to prove their virtue before their allegations would be believed. In the early '70s, however, advocates of rape victims worked to enact laws that would protect the victim and place the focus of rape trials on the accused. Sexual assault crimes were redefined on a graduated scale to increase the possibility of gaining a conviction, and defense attorneys could no longer use a victim's sexual history to impeach the victim's testimony.*

---

*Cuklanz, Lisa, Rape On Trial, *University of Pennsylvania Press, Philadelphia, 1996.*

Even though most states have rape shield laws which prohibit any non-relevant evidence of the victim's past sexual history from being used by the defense at trial, the crime is reported, on average, only 31% of the time. This means an alarming percentage of attacks go unreported. Each of us has experienced, to one degree or another, shame, embarrassment, or self-blame, and the fear of further injury or retaliation. But if only 31% of us reports the offense, this all but gives the sexual predator permission to strike again. If a rapist knows he stands a good chance of getting away with his crimes, he will continue to terrorize. While reading about this subject, I came across horrifying statistics published in an article on the *National Center for Victims of Crime* website that reported that *126* rapists had perpetrated *907* rapes against *882* separate individuals. The study referenced did not include the incidences of sexual preditory behavior, that include molestation, incest, and child sexual assault, that often result in repeated offenses and claim a huge number of victims.*

It is generally believed that women do not report the crime because they do not want to be put on trial by the defense attorney. I wasn't really afraid of the questions the defense attorney might ask me because I knew I didn't have anything to hide. What took place that night was a crime. Over the years, I have come to own my past and I was not ashamed about anything I had done. Good or bad, I can't undo history. It's all part of who I am now. No matter what might be brought up about me — my drinking or occasional cocaine use — none of this would make what that guy did okay. There wasn't anything for him to drag up to make me look bad or to undermine my confidence on the witness stand. Not reporting the crime does nothing to protect the victim or subsequent victims. Only getting the rapist behind bars can do that.

It never occurred to me *not* to report this crime. I believed that night, and I still believe, that my attacker needed to be stopped. I suspected he

http://www.ncvc.org/ncvc/main.aspx?dbName=DocumentViewer&Document ID=32369 had raped before, and I believed he *was* going to strike again. How I was going to be viewed by police or anyone in the justice system never entered my mind. I wanted the assailant who had tried to suffocate me and who had raped me taken off the streets. It was the only way to guarantee he would not victimize anyone else.

Women who have become victims of the crime of rape are immediately shrouded in a cloak of isolation once they report the assault. Although originally the practice of withholding a victim's name was established as a means of protection, the result is a misdirected veil of shame. The trauma from the crime, the shame inadvertently produced in the name of protection, and the fear of being made to look, in or out of the courtroom, like their behavior was the cause of the attack, keeps many women from reporting the crime. The thought of having to defend their honor in the courts makes many of those who do report the crime reluctant witnesses. The victim's protection laws are designed to prevent the practice of scrutinizing the victim while she is testifying against her attacker, but these laws are impossible to completely enforce. In order to cast doubt in the eyes of the jury, it becomes the role of the defense attorney to attack the victim's reputation.

No one likes to talk about rape. No one is comfortable talking to the victims about the crime. Even saying the word is taboo. It is time for victims of this despicable crime to be heard. I was empowered by the outpouring of support from the strangers who had written to me. I began to understand I was not alone in this endeavor. I knew I could walk into that courtroom without falling apart. I realized the picture was much bigger than I could have imagined.

During the endless months leading up to the trial, I was thinking it was about me facing my demon. In as much as the trial would be this, it was also much more. I had been too close to understand that there are women all over the world who needed to know they have a voice.

I would never have believed I would be the voice for countless women who would not or could not speak for themselves against this man and men like him.

And something else occurred to me. My attacker had only seen my face for a few minutes almost twenty-one years ago. I doubt he had been paying much attention to my features. He had been spying on me through the curtains of my back door, watching me count my tips and then change into my pajamas. And during the entire assault, he was either behind me or in front of me, pushing my head and face toward the floor. This creep had no idea what I looked like. He didn't know me at all. To him, I was a cowering, scared girl.

That's not who I am.

From the time I learned I would have to testify in court, I was afraid to be in the same room with my attacker. Although the prospect of relaying the events of the assault with him in the courtroom was unnerving, I realized I was not afraid of *him*. I was afraid of the memories I had of him. This realization was a huge breakthrough and was really enlightening.

Everyone kept saying, *"He can't hurt you; he'll be surrounded by guards; He'll be on his best behavior trying to impress the judge and jury;"* and *"You'll be great."* Up till now I would hear the words, but they didn't mean anything to me. What did they know? He'd hurt me once; he'd threatened my life. He was scary. So, therefore, I was scared of him.

The words, *"He can't hurt you,"* did not really sink in until after the calming power of the e-mails started to take effect. My fear of seeing this man again and being in the same room with him stemmed from whatever residual internalized fears of the assault I still had. My apprehension was coming from my feelings of powerlessness because of the control I had allowed him to have over me for so many years.

I was sure the creep expected me to be afraid of him. *He* knew what he had done to me that night. *He* knew how terrified I had been of him then, and I am sure he believed I would continue to be gripped by this fear. Creating fear in women made him feel powerful.

I could redirect the flow of energy simply by walking into the courtroom with an air of confidence and refusing to fall apart. Dave Cordle's words, *"You're ready. You may not believe it yet, but you're ready to have this done. You'll be great,"* echoed in my head. Dave was right. I was ready because I had finally begun to understand what was meant by, *"He can't hurt you."* By finally understanding this, I set in motion the very act of taking back what the rapist had stolen from me that night. *I* was in charge of my fate, and this time *he* would be powerless.

Check and checkmate.

I was ready to do what had to be done to expose this man and his crimes to the world, and in doing so empower all of the women he had terrorized. I was ready to speak out on behalf of all victims of rape who are unwilling or unable to take the stand themselves. I was ready to see, face-to-face, what my boogeyman looked like and to banish him from my nightmares.

54

Counsel From a Faraway Friend

I received an e-mail from my friend Susan on January 5, 2010. Although I was sad she was not going to be with me in the courtroom, I was so grateful to her for offering me her ear. At the time of my assault, Susan had been a lawyer. She'd left her practice of law to become a spiritual leader. The "Trials and Tribulations" e-mails we sent back and forth during the week of the trial were extremely helpful to me. I was able to take a few minutes every night and go over the events, thoughts, and feelings of the day. Susan was my confidant during this time. Because I was a sequestered witness, I could not share details of the trial with her, or anyone else, for the duration. However, I was able to relay many of my impressions and feelings to her, knowing they would be graciously received.

January 5 at 8:18am
Hey Kiddo — I can't believe that the trial is here already and actually going to happen...as it has now happened, I'm out of the country until Jan 25!!!! I am so sorry I won't be able to be there with you. I'd love to hear about this from your point of view, though...You've been so open about the whole process, will you be writing about it, do you think? And if not generally, perhaps you would enjoy writing about it to me — if only as a way to help process what you're going through, and to make a bit of a record of it? And perhaps my legal training will come in handy to help make sense of what's going on.

Anyway — I'm still a phone call away — but we're in Puerto Rico for the month.

I'll hope to hear from you when you can, and I'm praying that this time will be one of healing and forgiveness and new wisdom and insight for you. All the best!
Love,
Susan

January 5 at 1:30pm
Thanks so much Susan. I wish I were in Puerto Rico for the month! Ha! Ha!

Seriously though...I appreciate your ear and I think I'll take advantage of your offer right now!

I'm not as nervous this time as I was in October. But, that might change later this week after I meet with my lawyer and go over my testimony. I'm not really afraid to testify — except for stage fright, that is.

Although telling the story will be somewhat upsetting, the hardest part for me is seeing this guy for the first time. I've never seen his face (except for a TV news story photo), so for all these years there has been a black emptiness. Although I believe "knowing" will be empowering for me, acquiring the knowledge makes everything real. The fear and disbelief of being strangled and raped years ago has turned to a sort of surreal event that happened to a person who doesn't exist anymore, yet is one of the things that has largely influenced who I am today.

I think my court statement sums up a lot of my thoughts about the incident. I have always been fascinated with detective work and crime solving.

Once I separate myself from all of this, I find a story that is not too unlike many other victims' tales except for the strange string of occurrences that had to happen just as they did, when they did, to lead to this end.

That is what would make an interesting story. If it is a story that should be written, then I believe my guides will help me get the words out.

I will keep you posted on the developments. I may not have Internet access in Annapolis, but I have your # programmed into my phone.

Thanks again Susan!
Enjoy Puerto Rico,
Jen

January 12 at 9:10am
Thinking about you, Jen. And I hope that all is well and that you're holding up. Drop a note when you can. I've continued to think through all that you said. It's funny, because yesterday I was doing my usual walk to the point at sunset, and as I came back, there were several local men on the beach, just hanging around. I figured they were getting ready to do the evening fishing, but I also became so highly aware of how much we are dependent upon the good will of others for our safety. Women have little chance against even a small man...Especially if she is not expecting attack...

I hope that this process will be a positive one for you, and not a reliving or renewal of the fear and hatred... Much is said in the Christian writings about forgiveness — and its freeing power. I wish for you that seeing him will enable you to see how pitiable he is... And to see that he no longer has any sway in or over your life.

You've heard the story of Joseph and the multicolored coat? Where his brothers sell him into slavery because he's their father's favorite? He has a great line when he turns out to be the King of Egypt's 2nd hand man, and his brothers appear before him, trying to get food for their starving family:

"What you meant for evil, God meant for good."

I think God meant you to be an artist. Artists wrestle with monsters. You have wrestled well.

Much love and every blessing,
Susan (my thoughts are with you).

P.S. and I hope that the monster might also turn out to be redeemable back into a human...

January 12 at 12:44pm
Hi Susan,
For the past couple of days I have felt a sort of calm come over me. I am sure that some of this is from the amount of sleep I have been getting this week. (Making up the sleep deficit!), but even more so from the spiritual energy being sent from so many friends and family. There is a lot of strength to be gathered from this out-pouring!

Although I have been able to work through many of my fears through my artwork over the years, it is facing this demon that I have really needed. I believe that seeing him and telling this story will purge whatever hold he has left on me. Just making the decision to use this opportunity to release his grip on me has made me stronger. My lawyer and advocate have referred to this whole thing as a "Made for TV" case. From a legal standpoint, I guess it isn't very often lawyers meet up with someone who (at the advice of the police officer during evidence collection) has written a journal detailing everything that happened that night; everything that was said and done. There were many times over the course of 21 years when moving or cleaning I picked it up & tossed it into the trash. But, the voice in my head said, "No....keep it. You'll need it one day." I guess my eye for detail has provided them with even more than they could have hoped for.

I have learned to listen to the spirits who guide me. They are always right. For years, I cursed God and asked him to go pick on someone else. After Stephen died about a year after I was raped, I had had enough. Now it's a toss-up as to whether Stephen or my Grandmother can talk the loudest in my head; giving advice and reassurance! I said to my sister Debbie the other day, "It wasn't until recently that I realized that everything had to come to this end." This includes the creep choosing me as his victim. I was meant to stop him.

I have said before that he had done this before & would do it again. I can't help but wonder how many women and children he has abused through the years — doubtless many. With all the puzzle pieces now falling into place, I can understand why I was among his victims. I am the one who will speak for all of those who will not be in the courtroom with me tomorrow. That, in and of itself, is very empowering for me.

I am sure tomorrow will be full of tears and hugs and all of this will be very cleansing. Several new friends and a few old friends will be there in the courtroom with me. I will be OK. I've made my peace with God & hope that somewhere along the way this will bring hope to someone else who feels like [she has] been given more than [she] can handle.

The plan is to have the group stop in to Stan & Joe's on West Street and sing Karaoke tomorrow night. Some old Chart House friends and family & new friends will be there. (I saw Kevin & P.M. last Thursday when I was in town for pre-trial prep! How much fun was that?)

I have to hop in the shower & get ready to head to Annapolis. I'll call or e-mail later. Thanks for being such a good friend through this.

Lots of love to you,
Jen

THE TRIAL

Promise me you'll always remember:
you're braver than you believe, and stronger than you seem,
and smarter than you think.

~ Christopher Robin to Winnie the Pooh ~

~ Mollie to me ~

55

Tuesday, January 12, 2010

During the week before the trial began, I finalized arrangements to stay at a bed and breakfast in Annapolis. I wanted to be downtown and within walking distance of the courthouse. No way was I going to risk trying to drive into town to get to the courthouse before 9:00am and risk getting caught in traffic. I didn't need the added stress.

The Flag House Inn is at 26 Randall Street just down from the main gate of the Naval Academy. The owners became acquaintances of mine when I had been doing framing at a downtown gallery years ago. Although I had not seen Bill and Charlotte since I'd had my own gallery and frame shop on Main Street in 2003, I knew their bed and breakfast was where I wanted to stay. I was of the mind to surround myself with caring, nurturing friends and family, and couldn't think of a more welcoming place.

Marcus and I drove to Annapolis and checked into the Flag House Inn on Tuesday night. After we were settled into our room, we walked the couple of blocks to the city dock and had dinner at McGarvey's. I was struck by how odd it was to walk into the restaurant where I had worked years ago and not know anyone. The place looked exactly the same, except now I was the stranger in my own hometown. When we returned to our room, I laid the clothes out that I planned to wear the next day. I figured getting everything ready the night before would help to reduce the stress I was sure to face in the morning.

I had given quite a bit of thought to the layout of the courtroom and about how the defendant was going to be in my peripheral vision the entire time I was testifying. I really didn't want him to be staring at my face while I was on the stand, and I didn't want to see him out of the corner of my eye the whole time either. I decided to wear my hair all the way down instead of in a ponytail as I had originally planned. With it down and brushed to the left, it would shield my face. My hair is really curly, long, and *big*. When I have it down, it's really more "out" than "down" and it gets bigger as the day gets longer. He wouldn't be able to see much of my face and I wouldn't see him until I wanted to look at him. I knew I was going to have to put a lot of product on my hair to keep it under control. But this was the simplest way to solve my problem. I was ready.

I checked my e-mails while Marcus was in the bathroom and found notes from my dad and my sister-in-law Nancy:

It's not a pleasant experience, but, just remember, they can't hurt you. The lawyer will try to make it hard for you and make you uncomfortable, but your lawyer should be able to counter anything he comes up with. Also, the judge is not an ogre. I've had to do it several times in building disputes. Just keep the facts straight, no matter what they may be and how difficult to explain, and you'll be OK. Remember, everyone there knows what the trial is all about; you won't be telling them anything they're not expecting to hear. Just stay as calm as you can and you'll get thru it.

Take care and know that we'll be thinking about you. Keep us posted.
Love you,
Dad

Jennifer,
Todd and I will be with you in spirit. I am thankful that this time has finally come for you as there is an end — a REAL end in sight! I hope you feel the love we are sending you!
~ Nancy

After reading the e-mails, I heard my phone beep. Apparently while at dinner I had missed a call and there was a text message for me:

Get Tough! I believe in you, and though I can't be physically with you in the courtroom, I hope you know I'll still be there...beat him.
~ *Dave Cordle*

56

Wednesday, January 13, 2010
Morning

I didn't have any problem sleeping. I was "out like a light" and slept soundly all night. There were two alarms set just to be sure we didn't sleep through the morning. Marcus set one and I set one. We had plenty of time to have coffee and something to eat before we left for the courthouse. Charlotte had breakfast ready for us when we got downstairs. Although I didn't have much of an appetite, she made sure I ate something before we left for the day. She wished me luck, gave me a hug, and saw us out the door.

Marcus and I walked hand-in-hand up the hill to the courthouse.

It was a really cold morning. The sun was bright, but it wasn't offering any warmth. Glaring reflections of gold sparkled off the store windows and car bumpers shone with silver light. There were frozen puddles in the brick street. "Ego Alley," Annapolis' harbor area, was covered in a film of ice. A flock of seagulls circled around the boats in the harbor looking for a spot to make a clear landing. There were a few young people in the cyber café staring at their laptop screens and drinking coffee. Most of the stores on Main Street were not open. The street was mostly deserted, except for the trash men who were picking up bags from in front of the shops and a few men working on some telephone wires. Chick and Ruth's Delly was busy with people having breakfast. A line was forming at the ATM machine.

It was just like every other winter morning in Annapolis.

It was like no other day in my life.

It was a day I had never imagined dawning.

It was the day I would be seeing, for the first time, the face of the man who had raped me.

We met Cindy as she was walking into the courthouse. It was 9:00am and jury selection was supposed to be getting underway. She appeared to be frazzled.

After I introduced Marcus to Cindy she asked, "Did you two get caught in that traffic jam? Kathleen just called me to tell me she is still stuck on Rowe Blvd."

"No, we walked up from the bottom of Main Street," I said.

"Oh, that's right; you are staying here in town. Of all mornings for there to be a backup!"

Cindy hurried in ahead of us, telling us to let her know when we got downstairs. She wanted to get us set up in a waiting room and be available in case she had any questions for me and vice versa. First, she was going to see if the jury pool had started to arrive and let the judge know Kathleen was delayed in the traffic jam.

The courthouse had a security check-in station just after the main door. There was a pretty long line, but it was moving quickly. I was carrying an open bottle of seltzer with me. The top was on, but it was loose. I was afraid if I had to put it through the scanner it might leak, so, I twisted the cap to tighten it. I don't know exactly how it happened, but when I twisted the top, it flew off with an audible *"POP!"* Seltzer water sprayed all over me and the floor. The pressure behind the gusher was so fierce I couldn't get the screw top to catch hold. Instead, my efforts to replace the cap just made everything worse. Now the jet-stream of water was even more powerful and much more far-reaching. I was embarrassed. The woman behind me was pretty indignant even after I explained to her it was just water.

Of course, the two police officers at the security check-in looked over at the sound of the explosion, not sure at all what had happened. I recognized one of the officers from my pre-trial visit to the courtroom. He was the one who had told me that armed guards would be positioned behind the prisoner at all times. I explained to him what had happened and asked him if he had a paper towel I could use to wipe up the floor before someone slipped. He was very kind, telling me not to worry; he would take care of everything. No doubt they would remember me.

What a way to start this day!

Marcus and I made our way down to the State's Attorney's Office and I told the woman at the desk that I was meeting Cindy Haworth. A few minutes after she was paged, Cindy showed us into a room where we could wait until jury selection was finished. There were going to be quite a few people meeting us at the courthouse who were not sure where to go, so I sent text messages from my phone letting them know where to look for me once they got into the building. It wasn't a big room and before long it was standing room only.

Cindy came to pull me out of the group so we could go over a couple of questions Kathleen was going to ask me on the stand. I think she was surprised to see how many family members and friends had gathered in the room. There were at least seven at that point with more expected to arrive.

As we walked to her office, she said, "What a day to have forgotten my pass. I changed coats this morning and left my key-pass in my other coat. Now I have to be buzzed into and out of my office every time."

She still seemed a bit frazzled because of the unexpected traffic problems that had held Kathleen up and delayed the start of jury selection, but she reassured me things were getting underway in the courtroom upstairs. "Kathleen's up there doing what she does best," she said.

We went over all the questions on the paper. They were the same ones Kathleen had asked me during my pre-trial meeting.

"Always tell the truth," Cindy instructed me. "That's important. But don't offer any information when the defense lawyer asks you questions. Just answer his questions honestly. Also, only talk about things that happened to you when you are telling your story. Just talk about what happened, not what you think might have happened."

She didn't want me to mention things I had figured out after the fact — like how the attacker had gotten into the house or how he had unscrewed the light bulbs. She didn't want me to talk about how I thought the guy was spying on me through my back door or how he had climbed up onto the balcony using my car as a step-up. Anything that didn't happen directly to me would give the defense an opportunity to object and would not be admissible.

"Just talk about what happened to you after you got home that night."

Additionally, Cindy didn't want me to offer anything that would give the defense an opportunity to discredit me or to ask me questions that would create doubt. I really couldn't imagine what the defense lawyer could possibly ask me. Between the evidence against the creep and my story, there didn't seem to be much the defense could question.

"And, don't mention the T-shirt. We don't have it as evidence. It's lost. It's unfortunate because it would be great if we could include it as evidence. If you tell the story about finding it on the bridge and then we can't produce it, you will come off looking like a crazy lady. So, just don't mention it at all."

"Okay," I said. That was a damn shame. I would have loved to hear how the defense would explain away how it was found in the middle of the bridge, and how it came to have my name on the label. And, maybe even more importantly, how it had been used to suffocate me and to wipe off fingerprints as he made his way through the house. Damn Detective Leo for being such a screw-up.

"That sucks." I said.

"What did the nightgown look like?" she asked me.

I remember telling her about the nightshirt at our pre-trial meeting.

"It's red with yellow and blue piping around the cuffs."

"We still can't find this in the evidence," she said. "I think this is all for now. Can you think of anything else?"

"Nope."

I left my coat in her office, and as Cindy went to check on the jury selection, I made my way back to the waiting room. A few more friends had shown up during my absence.

We were getting pretty loud, but there didn't appear to be anyone else around who would be disturbed by the noise. When I walked into the room, Marnie was there laughing about how the women at the desk were now referring to me as, *"The woman with all the hair."*

"I couldn't find you and I didn't know where to go so I just asked them if they knew where I could find 'Jen,'" Marnie said. "One of the ladies said, "Oh, the one with all the hair? I just saw a lot of hair walking down that way," and I knew it had to be you!"

Great, I thought, *Now I'm known as "The woman with all the hair who sprays seltzer all over the place!"*

Around 10:30, Cindy came by to say the terrible traffic jam that morning was the result of a serious accident. Not only had Kathleen been stuck in the mess, but so were quite a few of the potential jurors, so jury selection was behind schedule. Now that everything was underway, the process was moving right along, but because of the late start, the jury would not be seated before lunch break. She promised to drop by and give us an update around lunch time.

A few minutes later, Dave Cordle popped his head in to say hello and he did a double-take.

"Wow, you've got a full house," he said. "Well, this is it. Today's the day; it will all be over soon."

He shook his head as if he could hardly believe the words he had just said. It really was unbelievable that after all these years we were finally heading into a courtroom. I asked him if he was going to be around.

"Oh, yeah, you know it. Don't worry, I'll be here."

It occurred to me that although I had known Dave for twenty-two years, no one else in the room knew what role he had played in bringing Trice to trial, so I introduced him.

"This is Dave Cordle, the man of the hour. The investigator who cracked the case and arrested..." Before I could finish, everyone started clapping. It was great!

"...the creep." As I said, "creep," Dave chimed in with, "Scumbag."

"Anyway," Dave continued, "I just wanted to stop by and see how you're doing. I see you have lots of support, so I'll let you get back to your friends and family. I'll see you later."

Just before he walked away, he said, "And don't worry; you're going to do great."

This time when he said it, I believed him. Tears filled my eyes.

The whole time I sat waiting in the small room for the jury to be selected I felt odd. I was disconnected from what was going on around me. I was exhausted and full of nervous energy at the same time. One minute I was shivering, and the next I was flush. By 11:00am there were at least ten friends and family members in the room with Marcus and me. All of them were talking at the same time and laughing. It was surrealistic. If this had been any other time or place, it would have appeared we were having a party.

I was happy to see how everyone was so at ease with each other, and I was really happy they were all there with me, but I had a tough time following any of the conversations. At any given moment, there were two or three going on at the same time. Everyone was talking across the room to someone. Confusion.

When questions were asked of me, I just felt befuddled. I couldn't think straight. Forming words was nearly impossible because I couldn't get all the thoughts and voices in my head to quiet down long enough to sort out an answer. I was concerned I wouldn't be able to clear my head before I took the stand and my testimony would end up sounding as confused as I felt right then.

It seemed like I was moving at a slightly different speed than the rest of my group. Or, rather...I felt like I was watching a TV show where the voices were out of sync with the action. By the time I made sense of the words, I'd forgotten who'd asked the question in the first place. It was really unsettling. Eventually, I decided to let everyone else do the talking, and I just kept quiet and tried not to clock-watch.

Whenever I did find my voice, no matter what I said, someone would tear up. Just for a second, the animation would die down. Then, quietly, the moment would pass and the conversations would start to flow again. Apparently I wasn't the only one who felt raw and overloaded.

Just before lunchtime, Kathleen and Cindy entered the room. They told us they were at a good breaking point, so the judge had sent the jury out for a lunch break a little early. Kathleen explained what was left in the process that still had to be done before witnesses would be heard. I didn't understand. I gathered from what she was saying that things were going as expected. Someone asked what courtroom we would be in and Kathleen answered, "3-D."

"Oh, darn! I forgot to bring my special 3-D glasses!" Marcus said.

"And that would be my husband, Marcus," I said, chuckling. Kathleen asked me to join her for another short meeting in her office. She held a huge bundle of documents in her arms. She was very focused.

When we got back to her office, she told me again that jury selection was moving right along. Then she showed me some of the evidence she would be presenting in the courtroom. She handed me a couple of photos of me.

"Do you remember when these were taken?"

I looked at two pictures of myself. I had taken the photos just a few months before I was raped. "Just a couple of months before, the spring of 1988 is about right," I told her.

She handed me a black and white crime scene photo of my Datsun B-210 parked in the carport.

"Do you recognize the car? And where is this parked?"

At first I did not recognize the car in the picture, but I knew where the photograph had been taken. After looking at the photo more closely and seeing that the licence plate was fuzzed-out, I realized it was my old car.

"Wow," I said laughing " I haven't seen this in quite a while."

As I handed it back to Kathleen, I said, "That's a photo of my old car and it's parked in the back of the house in the carport."

"Take a look at this one and tell me what it's a picture of."

"This one is of the DMV driver's license renewal papers on the front seat of my car."

Then Kathleen handed me one last photograph. Looking at this one sent a chill through me.

"Can you tell me what this is a photograph of?" she asked.

"Wow. This is my bedroom. Was it taken that day?" I felt cold.

"Yes," Kathleen answered.

The photograph was taken from the doorway and I could see the side of my bed, and my nightstand with the phone and the candle sitting on top of it. On the floor was the duffel bag I carried back and forth to work. Inside were my flowered dress and work shoes. Next to the bag was the bowl I had eaten my dinner from that night, a plastic cup, and a small trashcan. The book I had been reading was still lying on the floor right next to the bed where I'd left it.

"Can you point out the candle in this picture?"

I pointed to the candle on the nightstand.

"Wow," I said again. "I didn't know there were any pictures taken that day."

I had a hard time shaking the creepy feelings I was having. I realized as I was looking at the photograph in my hand, the guy who'd grabbed me — the one I could not see in the photograph, but who had been just out of frame to the right — was, today, upstairs in this building.

Of course, I knew he had been upstairs in the courtroom all morning while the jury was being selected, but when I looked at the photo, it was as if he had been upstairs lurking in the shadows waiting to strike, just like he had done in 1988. Seeing this photograph made me aware of how close he was. I couldn't see him, but I could sense he was near.

And now it seemed as if I was holding that night right there in my hand. The photo had been shot from the exact vantage point of the lasting image etched in my mind for all these years. This was the same scene I saw that night twenty-two years ago, just before I stepped into my room. I felt as if I had actually been transported back across time to that night. For a split second I thought, *Don't take the step, don't go in. If you don't walk into the room, all of this goes away.* By not going into the room, I could change my future. I could change "now."

But it was too late. I could sense my attacker was close. He was moving in toward me from the right and in a moment he would grab me...

A shiver ran through my body as I handed Kathleen the picture.

She had some other things she wanted me to look at, but she needed Dave to help her with showing me the items. Since he was the lead detective, she had to be sure the chain of command in handling the evidence was not broken.

Dave entered the room with a big box overflowing with sealed envelopes and bags of stuff — my stuff! — that I had not seen for twenty-two years. It was strange. He produced a dull razor blade and proceeded to saw open a manila envelope whose edge was covered in layers of red tape. He was having trouble getting through the thick layers of tape.

"Gonna have to get a new blade one of these days," he muttered.

"When you were in the hospital and gave them the tampon, did you see the bag you put it into? Can you describe it?" Kathleen asked me.

"Yeah, it was a clear bag, like a baggy."

"Do you remember if your name was on it?

"I don't remember seeing my name on it anywhere."

By this time, Dave had gnawed through the tape and produced a clear plastic bag. He handed it to Kathleen.

"Do you remember if this bag had this label on it when you were in the hospital?" Kathleen asked.

She showed me the bag indicating the label with my name typed on it. Inside the bag was a very old tampon. I started to laugh.

"Aw yuck, who would have known a tampon would still be around after all these years? No, I don't remember seeing the label, but the bag could have been facing the other direction when I dropped it in."

"Good answer," Dave said.

He took the bag from Kathleen and then resealed it with yet another strip of red tape, then picked up another, bigger manila envelope. This one was marked "Red Shirt."

"You said that your nightgown tore when you were trying to take it off," Kathleen said.

"Yeah, I heard it tear. I thought it had torn in the front where the buttons are. But, I couldn't see where it had torn because it was dark."

Dave handed me the nightgown and Kathleen said, "It's not torn."

I looked it over and I couldn't see any seams ripped or any tear in the button area. I was puzzled.

"I know it tore. I heard it. And, after it tore, I was able to get it off my shoulder."

I looked closer. Finally I noticed the loop that held the middle button was torn. Somehow the loop had ripped and the button was still attached. I showed this to Kathleen.

"This must be what ripped. This loop is torn."

I hadn't had the top button fastened that night. When the loop ripped on the second button, the nightgown loosened enough for me to slide it off over my shoulder.

"It sure sounded like the fabric had ripped. That's really odd," I said. We discussed the possibility that some of the threads of the fabric may have stretched and made a tearing noise, even though no seams were ripped open.

Kathleen mentioned again that the T-shirt was missing from evidence. She asked me to tell Dave about the last time I saw it. I relayed the story about going into the evidence room and how the young guy came out with the shirt, waving it around in the air and asking me if I wanted it back. "That was the last time I saw it."

Dave looked at me, shaking his head, and said, "You never told me this before."

I thought I had told him this story. I couldn't imagine how I would have forgotten. For years I had been mixed up in thinking it was Dave, not Detective Leo, who had told me it was okay to go get my blanket. That's why I must have thought Dave already knew. But, I should have realized my mistake a long time ago, as there was no way Dave would have ever agreed to retuning any evidence.

Next, Kathleen handed me another clear envelope with a DMV license renewal form in it.

"Really? This was taken as evidence?" I asked. "I could have sworn I had this with me when I went to the DMV that day. Wow." The yellowed paper had my name, address, and date of birth typed in the appropriate spaces — all the information the rapist had needed that night. I noticed the paper had a concave curl to it. He must have had this in his back pocket, I thought. It was indented like it had been pressed against his butt cheek. This was the last piece of evidence Kathleen and Dave needed to show me. I was free to go back to my group and decide what we wanted to do for lunch.

57

Trials and Tribulations
Afternoon

January 13 at 12:26pm

It's just after noon — (an hour later, here) — so perhaps you're on lunch break.

I'll be interested to hear how they treat you, as well as how you perceive their treatment of you. I send you every good wish and my prayer that you will walk in peace today, with clear thoughts, an open heart, and full of wisdom and understanding. Say hi to the gang at Stan & Joe's when you get there this evening, and sing 'Angel from Montgomery'...
love,
Susan

*I*t seemed to take forever to decide what to do for lunch. The state senate was in session and downtown would be mobbed. We would spend way too long waiting in line anywhere we went, so we opted to go to the cafeteria in the lower level of the courthouse. I have a feeling this was a typical day for the cafeteria and that is really too bad. There was a long line that wasn't moving at all. I overheard the gentleman in front of me tell one of my sisters he was in the jury pool. *Great*, I thought. *Would he have to dismiss himself if he got picked to be on the jury for my case because we stood in line together?* The cafeteria smelled like peas, overcooked peas. Mush-peas. The line had moved forward about two body lengths.

I had to text Jackie, Shirli, and Andrea to let them know the jury would be seated just after lunch and that they should come around one o'clock to be in the courtroom in time for the opening arguments. I couldn't get a signal while standing in line, so, I walked to the ladies' room, used the facilities, and sent my message from there.

When I got back to the snaking line behind Mollie, the air smelled like canned corn, overcooked canned corn that had gone from a pretty pale yellow to a glossy neon from being heated too long. The smell of overheated corn was quickly overpowered by the pungent odor of burnt toast. The line crept along. I wasn't hungry, but I was very thirsty. No one ahead of us could make a decision. I couldn't blame them really; the food looked awful. Did they want the mush-peas or the waxy overcooked canned corn? Just make a decision, I thought, or don't, but move so we can get past.

I bought a bag of almonds and some juice. We all sat at one of the tables talking about how bad the food looked and smelled. Even Marcus couldn't finish his chicken and he'll eat anything. I couldn't stop looking at my watch. Time was passing really quickly now. I was antsy and I was worried that we were going to be gone too long. I was afraid Kathleen would be ready to start and we would wander into the courtroom late, smelling like four-day-old Thanksgiving leftovers.

I managed to eat four or five almonds and I drank all of my juice. As soon as I finished it, I wondered if that had been the smartest thing to do. I was already nervous and the last thing I needed was a full bladder when I was on the stand. On the way back to our waiting room, I used the facilities again.

As soon as the group of us got back to the waiting room, Jackie, Shirli, and Andrea showed up. I had seen Shirli and Andrea during the Christmas holidays. We'd all gone caroling together. And I saw them again when I was in town for my pre-trial meeting. But this was the first time I had seen Jackie in twenty-two years. I instantly got teary. My mind flashed back to the days after I was raped when she, Jen, and Karen came to visit. It was so right for her to be here with me now. It was right to have all of my friends and my sisters with me. How incredible life can be!

I no sooner said hello to them when Cindy came to get me again. She wanted to talk to me one more time in her office and then we would head upstairs. The jury was almost ready and opening statements were going to start in a few minutes.

When we reached her office, Cindy reminded me again not to offer any information while I was on the stand and not to mention the T-shirt. While she looked back over the list of questions and made a couple of notes, I thought about how careful Trice had been to not leave fingerprints all over the house. And how the only real slip that I knew he'd made was when he picked up the candle. No way was I his first victim. No way could someone do all he had done that night for the first time and only have a couple of screwups.

With this in mind, I said, "I told Detective Leo he had done this before and he would do it again if he wasn't stopped."

Cindy paled. "Oh, no," she said. "You can absolutely not say that! If you even mention anything about any other victims or prior arrests, the judge will immediately throw out the case; right then and there it will be over. He will dismiss the case and we all go home. You cannot say this in the courtroom."

I reassured her I would not mention it, but I wasn't real sure she was convinced.

"Not a word about the other victim; nothing."

"Okay, I promise. Really, I won't say anything. Seriously, relax, I won't," I assured her.

Now Cindy was really concerned that I was going to talk too much or get off track. I usually do when I'm talking. But I was pretty sure I could answer the defense attorney's questions honestly and simply. I didn't think I was going to have a problem keeping my answers concise. And now that Cindy had pounded home that "mum's-the-word" about the creep's criminal history, I was sure I would stick to the story. I was more concerned about forgetting to mention important details than embellishing my testimony along the way. I left my purse in her office and followed her upstairs.

Our whole group was waiting to go into the courtroom when we got back upstairs, and Cindy took the opportunity to inform everyone of courtroom etiquette and especially about turning off cell phones.

"All the way off," she said. "Power them down. This judge will not tolerate cell phones going off in his courtroom. No talking above a whisper and no food or drinks are allowed in the courtroom. If anyone needs to get up and leave to use the bathroom, that's okay. Just be quiet about it."

Everyone checked to be sure their cell phones were off, hugged me, told me, "You're going to do great," and walked into the courtroom. Linda grasped both of my hands and said a quiet prayer before she went in last with Sherry. Everyone was teary. I was crying and my nose was running. *Great, my Kleenex™ is in my purse in Cindy's office,* I thought.

"Do I have time to go to the bathroom?" I asked Cindy. I had to go again and I had to blow my nose.

"Yup, plenty of time; maybe even time to go more than once."

Off I went....again.

Cindy sat with me on the bench outside the courtroom while the lawyers were making their opening statements. Within just a few minutes, Shirli flew out of the courtroom in tears.

"I'm so mortified!" she said.

I couldn't imagine what was going on in there to cause her to come running out. Of all the people I thought might not be able to handle being in there, Shirli was not on the list. As it turned out, she had not turned her cell phone off and got a call just as Kathleen got into her opening statement. The judge told her, "Get out of my courtroom!" She was a wreck.

"I thought it was off," she said. "I don't even know if I know how to turn it off. Oh, I'm so embarrassed!"

I took her phone from her and turned it off. Then I showed her how I'd powered it down. "Okay, no harm done."

Cindy said, "Just wait a few minutes and then go back in quietly."

The three of us sat on the bench together until Shirli calmed down enough to go back inside the courtroom. Cindy did her best to keep my mind off what was happening behind the closed doors by distracting me with small talk. She talked to me about traveling and asked me where my favorite place was.

"Italy," I said without hesitation. "Any day I get to spend in Italy is a great day." We talked about where we had been in Italy. I had been fortunate to have been there on three occasions and loved the country. I told her how Marcus and I would be going on a cruise in October and it would leave from Venice. I couldn't wait to go back. We chatted, sharing our Italian stories. The whole time we talked I was very aware that just beyond those heavy wooden doors sat the man who had raped me twenty-two years ago. I was getting nervous despite Cindy's best efforts.

58

The Trial

I was not allowed to be in the courtroom during the opening statements nor when the other witnesses took the stand. Several months after the trial was over, I discovered there were audio CDs available for each day of the proceedings. I was curious to hear what was asked of each witness and what their answers were. Listening to the direct testimony of the additional witnesses gave me a more accurate picture of the court proceedings.

I knew my lawyer was prepared for her role in the courtroom and I was eager to hear how she had presented the case to the jury. I was also curious to learn what the defense attorney had presented as evidence, *if* he'd had any to introduce. The legal ballet of our justice system is truly like an opera performed in a foreign language. Although one may get the gist of the plot, how the details are presented is often lost in translation. Hearing the CD helped me to understand a little better what Kathleen and Cindy do every day.

I knew that some of what took place and what I deduced about the early morning of August 21, 1988 would not be discussed on the stand. It was interesting to hear, or rather, not hear, what the detectives could and could not mention in the courtroom. I heard the actual testimony for the first time a few weeks after the trial was over while I was transcribing the audio CD of the court proceeding to include in this book.

Hearing the audio transcripts gave me insight into what went on inside courtroom 3-D while I sat on the bench outside. It has given me, for the most part, the first glimpse as to the roles each witness played in solving my case. There were quite a few discussions between the lawyers and the judge that were masked by white noise and were difficult to hear. Also, there were a few discussions between the lawyers and Judge Hackner that got very technical; I have not included many of these private exchanges.

Much of the reluctance of victims to report rape is, in part, due to a fear of being grilled on the stand and made to defend their honor. I am convinced there were times during my time on the stand when the defense lawyer was trying to do just that. Following is my testimony, thoughts I had about the questions asked, and excerpts from the audio transcripts of the trial.

What follows are excerpts of what took place and what was said by some of the key witnesses during the trial. I typed the proceedings directly from the audio CD. If any motions or arguments struck me as important or interesting, I included at least a portion of them. In addition, I include some testimony from most of the witnesses, but I have not included everything that was said by everyone. Whenever something was mentioned that I felt deserved a comment, I added my thoughts and comments. At times, it may appear as if I must have missed words or forgotten to include whole sentences; rest assured I typed out the recorded transcripts with great accuracy.

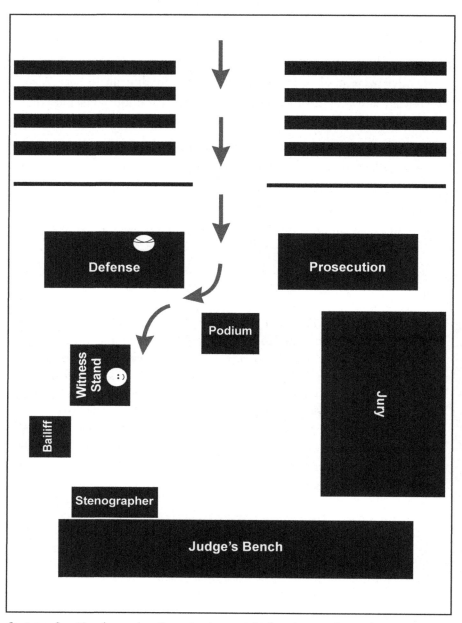

Courtroom floor plan. Arrows show the route witnesses take from the entry door to the witness stand, passing by the benches where spectators sit and the defense table.

59

Opening Statements

Bailiff:	*All rise.*
Judge Hackner:	Be seated, please. Ladies and gentlemen, would you please check and make sure your cell phones are off. And please don't talk in the audience. Not a peep. If you've got to talk, step outside, please. State of Maryland vs. William Joseph Trice K-08-00281. Counsel identify yourselves, please.
Ms Rogers:	*Kathleen Rogers on behalf of the State.*
Mr. Szekely:	*Andrew Szekely on behalf of Mr. Trice, who is present to my right.*
Ms Waters:	*And also Gwendolyn Waters on behalf of Mr. Trice.*

Opening Statement: Kathleen Rogers
2:26pm

Jennifer Wheatley has been looking over her shoulder for twenty-two long years. The crime that brings us here today to this courtroom took place on August 21, 1988. Most of us probably have no idea where we were or what we were doing on that particular day. But it is the one day in Jennifer Wheatley's life she would most like to forget, but never will.

Jennifer Wheatley was born in 1958. She grew up right here in Annapolis. In 1988, when this crime occurred, she was twenty-nine years old. She was living with her mom in the Eastport section of Annapolis. She was working as a waitress at the Chart House; a local restaurant in Annapolis. The home that she and her mom shared was in a community called Chesapeake Landing. It was a little gated community. They had a condominium that they shared. It was three floors. Jennifer's bedroom was on the bottom floor in a basement-type area. The middle floor had a kitchen, and she and her mom shared that area. Then her mom's bedroom was on the top floor of the condominium. Jennifer had her own entrance on the bottom level of the condominium. She would get home, she was a waitress, she would get home at late hours. And she would enter through that door.

On August 20th of 1988, Jennifer's day began like any other day in Jennifer's life. She was scheduled to work at the Chart House late that afternoon, early evening. She went to work. Absolutely nothing was different; nothing unusual about that day. She got off work at the usual time. She may have stayed and had a beer with her friends or coworkers before heading home. She got home at about 2:30 in the morning. She parked her car in front of their garage, walked around into her entrance and entered her home. She didn't see her mom. She assumed she was asleep upstairs as she always was when Jennifer got home at that hour. It was a cool night. It was August, but the windows were open in the condominium, she noticed when she got there. She said it was a very cool night for August.

She went into her bedroom. She changed out of her work clothes, got into her nightgown. She decided to go into the kitchen upstairs to make herself something to eat. She noticed when she went upstairs that a sliding glass door on the middle level was cracked open and a kitchen window was open. So she assumed the air conditioning was not on at that time. She made herself something to eat and went back to her bedroom downstairs. She lit a candle and began reading a book. She thinks it was a Stephen King book. She was eating her food, reading her book, lying in bed when at about 3:00am her phone rings. She picked up the phone and the caller said, "Jennifer you have a beautiful body." She didn't recognize the voice and hung the phone up. Picked her book back up and began reading again feeling a little bit apprehensive, but really not too worked up about it.

The phone rings again. The same male voice — the same voice she doesn't recognize — and this time the voice says, "You were born to live in 1958." She hung up immediately. At that point she's feeling a little spooked. This person with a voice she does not recognize knows her name and the year she was born. But in her head she's saying, "I'm in the house, I'm safe. Nothing can happen here." The phone rings again and she just doesn't answer. She takes it off the hook. The beeping is driving her crazy so she slips it under her pillow; she hangs it back up. She's feeling spooked, restless.

She gets out of her bed and walks around the corner — on the same level there is a bathroom. She goes into the bathroom and closes the door. When she comes back out of the bathroom and goes around the corner into her bedroom, she notices the overhead light is off. She is sure she left it on, pretty sure. She wouldn't turn it off. She gets closer to her bedroom and the candle that she lit is still lit. She can see a little bit of light coming from her bedroom. She steps into her bedroom and as soon as she does she is grabbed from behind in a choke-hold around her neck. Something is being wound around her neck. Her head is being yanked backwards; something is shoved into her mouth like a gag. She can't breathe. Her neck is being so extended that she is in a great deal of pain. And she is sure she is going to die.

He said, "If you scream, I'll kill you."

She still is trying to scream. She doesn't know what to do. She's struggling. She can barely breathe. She feels as if maybe she's slipping away because she can't get any breath through her throat. And her neck is so far back that she also can't breathe through her sinuses. Because he's yanked her head so far back, her jaw became dislocated as this was occurring. After what seemed like an eternity, he said something again about, "If you won't scream, I'll take the gag out." She's trying to nod to let him know because she thinks it's her only chance at living.

He says to her, "You are alone."

And the way that he said this to her, she thought he had probably already killed her mother. It didn't sound like a question to her — it sounded like a statement. And she thought, "It's too late for me to scream now, no one will hear me." Thankfully, her mother was fine. He ordered her, still behind her, holding her tightly around her neck, to remove her nightgown. She was struggling. She had one hand. She could barely get it down. She got it off. He then forced her over to the bed, sat her down, making sure she did not look at him.

And, again, the only light in the room is the candlelight. And he forced her to perform oral sex on him. He then made her lie down on her stomach on the bed and inserted his penis into her vagina and raped her vaginally as she was on her stomach. When he was done, he said, "Do you want to know how I know you?" She said, "Yes." And he said, "I'm your DMV man," and put something on her pillow. What he tossed on her pillow was her license renewal form that had been on the front seat of her unlocked car parked outside her condominium. They contained her name and her date of birth. He told her to lie on the bed and not to move and not to call the police. And then he left her home.

Jennifer could not believe what had just occurred. She was in her own home. It couldn't have possibly have happened. He jumped out in her bedroom, he grabbed her, he raped her. He was a complete stranger in her home. He knew her name. He must have been watching her. This was like something out of the movies. But it was real. It was as real as the semen and the fingerprint that the defendant left behind. He had ejaculated into her vagina when he raped her. That was his first mistake. His second mistake was that at some point he asked her if she had any drugs or money, and he picked up the candle on her nightstand. The two mistakes that Jennifer

Wheatley's attacker made left his identification for the police to find in two different ways. A latent print was lifted from that candle that he had picked up off her nightstand. It was stored for many years as part of this case. It was lifted when the crime scene was processed in 1988.

Jennifer Wheatley called 911, the police arrived and she was taken to the hospital. At the hospital, a rape kit was done and vaginal swabs were taken and sperm was found. The DNA technology that we have available to us as we sit here today in 2010 is not the technology that existed back in 1988. But the vaginal swabs were stored as a part of this case. The defendant had left his identification in two very different places and in two very conclusive ways. It was only a matter of time when his name would be found and matched to the fingerprints and the DNA. He made two mistakes that would ultimately lead to his apprehension.

This case sat dormant for many years. But science was not dormant. Science marched forward and DNA became the most powerful tool in the police officer and prosecution's arsenal. Reviews of old cases began to occur. And in the State's Attorney's Office in Anne Arundel County, all the old cases were being reviewed. It was determined, when this case was looked at, that there was evidence that was suitable for DNA testing. The vaginal swabs were sent out to be tested, the process began. But remember, there is still no suspect at this point. The vaginal swabs are processed and a DNA profile is obtained of Jennifer Wheatley's attacker. So we know...

(Shirli's phone rings.)

Judge Hackner: **You, get out with the phone right now.**

(Ms Rogers continues:)

....So we know the attacker's exact profile, but we still don't have his name. The only thing left to be done is to find a name to match that profile. Whose DNA is it? Who was Jennifer Wheatley's attacker?

A complete review of the entire case was done in 2008, and the police realized there was a latent print that had been lifted from the candle and it was in that file. That print was eventually compared to a known latent print of William Joseph Trice and it was found to be a match. So known DNA of William Joseph Trice was then obtained and then compared with the DNA of 1988 that had the profile of Jennifer Wheatley's attacker. Again, a match to William Joseph Trice. Whose fingerprint? The defendant's. Whose DNA? The defendant's. Two mistakes and two identifications.

Jennifer Wheatley will be walking into this courtroom in just a few minutes and she will not be looking over her shoulder any longer for an unknown attacker. She will be facing forward and she will be looking at William Joseph Trice, the person who broke into her home and brutally attacked and raped her in 1988. Thank you.

Judge Hackner: **Thank you, Counsel. Mr. Szekely would you like to make a statement?**

Mr. Szekely: *I would. Thank you, your honor; if I may approach the jury.*

Opening Statement: Andrew Szekely
2:38pm
Good afternoon. My name is Andrew Szekely and I, along with Gwen Waters, represent William Trice in this matter here today. What you just heard from the State's Attorney is not the evidence in this case. As you heard earlier from the court, the only evidence you are going to hear in this case is going to be the testimony from the witness stand, any photographs, documents, or any other evidence submitted to you for your review. What the state gave you is an outline or a summary of the evidence the State expects to present in this case. It is not, however, the evidence in this case.

In sitting here as jurors, it is going to be your job to diligently listen to the evidence and think about the evidence. And I'm going to walk you through some of that evidence now. The State's theory in this case is there was a burglary in this case. That the — Mr. Trice entered the room through a sliding glass door on a balcony. However, you're going to hear from a witness named Mary Pat Whiteley. Ms Whiteley is going to come in and she's going to testify that she's a crime scene investigator, a crime scene technician. And when she comes in, it's her job to look around the crime scene for evidence. And she was able to locate a fingerprint on a candle.

You'll also hear from Ms Whiteley that she checked the sliding glass door from the balcony, the gate, or the control panel that controlled access into the gated community, for fingerprints. She checked banisters, she checked railings, and she checked the other door in the apartment. And there were no fingerprints found there that matches with Mr. Trice. You're also going to hear that they did, in fact, check — this will be from Ms Whiteley as well as from Mr. Lowman, who you are going to hear testify early next week — you're going to hear that the piece of paper that was on Ms Wheatley's bed was checked for fingerprints and there was not Trice's fingerprints. There was some unidentified person's fingerprints on there.

You're also going to hear that Ms Wheatley was taken to the hospital after she reported the crime. Now, it's important to note that there was over an hour from the time that Ms Wheatley said that her attacker left and the time she called the police. And she was then taken to the hospital and she was examined and you're going to hear testimony from a nurse who was there and most likely medical records. And what those medical records and the nurse's testimony will show is there was no sign of trauma on Ms Wheatley's neck. Nothing to suggest that her neck was pulled back or that she was choked in the manner she described. You're also going to hear that there wasn't the sort of trauma around her genital region that would likely be associated with this sort of attack.

In this case, the police did an investigation that began in 1988, and then the case sat idle for a long time. Now the investigation the police did, did not, was not as thorough as we would like it to be. And, there's going to be some holes in this case; some gaps in the evidence. And it's going to be your job as jurors to sit here and critically think and review the evidence that is presented to you.

You heard earlier when Judge Hackner, during the jury selection process, [said] that there is a rule of all presumption to innocence; that as we sit here right now Mr. Trice is presumed to be completely innocent of these charges. But as you sit here over the next several days and you hear the evidence in this case and you do what I believe you will do in good faith, listen to the evidence, think about the evidence, and when you deliberate, you're going to see that Mr. Trice is not only presumed to be legally innocent in this case, you will see that he is, in fact, factually innocent of these charges. And in the end of this trial, I'm going to stand here before you and I'm going to ask you to return a verdict of "Not Guilty."

Judge Hackner: **Okay, thank you Mr. Szekely. Ms Rogers, would you like to call your first witness?**

Ms Rogers: *I would, your honor. The state would call Jennifer Wheatley.*

60

Taking the Stand

*D*o I have time to pee again?" I asked Cindy.

"Yeah, but don't be long. Come right back. Kathleen will be ready for you in just a few minutes." So, I went...again.

2:44 pm

Ms Rogers: *She's in the bathroom, your honor. I sent someone to get her.*

Judge Hackner: **Okay, that's fine.**

When I came out of the bathroom this time, Kathleen was indeed waiting for me.

I looked to my right and saw Marcus, Scott, and Art walking quickly down the hall away from me. They didn't even look back.

"Are you ready?" Kathleen didn't wait for an answer. I didn't have one.

"Go in ahead of me and walk to the court stenographer to be sworn in."

She opened the heavy wooden door and I stepped into the room.

I could have heard a pin drop when I walked through the door. I was alarmed at how much bigger the room appeared to be now that it was full of people. *It didn't seem this large the other day,* I thought. How could that happen? Shouldn't it feel smaller? Closer?

In fact, the room had taken on the feel of a fun house. Judge Hackner sat at his bench straight ahead, but he looked to me to be out on the fifty yard line of a football field and sitting way up high on a mountaintop. I was feeling small. I felt I would be engulfed by the space.

I quickly glanced at the benches where the jury sat. They had all turned their heads to look at me as I entered the room. I looked away and my gaze passed over the benches where my friends and family members sat, behind the State's table where Kathleen was headed. I didn't want to look at anyone here too closely because I thought I would get too emotional. I didn't want to fall apart. My eyes darted to the opposite side of the room and I couldn't help but notice there were very few people sitting on the benches behind the defendant.

The balance of the room felt all wrong. Physically there were many more people sitting on the left side than the right and yet the floor seemed to be listing toward the right; tipped as if being weighed down by an invisible force toward the defendant's table. The area around the defense table looked dark and uninviting, but I felt myself leaning into the tilt of the floor as if being sucked toward the shadow that hung there. I tried to straighten myself.

As I passed the seats where all my supporters sat, I was aware of a charged energy that was light, warm, and safe. I walked into this light and wanted to stay there. I couldn't. I was being instructed by someone to approach the bench where the court stenographer sat. I didn't want to walk toward her because I would have to pass through a section of the room that was dark and oppressive.

I felt dwarfed by the judge sitting way up high. I was being swallowed by the room with its heavy mahogany wood and thick carpet. I felt overwhelmed by what was expected of me. I took a breath and walked forward, being careful not to stumble.

Whatever you do, don't trip. Try to stand up straight, I thought.

All eyes were on me. I could feel them. It was so quiet. I heard only a sniffle or two.

There was nothing inviting about this. The whole room seemed to be pitched in the direction of the defense table. The air felt heavy and thick.

I saw his face in profile. He was staring straight ahead with his hands in his lap. His features were sharp; a thin face with protruding cheekbones, a goatee, a widow's peak, and a receding hairline. His complexion was pale. Way too pale to support hair and a beard that looked to be poorly dyed with inky-black shoe polish, and slicked back with Vaseline. Unnatural. Instantly I understood completely why he'd dyed his hair. I was sure it would soon be very clear to the jury.

As I walked by the corner of the defense table, I was careful not to brush the edge. Darkness hung heavily in the air around the three people sitting there. I did not want to pass through it.

The stenographer stood and started to speak. Even this was odd. Instead of looking into my eyes when she spoke, she seemed to be looking at something just above my head behind me. I resisted the temptation to twist around to look up and see what her eyes were fixed on. *Is she blind?* I wondered.

"Ma'am, would you come up here and stand next to this gentleman, please?" the judge asked. "Face the clerk up here, please, and raise your right hand."

"Do you solemnly declare and affirm under the punishment of perjury that the testimony given will be the truth, the whole truth, and nothing but the truth?

"I do."

"You may be seated."

"Pull up the chair and as you sit, sit in the chair about a foot away from the microphone, please. Thank you. Everything including your voice is being recorded. Okay."

"Can you hear me?" I asked.

"Madam clerk —"

"Please can you spell your name for the record?" Judge Hackner asked.

At least, I thought it was he who spoke and I thought that's what he said. Even now that I was in the center of the room, the judge didn't seem to have gotten any closer. His voice sounded muffled, miles away, and hard for me to understand. I spelled out my name, speaking slowly into the microphone.

"J-e-n-n-i-f-e-r W-h-e-a-t-l-e-y."

I sat down in the chair and realized right away the support once offered by the seat had disappeared about two hundred witnesses ago. To sit back in the chair was a risky commitment. There were no springs under what was left of the cushion. I could feel myself getting sucked into the depression and it seemed like I wouldn't stop falling until I hit the floor. I made the decision to perch on the edge of the chair since I wasn't sure I would be able to get out of it at all when I was finished testifying.

I was thirsty. I was beyond thirsty. My mouth was so dry I was afraid I was going to start to cough uncontrollably. I wanted something to drink; I wanted a mint in my mouth. Kathleen started asking me her questions:

Ms Rogers: *Jennifer, how old are you?*

Me: Forty-nine.

I did say forty-nine. I can only say I heard fifty-one in my head. I have no idea how or why forty-nine came out.

I thought how crazy it was to be here. Twenty-two years since the attack and here I was sitting in an uncomfortable chair in a courtroom getting ready to tell what happened that night. Fifty-one sounded really old to my ears; a lifetime ago.

Ms Rogers: *And are you working at this time?*

Me: Yes. I'm an artist.

Ms Rogers: *What sort of artist are you?*

Me: I work in fabric. I sort of do paintings in fabric.

Ms Rogers: *You also do photography?*

Me: Yes. I do photography.

Ms Rogers: *And are you married, Jennifer?*

Me: Yes, I am.

Ms Rogers: *How long have you been married?*

Me: I've been married for six years now.

Ms Rogers: *Jennifer, where did you grow up?*

Me: In Annapolis, Maryland.

Ms Rogers: *What part of Annapolis?*

Me: Eastport.

Ms Rogers: *And do you have any brothers or sisters?*

Me: Yes, I do.

Ms Rogers: *Tell us who they are...about them.*

Me: I have two sisters and two brothers. Two older sisters, one older brother, and a younger brother.

Ms Rogers: *Okay. And did they all grow up with you...?*

Me: Yes.

Mr. Szekely:	*Objection, your honor.*
Judge Hackner:	**Overruled.**
Ms Rogers:	*Your honor, may I approach the witness to pour some water?"*
Me:	Thank you.
Judge Hackner:	**While you're at it, can you move another six more inches or so?**
Me:	Closer?
	(I shift in the witness chair.)
Judge Hackner:	**Yeah, that's okay. Thank you.**
Ms Rogers:	*I'm going to show you two pictures. State's Exhibit #1 and #2, and could you tell me who they are pictures of?*
Me:	*(I giggle.)* Me.
Ms Rogers:	*And when, approximately when were those pictures taken?*
Me:	Um, when I was twenty-nine. 1988.
Ms Rogers:	*Okay.*

(Ms Rogers takes the photos over to the jury box for them to pass around.)

Ms Rogers:	*Jennifer, in 1988, were you still living in Annapolis?*
Me:	Yes.
Ms Rogers:	*And where were you living at that time?*

Me:	I was living with my mother in Chesapeake Landing.
Ms Rogers:	*And is that in Eastport?*
Me:	Yes. It's at Horn Point.
Ms Rogers:	*Horn Point. And how old were you then?*
Me:	Twenty-nine.
Ms Rogers:	*Twenty-nine, okay.*
	And were your sisters still living in the area at that time?
Me:	In the area, but not with my mother.
Ms Rogers:	*Okay. In Annapolis. And were you working, Jennifer?*
Me:	I was working at the Chart House. Yes.
Ms Rogers:	*And about how many days a week did you work, if you know?*
Me:	Five, usually.
Ms Rogers:	*Can you describe for us the home that you and your mom shared?*
Me:	It was a four-story condominium. Basement level was my bedroom, what I called the second floor was where the living room, dining room, and kitchen area was. My mother's bedroom was on the third floor, and the top floor was a studio for me.

Ms Rogers:	*Okay. And, um, what type of community was that or is that?*
Me:	It's a gated community.
Ms Rogers:	*Can you describe the entrance of the community for us?*
Me:	When you drove up to the gate, there were two metal gates with bars. There was a panel where you had to either type in a code or call into the house to get the gate to open, to let you in. There was also a pedestrian gate that had its own code."
Ms Rogers:	*Okay. And, I'm going to show you a picture and you tell me if you recognize it. State's Exhibit #6.*
	What is that?
Me:	This is the panel, the phone panel that you had to punch your number into to get the gate to open.
Ms Rogers:	*Okay. And Jennifer, it appears to be something to the sides of the panel. And what is that?*
Me:	What they would do is have a two-letter or two-number code and the person, resident's name next to that.
Ms Rogers:	*And would it have been a first name or last name? Or do you recall what name was on that?*
Me:	It was generally, it was in my mother's name. So it was "Wheatley" and her first initial. They never put the first name on there. But the last name was spelled out.

Ms Rogers:	*Okay. And that was right next to the phone?*
Me:	Right.
Ms Rogers:	*Enter State's Exhibit #6.*
Mr. Szekely:	*No objection, your honor.*
Judge Hackner:	**Six is admitted.**
Ms Rogers:	*Now, Jennifer, what were your normal work hours at the Chart House?*
Me:	Usually 4:00pm till closing. Closing was 2:00am. And then we had some bookkeeping-type stuff to do afterward. So generally 2:30 would be the time I'd get out of there.
Ms Rogers:	*And on August 20th of 1988, did you work that particular day or evening at the Chart House?*
Me:	I did.
Ms Rogers:	*And what time you started?*
Me:	I started at four o'clock.
Ms Rogers:	*And about what time you got off?*
Me:	What time did I get off? About two o'clock.
Ms Rogers:	*Okay. Do you recall if you hung around for a while or…*
Me:	I believe I hung around and had a couple of beers and finished my paperwork and drop tips, things like that. We had to report tips and then drop them in a safe for

the girls. We usually pooled our tips, so we'd do the paperwork together.

Ms Rogers: *Okay. And about how long would it take you to get home? Did you drive?*

Me: Yeah, I would drive. Five minutes would be a long haul. It was only a couple of blocks.

Ms Rogers: *So on the morning of August 21st of 1988, about what time did you get home?*

Me: About 2:30.

Ms Rogers: *And when you got to your house describe where you parked your car and what you did.*

Me: I came through the gate. I put the code in to open the gate. And then I had to drive sort of around a block of condominiums to get to our carport. And I pulled my car into our carport area.

Ms Rogers: *And after you pulled your car in, did you get out of your car?*

Me: *(I giggle.)* Yeah.

Ms Rogers: *Okay. And did you leave your car unlocked?*

Me: Yes.

Ms Rogers: *And was that normal for you?*

(I nod.)

Judge Hackner: **Say "yes" or "no" because...**

Me: I'm sorry. Yes. Um, yes, it was a gated community so I figured it was pretty safe being unlocked. And it was an old car so...

Ms Rogers: *Do you know — did you see your mom when you got home?*

Me: No. She was in bed.

Ms Rogers: *What was the weather like that evening into the early morning?*

Me: It was pretty cold.

Ms Rogers: *When you say cold, it was August...*

Me: It was August, but it was probably anywhere from 55-65 degrees. It was, it was unseasonably cold.

Ms Rogers: *Okay. And when you got home, what entrance did you go into?*

Me: What's considered the back of the house where the carport is. There was a door right there, and I would get out of the car and go right in that door.

Ms Rogers: *And when you enter that door, does it go to the level that your bedroom is on?*

Me: Yes.

Ms Rogers: *So you don't go up or down any stairs from there?*

Me: No.

Ms Rogers: *After you entered your home, did you — was the door locked when you got there?*

Me: Yes, that door was locked.

Ms Rogers: *And you unlocked it to enter?*

Me: Yes.

Ms Rogers: *And after you entered, did you lock that particular door?*

Me: Yes.

Ms Rogers: *You described the weather for us. What, if anything, after you got home did you observe regarding windows or doors in the home?*

Me: My mother had left the sliding glass door on the second floor open. Which is also on that same end of the house where I could come in. And also the kitchen window was open.

Ms Rogers: *Okay. And what did you do when you first entered the home? Where did you go? What did you do?*

Me: The first thing I did was I walked into my bedroom and put on my pajamas and counted out the tip money that I had made that day. And, took some out and put it in my purse — like twenty or thirty dollars. And took the rest of it and put it in a ceramic pot that's on a book shelf. And I'd hold that until I could get it to the bank.

Ms Rogers: *Okay. And after you counted, changed into your pajamas and counted out your tip money, what did you do?*

Me: I went upstairs, fixed myself something to eat, and got myself a beer.

Ms Rogers: *So you went to the main level?*

Me: Yes, to that, the second floor.

Ms Rogers: *Did you eat your food up there? Or what did you do?*

Me: No, I came back downstairs to my bedroom, sat on my bed. I believe I was reading Stephen King. I sat on my bed, started to read my book and eat my diner.

Ms Rogers: *Okay. What was the lighting in your room?*

Me: I had the overhead light on and a candle lit. I used to light candles all the time back then and I had a candle right on the nightstand next to me.

Ms Rogers: *Was the air conditioning on when you got home?*

Me: No. It was too cold for the air conditioning.

Ms Rogers: *As you sat on the bed eating and reading your book, what happened?*

Me: Um, the phone rang and I...

Ms Rogers: *About what time was that Jennifer?*

Me: I'm guessing, close to 3:00. Close to three o'clock in the morning the phone rang. I, I thought it was somebody from work. I grabbed it real fast and I heard someone say, "Jennifer you have a beautiful body." And I just hung up. I was...

Ms Rogers: *Did you recognize the voice?*

Me: No. I was just a little annoyed. You know? Three o'clock in the morning. I didn't know who it was, so I just hung up on him.

Ms Rogers: *And then what happened?*

Me: A few minutes later, the phone rang again. The same voice — I recognized it as the same voice — said, "You were born to live in 1958," and I hung up the phone again.

Ms Rogers: *And that was the year you were born, Jennifer?*

Me: Yes.

Ms Rogers: *Did you, at that point, recognize the voice?*

Me: [I] did not recognize the voice, but I was a little concerned wondering how he would know what year I was born. But I figured it was just annoying at that point. I just hung up again. Um, a few minutes later, the phone rang again. This time, I didn't listen to it. I just laid it face down on the bed next to me. Then eventually it started making, you know when you leave a phone off the hook? It made that noise? That beeping noise? It used to do? I don't know if they do that anymore. So I hung it up. And the fourth time it rang, I just slid it under my pillow and ignored it.

Ms Rogers:	*Could you hear anybody's voice or anything being said?*
Me:	[I] couldn't hear anything at that point. But again, it started making that beeping noise, but I just left it under the pillow at that time.
Ms Rogers:	*Were you still reading your book?*
Me:	Um...I was still reading my book, but shortly after that last phone call, I think it was like maybe five minutes, I heard the air conditioning come on. And, the air conditioning unit — the motor part — was right down in my bedroom so I could hear it coming on. And I thought that was really strange because when I had been up in the kitchen to get my food, I actually closed the kitchen window because the wind was blowing through the house. It was really cold. So I closed the window. I had considered at that point, when I heard the air conditioner coming on, I had considered going upstairs to turn it off. But I thought maybe Mom's hot and she got up and turned it on. I didn't know.
Ms Rogers:	*Did you hear her get up?*
Me:	I didn't hear her. But I figured she must have had a reason to turn it on, so there was no sense in me turning it off. So, I got up and went over to my dresser and got some socks and I put them on. And I had also turned my stereo on when I got home and I turned that off. Then I went into the bathroom.
Ms Rogers:	*Describe where you walked to get into the bathroom.*

Me: Um, you have to go out my door, take a right and take another right. It's just a couple of steps, but it's a very close, sort of U-turn, if you will.

Ms Rogers: *When you went into the bathroom did you leave the bathroom open or closed?*

Me: I believe the door was closed then.

Ms Rogers: *I mean the door to the bathroom.*

Me: The door to the bathroom? You know, I don't honestly remember.

Ms Rogers: *Okay.*

Me: I probably, maybe not completely latched shut, but I probably pushed it shut. You know.

Ms Rogers: *About how long were you in the bathroom?*

Me: Just a couple of minutes and then I came back out of the bathroom and sat back down on my bed for a few minutes and continued reading my story. I'd finished eating, but I hadn't taken my dishes upstairs. I probably should have, but...they were sitting on the floor at the bed, next to the bed at that time. And I heard a "crack" on the step going down to the landing in the front of the house.

Ms Rogers: *Was that something you'd ever heard before?*

Me: I'd heard it, but usually you only hear it when somebody actually stood on that step. You know?

It didn't just randomly happen. Somebody had to be walking on that step. And I thought for a second maybe it was my mother, so I didn't really react to it. But I was a little taken aback by hearing it. But then I also thought I was just making myself nervous because I was reading Stephen King. So, I made the decision that I'd had enough, I'm going to bed. So I got up, walked back into the bathroom, pushed the door maybe not all the way shut but probably ajar, but — a little bit — Sorry.

I went to the bathroom, brushed my teeth, and came back out of the bathroom, and when I walked toward my bedroom door...

I'd told the whole story up until now and I was surprised because my voice didn't fail me. I didn't feel afraid or nervous. I could feel Trice's eyes on me, but I didn't falter. Through all of this, I held myself together. This was the easy stuff. I had my cup of water, and when my mouth felt dry I would take a small sip and continue. I still had to tell the part of the story that was going to be hard. I didn't want to tell this part, so I stalled. All eyes were on me. Everyone was waiting for me to continue. I could feel him willing me to walk out of that bathroom and into the bedroom again. He was there waiting. I hated this. We all knew he did it; he knew he did it. Why couldn't we just skip over this part? I wanted to leave. I didn't want to turn that corner again. I especially didn't want to turn the corner with him sitting right there.

Maybe he would jump up and shout out, *"I'm guilty, I did it!"* and I wouldn't have to say the rest. I paused for a second, hoping.

He didn't.

I wasn't sure I could say what I had to say with him sitting less than six feet away from me. I knew this time what was going to happen when

I turned that corner and I wasn't entirely sure I could go through with it. I felt raw and shaky.

I began again.

Me: I noticed the light was off. The overhead light was off.

Ms Rogers: *Had you turned it off?*

Me: I didn't remember turning it off. I hesitated, just for a second and then...

I couldn't talk. There was a huge pressure in my chest. It was pushing against my breast bone trying to come out. I tried to talk, but there were no words. It was difficult to breathe in and out. I began to cry.

For the second time that day, I felt as if I was walking back into that room. Only this time it was as raw and as terrifying to me as it was on the night of the assault. I knew what was going to happen next. And the person responsible was sitting just a few feet away.

The courtroom was quiet except for a few sniffles from my group who had started to cry with me. Everyone in that room knew what was going to happen and none of them wanted me to have to go through that experience again. No one wanted me to walk into that room. No one wanted to hear the rest of this story.

No one, that is, except for one.

Over my left shoulder, I felt — sensed? heard?— a laugh. It was the sound of joy like the giggle of a child when he receives an unexpected gift. Sheer pleasure. I resisted the temptation to turn toward him. Did anyone else hear this? Was no one else appalled by this? I sat on the edge of the uncomfortable chair with the horrible tightness in my chest and his laughter in my head. It was too much. He was happy, no, delighted, to be in the room, watching me with anticipation. He couldn't wait for me to take that step. He couldn't wait to spring from the shadows once more. He was relishing this opportunity to experience, through my eyes, the terror he had inflicted. This was a first for him. He knew what was in store for me once I stepped forward.

And at that moment he was like a painter applying his signature to the canvas then standing back and observing his work. His pleasure was made all the greater because, this time, it wasn't just the two of us. Today, he got to shock an entire roomful of people. He was delighted there were so many here to witness the terror he was responsible for creating.

I had to get out of his head.

It was disturbing.

I had to continue talking.

I had to tell what happened next.

My voice would not come.

I closed my eyes for a moment and opened my mouth slightly.

Everyone was waiting.

I felt like it was taking me forever to find my voice.

I have used words to describe what happened from this point on in my testimony like "amazing," "spiritual," "empowering," and "strengthening." No matter how many times I say this, or what words I come up with to describe what was happening, the whole experience still sounds crazy. It was profound, unearthly. Time didn't even seem to be passing. Everything slowed down. A second felt like minutes and a minute felt endless. I have no idea how long I was on the stand. The collective energy I felt when I entered the courtroom, coming from the women there with me, grew stronger as I got further along in retelling the events of August 21, 1988. What I recognized as a comfortable and inviting light when I entered the courtroom became an energizing wave that continued to roll toward me — like an ocean — while I was on the stand. This wave calmed me and filled me. It was wild!

I believe there was no coincidence in receiving the *"Twelve Strong Women"* e-mail from Andrea when I did. The women who were in this courtroom with me were there because each of them had touched my life. Every one of them was dear to me. I believe it was the combination of their love and their wish to see me released from the grip this man still held on me that created the energy that filled the room. With them, nothing was impossible. Because of them, I could feel, see, and hear clearly.

I remembered the words from the e-mail:

May today there be peace within.

May you trust that you are exactly where you are meant to be.

May you not forget the infinite possibilities that are born of faith in yourself and others.

May you use the gifts that you have received, and pass on the love that has been given to you.

May you be content with yourself just the way you are. Let this knowledge settle into your bones, and allow your soul the freedom to sing, dance, praise, and love. It is there for each and every one of us.

I had made deliberate choices that day in the clothes and the jewelry I wore. I had on my favorite skirt with its handkerchief hemline and my lace-up "witch" shoes for comfort and artistic flair. I wore a deep plum sweater to go with the skirt. Shirli pointed out it was the color of power and strength. I selected pieces of jewelry that belonged to women whom I loved who could not be with me in the room. I believed wearing each piece would bring them near. I chose my grandmother's watch, a dogwood pin that my mother had given me, a ring from my aunt, and a favorite scarf that belonged to Marnie's mother. And, knowing Marcus was not going to be in the courtroom with me when I testified, I chose a small heart pendant he had given to me to wear around my neck. It's covered in tiny sapphires. Sapphire is the gem of fidelity, trust, honesty, purity, and loyalty. Its powers include spiritual enlightenment and inner peace. It is also considered an antidepressant and an aid to psychokinesis, telepathy, clairvoyance, and astral projection.

I clearly heard my grandmother's voice in my head telling me, *breathe in*, just as the wave of light and energy carrying Andrea's fortifying breath reached me from across the room. I could sense figures and voices of women I did not recognize in a circle that swirled above me and I felt comforting arms around me. Stephen, my guardian angel, was there. Although I had heard his voice along with my grandmother's during the many months of waiting for the DNA results, for the most part he had been quiet for twenty years. He was standing to my left between me and the defendant. Stephen had assumed the role of "The Protector." I could feel that he finally realized just how important it was for me to take back my spirit and purge the fear and shame I had felt for so many years.

I breathed in just as another fresh wave moved toward me, filling my lungs. As I exhaled, I felt some of the intense pressure leave me. I didn't swallow it, I let it go. Another deep breath in and I started to talk again.

Me: ....And then, when I took that first step into the room, I was grabbed from the right-hand side. And this person was saying to me, "Why did you hang up on me? I told you if you hang up on me I'm going to kill you?" I was confused, I was scared, I screamed, and I tried, I tried to pull away, but he already had a hold of me. I couldn't get away from him.

*(Judge Hackner hand the bailiff a box of tissues,
and he places them on the ledge in front of me.)*

Me: Thank you so much.

Ms Rogers: *Jennifer, how was he holding you?*

Me: He had one arm around here, and the other arm, I believe, came up and gripped his own arm. So he had me like in a bear hug. He was standing back several inches and pulled me towards him.

Ms Rogers: *Were you facing away from him?*

Me: I was facing — yeah, he was behind me at this point. He'd come up from the right-hand side and immediately got behind me. I screamed once and I realized at that point that something was being wrapped around my neck. And then I really tried to pull away and I couldn't get out of his grip. When I went to scream again, he had gone around twice with whatever he was wrapping around my neck and he jammed it into my mouth and down into my throat. He pulled me back pretty far. I, I can't pull my neck back as far as he had me pulled. And my jaw was off to the side so he had a hold of me with my jaw jammed wide open and down toward my chest and it was dislocated. I couldn't breathe. Because my head was back so far, when he jammed this gag in my mouth, it pushed against the back of my nasal passages and I couldn't get any air.

I kept telling him...telling him in gestures and noises I was making, that I couldn't get any air. I could get a tiny bit in the side of my mouth. I was trying to move my tongue to get this thing out of the way. But it wasn't working. He kept a hold of me. He was asking me, "Do you have any drugs? Do you have any money?" I just kept saying no. And then he said, "Are you here alone?" And I said, "No." And he said, "Oh, yes you are." And I got terrified because I knew my mother was upstairs and um, when she didn't come downstairs when she heard me scream, I thought he'd, I thought she was dead. So I really got scared and I was...I wasn't...I couldn't breathe and I tried to communicate with him that I need air. Basically, I need air, I can't breathe. And he pinched my nose shut and said, "This is what it feels like not to be able to breathe."

I think I was starting to get lightheaded and I stopped struggling. Because I knew if I continued to struggle he could easily break my jaw or my neck and I didn't, couldn't fight it. There was no way I could fight him, he had a hold of me. I'm not sure when, if I stopped fighting him and relaxed, something changed, and he said, "I'll take the gag out of your mouth if you promise not to scream again." This took a few minutes. Probably, maybe five minutes to get to this point. So, yeah, I want air, I want to get this gag out of my mouth. He took the gag out of my mouth and I couldn't shut my mouth. I had to take my hand and push my jaw into alignment.

Ms Rogers: *Did he let you do that? Or were your hands free to do that?*

Me: I just did it. I honestly don't remember how I had two free hands, but I did it. I pushed both of them. I must have pulled this one around and just pushed it up, because there was no way I could close my mouth, it was stuck open. And, I almost did scream because it hurt really bad.

I went on to tell the jury the entire story, in detail, of what the defendant did to me. Every time I came to a place in my testimony that was difficult to relate, I would pause and cry. And each time, I would wait until I felt the bright wave swirl toward me from across the room. Then I would breathe in deep and exhale. As I let each breath out, I felt the knot grow smaller and smaller. The sensation was not unlike the ebb and flow of the ocean. With each approaching wave came a strengthening breath. And with each ebbing, a bit of my repressed anger and fear was washed away. I was regaining control. Each time I re-entered my story after a clarifying exhale I felt stronger and bigger. The room didn't seem quite so large and overwhelming anymore. Or maybe I was growing to fill it.

There were several times during my testimony when I had the opportunity to look at the jury. I was shocked to see that nearly all of them were men. There was a wide range of ages and races. I was surprised and moved to see many of these men with tears in their eyes trying to gather up their emotions as I told of the events of that night. I felt I shouldn't look at them too much. But when I did meet the eyes of several of the jury members, I had no doubt they felt the pain I had experienced that night. I caught the eye of one of the women jurors openly weeping and having trouble collecting herself. I turned my head toward the defense table.

Trice never met my eyes. It was uncanny how, no matter when I looked at him, he was always focused on something else in the room. Maybe his lawyer told him not to look at me at all. Maybe he didn't want to look at me. I wondered as I looked at him, "Does the face you are born with determine your fate? Or, does the life you lead imprint itself onto you? Do lines etch and features reposition until you look the part of the role you have chosen for yourself? I'm not sure. But I was struck by how his face told the story of his life. If I knew nothing about this man, and had seen him walking toward me, I would cross the street. If our meeting were in a dark alley, I would run in fear.

Each invasion, every surprise attack, and every scream he elicited from a terrorized victim echoed from his eyes. His eyes were light in color and ice cold. What must have once been smile lines in childhood had become twisted and carved into a sneer. His jaw was set and closed tight, giving him an angry look. If he had been a Hollywood actor, he would have been type-cast to play every role of sexual predator that came along. His face was one that conjured nightmares. No matter who he was as a child, his choices in adulthood had made him the boogeyman. He was surrounded by dark and evil-looking shadows.

The longer I spoke the more I felt his happiness fade. What had been joyful for him at the start had become a disappointment. I have no doubt he sensed the strength I garnered from telling this story. He had to have been aware of the purifying energy that surrounded me, but never made its way to his table. I have no doubt he realized, by the time I reached the end of my testimony, that I was not the small and frightened girl he had left face down on the bed twenty-two years ago.

The longer I talked, the further along I got in my story, the darker the air around him became. In contrast, the rest of the room was alive in a bright light. This light swirled and danced around the room touching every other person. There were no windows. It wasn't coming from outside. The light was, I believe, the collective energy, love, and strength of the women in the room. The light was freeing, empowering, and uplifting.

And then I was finished.

Ms Rogers: *Jennifer do you know or have you ever known a man by the name of William Trice?*

Me:	No.
Ms Rogers:	*I have no other questions.*
Judge Hackner:	**Counsel, could you come up.**

The judge flipped the switch to turn on the white noise, and Kathleen and Mr. Szekely walked to the front of the room. As the three of them talked, the crackly noise filled the air.

Then the judge addressed the members of the jury. "Ladies and gentlemen, we're going to take a ten minute recess. Leave your notes, please, don't talk about the case, and step out into the jury room."

Looking at me, Judge Hackner said, "Okay, thank you, you can step down. Please don't discuss your testimony at this point until your testimony is over. Okay?"

"Okay," I said. "Thank you."

The bailiff called, "All rise."

I was unsure of what to do. I looked over at Kathleen who had made her way back to her table. She shook her head "No" as I started to get up. I perched on the edge of the worn out chair and I watched as the jury walked single file out of the room. Many of them looked over at me as they exited. A few were still trying to compose themselves. All of them looked shell-shocked.

Then it came time for me to exit. I met with Kathleen at the edge of her table and she whispered, "The judge thought you might like a few minutes to collect yourself."

I thought that was really nice of him, and I headed to the bathroom. I wanted to touch up my makeup, but settled on patting my eyes with a paper towel.

I think it was Hope, it might have been Marnie, who came into the bathroom while I was in there. She had red eyes from crying. I don't remember what we talked about. Maybe nothing.

61

Body Language

I don't remember when his posture changed...just that it was different from before and after. When you were on the stand, his legs were outstretched and crossed at the ankles. Occasionally, he would wiggle the top foot, or bounce it up and down. When you were not on the stand...before trial began, opening statements, other witnesses, he had his feet tucked under his chair and crossed at the ankles. His upper body didn't change...just the positioning of his legs. It was strange.
~Andrea

HOW THE LEGS REVEAL WHAT
THE MIND WANTS TO DO:

Over three decades of interviewing and selling to people, we have noted that when an interviewee locks his ankles, he is mentally 'biting his lip.' The gesture shows that he is holding back a negative emotion, uncertainty, or fear. The feet are usually withdrawn under the chair, showing that the person also has a withdrawn attitude. When people are involved in a conversation, they also put their feet into the conversation. Our work with lawyers showed that defendants who sat outside the courtroom just prior to a hearing were three times more likely than the plaintiffs to have their ankles tightly locked under their chairs as they tried to control their emotional state.

The person who sits with his legs crossed and kicks is usually bored. Look for the direction in which the feet are facing — toward you indicates interest. *

---

* *From 'http://westsidetoastmasters.com/resources/book_of_body_language/chap10.html' Chapter 10.*

62

Sidebar

4:00pm

Bailiff:	*All rise.*

Judge Hackner: **Please check your cell phones and make sure they're off. This is State vs. William Joseph Trice K082821.**

The jury isn't in the courtroom yet. Do you want to address the issue we talked about earlier?

Ms Rogers: *Your honor, we spoke with Investigator Cordle and he indicated that those were thoughts that Jennifer Wheatley shared with him. So...*

Judge Hackner: **Alright, so, you want to make any further argument on the point?**

Ms Rogers: *Oh, I'm sorry, your honor.*

Judge Hackner: **I believe it would be appropriate for counsel to ask Ms Wheatley her recollection of those events. And if she doesn't recall or testifies inconsistently, then they're subject to impeachment, I guess. In the extent that she told something to Mr. Cordle. I think there is relevance to it, and A, could potentially have some bearing on the outcome of the case.**

Ms Rogers:	*I'll bring Ms Wheatley back in, your honor.*
Judge Hackner:	**Actually, I guess we should go ahead and get the jury back in.**
Ms Rogers:	*Oh, yeah.*
Judge Hackner:	**Might help.** *

---

*I later learned, while transcribing the audio files of the trial, the reason for this discussion between Kathleen, Mr. Szekely, and Judge Hackner. Mr. Szekely believed I had done cocaine with George the night before I was raped, instead of the two years previous when George had helped me move. He also believed that I had accused George of committing the crime in my statement to Detective Leo. Apparently he arrived at this conclusion after misreading some notes Dave Cordle had written sometime during his investigation.

I guess Mr. Szekely hadn't been able to read Dave's notes very well — because of poor penmanship? In any case, believing the incident took place the night before I was raped, Mr. Szekely planned his entire defense around this one night with George that took place in 1986. I believe Mr. Szekely intended to present me to the jury as an habitual drug user in hope that this would destroy my credibility. I had no knowledge of this conversation when I was called back into the courtroom for cross-examination.

63

Intermission

Cindy was sitting on the bench in the hallway when I came back from the bathroom.

"Kathleen and the defense lawyer had to go down to Dave's office to speak to him about something, so it will be a few minutes longer before you get called back in."

"Okay." I figured there was no sense in asking what the meeting was about. Even if she wanted to tell me, she wouldn't be able to.

"That whole thing with George and Jeff, was that just you giving Dave a suggestion, a possible avenue to pursue?" she asked.

"Yeah, I didn't have any idea who had done this, but I did tell Dave at one point, before he had a suspect, that it might be George because he fit the vague description. In 2008, when he told me they had another victim and how she worked in a yacht yard in Annapolis back in the '80s I told Dave he might want to look into Jeff. He was a drug dealer and drove a truck delivering sailboats all over the country for a local yacht yard back then. When Dave and Tracy told me about the fingerprint match, they told me Trice was a courier back in the '80s. I thought the creep might know Jeff — maybe he delivered stuff to the yacht yard or bought drugs from Jeff."

Cindy and I talked a bit more. I was still incredibly thirsty, although I had drunk the entire cup of water Kathleen had given me.

"Do I have time to get a drink?"

"Yeah, just don't be long," Cindy answered.

I walked back to the water fountain to get a drink and I went in to use the bathroom again. I was again feeling antsy. I needed to blow my nose, but I didn't want it to look any redder than it already was. My next part on the stand was to be with the defense attorney, and I could not imagine what he was going to ask. The good thing was that his questioning probably wouldn't take long.

Just as I was finishing up in the bathroom, both Kathleen and Cindy opened the bathroom door looking for me. I heard Kathleen's voice. She was irritated. She said something like, "Enough with the bathroom," or "No more trips to the bathroom." When they came in, she said something about the judge waiting for me and how I needed to hurry. One of them told me to forget about washing my hands.

"Do you think he's going to care if you wash your hands?"

What an odd question, I thought. *"He" who? The judge or the creep?* I washed my hands anyway thinking, *I cared*, and then I followed them back to the courtroom.

64

Cross Examination

4:05

Judge Hackner:	**Ms Wheatley, you can come up and have a seat in the witness box. The jury is coming in in a minute.**

The judge reminded me I was still under oath as I sat down on the edge of the chair again.

Me:	Thank you.
Judge Hackner:	**Pull up the chair a little bit, please.**
Me:	Could I get some more water?
Judge Hackner:	**Sure, ah, I don't have a pitcher. But, Ms Rogers, if you have a pitcher, you're welcome to it.**
Ms Rogers:	*Oh, sure.*
Judge Hackner:	**And ma'am, could you just restate your name.**
Me:	Jennifer Wheatley.
Judge Hackner:	**You don't have to talk right into the microphone because then it...**
Me:	Then it reverberates?
Judge Hackner:	**Yeah, just sort of...fine. Please be seated now,**

ladies and gentlemen. Okay, the jury is now in the
courtroom. Counsel, you may have a seat.

The defense lawyer said hello and then started with his questions.
He seemed really excited. I was reminded of Perry Mason just before he
revealed to the jury some important detail that would shift the thinking
of the jury. A big revelation. I was curious.

Mr. Szekely: *Ms Wheatley, you were initially interviewed by Detective
Leo on the early morning of the 21st of 1998?*

Me: That's right.

(*No*, I thought, *actually it was in 1988.*)

Mr. Szekely: *During that time, if you remember, was Detective Leo
taking notes?*

Me: No, he had a tape recorder and he recorded my statement.

Mr. Szekely: *And this was taken at the Annapolis Police station?*

Me: Yes.

Mr. Szekely: *They took you there after you had gone back to
your apartment?*

Me: That's correct.

Mr. Szekely: *And then you then met with Mr. David Cordle in 2005?*

Me: Um, just about a year later, actually.

Mr. Szekely: *In 1989?*

Me: Yes.

Mr. Szekely: *And at that time, did you, ah, did you, ah, give another*
                   statement at that time?

Me: Um, we talked about the case together and I gave him
                   the information. I don't know if it was considered a
                   formal statement.

Mr. Szekely: *If you remember, was he taking notes during that time?*

Me: I'm sure he probably was, I don't remember.

Mr. Szekely: *Was that one audio recorded?*

Me: I don't think so.

Mr. Szekely: *And then you met again with Mr. Cordle in 2005.*

Me: Yes.

Mr. Szekely: *And you gave another statement at that time recounting*
                   the events of the 21st of August.

Me: Noooo, um, he met with me then to discuss, um,
                   actually, I don't remember. I don't remember why we
                   met that time...

I stalled. *Here it is,* I thought. He was trying to trap me into saying
something I shouldn't. Dave had called me into his office in 2005 to
discuss a possible suspect and a cold hit. At the time, I didn't know what
that meant, but I did now. I was sure Szekely was trying to trap me
into saying something I shouldn't. I guessed this was his whole defense
strategy. Getting me to mention another victim or previous arrests of the

defendant was his best defense. Matching DNA and fingerprints didn't allow for any wiggle room. But he'd underestimated my counsel. I knew better. Mr. Szekely's plan might have worked had I not talked with Cindy earlier. I knew the consequences of voicing the answer he wanted to hear. I wasn't going to give him what he wanted.

But, I had a problem. How could I answer the question without talking about the other victim? I had to answer the question honestly.

In 2005, during my meeting with Dave, he didn't tell me all the details of the investigation. However, when he met with me in 2008, he told me about the fingerprint, and Detective Morgan told me how the DNA evidence linked to another victim. If I said anything about the other woman who had been raped by the defendant, it would prejudice the jury and the case would be thrown out. The defense would win.

I was feeling panicky and I couldn't think. How could I tell the truth without telling Szekely what he wanted to hear? If I didn't choose my words carefully, it would all be over. Case dismissed! The creep would win. Crap. Help!

I needed help and I needed it fast. Now would be a great time for an objection. I look over at Kathleen, but she was quiet. I was in trouble. Why wasn't she helping me? She had to know I was feeling trapped. My heart raced so fast I could hear the blood rushing in my ears.

I saw Mr. Szekely looking at me with smug anticipation on his face. He repeated the question.

I took a breath in and tried to calm myself. *"You have to tell the truth."* I could hear Cindy's words echo in my head. *"You absolutely cannot mention the other victim or it's all over right then and there."* Shit, I couldn't think. There had to be a way to answer this honestly and not give anything away, but I'd be damned if I could come up with anything. I was feeling confused, trapped. Damn. Couldn't Kathleen object to something, anything?

I realized the defense attorney was talking to me again.

Mr. Szekely: But, you discussed the case.

Me: Right, right...

Mr. Szekely: *I mean...*

Me: Right, we weren't having lunch. No.

Mr. Szekely: *That's what I mean, it was about this case.*

Me: Right, yes.

He had stopped talking again and was waiting for an answer. I had to say something. I took a deep breath and started:

Me: No, it wasn't to give a statement...

And, out of nowhere, I heard my grandmother's voice in my head say, *"Tell him he re-opened the case."* Thank God! Thank you, Nana!

Me: ...I think he had opened the case again.

I let out a huge breath. Wow, I hated that. Thank God! I took a couple more deep breaths and began to feel calmer. I had just enough time to wonder about my last conversation with Cindy in her office, about how my thinking out loud, *"He's done this before and he'll do it again,"* seemed so random at the time and yet proved here to be essential in helping me through this line of questioning. I doubt I would have known I was *not* allowed to talk about the other victim, and I'm sure Mr. Szekely was counting on just that. *No such thing as coincidence,* I thought. Thank You! Thank You! Thank You! I'd answered the question honestly and had not given him what he was hoping for. Suddenly, Mr. Szekely didn't seem quite as excited as when he'd started questioning me.

Mr. Szekely: *And then you met again with Mr. Cordle and a Detective Morgan in 2008.*

Me: Right.

Mr. Szekely: *And do you remember if either of them, Detective Morgan or Mr. Cordle, was taking notes?*

Me: I don't remember.

I wondered, what possible difference could it make who took notes or when they took them?

Mr. Szekely: *Where was that other, where was the 2005 meeting?*

Me: I came here for that one. It was very short.

Mr. Szekely: *Downstairs in the State's Attorney's Office?"*

Me: Yes.

Mr. Szekely: *And how 'bout the 2008 meeting?*

Me: The other one was at my house.

Mr. Szekely: *Okay. Now, when you met with Mr. Cordle in 2008, you stated that you did talk about August 21, 1988, with him that day.*

Me: Briefly, yeah.

Mr. Szekely: *And you also spoke with him about your life, sort of, in general at that time.*

Me: Sure.

What the hell was all of this really about? My life in general? No, they didn't drive all the way to my house just to talk about my life. I was beginning to feel like he was trying to trip me again. But how? I'd already mentioned that Detective Leo had taken a tape-recorded statement, and Szekely knew about the journal. He had a copy of it in front of him. I didn't really know about any notes or why he was so interested in them. What, if anything, was in these notes, and what, if anything, did they have do with the night I was raped?

Mr. Szekely: *And you told him that before you worked at the Chart House, you worked at a raw bar named McGarvey's?*

Me: That's correct.

Mr. Szekely: *And there was a gentleman named George, and you weren't quite sure about his last name.*

Me: Right.

Mr. Szekely: *And he worked there with you.*

Wow, where had he gotten George's name? Okay, I thought, where was he going with this and why? Did I know Trice through George? Had I met him when I was working at the raw bar in 1986? I could see how the two of them might have been friends. George liked to do drugs. The creep had asked me for drugs, so I presumed he liked them, too. George had a wicked temper and clearly so did my attacker. Was he one of George's friends? Had he been one of my customers at the raw bar? I didn't remember meeting him, and I was certain I would not have forgotten a face like his. I answered with a slightly drawn out and questioning, "Right."

Mr. Szekely: *And that George was somebody who you spent some time with outside of work. Either romantically or socially?*

Me: Right.

I probably should have said "No." But, technically, I guess you can
call sitting at the bar together after work "social." But, no, I did not
really hang out with him on a regular basis or anything. I was scared of
the guy. He'd helped me move *once*. I guess that counted. Well, whatever
I thought, George didn't have anything to do with this. I hadn't seen him
since I quit working at McGarvey's.

Mr. Szekely: *You told Mr. Cordle you'd done cocaine with George*
                 on an occasion?

Me: I had. Yeah.

Mr. Szekely: *So, now and again, every now and again you used*
                 cocaine with him.

Me: Right.

What the hell did I say that for? I'd only done it with him once, that
night, at his suggestion, after he helped me move in 1986, two years before
the attack. Why did I say from time to time? Too late to take it back. Let
it go. I'd look like I was trying to hide something if I backtracked now.
Besides, none of this had anything to do with anything.

I sat perched watching and waiting as the defense attorney checked
his list of questions trying to create something out of nothing. I
attempted to keep my expression set. The further into his interrogation
he got and the more bizarre his questions became, the more frequently
I felt my brows furrow together or lift up in disbelief or puzzlement. I
was curious about what he thought he was going to spring on me and
the jury.

Mr. Szekely: *And was there a specific occasion when you and George did cocaine that he was holding or was supposed to deliver to somebody else?*

Me: Yes.

"*One* time in 1986," I should have said. Stupid! I should have cleared up the "now and again" mistake. What an idiot I was. But really, what had this got to do with anything that happened in 1988? Why wasn't Kathleen objecting to the defense implying I was some sort of drug addict? Or, better yet, object to something that happened two years previous? Did he know something about George that I didn't, or something about the creep?

Mr. Szekely: *And that cocaine was supposed to go to Jeff S.?*

Me: Yes.

Crap! Did Jeff have something to do with this, after all?

Mr. Szekely: *Ultimately, obviously you and George used that cocaine together.*

Me: Yes.

Mr. Szekely: *Now, was George selling that cocaine to Mr. S. or was he just supposed to deliver it?*

Me: I think he was delivering it. I really don't know.

Mr. Szekely: *Okay. But that was Mr. S.'s cocaine that you used with George that night.*

Really, I thought, *Is this what he was going with? Make me out to be a habitual drug user?* Okay, so I didn't know the defendant from McGarvey's. That was a relief. Apparently he wasn't a friend of George's, after all. But if I didn't know the defendant from my days working at McGarvey's, I couldn't for the life of me figure out why I was being asked about this. Did Jeff and Trice know each other? How crazy would that be? Maybe Jeff *did* set up my assault? Maybe the long-shot suggestion to Dave years ago hadn't been so crazy after all.

It seemed doubtful. More likely, Mr. Szekely just wanted to make me look bad in the eyes of the jury. That must be the reason he was asking these questions. Discredit the witness to make her testimony less believable. Why wasn't Kathleen objecting at this point? I paused hoping to hear "Objection-Relevance" like you see on TV, but she stayed quiet. So I continued.

Me:	Right.
Mr. Szekely:	*And did George ask you for money to pay for it so you could at least give the money to Jeff?*
Me:	Um, I don't think that came up. I don't remember that.
Mr. Szekely:	*You later met Mr. S. when you worked at the Chart House?*
Me:	I knew him. He was a regular customer there.
Mr. Szekely:	Oh, so you knew him from the Chart House?
Me:	Um-hmm.
Mr. Szekely:	*Now did you...*
Judge Hackner:	**Say yes or no, please.**
Me:	I'm sorry, yes.

Mr. Szekely: *And you told Mr. Cordle that...*

Ms Rogers: *Objection.*

Now, she objects. Damn, what took her so long?

Judge Hackner: **Counsel can you approach, please?**

When Mr. Szekely returned to his questions, he didn't seem quite so excited. Apparently Kathleen's objection took some of the air out of his sails. I had no idea what she was objecting to or what the discussion with the judge was all about. I was just glad she had finally objected to something.

Mr. Szekely looked over his notes with the other defense lawyer and then started again.

Mr. Szekely: *If I could withdraw that question and rephrase it, your honor.*

Judge Hackner: **Yes.**

Mr. Szekely: *Did you believe that Mr. S. was a narc? Or did he believe that you were a narc? It's not; I'm not clear which one...*

Ms Rogers: *Objection.*

Ha, ha, I thought, What was up with that? He couldn't ask me a question like that. He'd lost. He had nothing. Sorry, dude. This was not looking good for him. I kept my mouth shut.

Judge Hackner: **Sustained.**

I didn't have to answer this one, but no, I did not think Jeff was a narc, although there were people in town who thought he was. Just the opposite — I believed he was one of the biggest drug dealers in Annapolis. This was really sad to watch. Except for revealing that I had done cocaine back in the 1980s and trying to make me look bad to the jury, he had nothing.

Mr. Szekely:	*Now, at one point, you had given George's name to the police in connection to August 21, 1988.*
Me:	No. I don't remember doing that. Because I didn't know who, I didn't know who had raped me.

Seriously, wasn't he finished with this yet? I'd suggested to Dave he might want to look into it in 2005 because George was the only one I could come up with who fit the description. Maybe Jeff was behind it, maybe not. End of the story, let's move on.

Mr. Szekely:	*Do you remember an incident when Jeff asked you whether the police had found anyone and he mentioned George's name?*
Me:	I remember him asking me, but I do not remember him saying it was George. No.
Mr. Szekely:	*And you don't remember being nervous because you had given the name "George" to the police and you were concerned how Jeff found that out.*
Me:	But I didn't give the name to the police.

Wasn't he listening? Didn't I just say I didn't tell the police about George? And why was he still going on about this, anyway? An isolated incident in 1986 had bearing on this case? Seriously? Okay. He'd made his point. So much for victim's rights.

I shifted my weight in the unstable chair and looked toward the floor to get my face composed before I looked back up.

I glanced at Trice while Mr. Szekely fidgeted with some notes. At that moment, I almost felt sorry for him. His fate was in the hands of an incompetent attorney. I didn't know what evidence Mr. Szekely thought he had. Clearly, when he started with this line of questioning, he thought he was setting me up for a real zinger. Truth was, there was no story here. Whatever he was trying to do wasn't working. And, apparently he wasn't getting any of the answers he was looking for.

Mr. Szekely: *And when you met, ah, when you spoke with Mr. Cordle in 2005, did you indicate to him that...*

Ms Rogers: *Objection.*

Judge Hackner: **Same basis as earlier?**

Ms Rogers: *Yes, your honor.*

Oh, now she objects to a question about the 2005 meeting. Why couldn't she have done this a few minutes ago when I was backed into a corner? I object! I objected to being made to look like a drug addict. I objected to being asked questions that might make me say something to prejudice the case. I wondered what Kathleen could be objecting to? What, if anything, had I said to Dave in 2005?

Mr. Szekely: *Okay, then I'll withdraw and rephrase the question. Did you believe that Jeff had set you up to be raped?*

Me: Um, I did mention that to Dave Cordle. Yes.

Yeah, I'd thought it might be possible, but why would he even think to ask? Had the creep told him he was hired to do the deed? That wouldn't make him any less guilty of the crime — DNA doesn't lie.

(Mr. Szekely hands me a photograph.)

Mr. Szekely:	*Now, Ms Wheatley, this is what you have marked and identified as State's Exhibit #3?*
Me:	Right.
Mr. Szekely:	*And just to recount, since the jury can't see while we're looking at it...*
Me:	That's my car in the carport, the balcony, and that's the sliding glass door down into the living room area.
Mr. Szekely:	*Now, this sliding glass door when you came home, this sliding glass door, now was it open?*
Me:	Yeah, about four or five inches.
Mr. Szekely:	*About four or five inches. And that's the door you say created that sort of cross flow from the living room into the kitchen.*
Me:	Right.
Mr. Szekely:	*Now that door was, if you remember, is this how the door was, how it looked that night. If you remember, if you don't remember, that's exactly the way the door looked later that night.*

Was this a question? Maybe I should ask him to repeat it. No, the door didn't look exactly like it did that night. We just went through this... remember, four or five inches? I was feeling irritated. I needed a break.

I took a couple of slow breaths to calm myself. I heard the words, *"It'll be over soon,"* go through my head. My grandmother's voice again?

Me: I, um, I think it's open further now than when I saw it. Because, obviously this is open further than a few inches. Yeah.

Mr. Szekely: *Now, that door has a screen there?*

Me: Right.

Mr. Szekely: *So, even if the door's open, you can't just walk in, somebody has to actually open...*

Did I really have to answer this? Did he just ask me if someone had to open the screen door before he could walk through it? Let's review:

Screen Doors 101:
Step 1. Open door
Step 2. Enter.
Caution: Skipping step one, will result in complications.

I had to calm down. He was bugging me by asking questions that didn't make any sense, but I didn't want to get into trouble. I composed my voice before I answered.

Me: No, you have to open the screen and open the rest of the sliding door to fit through.

I couldn't help the slight smile that crossed my lips.

Mr. Szekely: *And is it one of those doors, I know they come two ways, is it one of those doors where the screen is outside the glass or inside the glass?*

Me: If you were on the balcony, the screen would be first
                       and then the sliding door was on the inside. It was a
                       storm door.

Mr. Szekely: *And there's a latch and you pull that and slide the*
                       screen open and you can step inside and the screen...

Me: Right.

Mr. Szekely: *Is the screen like a spring, and does it shut behind*
                       you automatically, or do you need to pull that
                       shut? If you remember?

Me: I think you had to pull it shut.

Mr. Szekely: *Okay. Now, Ms Wheatley, you testified that at one*
                       point during the attack, your attacker picked up
                       the candle.

Me: Yes.

Mr. Szekely: *That candle came from your employer?*

Me: Correct.

Mr. Szekely: *You had stolen that from your employer?*

Oh, good. I was afraid he might disappoint the jury and stop with
the drugs. I remembered I had written in my journal that "I stole it,"
and I was sure the defense lawyer wanted to add the brand of "thief" to
his list of my character flaws.

Speaking of which...Why was he allowed to ask questions about how
I got the candle at all? And why did he get to use the journal — that I
hadn't mentioned writing — to ask how I'd gotten that candle? I hadn't

mentioned in my testimony how I'd acquired it or from where. What possible difference could it make where the candle came from?

Kathleen had not asked me where the candle had come from. I only testified that the creep had picked it up. I'd said, *"I used to light candles all the time back then, and I had a candle right on the nightstand next to me,"* and later, *"He picked the candle up..."* So, why wasn't Kathleen objecting to this? Okay, I had to prepare myself for being made to look like a thief in addition to a drug addict. This would have been pretty entertaining if it weren't happening to me.

Again I took a breath before starting my answer and hoped my frustration wasn't obvious.

Me:	I, there was a storm about a week before this happened and we had put out, I don't know, a couple extra cases of candles around the restaurant because we lost power. But we'd thrown out all the extra boxes. So when we opened on the next day, management said, "Go ahead and take one."
Mr. Szekely:	*So, you had taken that with permission?*
Me:	I took it home. I took it home with me.

There was a lot of whispering between Mr. Szekely and the other attorney as they flipped through pages of the diary. I think they were trying to find my entry about taking the candle home. I heard him ask in a whisper, "What page is that on?"

Mr. Szelely:	*Brief indulgence, your honor.*
Mr. Szekely:	*What page is that on? I have my own copy. I don't know, doesn't have a page number on it. It's not that...*

Apparently he couldn't find what he was looking for and continued:

Mr. Szekely: *Ms Wheatley, at the time of this...*

Mr. Szekely: *Court's indulgence.*

Mr. Szekely: *Your honor, I'm going to withdraw that, withdraw that question.*

Judge Hackner: **Okay.**

What was wrong? Were his plans to make me look like a thief fizzling? Too bad his assistant wasn't actually assisting him with that one. I couldn't wait to hear what he would come up with next.

Mr. Szekely: *Um, Ms Wheatley, I just want to go over the timeline of that night with you one more time. You said you came home around 2:30?*

Me: Correct.

Mr. Szekely: *And you had had a couple of beers with your coworkers after. Now, is that a couple like two, or is that a couple like sometimes they say a couple, but they mean more than two.*

Oh, yeah, here it was, and I hadn't had to wait too long for another attack on my character... Now, I was a drunk, too. What had happened to victim's rights? He was going to imply because I had been drinking I deserved to be raped? Or was he just trying to suggest that I was drunk, and in my drunken state I'd let the defendant into the house? However, rather than letting him in through the door, I'd made the creep hop onto the hood of my car, shimmy up a wooden post, and flip onto the balcony to come in the sliding glass door on the second floor. Don't forget to open the screen door first and take your shoes off! Rapunzel, I'm not!

And what was with his flippant tone? What difference did it make if I'd had one or a hundred and one beers? None. No matter how much I'd had to drink, nothing made it okay for the creep to do what he did to me.

I hesitated, wondering if Kathleen was going to jump up at this one. Maybe she was thinking along the same lines I was. Nope. Nothing. I guessed I was on my own in protecting myself from the "She's a drug addict, a thief, and a drunk" flag he was waving to the jury. Hey, at least I wasn't a slut; that was something. However, come to think of it, I probably would hear, *"Objection, your honor,"* if he were to attack my sex life. The defense lawyer wasn't allowed to attack my character. Good thing there are laws which prohibit any non-relevant evidence of the victim's past sexual history from being mentioned by the defense at trial.

Me:	No, it was a couple, like two.
Mr. Szekely:	*You had two beers, then you came. If you left work around 2:30, you got home around, ballpark, 2:35.*
Me:	Right.
Mr. Szekely:	*You went, um, upstairs to the kitchen and got yourself something to eat and got a beer.*

Okay everyone, can we all count to three? It's the number of the day on Sesame Street. Three! Three beers and you're a drunk who deserves to be raped?

His tone was pissing me off and I was having a real hard time maintaining my calm. Thank goodness my grandmother's voice continued to remind me to breathe and, *Check your tone. You don't want to sound as pissy as you feel right now — it won't help a thing.* I did my best to keep my face composed as I answered.

Me: Right.

Mr. Szekely: *What time was that — quarter to three?*

Me: That sounds about right — quarter of three.

Mr. Szekely: *Now, you had that food, you went back down.*

Me: Back down to the bedroom. Yes.

Mr. Szekely: *And what time was that first phone call?*

Me: Three o'clock.

Mr. Szekely: *Okay. If you remember, what time did the entire incident end?*

Me: End?

Mr. Szekely: *End. What time were you left on your own?*

Me: I believe it was close to four o'clock.

Mr. Szekely: *So the, the incident lasted roughly an hour.*

Next week, kids, we will try subtraction now that you have addition down. Crap, he was bugging me. Take a breath in and let it out.

Me: Right, from the first phone call until he left.

Mr. Szekely: *From the first phone call until he left. Okay. And from, how much time was there from that first phone call till you thought someone was in your house?*

Me:	I think probably close to a half hour.

Actually, that wasn't right. It was about half an hour from the time he grabbed me to the time he left. But he was in the house and had turned on the air conditioner at 3:15. That meant the defendant was in the house for almost forty-five minutes and the attack lasted fifteen to twenty minutes. But no biggy, not worth backtracking on this. I had made the mistake of saying it was 3:30 when I'd called Deborah, but the jury was taking notes; they would realize this was about the time I was grabbed — when I walked into my room. They would see that I was just mixed up.

Mr. Szekely:	*And you say the incident ended at 4:00. And you sat on your bed.*
Me:	About four o'clock.
Mr. Szekely:	*And you sat on your bed and had a cigarette.*
Me:	Right.
Mr. Szekely:	*And you said you sat there for two or three minutes trying to gather yourself, trying to figure out what to do.*
Me:	A couple of minutes. Right.
Mr. Szekely:	*Then you went into the bathroom. Then you came out of the bathroom and called your sisters.*
Me:	Right.
Mr. Szekely:	*And it was only after you called your other sister that you called 911.*

Me: Correct.

I learned after the trial that the defense attorney claimed it took me over an hour to call the police after the attack. In his opening statement, he had claimed he was going to illustrate how I had set up the defendant. He planned to show the jury that I had plenty of time — almost an hour — to remove all the fingerprints around the house except for the fingerprints on the candle. And after having removed all the prints except for those, it would be easy for me to point out exactly where the defendant's prints would be found.

Since I was not allowed to mention the T-shirt in court, this was the only way the defense attorney could explain why there were no other prints from the defendant in the house. However, with my retelling of the timeline, he had to see he was mistaken. He had been given a copy of my journal well before the trial started, and in it I state exactly how much time had passed from the time the defendant left until I dialed 911:

I'd tried to remember Debbie's number and it had finally come to me. I guess about five to ten minutes had passed since he'd left and I'd called 911, but it felt like a lifetime.

I could only guess Szekely hadn't read the journal carefully or he was trying to confuse me.

Mr. Szekely: *Now, you testified earlier that your mother was upstairs sleeping?*

Me: Yes.

Mr. Szekely: *And you say that you let out a scream.*

Me: I screamed. Yes.

Mr. Szekely: *And it was because your mother didn't come down when you screamed that you thought something had happened to her.*

Me: Right.

Mr. Szekely: *Because typically, if your mother heard you scream, she'd come down to see what was wrong.*

I was not even sure how to react to this question. This time I was unable to keep my reaction from reaching my face or the sarcasm out of my voice.

Me: That's what I would think. Yeah.

Mr. Szekely: *You said the air conditioning was turned on?*

Me: Yes.

Mr. Szekely: *Now, was that a wall thermostat or was that sort of one of those against the wall and you go and turn the knob.*

Me: No, it was in the living room — wall controlled. The thermostat was in the living room. So you could turn it on from there.

Mr. Szekely: *And that controlled the whole house?*

Me: The whole house. Yes.

Mr. Szekely: *Court's indulgence, your honor.*

Mr. Szekely: *Nothing further, your honor.*

Judge Hackner: **Ms Rogers, anything else?**

Ms Rogers:	*No, your honor.*
Judge Hackner:	**I want to thank you. Would you expect that Ms Wheatley might be called again; that she should remain outside?**
Ms Rogers:	*Not today, your honor.*
Mr. Szekely:	*We'll figure it...I don't expect to be calling Ms Wheatley today. If she can be held; kept available.*
Judge Hackner:	**You don't object to her going back out?**
Ms Rogers:	*No.*
Judge Hackner:	**Okay, very good. Ms Wheatley you can step out please.**
Me:	*Thank You.*

And, just like that, I was finished.

I glanced at the defendant one more time before I stood up to leave. He looked small. For years, I had been terrified of this man. Now, I felt sad, disgusted, and sickened. He had caused so much pain for so many for decades. Only he knew how many women should be having their day in court. I doubted he really had any idea just how far-reaching his selfish and shameful behavior really was. What a waste his life was; pathetic.

65

An End to a Long Day

I walked out of the courtroom feeling like I had grown twelve feet taller than I was when I'd walked into the room. My head swam from everything that had taken place in there. It was going to take some time to digest it all. I knew everyone was going to sit and listen to the next witness, so I headed to the bathroom. *I could use a cigarette,* I thought. *And a beer.*

When I finished in the bathroom, I walked back to the bench outside the courtroom. There was a police officer sitting at the far end. Knowing I was not supposed to talk to anyone, I just nodded to him and smiled. I sat down a few feet away from him. I sat with my head in my hand and thought about my testimony and the crazy energy exchange between myself and the girls. Dave Cordle approached and greeted the officer and said hello to me.

Then Dave said, "I bet you don't remember this guy. Officer Neutzling. He's a captain now." As soon as Dave said the man's name I knew exactly who he was.

"You took me to the hospital that day?" It was really more of a statement than a question. I smiled. "I never thought I'd see you again. Thank you."

The police officer smiled and said, "Yes, I did... Good to see you again."

He and Dave talked between themselves for a few minutes and then the officer went into the courtroom. I was tired and yet completely pumped up on adrenaline.

Dave stayed with me while we were waiting for the police officer to finish with his testimony. Sitting on the bench, I wondered how long I had been on the stand. I thought back on all I'd said, hoping I'd remembered everything. There were a couple of times when I had forgotten something and had had to backtrack.

In just a few minutes, the officer was finished and he exited the courtroom. He paused in front of me, extended his hand, and looking me in the eye, he said, "Thank you. Good luck to you."

I smiled with tears in my eyes.

"Thank you," I said as we shook hands.

Then, one by one, everyone filed out of the courtroom.

Mollie walked up to me in tears and hugged me saying, "You did so great. I'm so proud of you. Why did you tell them you're forty-nine?"

"No, I didn't," I answered, confused.

"Yeah, she asked you how old you are now, you said forty-nine."

"I did? No, I heard myself say fifty-one."

Cindy was standing next to me. "No, you said forty-nine. I remember thinking, 'What is she doing? This isn't any time to make jokes.'"

"Really? I swear I said fifty-one. I heard myself say fifty-one."

My sister Debbie hugged me, saying, "No, you said forty-nine. You did great."

I hugged all my friends. We all cried. All of us were exhausted and pumped up at the same time.

I heard Cindy say, "Okay, ladies. Get it out of your systems now. You can't discuss Jennifer's testimony with anyone."

Marnie and I walked to the bathroom together. I asked someone to let the boys know we were finished since I didn't have my phone with me. I looked at my watch. It was almost 4:30. Wow! It was a lot later than I'd thought. Marnie and I walked back to the group with our arms around each other singing the Sister Sledge song, *We Are Family*.

Everyone was ready for a stiff drink. I said I could use a smoke. Shirli suggested maybe I should have "just one."

"Yeah, that won't happen. If I have one, I'll be buying a carton before we get to the restaurant!"

Jackie had to leave to pick up her kids and get home, so I gave her a hug and thanked her for being there with me.

"I'm so glad you were here today — it was right that you were here."

I told her I'd let her know what time closing arguments would be on Tuesday, and then I walked downstairs with Cindy to get my coat and purse.

The group of us walked downtown to one of the restaurants for drinks and dinner. Dad called my cell phone while we were there and I told him it went well, but that I couldn't give him any real details. Then I mentioned we were all having dinner together.

"Oh," he said, "you're having dinner now? For crying out loud, I didn't know you were in the middle of dinner!"

Before we hung up, I told him I would call him Tuesday after the verdict.

I went upstairs where it was a bit quieter to call my mother. I told her how creepy the defendant was and how nervous I'd felt when I started talking.

"By the time I got to telling about the rape itself, it was as if it was 1988 and it was happening all over again," I said. "It was really weird to be telling the story in front of him. But I made my way through it all." I told her how many of my girlfriends from the Chart House had been there with me. "...and Mollie and Debbie and a few other girlfriends."

"Was Marcus in there with you?" Mom asked.

"No, I made the decision not to have any of the guys in the courtroom with me when I told the story. He and the rest of the guys went to a bar on Main Street until I was finished. They were there for the opening statements. Apparently, my lawyer painted a pretty graphic description of what happened, and they all got to see the guy."

"Well, I'm glad the hard part is over," Mom said. "Keep me posted. Give Marcus a hug from me. I love you. Now go have fun with your friends."

We all had a difficult time not talking about what had taken place in the courtroom. It was one of the most frustrating parts of this whole process. Everyone had questions and comments and we had to keep quiet about all of it because I might get recalled. I think we camped out in Middleton's for almost three hours. It was a great time. I felt relieved that my time on the stand was over. The experience had been uplifting and powerful. I'd witnessed strong bonds joining all of us in a united objective. I felt free — released from the grip of my attacker. Sharing this unbelievable day with my family and friends was overwhelming.

After a late night out with friends, I had an even later night tossing and turning. Marcus and I got back to the B&B around 1:00am. Marcus fell asleep immediately. I checked my e-mails and then went to bed. I couldn't fall asleep. The voices in my head would not be silenced. Over and over again, I went through my testimony. Then I started thinking about the questions the defense attorney had asked me. No matter how I looked at it, I couldn't figure out the purpose of most of his questions. None of the references to George and Jeff made any sense. If there were no connections between something that happened in 1986 and 1988, then what was the point?

It was disturbing to discover just how ineffective the rape shield statutes really are — well, actually, maybe they were effective, since my lack of a sex life was not mentioned in the courtroom. But the defense attorney made a point of making me appear to be an addict and a drunk. Unfortunately for him, his plan to add "thief" to this list had failed.

I needed sleep.

Although I didn't have to be in the courthouse the next morning, I did want to be there while everyone else was sitting in on the testimony. Around 4:00am, I got up and took a bite off an antihistamine tablet. *Ha, ha,* I thought as I bit off a quarter of a pink Benadryl tablet. *I wonder if the defense attorney would think taking this to help me sleep makes me an addict?* I was asleep in minutes.

Jenny,

Please accept my words of heartfelt support. You have the heart and courage of a lion — bar none. Your testimony today was a testament of your will and strength to meet treacherous challenges. Everyone who knows you is mightily proud of your efforts today — including me.

You make all women proud, and you've advanced all our efforts to make right one of the most egregious crimes of all time. Thank you, Jenny. You deserve all the support you need and more. Please tell me if there is anything I can do to help.

Please know how personally proud I am of you for your outstanding testimony today. More support is here if you need it. All you need to do is ask.

White light, Jen.
~ Ruth & Sweet Pea

66

Thursday, January 14, 2010

I wasn't going to be allowed in to hear any of the other witnesses testify, but Marcus, Art, Hope, and Kathie were able to listen in and wanted to go to the courthouse after breakfast. I wanted to be close in case the creep decided to plead guilty somewhere along the course of the day. As we sat in Chick and Ruth's eating breakfast, Marcus got a text message from Scott. He and Sherry had arrived at 9:00am and were already in the courtroom listening to testimony. Sherry had asked Cindy if it was okay for her to take notes to show me after the trial was over. Cindy said it was okay.

After we finished eating, we got to the courthouse and the rest of my group went into the courtroom while I stopped off in the bathroom. As I walked back to the bench outside of the courtroom, I saw Dave Cordle. He had just finished testifying. Cindy had told me not to talk to anyone, so I was hesitant to say too much.

Dave said, "Hey, I have a question I'm dying to ask you, but I'm not allowed to."

"Am I allowed to talk to you?" I asked him.

"Oh, yeah, we can talk. We just can't say anything about the trial."

I sat down on the wooden bench and we started talking about vacation spots and preferred retirement locations. I was telling Dave about a condo in Florida that Marcus' cousin had owned that was on the market. "....We decided not to buy the place because the annual fees and taxes would end up costing us more than the condo in just a few years...." As I was talking, I noticed the jury was walking out of the courtroom for their lunch break and passing in front of us. As they walked by, I tried not to make eye contact with any of them because I did not want them to recognize me. Even though I had my hair braided and was wearing jeans, I'm sure a couple of them realized I was the same person they'd seen in court the day before.

Just after the jury filed out, everyone who was with me walked out of the courtroom. How did it get to be lunch time already? Didn't we just finish breakfast? All of us headed back out of the courthouse so Scott and Sherry could get something to eat. Downtown was mobbed with the people from the State House because the state senate session had just started. Every place we tried to get into had lines that were crazy long. So we walked back down Main Street and ended up back at Chick & Ruth's. Although we had a different waiter this time, the guy who seated us was the same. He recognized us right away.

"Welcome back!" he greeted us.

During lunch, I heard who some of the morning's witnesses had been. Unfortunately, no one was able to give me any details. I was envious. I wanted to listen in on the testimony, but I didn't want there to be a problem if I got called back onto the stand. Sherry said she would give me a copy of her notes after the trial.

As we were leaving the restaurant, I heard the host say, "See you later for dinner!"

I laughed and thought, *I hope not.*

67

Morning Witnesses
Mary Pat Whiteley — Evidence Technician

9:35

15 pieces of evidence removed from the scene:

#1. Driver's Registration

#2. Miscellaneous papers from the front seat of the car

#3. Red shirt (on the victim's bed)

#4. 2 Candles (from the nightstand)

#5. Victim's panties (on the bed)

#6. 2 Grey-blue socks (recovered from the bed)

#7. Green plaid flannel shirt

#8. Driver's license paper (from the bed)

#9. 1 Paper towel (from the bed)

#10. 1 Kleenex[TM] (from the bed)

#11. Quilt and Bedspread (from the bed)

#12. A pillow case, yellow in color (from the bed)

#13. Quilt, brown & yellow (from the bed)

#14. Victim's pillow (from the bed)

#15. Hand-held mirror (from the bed)

#16. Red Scarf & Brown Nylon Belt (found on the bottom bed rail)

Ms Whiteley: A red scarf and a nylon belt. They were, like, intertwined.

Ms Rogers: *And did you take each of those items and package them separately, Ms Whiteley?*

Ms Whiteley: Yes, I did.

After the trial, in the beginning of March 2010, I was in Annapolis to meet with Dave Cordle to gather crime scene photographs, documents, and evidence to photograph so we could include them in this book. When I stepped into his office, Dave was looking through a huge binder with "Wheatley Rape" written on the spine.

"Wow!" I said. "Is that all me?"

"Actually, I have two this size," Dave chuckled.

"Did I ever show you a picture of Trice, back in the day?" he asked.

"No," I answered, "you never did."

I was equally curious and nervous about seeing his picture. I wondered if I might remember having seen Trice's face in a crowded bar or restaurant. Had he been stalking me before he'd finally attacked?

Dave handed me the photo.

The face in the picture looked like so many faces in so many photographs taken in the '70s and '80s. It was familiar only in that the mullet hairstyle was popular in those days. I was sure I did not know Trice, but I came to a frightening realization: If he had approached me in a bar back then and asked if he could by me a drink, I probably would have said, "Sure," making his job of securing a victim much easier.

I had a hard time reconciling the picture in my hand with the face I remembered seeing in the courtroom not more than a month ago. Because of his chosen lifestyle, Trice hadn't aged well. Looking at the picture again, I wondered what drives someone to make such evil choices in life. Then I noticed something.

"Wait, Dave..." I said, "This picture is dated 7-23-1989. This is an arrest photo! What was he arrested for that time?"

"That was a Peeping Tom charge," Dave answered.

I felt a chill run through me as I realized how close another woman had come to being one of his victims. No doubt his plans to rape that night had been foiled because he was caught spying on his prey. I also felt a surge of anger. At the time of that arrest, 1989, there was really no way to connect him to my case. I wondered how many more women he had stalked and raped before he was finally picked up in New York.

Handing the picture back, I said, "We are definitely including that one in the book."

Together, we went through some of the evidence that was sitting in a big box in his office. I stood next to Dave as he picked up a few of the bags, reading the notes on the outside that told what the contents were. It felt odd to know that pieces of my life had been neatly bagged, labeled, and stored away in a cavernous warehouse for more than twenty years. Dave picked up a small paper sack marked "Red Scarf-From the bottom bedrail," and another labeled "Brown Nylon Belt-From the bottom bedrail." I asked if I could see these.

First, he opened the bag with the red scarf in it and handed it to me. It was about eighteen to twenty inches long and about three and a half inches wide, made of very soft, red, lightweight silk. I put the scarf in my left hand and pulled one end of it slowly through my fingers. An intuitive vision came to my mind of a woman with long, straight, soft brown hair standing in the sun on a beach with her back to me. For a few seconds, I swore I could feel a breeze and smell the slightly salty air. It was quiet and sunny.

Dave then took the brown nylon belt, about eighteen inches long, out of its paper evidence bag. It had a brass buckle on one end that you weave the belt end through and over a bar in the center of the buckle. When Dave dropped the belt into my hand I experienced a jolt not unlike an electric shock. In my head, I clearly heard a confusion of screaming and yelling. An image of a young boy, about ten to thirteen years old, crying, flashed through my mind. He was running, or trying to run, away from someone. Who was he running from? Why? I couldn't see this person, but I felt the child's panic. He was scared, really scared. Both images were so clear to me. This image of the frightened child made my heart race. Touching the belt sent a chill through me that I could not shake for days. The images I received from both of these objects continue to haunt me. Who were these people I had envisioned? What were their connections to these items?

"Dave, these are not mine," I said quietly. I felt shaky.

"Sure they are. It says right here they were collected from the end of your bed — 'Draped over the bottom rail.'"

"I have no doubt they were collected from the end of my bed. But they are not mine. They don't belong to me," I answered.

"That's odd," Dave said.

"Here, take this, it's really creeping me out." I handed him the nylon belt and felt a shiver run through me again. My stomach was queasy. I ran the silk scarf through my fingers again. I considered keeping it, but then I handed it back to him. It didn't feel right for me to have it. "He must have brought these in with him thinking he was going to use them to wrap around my neck and gag me, but he decided to use my T-shirt instead." I guessed he'd forgotten to take them with him when he'd left. I hadn't seen them that night.

Listening to the audio transcript of Ms Whiteley's description of how the scarf and belt were "intertwined" when she'd found them gave me a chill. Were these trophies from previous crimes? Had they belonged to the people I envisioned? Although I did not sense a feeling of violence from the red scarf, I did get a feeling of close observation, like I was watching this woman go about her business without her knowledge. The brown belt, however, made me feel instantly bad. I was certain it had been used to inflict pain. The screaming I'd heard in my head when I held the belt in my hand was that of a terrified child. Was he another victim? Or had the belt been used violently against Trice at some point in his life?

I met with friends for dinner after my visit with Dave and I was unable to shake the sickening feelings the belt had left with me. It was disturbing for me to think these seemingly normal items might have been used to bring harm to others. It was also unsettling to imagine how my attacker reasoned they would not be adequate weapons to use to strangle me, even after he'd twisted them together. I doubt he intended to leave them behind, but apparently he'd forgotten he'd draped them over the footboard of my bed.

68

Morning Witnesses
David Cordle — Chief Investigator

10:47am

Ms Rogers: *Investigator Cordle, what are your duties as the Chief Investigator for the Anne Arundel State's Attorney's Office?*

Inv. Cordle: I handle cold case homicides and rapes for the city of Annapolis. One for the county. I also do domestic violence lethality assessment, danger assessment, as well as run our witness security program.

Ms Rogers: *How long have you been with the State's Attorney's Office?*

Inv. Cordle: Over twenty-nine years.

Ms Rogers: *Did you have occasion to become involved in the investigation of a case involving Jennifer Wheatley?*

Inv. Cordle: Yes, I did.

Ms Rogers: *When did you first become involved with that case?*

Inv. Cordle: It was in May of 1989.

Ms Rogers: *And in what capacity did you become involved with that case?*

Inv. Cordle:	I was assisting another one of the investigators that was involved with the case.
Ms Rogers:	*Throughout the years, did you occasionally review this case, as well as other cold cases, as part of your job at the State's Attorney's Office?*
Inv. Cordle:	Yes, I did. That's a regular practice in cold cases based on change[s] in technologies.
Ms Rogers:	*And what was your purpose of periodic reviews? You may have just said it, but in this case?*
Inv. Cordle:	In this case, just looking at the changing technologies as it relates to whatever DNA evidence there may have been in any of the cases.
Ms Rogers:	*And now that was basically because, throughout, from 1988 throughout the years, DNA technology was changing. Is that correct?*
Inv. Cordle:	It changes almost as fast as software programs.
Ms Rogers:	*Okay. And did there come a time when the entire file, not just the DNA evidence, was reviewed?*
Inv. Cordle:	Yes, that was in July of 2008.
Ms Rogers:	*And why did that review take place?*
Inv. Cordle:	A detective that is detailed to our office to assist in working cold cases had been freed up from doing a lot of his normal duties that had kept him from assisting in a full-time manner. And I asked him to review a number of the cases we had pending.

Ms Rogers: *And did he, in fact, under your direction, review the entire "Jennifer Wheatley" case?*

Inv. Cordle: Yes, he went through the entire case on July 1st.

Ms Rogers: *And as a result of that review, what, if anything, did he discover?*

Inv. Cordle: He asked me if I knew there were latent prints, ah, in the file.

Ms Rogers: *And did he, in fact, show you a latent print that was in the file?*

Inv. Cordle: I eventually was; he explained to me that latent prints had been recovered at the scene.

Ms Rogers: *I'm going to show you what has been marked as State's Exhibit #13 and ask if you recognize that.*

Inv. Cordle: Yes, this is one of a number of latents that were placed in the file and that were collected from the original scene.

Ms Rogers: *Okay. Did you, in fact, do anything with this particular latent State's Exhibit #13?*

Inv. Cordle: Yes I did. Based on Detective Johns' inquiry, I delivered the whole packet of the latent prints from the original crime scene up to Technician Lowman at the Anne Arundel County Police Crime Lab. He's a latent print examiner.

Ms Rogers: *And why did you deliver that particular latent that had been lifted from the candle to Ernie Lowman?*

Inv. Cordle: Because he is an expert, well, I can't say that. He is a latent print examiner. We wanted to compare that and take a second look after all the years had passed by.

Ms Rogers: *Okay. Did there come a time when you began to try to locate a man by the name of William Joseph Trice?*

Inv. Cordle: Yes, there was.

Ms Rogers: *And when did you begin trying to locate William Joseph Trice?*

Inv. Cordle: I have to refer to my notes.

Ms Rogers: *Go ahead.*

Inv. Cordle: Thank you. Probably in late July, early August, 2008.

Ms Rogers: *August, 2008? And were you, in fact, able to locate him?*

Inv. Cordle: Yes, I was.

Ms Rogers: *And where did you locate him?*

Inv. Cordle: He was residing in upstate New York. I believe in Eagle Bridge, New York.

Ms Rogers: *Did you make contact after discovering that with the New York State Police?*

Inv. Cordle: Yes, I did. I contacted the New York State Police detective division out of Albany.

Ms Rogers: *And what, if any, information did you relay to them?*

Mr. Szekely: *Objection.*

Ms Rogers: *I'll withdraw it, your honor.*

Judge Hackner: **Sustained.**

Ms Rogers: *Did there come a time when you obtained an arrest warrant for Mr. Trice?*

Inv. Cordle: Yes, I applied for an arrest warrant for Mr. Trice.

Ms Rogers: *Did you provide that information to the New York State Police?*

Inv. Cordle: Yes, I did.

Ms Rogers: *And did there come a time when you actually traveled to New York to speak with William Joseph Trice?*

Inv. Cordle: Yes, that was on November 20, 2008.

Ms Rogers: *And who went with you?*

Inv. Cordle: Detective Tracy Morgan.

Ms Rogers: *Do you see the person we have been discussing, William Joseph Trice, in this courtroom?*

Inv. Cordle: Yes, I do. He's seated between his two attorneys with the yellow tie.

Judge Hackner: **He's identified the defendant, for the record.**

Ms Rogers: *I have no further questions, your honor.*

10:53am

Cross Examination:

Mr. Szekely: *Thank you, your honor.*

Mr. Szekely: *Investigator Cordle, you first were assigned to this case in 1989, you said?*

Inv. Cordle: Yes, May of 1989.

Mr. Szekely: *And you were referred to this case by Detective Leo — is that correct?*

Inv. Cordle: I'm sorry?

Mr. Szekely: *Do you remember the name of the detective who assigned you to the case?*

Inv. Cordle: Actually, it was a different detective.

Mr. Szekely: *It was not Detective Leo? Do you remember the name of that detective?*

Inv. Cordle: Well, Detective Leo, I believe was working it. But I believe it was also Detective Lykken.

Mr. Szekely: *At the time you were assigned the case from Detective Leo and Detective Lykken, did you receive any reports they had generated at that time?*

Inv. Cordle: No, I did not.

Mr. Szekely: *Did you receive an audio recording of a statement given by Ms Wheatley?*

Inv. Cordle: No, I did not.

Mr. Szekely: *Did you, yourself meet with Ms Wheatley in 1989?*

Inv. Cordle: Yes.

Mr. Szekely: *Did you take any notes from that meeting?*

Inv. Cordle: Not that I'm aware from that initial meeting. No.

Mr. Szekely: *Court's indulgence.*

Mr. Szekely: *Then you said that you periodically reviewed these cases for, to see if anything changed in the technology?*

Inv. Cordle: Yes.

Mr. Szekely: *Did you conduct one of these reviews in 2005?*

Inv. Cordle: Referring to my notes again, please. Did I...

Ms Rogers: *Your honor, may we approach?*

Judge Hackner: **Yes, you may.**

(White Noise)

Ms Rogers: *I'm just concerned with that question that he's going to throw it out that there, there was an additional case in 2005.*

Mr. Szekely: *I can just not ask it.*

Ms Rogers: *Okay, if you want to lead him, lead him. But I just don't want him, his response might be ...*

Mr. Szekely: *Yeah, I got you...*

(End White Noise)

Mr. Szekely: *Mr. Cordle, I'm going to withdraw that question and just ask, did you meet with Ms Wheatley in 2005?*

Inv. Cordle: Yes, I did.

Mr. Szekely: *And at that time, you met with her and you took notes from a conversation you had with her.*

Inv. Cordle: Yes.

Mr. Szekely: *I have a copy of those notes, I don't know if you have a copy there. I know the State has your original handwritten notes, unless that's what you have in front of you. So, if you need to refer to them at any time, just let me know. I just want to ask you a few questions. During that interview with Ms Wheatley, did she indicate that...*

Ms Rogers: *Objection, your honor.*

Judge Hackner: **Come on up, please.**

(White Noise)

Judge Hackner: **I think I know what your intention...and I ruled to impeach.**

Mr. Szekely: *I'm going to withdraw that question.*

(End White Noise)

Mr. Szekely: *Investigator Cordle, you did obviously [take] notes at that meeting.*

Inv. Cordle: Yes.

Mr. Szekely: *And there came a time in 2008 when you and Detective Morgan met with Ms Wheatley again.*

Inv. Cordle: Yes, that's correct.

Mr. Szekely: *Okay. Did you take any notes during that meeting with Ms Wheatley?*

Inv. Cordle: I don't recall if I did or did not. I don't have copies of my notes with me right now.

Mr. Szekely: *In general, in the course of working on this case, one of the tasks you worked on was assembling all the materials related to this case.*

Inv. Cordle: Not initially, no.

Mr. Szekely: *But, at some point, you helped to retrieve the physical evidence and the previous police reports, and you put all that together into a case file.*

Inv. Cordle: Everything that I could locate, yes.

Mr. Szekely: *Everything you could locate. You conducted a search and you asked Annapolis Police, "Can you look for these items, anything you have related to this case?"*

Inv. Cordle: Yes. Myself and Detective Johns.

Mr. Szekely: *Court's indulgence.*

Mr. Szekely: *Excuse me if I already asked you this, I'm not sure if I asked you this or not, but were you able to get a full sort of main report from either Detective Leo or Detective Lyyken in this case?"*

Inv. Cordle: No, I was not. The only reports that I received seemed to be supplemental reports.

Mr. Szekely: *No further questions, your honor.*

Judge Hackner: **Ms Rogers, anything else?**

Ms Rogers: *No, your honor.*

Judge Hackner: **Mr. Cordle, you're excused.**

Inv. Cordle: *Thank you, your honor.*

69

Morning Witnesses
Detective Tracy Morgan

11:01am

Ms Rogers: *I'm going to show you what has been marked as State's Exhibit[s] #1 and #2, and do you recognize those?*

Det. Morgan: Yes.

Ms Rogers: *What are those?*

Det. Morgan: Those are the photographs we showed Mr. Trice.

Ms Rogers: *And the photograph's of whom?*

Det. Morgan: Of the victim.

Ms Rogers: *And what did you say or do when you showed him those pictures?*

Det. Morgan: I asked him if he recognized her.

Ms Rogers: *And what did the defendant respond when asked if he recognized Jennifer Wheatley?*

Det. Morgan: He said that he did not.

Ms Rogers: *What was the next thing you asked him?*

Det. Morgan: I showed him another picture of the Chart House restaurant where she was employed and he advised he did not recognize that, either.

Ms Rogers: *Okay. And then what did you do?*

Det. Morgan: He actually told me that that was not one of his hang-out spots — that he hung out elsewhere.

Ms Rogers: *Did he tell you where he hung out during this period of time?*

Det. Morgan: Yes, he advised that he hung out at the American Legion Hall in Edgewater, Maryland.

Ms Rogers: *Okay. And did he tell you what road that was on?*

Det. Morgan: Mayo Road.

Ms Rogers: *Okay. When you asked him where he hung out, were you directing it towards the timeframe of the rape?*

Det. Morgan: Yes, I was.

Ms Rogers: *And what else did he tell you he was doing in August of 1988, or around that timeframe?*

Det. Morgan: He advised that he was employed at the time. And he was employed with a courier service.

Ms Rogers: *And what was his job at the courier service?*

Det. Morgan: His job was based in Washington, D.C. And his job was to take paperwork from D.C. to whatever business required the paperwork or vice-versa.

Ms Rogers:	*After he told you about his employment, what was the next thing you asked him?*
Det. Morgan:	Um, we actually showed him another photograph.
Ms Rogers:	*And what was that photograph of?*
Det. Morgan:	That was of Ms Wheatley's apartment complex.
Ms Rogers:	*Chesapeake Landing?*
Det. Morgan:	Yes.
Ms Rogers:	*And when you showed him that picture, what, if anything, did you ask him or did he say?*
Det. Morgan:	[I] asked him if he had ever been there, and he said no, not that he could recall.
Ms Rogers:	*What was the next thing that he told you?*
Det. Morgan:	He advised that he actually had another family member that lived in Maryland.
Ms Rogers:	*And who...?*
Det. Morgan:	His father lived in Davidsonville, Maryland.
Ms Rogers:	*Where specifically in Davidsonville?*
Det. Morgan:	Riverwood Estates.
Ms Rogers:	*And after he provided that information, what was the next thing you asked him?*
Det. Morgan:	I asked him where he spent his free time.

Ms Rogers: *And what did he say?*

Det. Morgan: He advised that in the late '80s he often went bar-hopping in Rockville or Washington, D.C.

Ms Rogers: *Okay. And what did you do then?*

Det. Morgan: Then I advised him that evidence indicated that his fingerprints were found on an item in Ms Wheatley's apartment.

Ms Rogers: *Okay, did you tell him what the item was?*

Det. Morgan: Yes. That it was on a candle.

Ms Rogers: *And did you tell him where the item was located in the house?*

Det. Morgan: Yes.

Ms Rogers: *Had you informed him, you said earlier you had told him he was a suspect in an assault — at some point in time, did you tell him that the allegation was rape?*

Det. Morgan: No, not at this point in time.

Ms Rogers: *Okay. So you told him his fingerprint had been found in her home on the candle, correct?*

Det. Morgan: Yes.

Ms Rogers: *And what, if anything, did he say? Or did you keep talking?*

Det. Morgan:	He advised that he did not know how his fingerprint could have gotten on the candle.
Ms Rogers:	*Okay. And then what did you tell him?*
Det. Morgan:	Then we again showed him a photograph of the apartment complex where Ms Wheatley lived and he advised that that was a place where he would not have hung out.
Ms Rogers:	*Did he say why that was a place where he wouldn't have hung out?*
Det. Morgan:	Because it looked quote/un-quote, [like a] "Money Place."
Ms Rogers:	*Okay. Then what did you tell him?*
Det. Morgan:	Well, he was actually looking again at Ms Wheatley's photographs, and he advised that he had dated a lot of girls in the past, but he would have remembered if he had dated her.
Ms Rogers:	*He would have remembered?*
Det. Morgan:	Yes.
Ms Rogers:	*And then what happened?*
Det. Morgan:	And I again told him I thought he assaulted Ms Wheatley, and he said that if he had done something to her, he would have remembered it.
Ms Rogers:	*And then what did you ask him, or what did you say to him?*

Det. Morgan:	I explained to him that we also found that his DNA was found on Ms Wheatley's body. And he made a statement to me of, quote, "Oh my God, no way! I'm worse than I thought I was."
Ms Rogers:	*What did he do after he said those words?*
Det. Morgan:	He put his head on the table and began to cry.
Ms Rogers:	*If I could just ask a couple more questions. Detective Morgan, did there come a time when you met with the defendant again?*
Det. Morgan:	Yes.
Ms Rogers:	*And when was that?*
Det. Morgan:	On January 16th of 2009.
Ms Rogers:	*And what was the purpose of meeting with him at that point in time?*
Det. Morgan:	I had a court order that was signed by a judge, and I, actually, it was ordering me to collect his DNA evidence by saliva sample.
Ms Rogers:	*And had you been trained in how to collect DNA evidence by a saliva sample?*
Det. Morgan:	Yes.
Ms Rogers:	*Okay, and tell us exactly how you do that; how you did it.*
Det. Morgan:	After presenting the paperwork to Mr. Trice, I wear gloves, I utilize sterile equipment, and I take swabs.

And I ran it inside the defendant's mouth, put it in another sterile environment in a box, sealed it up, marked it as "Evidence" indicating the date, time, and location where I took it and I turned it in to our lab.

Ms Rogers: *I have no other questions.*

There was at least one comment made by the defendant at the time of his arrest that was not allowed into Detective Morgan's testimony because the judge ruled it prejudicial.

Afternoon Waiting

*T*here were a few more witnesses scheduled for the afternoon and my group went in to listen to the testimony as I sat on the bench outside. I wasn't alone for very much of the time. Dave Cordle came by; Tracy Morgan came over to talk to Dave and gave me a hug. They were discussing parking places and who was parked in whose spot. With so many witnesses scheduled to appear and the House in session, parking was at a premium. I overheard Tracy mentioned she was parked in "Bill's spot" and there was a lengthy discussion of how he was going to react to this when he got back from lunch.

Someone approached Tracy carrying a large foam-core sheet with numbers in columns printed all over it. I thought I saw "Vaginal Swab," "Tampon," and "Defendant" at the top of the sheet. I assumed this was the DNA specialist. I wondered if this was the woman who'd had the baby in August, the one responsible for the first postponement.

Scott came out of the courtroom a couple of times and raced out of the building to move his car. During the course of the trial, he repeated this action every two hours. He must have great parking karma, because he was never gone for more than a few minutes at a time.

Around one o'clock, Art and Hope came out and said goodbye. They wanted to stay for the duration, but had pressing business they couldn't miss back home in Pennsylvania. I hugged them, promising I would let them know when closing arguments were scheduled. They planned to drive back down to be with me when the verdicts were announced. Art was disappointed he couldn't stay longer. Like me, he loved court proceedings, and since this was a case close to his heart, he was even more interested in seeing how the proceedings went.

Afternoon Witnesses
Annette Box — Forensic Chemist
Anne Arundel County Police Crime Lab

1:58pm

Ms Rogers: *I'm going to show you what's been marked as State's Exhibit #21 and ask you if you recognize that?*

Ms Box: Yes.

Ms Rogers: *Ms Box, does this chart fairly and accurately depict the results you were asked to compare in this case?*

Ms Box: Yes.

Ms Rogers: *Ms Box, could you explain to the jury what it shows?*

Ms Box: Sure. The vaginal swabs were tested at Bode Technology along with the tampon. And I took those results and compared it to the swab that I received for William Trice. And here are the sixteen genetic locations I was discussing earlier. This is the sets of genes — one from mom, one from dad. So we can expect to see two numbers at each location. And as you can see as you go down the line — this is genetic location #1. William Trice is a 14-15, the sperm fraction from the tampon is 14-15 and the sperm fraction from the vaginal swabs is also a 14-15. And if you follow down each location, you can compare the types from William Trice, and you can see that they match the types in each of these samples.

Ms Rogers: *Ms Box, based on the results, did you calculate a statistical frequency?*

Ms Box: Yes, I did.

Ms Rogers: *And what is that frequency?*

Ms Box: The frequency for the Caucasian population is one in forty-one quadrillion individuals, and the frequency for the African-American population is one in forty-three quadrillion individuals.

Ms Rogers: *And what exactly does that mean?*

Ms Box: This will tell us the frequency we would expect to see that particular DNA profile pop up in the population. So, basically, the profile that was on the chart for William Trice, which matched the two samples, we will expect to see that particular profile only one time in a population of forty-three or forty-one quadrillion individuals.

Ms Rogers: *Do you have an opinion, Ms Box, to a reasonable degree of scientific certainty, as to the male DNA on Jennifer Wheatley's vaginal swabs and the defendant?*

Ms Box: Yes.

Ms Rogers: *And what is that opinion?*

Ms Box: The source of the DNA from those two samples was from William Trice.

Ms Rogers: *When you say those two samples...*

Ms Box:	The sperm fraction from the vaginal swabs and the sperm fraction from the tampon sample.
Ms Rogers:	*No other questions, your honor.*

Cross-Examination:
2:15pm

Mr. Szekely:	*Ms Box, as you do your testing in this case, part of your comparison was looking at the non-sperm fragments from both the tampon and vaginal swabs in this case.*
Ms Box:	Correct.
Mr. Szekely:	*And in doing that, you relied on the profile worked up by Bode Technology.*
Ms Box:	Yes, that's right.
Mr. Szekely:	*And similarly, in terms of the sperm fragment from the tampon and vaginal swab, you also relied on the work-up done by Bode.*
Ms Box:	Yes, correct.
Mr. Szekely:	*So the, the, I'm using work-up, I'm sorry that's not the right term, but in terms of the PCR process, you only executed that process as to the known sample from Mr. Trice.*
Ms Box:	Yes.
Mr. Szekely:	*And you say that your test looks at sixteen different loci? And each [locus] is sort of like a test site?*

Ms Box:	Correct.
Mr. Szekely:	*Within each cell in each human being, there's hundreds of thousands of these different loci.*
Ms Box:	Yes.
Mr. Szekely:	*Now, I'm going to propose for you a hypothetical. If you had a situation where you looked at the sixteen and sometimes fourteen out of the sixteen match but two definitively don't match. In that case, you can rule out a match in that case.*
Ms Box:	Well, it depends on the sample. If you're talking about a mixture of more than one person, obviously at least two people, it would really depend on why you're not seeing those particular markers. There are certain areas where you can see some degeneration and maybe some markers may have dropped out.
Mr. Szekely:	*But you would lower that, in terms of the statistical analysis you did, it would result in a lower number.*
Ms Box:	Correct. The only time we can actually call a match is when you see all sixteen match up with the evidence between, the evidence and the known standard.
Mr. Szekely:	*Now, the way you reach that statistical conclusion is by, through the use of a database that is assembled by the FBI.*
Ms Box:	Yes.
Mr. Szekely:	*And that is based on, on, ah, DNA sampling and*

statistical sampling throughout the population of the United States.

Ms Box: Yes.

Mr. Szekely: *And there's about, ballpark, 300 million people in the United States, fair to say?*

Ms Box: About 6.5 billion.

Mr. Szekely: *In the world?*

Ms Box: Yes.

Mr. Szekely: *Now, is that database based on the world population or the American population?*

Ms Box: Well, the FBI database is based on just random sampling of [a] certain number of individuals. It's not necessarily, they basically have taken about a hundred or so people for each location, genetic marker, and they have extrapolated out from that statistically what they could expect to see in the population.

Mr. Szekely: *So, just to be clear. You said one hundred people for each test site, does that mean one hundred overall or sixteen hundred overall?*

Ms Box: Well, I am not exactly that familiar with exactly what the FBI did to create this database, and exactly how many people are exactly in there. I would have to look that up.

Mr. Szekely: *But, safe to say it was well under a thousand people.*

Ms Box:	I would think that would be correct. Yes.
Mr. Szekely:	*And from that they could extrapolate to the entire world.*
Ms Box:	Right.
Mr. Szekely:	*No further questions.*
Judge Hackner:	**Ms Rogers?**
Ms Rogers:	*Are you aware or not whether the way the FBI formulated this database and then extrapolated it — is it a scientifically acceptable method of doing that?*
Ms Box:	Oh, yes.
Ms Rogers:	*I have nothing further.*

I found it particularly curious that rather than let the devastating effect of Ms Box's statement — *so basically, the profile that was on the chart for William Trice which matched the two samples, we will expect to see that particular profile only one time in a population of forty-three or forty-one quadrillion individuals* — had on the jury fade, Mr. Szekely felt the need to propose a hypothetical that did nothing less than punctuate the implication of Ms Box's testimony.

DNA Results

Genetic Location	Vaginal Swabs (a and b) Sperm Fraction	Tampon Sperm Fraction	William Trice
D2S1358	14, 15	14, 15	14, 15
THO1	7, 9.3	7, 9.3	7, 9.3
D21S11	28, 32	28, 32	28, 32
D18S51	16, 17	16, 17	16, 17
Penta E	7, 14	7, 14	7, 14
D5S818	11, 11	11, 11	11, 11
D13S317	12, 14	12, 14	12, 14
D7S820	10, 12	10, 12	10, 12
D16S539	11, 13	11, 13	11, 13
CSF1PO	10, 12	10, 12	10, 12
Penta D	N/A	N/A	N/A
Amelogenin	X, Y	X, Y	X, Y
VWA	16, 19	16, 19	16, 19
D8S1179	14, 14	14, 14	14, 14
TPOX	11, 11	11, 11	11, 11
FGA	20, 23	20, 23	20, 23

DNA results presented by Annette Box, Forensic Chemist for the Anne Arundel County Police Crime Lab.

Complications

$\mathcal{A}$round 4:00pm, Cindy came out of the courtroom to tell me that all of the witnesses were finished until Tuesday. Apparently the defense attorney didn't have many questions to ask any of the witnesses. There was a private session with the judge in his chambers scheduled for Friday with Kathleen and Mr. Szekely to discuss some legal stuff. She explained what they would be talking about, but I don't think I understood. Cindy told me the last witness would be called on Tuesday morning since Monday was a holiday.

"We want you here around 9:00am. You may be called back on the stand after our fingerprint expert is finished," she said.

"Okay, no problem."

Before she went downstairs to her office, Kathleen told everyone, "I want to remind all of you not to discuss the case. There has already been an incident reported to the judge. Someone on the defense team overheard some of you talking. Do not talk among yourselves about anything. This could be a big problem if it happens again."

Both Kathleen and Cindy walked to their offices together.

I was really beginning to feel tired. Actually, I was exhausted. The hours of adrenaline that had kept me going well into the night had long ago worn off. I could hardly keep my eyes open. I was sitting on the bench while everyone talked amongst themselves. I figured, if I sat by myself, no one would be tempted to talk about the court proceedings of the day. Scott had been talking with Dave and Marcus was chatting with Sherry and Kathie. I walked to the ladies' room and got a drink. I was ready to drop. When I got back to the bench, I sat with my head in my hand for a second and felt myself dozing off.

I snapped awake when I heard Marcus talking excitedly to someone. I looked up and saw a gentleman walking toward our group. I thought he had just exited the courtroom. Before I knew it, Marcus was introducing me.

"Hey Bill, I'd like you to meet my wife, Jennifer."

I shook my head a bit. *I shouldn't be talking to him if he is a witness,* I thought, remembering Cindy's warning. I was afraid this guy was a witness and I would get in all kinds of trouble if I were seen talking to him. I figured it wouldn't hurt if I just said hello.

"Nice to meet you," I said.

"Bill and I were best friends growing up. He lived down the street from me and came by the house all the time. I can't believe it. I haven't seen him for almost twenty years," Marcus said.

I didn't think Marcus realized this guy might have something to do with the case. He was so excited about seeing his old friend I think he forgot about the case altogether. Before I knew it, Scott and Sherry had joined in the conversation. Apparently Bill Johns had been in their fifth grade class, and all of us had gone to high school together. I hadn't known him; we'd had almost seven hundred and fifty kids in our graduating class. I hung back for a few minutes until Dave Cordle mentioned it was Bill who'd helped him with my case.

"I had given him your file to read over. It was Bill who asked me if the fingerprints had ever been run through AFIS," Dave said.

"No kidding?" I said. I gave Bill a hug and thanked him. I couldn't believe this. Here was yet another crazy connection to this story. What were the chances that the detective who'd helped solve the case had been a childhood friend of my husband? This was crazy!

Marcus, Scott, Sherry, and Bill chatted among themselves for a while. They talked about the usual stuff people talk about when catching up after not seeing each other for so long: "Where do you live?" "What do you do?" "How many kids do you have?" I stood listening to the conversation thinking how odd all of this was. I nodded to a woman who passed by us to go down the stairs. It was getting late and I was sleepy, but I was happy to wait while Marcus visited with his old friend.

My cell phone began to ring. I answered.

"Jennifer, this is Cindy Haworth. Are you still in the courthouse?"

"Yes, Marcus is talking with Bill Johns, so we haven't left yet."

"Kathleen just told me someone from the defense team just walked past your group and heard you discussing the case together. Kathleen is really concerned; she just finished telling you not to talk to anyone. I don't think you realize how serious this is. This person is taking the information to the judge. I have no idea how this might impact the case."

"But they aren't talking about the case at all. It is a completely benign conversation — old friends catching up with each other."

"I realize that. But you have to understand how it looks to other people. You have one person attending the trial and taking notes and now you all are congregating outside the courtroom talking. It doesn't matter what you are saying. It's all how it looks. It's about appearances. You don't know who is watching and how they will interpret what they see."

"Okay, I understand. I'll tell them you called and let them know what happened. But, it really was nothing."

"Okay. It would be best if you don't talk to anyone. I'm not sure what the judge is going to do with this latest development. I hope it doesn't cause any problems."

"Marcus is going back home tonight and then returning next week, so there won't be anyone around for me to talk to."

"Okay. I'll see you Tuesday morning. Have a good weekend."

"Thanks. Bye."

I hung up feeling angry and scared. I was really angry with the woman who had walked past us to go down the stairs. I was sure it was she who ran to Kathleen with what she thought was a juicy tidbit. I couldn't believe two or three words overheard and out of context could cause so much trouble. I was scared the judge was going to throw out the case. I rejoined the group explaining that I'd just gotten into trouble because we were standing around talking. I suggested we leave the courthouse. Marcus, Scott, and Sherry said goodbye to Bill while I started walking down the hall with Kathie. I was really shaken up by all of this. I asked Marcus if he would stay and keep me company that night and head back home in the morning.

We said our goodbyes to Scott and Sherry. They promised to be back on Tuesday for the last witness. Marcus and I walked with Kathie back to her hotel, promising to call her later to meet for dinner. Then we went back to the B&B. I lay down as soon as I got my shoes off and fell instantly asleep.

After several hours of much needed rest, Marcus and I walked back up Main Street and met Kathie at the Maryland Inn. We had dinner at one of the restaurants on West Street. I think we were all feeling worn out from the events of the past couple of days. The two of them had been sitting in on some of the court proceedings and I could tell they wished they could talk about some of what they had heard. I knew Tracy Morgan and a DNA witness had been on the stand, but we couldn't talk about their testimony, so we tried to keep our conversations about general topics and away from the trial.

Marcus talked about how wild it was to have run into Bill Johns and how, of all the detectives in Annapolis, it was he who was involved in my case with Dave. Although I was glad Marcus and Bill had a reunion of sorts, I was still very upset about the huge misunderstanding. I was worried and preoccupied and could not help wondering how the judge was going to react to what had been reported to him. I figured if he was really angry about it, I would hear from Cindy or Kathleen first thing in the morning. It was going to be a long night for me. I wished I could explain to the judge what had really gone on outside his courtroom.

After our dinner together we all walked back to our rooms. Along the way, Marcus and Kathie purchased newspapers while I stood several yards away. I certainly didn't want anyone reporting to the judge that I had read the story on the front page. Although I did wonder what difference it would make; I knew more about the case, the defendant, and his history than most of the reporters did. We said our goodbyes to Kathie as we saw her safely into her hotel. Since there were no witnesses to be called until the following Tuesday, she was heading back home the next morning. I promised to e-mail her with news and developments to keep her in the loop.

An Official Perspective

On January 13, 2010, the case of the State of Maryland vs. William Joseph Trice began. Jennifer's day in court had finally come.

As has been common over my career, I have been excluded from the courtroom during the trial phase of cases I have investigated, including Jennifer's case, except for when giving my own testimony. I may need to be called as a "rebuttal" witness or even as a "rehabilitating" witness. The former disputes a defense witness's testimony. The latter attempts to rebuild the credibility of a state's witness when the defense team has created doubt as to their truthfulness, veracity, and/or reliability in the testimony they have provided. Even though I am excluded from the courtroom after my initial testimony in a trial, I must be constantly available in case I am called to provide additional testimony.

Every day during the trial, Judge Paul Hackner instructed the jury and visitors in the courtroom not to discuss the trial proceedings with anyone. One afternoon during the course of the trial, concerns were raised by the defense attorney about whether or not the group of Jennifer's family members and friends standing outside courtroom 3-D had discussed their observations and opinions about what had happened during the trial and the testimony of witnesses who had already testified.

I had been keeping Jennifer and her entourage company in the hall outside of courtroom 3-D, and was present in the hallway when these alleged discussions took place. Many of us had known each other since grade school or high school. We talked about events that had happened when we were growing up and in our current lives. Speaking as a representative of the law and as a person well-versed in trial procedure, I know that the discussions taking place outside courtroom 3-D that afternoon did not include any discussions about the trial or the testimony given by witnesses. We had complied with Judge Hackner's orders not to discuss the trial.

74

Reunion

Marcus Wolf:

On the morning of January 14th, a group of us went to Chick and Ruth's Delly, a famous Annapolis restaurant, for breakfast and we missed some of the expert witness testimony. Scott and his wife Sherry had come into town from Baltimore and went straight to the trial.

When we arrived at the courthouse, Jennifer had to wait in the hall and several of us were standing around chatting and keeping her company. Scott came out of the courtroom and pulled me aside. He told me he had something very interesting to tell me that Jennifer couldn't hear because she was a sequestered witness in the case.

So we walk out of earshot and Scott told me that he heard in the morning testimony that the investigator working with Chief Investigator Cordle on this case — the guy who actually broke the case — was our old friend Bill Johns. Incredible! I was surprised — pleasantly so. I hadn't seen Bill in about twenty years. I knew that he had been a policeman with the Annapolis Police Department, but who knew he worked for Anne Arundel County as an investigator?

I excitedly said, "Is he here now? Can we go see him?"

Scott was excited, too. He said, "I don't know, let's find out."

Scott and I ran downstairs to the office where Bill works, but he wasn't in. We left a message.

Scott, Bill, and I had been very good friends in school starting in fourth grade. Bill lived right down the road from me, and especially during the summers, I would go over to his house or he would come to mine to hang out. Bill was a great guy to be friends with. He was (and still is) an intelligent, fun-loving, patient person with a generous spirit and a wicked sense of humor. After high school, I moved away, and we lost touch, for the most part. I had been unhappy about that and this looked like a great opportunity to rectify the situation.

After court was over for the day, as we were again standing around chatting, Bill walked up and gave me a big hug. Under any circumstances, I would have been absolutely delighted to reunite with an old friend. And I was. But this was even more special because of the role Bill played in helping to bring William Trice to justice. It was an honor to be able to introduce Bill to Jennifer as a personal friend of mine. And it was great to catch up with him — with Scott there, too. We will certainly be seeing more of him from now on.

Bill Johns:

In 2005, Dave Cordle applied for the grant to reopen cold cases and asked me to help him out with the workload. Although I was excited to be able to work with him on these cases, I was tied up with nine homicides we'd had that year. So, at first, I was not able to do as much from the start as I would have liked. But I did what I could.

It was a bit tough to find cases to work because the Annapolis Police Department's (APD) older cases are not well computerized. During the time we were looking through the evidence of cold cases, the APD was under renovation. The two of us had to search through shipping containers stored in an underground facility for hours in the heat of summer. But we found a few with viable evidence we could send in for testing.

Dave kept me updated, and it was quite exciting when we started getting "hits" back. A "hit" is the term used when a DNA sample matches a profile stored in the national database.

I had heard Jennifer's name mentioned many times as Dave updated me on "the Wheatley case."

In the spring of 2005, we received the cold hit to the Anne Arundel County case. We were left with mixed feelings. It was good to get the match, but we did not have a name to put to a suspect.

As I was able to free up more time in 2008, Dave had me take another look at the files. Although we had been successful in solving some of the cases we pulled in 2005, some remained open. I wanted to re-read through all the cases to see if we had missed anything.

I especially wanted to become more familiar with Jennifer's investigation.

While reading through the file, I noted that latent fingerprints had been recovered in 1988.

It dawned on me that maybe no one had ever submitted them to the fingerprint database.

My part was small, but I was happy to play it.

The day of the trial came, and it appeared that I would not be needed to testify.

I was down in my office working on other cases when Dave came down from the courtroom and casually mentioned that he thought I might know Jennifer's husband — that I may have gone to school with him.

"What's his name?"

"Wolf."

"Marcus?"

I couldn't believe it. I had never known that Jennifer had a different last name other than Wheatley.

I asked if trial was over for the day and Dave said it was, but that Jennifer had been talking in the hallway and might still be there.

So off I went. I was excited about seeing Marcus again after so many years. But on the way up, I also had second thoughts.

What if Jennifer were keeping this incident private? What if Jennifer did not want friends knowing what had happened?

What if my showing up would embarrass Marcus and Jennifer? The prime directive, if you will excuse the Star Trek reference, is to protect the victim. I wondered if I was about to violate that. But when Marcus saw me and broke into a smile, I knew it would be okay.

And then to see Scott and Sherry...I recognized them immediately...was quite a bonus. And then I was introduced to Jennifer.

I am proud to call her a friend now, too.

Marcus, Scott, Sherry, and I have known each other since grade school. We grew apart in later years. I knew Marcus had moved out of state and I did not think I would see him much. I did bump into Marcus once or twice while working as a police officer. But the meetings were always short.

Marcus, Scott, and I spent a lot of time together in elementary school. I spent more time with Marcus after school because I could walk the mile to his house, but Scott lived too far away. Scott was, of course, the creative one. Marcus was very bright with a great sense of humor (still is) and, though I was not nearly as creative as them, I was the one willing to do almost anything to get a laugh. (I still have that reputation!) We would put on skits or short plays which Scott often wrote. I still remember silly little songs that Scott taught us.

In our "Mad Professor" skit, Scott tells me, Igor, to "feed his latest invention." I beg him not to make me, but he sends me off to do it. There are growls and screams from off stage, and pieces of clothing come flying out...including my pants. And then I come sliding out with just a towel wrapped around myself.

The crowd went wild and I loved it.

I was also the one who had the mouth. Though afraid of the bullies, I was not above provoking them with insults.

I took a few punches. But it still seemed like a moral victory knowing that a punch was all they had to offer.

I'm not sure Marcus always agreed with my philosophy, especially when he was with me when I did it.

I wonder if he even remembers.... LOL!

A Tourist in My Own Hometown

January 15 at 12:13pm

Thank you for what you could tell me now, and I'll be waiting to hear the details when you are allowed to discuss them! Wow... SO pleased to hear the spiritual element of your testimony. I — and I see now, so many others — will continue to be praying. Sometimes the most important spiritual part of the battle takes place AFTER what seems to be the big battle! Weird. . . . Stay alert; call for help if you need it! Many, many blessings to you.

Wow, is all I can say.
love,
Susan

$\mathcal{H}$ave you ever been a visitor in your own hometown? By that, I mean have you ever had the opportunity to see the place where you grew up as if through the eyes of an outsider? The long holiday weekend between the trial days afforded me just such an opportunity and I looked forward to it. This was the first time in my life when none of my family actually lived in Annapolis. Although a few of my friends offered their hospitality, I opted to stay at the Flag House Inn right in the historic district.

After Marcus left to return home for the weekend, I headed to Main Street. Although I hoped to meet a few friends later in the afternoon, I had the whole day to myself. I wanted to buy a new pair of shoes and a skirt to wear into the courtroom on Tuesday. I had been warned by Cindy that I may be recalled as a witness, and the only other outfit I had with me was a skirt just like the one I'd worn on Wednesday in a slightly different color. It was fine to wear just walking in and sitting on one of the benches, but not if I had to take the stand again. I didn't want the jury to think I was wearing the same clothes.

I knew there were at least two shoe stores on Main Street, so I figured I'd start my day shopping for shoes and then look for a skirt. It was really amazing to see the store where I got my grammar school uniform saddle shoes still open for business. I walked in and was greeted by a very attentive sales woman. After trying on about a dozen pair of shoes and boots, I finally picked out leather clogs that I could wear with a skirt or pants with dark hose. Yes! Now off to find myself a skirt.

I went into every store on Main Street and nearly all of the shops on Maryland Avenue, and very few of them had any skirts. None of them had something that was appropriate to wear into a courtroom. I realized I was about twenty years too old to be clothes shopping in Annapolis — unless I wanted Irish linen. I was getting discouraged. Maybe I could get a different kind of top to go with the skirt I'd packed and it wouldn't look like I was wearing the same outfit, I reasoned. So, changing tactics, I revisited a few of my favorite stores and checked out their sweaters and tops. I did have some success in finding a couple of pretty tops, but, once I got them back to my room I realized they didn't look so great with the skirt. Crap! They did, however, go with jeans just fine. So I showered and changed, and then headed out to meet my friends.

Even though my hometown had grown larger and had undergone a "face-lift" in some areas, I was pleasantly surprised to learn that in some ways, it was just as I remembered. Andrea, Jackie, and I had planned to meet at McGarvey's after the two of them got off work. I arrived early and walked up to the bar. I was immediately transported back to 1986 when I realized the bartender who greeted me was one I had worked with when I manned the raw bar all those years ago.

Guido handed me my tonic with a slice of lime and asked, "Didn't you used to work here?"

I laughed as I answered, "Yeah, I sure did. Brace yourself — I think it was about twenty-three years ago." We chatted for a few minutes while I waited for my friends to arrive. It was odd in some ways to see Guido still there; a real "time warp." When I worked there, we used to joke, "It must be the weekend because Guido is working." And indeed, it was the weekend. I am sure he had seen many changes over the years, but he chose to stay. Seeing him still bartending brought an air of familiarity to the place I had known all those years ago. In the midst of the numerous changes I was experiencing and craziness of the past few days, I welcomed the feeling of comfort I got from seeing a smile from an old friend.

Saturday, I had the entire day to myself. Marcus wasn't coming back into town until Sunday morning, Andrea was attending a play out of town, and my other friends were working. After checking e-mails and letting everyone know I would have my phone with me if they needed to contact me, I headed out. I stopped for breakfast at a small restaurant and then I walked around town for hours with my camera, taking photos. I wove around through all the side streets, snapping pictures and window shopping. Occasionally, I had to pop into one of the shops to get warm because, in spite of the bright sun, the temperatures were hovering in the low forties. As the sun began to lower in the sky, I found myself on the Eastport Bridge in time to witness an amazing sunset.

I couldn't help thinking about the T-shirt that was dropped in the middle of the span twenty-two years ago, and how now, because of forensic advances and good fortune, the defendant would never see a sky as beautiful as this one again. It was astonishing to me how fingerprints, two tiny fingerprints in the universe, could change the course of so many lives. Before heading back to the B&B, I went to Chick and Ruth's for dinner. I was freezing by then and my nose was running, but I'd had a great day.

Sunday dawned rainy and really cold. Miserable weather. I'd rather have snow. *A perfect day to spend by a roaring fire,* I thought as I got dressed and ready to go out. Marcus was driving in to Annapolis, and we were meeting Andrea for brunch at Galway Bay. I think we might have been the first customers to arrive. We had our choice of seats in the dining room. Andrea had recommended the Irish restaurant for brunch because, "It's wonderful and Rob Levitt plays guitar from 11:00-2:00. You'll love him!" She was right. After we cleared our plates, we moved into the bar and Andrea and Marcus had a cocktail while we discussed what to do for the rest of the day.

"How about seeing a movie?" Andrea asked.

"I can always see a movie," Marcus said.

I got to thinking about the matinees at Colonial Players and asked if the theater had a show that afternoon.

"Yes," Andrea said, "They are doing *A Lion in Winter* and have a matinee at 2:00. If we queue up early, we could probably get tickets." I asked Andrea if anyone I might know was in the play and she started naming the cast. "....and Kevin Wallace is playing the king."

"Kevin Wallace? Where do I know that name?" I wondered.

She ran through a list of plays Kevin had been in and I hadn't seen any of them. Then it came to me. "Is he also an artist?"

"Yeah, he's done set design work for various productions."

"I know him, or at least I think I do. I used to work with Kevin at either Michael's or MJ Designs. He did all the signage for the store, and he was also an actor. It has to be the same guy!" It was settled. We were going to see the play.

I love Colonial Players Theater, and until I walked through the front door, I had forgotten how much. It really had been a long time since I had seen a play there. I noticed a few renovations and expansions had been made to the building's lobby, but the stage remained as I remembered. The theater-in-the-round holds about a hundred people, and with the stage centrally located, every seat is great.

Kevin was wonderful, and I was very happy we'd made the decision to catch the play. I had never seen him act before and found he had the ability to really draw me into the story with his powerful voice and emotional delivery. I didn't want the play to end.

After the ovation, Andrea suggested we hang around for a few minutes to say hello to Kevin. He walked into the lobby after he changed into his street clothes, and she went up and gave him a hug. He was very excited to see her as they had not gotten together for a while.

As they chatted, I stood few feet away while Andrea tried to work an introduction into the conversation. I heard her say something like, "Here is someone you haven't seen for a while," and it seemed like Kevin spied me standing off to the side at the very same time. His face broke into a huge smile as he realized who I was.

"Jen! Oh, my God, it's sooo good to see you!" He gave me a big hug. "What are you doing here? Where have you been? What are you doing with yourself?" He was firing off questions faster than I could answer them.

"Hi, Kevin," I said smiling. "This is my husband, Marcus. We are spending the day with Andrea and she told me you were here. I had to come and see you perform; couldn't miss it. You were great!"

The four of us stood in the lobby catching up on fifteen years of our lives in about a half hour. Kevin had another show later that night and was eager to run out and grab something to eat before it started. We mentioned that we were going to get something to eat and then head to Main Street for karaoke later at 9:00pm.

"Please join us for a drink after your show," I said.

"Yeah, Jen's going to sing tonight!" Andrea added.

After dinner, Marcus and I headed back to the B&B for a nap. Around 8:45, I got a text message on my phone: "I'm here. Meet me for karaoke!"

By the time we made it to the top of Main Street, Andrea had secured a table for us and had put in the first song she wanted to sing. "You have to put your song in before 11:30 because the bar closes at midnight," she told me.

I was nervous. It had been twenty-one years since I'd stood in front of a crowd to sing. And back then, I wasn't alone on stage — my friend Tim King was always playing guitar next to me. Tonight, I would be up there by myself.

"You *are* going to sing tonight?" Andrea's words were more a statement than a question.

"You can put me down for *Angel from Montgomery* and hand the paper in when you take yours up," I told Andrea. I reasoned if I could overcome all kinds of fears and anxiety about facing a rapist in court, this would be easy. What the hell, I'd just done the hardest thing I've ever done in my life — this should be a breeze.

When the DJ called my name, I stood up quickly. Too quickly, I realized. The weight of my jacket knocked my chair over. *Oh, great. Good way to start*, I thought as I took the microphone. But as the music started, the familiar words came easily and my voice was strong.

> *I am an old woman, named after my mother.*
> *My old man is another child who's grown old.*
> *If dreams were lightning, thunder was desire;*
> *this old house would have burned down a long time ago.*
> *Make me an angel who flies from Montgomery...*
> *~ John Prine*

76

January 19, 2010

Cindy had not called me on Friday with news from Judge Hackner concerning the report of our alleged discussion of the case. I was still nervous about it, but reasoned she would have called first thing in the morning if the judge had made the decision to call a mistrial. Since the inn had not received any calls and there were no messages on my cell phone, Marcus and I got dressed and made our way to the courthouse just before 9:00am.

I managed to get through security without incident. Marcus went straight to the courtroom to sit with Scott and Sherry, and I went with Cindy to her office to drop off my coat. The final witness, Mr. Lowman, was late getting to the courthouse, and Cindy was getting nervous. Apparently, she had not been able to reach him on his cell phone and was worried he might have forgotten he was supposed to testify. I opted not to ask her about anything the judge might or might not have decided; she seemed very preoccupied and didn't need any more distractions.

On our way back upstairs to find Kathleen and let her know I had arrived, we saw Mr. Lowman walking in the door to State's Attorney's Office. As we approached, he mentioned he'd had a bit of trouble finding a parking place. He and Cindy chatted about the Caribbean cruise he had just returned from as they walked up the steps to the courtroom together.

I sat down on the bench as they went into the room. I was feeling restless. I really didn't want to be recalled to the stand. I couldn't imagine what Mr. Szekely could possibly have left to try to denigrate my character with. Maybe poor housekeeping habits? Nah, if he pointed out I was such a bad housekeeper, then he would have a hard time explaining why there were only two fingerprints belonging to the defendant in the house. Seemed to me he had covered all the bases pretty well on Wednesday.

Just after I sat down on the bench, a bearded man in a blue and green shirt walked up and sat down at the far end. I nodded to him and said good morning, then looked away. I could feel his eyes still on me and I tried to ignore them. He wasn't carrying a clipboard or notebook, so I figured he wasn't a reporter, and he didn't look like a law student or clerk. I felt he might be a relative of the defendant's; maybe his brother or uncle? Maybe he was a friend? I didn't feel comfortable under his gaze.

"Are you here for the trial?" I asked him.

The man nodded.

"I believe they have started already. You can go in if you want to." I said to him. To my relief, he got up and walked into 3-D. I was alone in the hallway. The courthouse was quiet. *Not too many people walking around today,* I thought. I supposed the other cases being heard had started at 9:00am and everyone was already inside.

I wanted to go into the courtroom, too. I'd spent too much time on this hard bench sitting by myself. I tried to imagine what the defense attorney could possibly come up with for his closing argument. What story was he going to try to weave together to create doubt in the minds of the jury? None that I could think of. For a second during his cross examination, I'd thought he was going to say I knew the defendant from McGarvey's. But that wasn't the case. I didn't know him, and that line of questioning seemed pointless. Was he going to say I knew the creep and let him into the house? That was not going to work for him since there was that pesky photo of those shoe prints on the hood of my car. Those are hard to ignore. It would be difficult for him to fabricate a story that could completely disregard my testimony. And, of course, there was the DNA and the fingerprints that matched the defendant's. Those two pieces of evidence didn't leave me with any doubt — reasonable or unreasonable. And I was pretty sure the jury wouldn't doubt them, either. It would be interesting indeed to hear what the public defender came up with.

77

Last Witness
Ernest Lowman — Latent Print Examiner
Anne Arundel County Police

9:39am

Ms Rogers: *Mr. Lowman, can you describe for us the nature of the work you do?*

Mr. Lowman: Yes. Basically what I do is examine different types of prints that are recovered from different types of crime scenes. And I compare them with known "Ink" prints to determine if those known ink prints are identical to the latent prints that are recovered.

Ms Rogers: *And how long, Mr. Lowman, have you engaged in this type of work?*

Mr. Lowman: Over thirty years.

Ms Rogers: *Mr. Lowman, can you tell the jury what a latent fingerprint is?*

Mr. Lowman: Yes. A latent fingerprint is a reproduction of the friction-ridge detail on your fingers, palms, and soles of your feet. And when those items come in contact with a surface, what you're doing is leaving that outline — that ridge outline — on that surface. And latent means invisible or hidden. So you need to use a fingerprint powder, chemical, or a dye to enhance it to make the print visible.

Ms Rogers: *And, Mr. Lowman, what is a "known" fingerprint?*

Mr. Lowman: A "known" fingerprint is usually on an 8x8 fingerprint card. It's called "known" because it is a deliberate reproduction of the friction ridge using printer's ink. Now we scan them because of new technology. We, you put your hand on a scanner and it scans the print. Well, in my time we always used printer's ink and you rolled "nail-to-nail." And there's a certain block for each finger. It's called "Known" because the person's name, date of birth, usually SSN, address, and description is on that card.

Ms Rogers: *How is it possible for a person to leave what you've described as a latent fingerprint?*

Mr. Lowman: Well, you have pores on your fingers, palms, and the soles of your feet and you're sweating. So when you're touching an item, what you're doing — that's what will adhere to that surface. And that's how you can leave your print. Of course, if you touch your forehead, you get grease and stuff, that makes it more possible to leave your print. And just by touching a surface or picking a piece of paper up, you're leaving your ridge detail on that surface.

Ms Rogers: *Is it possible for a person to touch a surface and not leave a fingerprint?*

Mr. Lowman: Yes, if the surface is not clean, like a window that hasn't been cleaned for a long time. What you're doing is, you are leaving your impression on there, but you are leaving it in the dirt. So all that moisture is absorbing into that dirt. So when you try to use a fingerprint powder to try and lift it, it won't show up.

Ms Rogers: *Are fingerprints and palm prints specific as to each individual person?*

Mr. Lowman: That's correct.

Ms Rogers: *Now, based on your years of training, experience, and analysis, have you ever know two persons with the same fingerprints?*

Mr. Lowman: No.

Ms Rogers: *How many comparisons have you done in your career?*

Mr. Lowman: I do thousands each year.

Ms Rogers: *What is the method you use to do a comparison?*

Mr. Lowman: The ACE-V Method.

Ms Rogers: *Is that the method for analysis that you used in this case?*

Mr. Lowman: Yes.

Ms Rogers: *And can you explain to us what that method is?*

Mr. Lowman: The ACE-V method is the analysis of the print, the comparison, and the evaluation, and the last thing that is done is the verification of the latent print that's found. You have Level 1, Level 2, and Level 3. Level 1 is the ridge flow. The way the ridge is flowing. So these are flowing in and out in front of the papillae and delta, that's what's part of the comparison. Number 2 is the individual ridge detail.

Like short ridges, you can have an island which is one ridge that splits into two and returns to one. You can have bifurcations. That's a ridge that comes up, bifurcates, and these are the points I'm looking at to do my examination. And they are different in everybody's finger. And then the 3rd level is pores and dots. Sometimes you have a little dot or incipient ridge. The ridge is thinner than the ridges between them. So you can find some real thin ridge detail. And the third level is not always present because usually these are a lot lighter so, on a "known" print, if you don't use enough ink, it won't show up. And same with a latent print — if you don't put enough pressure, it won't show up. But if there is enough pressure, those incipient ridges will show up. So Level 3's not always there. And just like a dot, if the dot's real light, if it's barely on your finger, you won't see it unless you have a lot of ink on that known print or on the latent print. If you don't put on enough pressure, they usually won't show up.

Ms Rogers: *Mr. Lowman, in terms of reaching a conclusion, what's the significance of whether there's Level 3 there or not?*

Mr. Lowman: Well, Level 3, you can use Level 2 and Level 3 to make your identification. Level 3 is, to me, it's just a bonus, because lots of times it's not there. But most of your exams are done on Level 2, which is your bifurcations and short ridges and things like that.

Ms Rogers: *Mr. Lowman, I'm going to show you what has been admitted into evidence as State's Exhibit #13 and I'm going to ask you if you recognize that?*

Mr. Lowman: Yes, I have.

Ms Rogers: *And can you tell us what that is?*

Mr. Lowman: This is a latent print. A latent print on a latent print lift card.

Ms Rogers: *And when did that come into your possession?*

Mr. Lowman: I believe, check my notes, 7-14-08.

Ms Rogers: *And did you have occasion to examine that latent print?*

Mr. Lowman: Yes.

Ms Rogers: *Can you describe for us, with regard to that examination, what you were able to determine?*

Mr. Lowman: Yes. Basically, what happened was — I was given this by Dave Cordle and he asked me to put it into our AFIS system.

Ms Rogers: *Mr. Lowman, if you could just tell us specifically what you did with regard to the print.*

Mr. Lowman: Oh, I looked at the print, made sure there's enough significant ridge detail to do an examination. And then I entered the print into the...

Ms Rogers: *Okay. Did you determine that there was enough to do the examination?*

Mr. Lowman: Yes.

Ms Rogers: *I'm going to show you now what's been marked as*

State's Exhibit #22, and do you recognize that?

Mr. Lowman: Yes.

Ms Rogers: *And what is that?*

Mr. Lowman: These are the "known" prints of William Joseph Trice that I took.

Ms Rogers: *Okay. Do you see the person in the courtroom who you obtained those prints from?*

Mr. Lowman: Yes.

Ms Rogers: *And where is he?*

Mr. Lowman: In the middle of the defense table.

Judge Hackner: **He has indicated the defendant for the record.**

Ms Rogers: *And when you say you took those prints, tell us what procedure you used to obtain those print.*

Mr. Lowman: Well, basically, I came to court and I brought my fingerprint kit.

Ms Rogers: *And did you meet with the defendant?*

Mr. Lowman: I met with the defendant in this courtroom. And I took his prints in this courtroom.

Ms Rogers: *Okay. And once you had obtained the defendant's prints and you also had the latent print, did you conduct a comparison between those two items?*

Mr. Lowman: Yes, I did.

Ms Rogers: *And tell us about the comparison.*

Mr. Lowman: Okay. There were two prints of value that I could do a comparison on. And once I did my examination it was determined that two of the prints were identified to be Mr. Trice's prints. It was the rolled left middle finger and his rolled left little finger.

Ms Rogers: *Those two rolled fingers were found to be consistent...*

Mr. Lowman: Matched.

Ms Rogers: *...matched the known rolled that you had physically done yourself of the defendant. Is that correct?*

Mr. Lowman: That's correct.

Ms Rogers: *Okay. And did you come to that conclusion to a reasonable degree of scientific certainty?*

Mr. Lowman: Yes.

Ms Rogers: *Mr. Lowman, as part of the ACE-V procedure methodology that you used in this case, that you indicated that the last step of that is the "Verification" procedure. Is that correct?*

Mr. Lowman: That's correct.

Ms Rogers: *And, um, is part of your opinion based, or is your opinion based on the entire procedure that you used in this case — the entire ACE-V?*

Mr. Lowman: Yes.

Ms Rogers: *And did you, in fact, use the verification procedure?*

Mr. Lowman: Yes.

Ms Rogers: *And were your results verified by another person?*

Mr. Lowman: Yes, it was.

Ms Rogers: *No other questions.*

Cross Examination
9:55am

Mr. Szekely: *Mr. Lowman, you stated that certain surfaces, well, are certain surfaces better than others for recovering a print?*

Mr. Lowman: Yes.

Mr. Szekely: *Particularly smooth surfaces are ideal?*

Mr. Lowman: Yes.

Mr. Szekely: *And you also stated that pressure makes a difference.*

Mr. Lowman: Yes, it does.

Mr. Szekely: *So, if someone were to be obviously leaning on something like I'm leaning on the table right now, I'm more likely to leave a usable latent print behind than if I simply, sort of graze the table with my fingers?*

Mr. Lowman: Yes.

Mr. Szekely: *Court's indulgence.*

Mr. Szekely: *No further questions.*

Judge Hackner: **Ms Rogers?**

Ms Rogers: *No further questions. And with that, your honor, the State would rest.*

Judge Hackner: **Mr. Lowman, please be sure somebody has the exhibits so that you don't take them with you. You are excused.**

Mr. Lowman: Almost took 'em.

78

"State Rests"

Cindy came back out to the bench and sat with me when Mr. Lowman had finished testifying and said, "It was close there for a while, but you don't have to go back on."

"That's good," I said. "I couldn't imagine what else he would want to ask me. When do closing arguments start?"

"Soon, in just a few minutes. The judge has some paperwork he's getting together for the jury."

I sent a text message to Jackie and Andrea telling them that closing arguments were supposed to be starting very soon. I called Marnie.

"They're getting ready to do their closing now. Where are you?"

"I'm at my gynecologist's! I keep telling him to hurry because I have someplace important I have to be!" She laughed.

"Okay, well, get here when you can. I'm turning off my phone and heading in now, so you won't be able to reach me. We're in the same courtroom — 3-D."

"Okay, Jen, see you soon!" I heard her yell to her doctor. "Will you please hurry," as I hung up my phone.

Mr. Lowman walked out of the courtroom and said goodbye to Cindy. As they were speaking to each other, I noticed the man in the blue and green shirt walk past us heading toward the exit. His shirt reminded me of my flannel shirt that had been taken into evidence. I wondered again who the man was as I watched him walk out. Odd, he wasn't staying around for the closing arguments.

"Can I go in and listen now?" I asked Cindy after Mr. Lowman left.

"Yes. You can sit in the front, if you want to. It's customary for the victim to sit in the front row of the benches. But if you don't feel comfortable doing that, you can sit wherever you want to."

I did want to sit right in the front. I walked in and sat down with Marcus in the first row. Tracy Morgan sat to my left.

Jennifer Wheatley
After being shown two photographs of the victim taken in 1988, the suspect was asked if he knew the then twenty-nine-year-old smiling in the pictures. He replied, "I've dated a lot of girls and if I went out with her, I'd remember." Later, during the interrogation, he said, "If I had done something to her, I would remember."

**Chesapeake Landing Gate,
Entry Phone, and Directory**
Crime Scene Photograph
August 21, 1988

Phone the defendant used to make the calls to the victim. The directory listed all occupants preceded by a two-digit number. The number was not the house number, but instead a code that would dial the phone of a particular resident. To contact a resident, the caller had to know the last name of the person being called. Believing the two digit number was a house number, William Joseph Trice picked up the phone and dialed "10," expecting to be connected to his intended victim. He was not. He then proceed to the victim's car to learn her identity.

Carport
Crime Scene Photograph
August 21, 1988

After making several phone calls to his victim, Trice made his way into the house by hoisting himself onto the victim's car and entering through the sliding glass door on the second floor balcony.

Interior of the Victim's Car
Crime Scene Photograph
August 21, 1988

Trice was able to learn the identity of his intended victim from the Department of Motor Vehicles forms on the front seat of her car.

Hood of the Victim's Car
Crime Scene Photographs
August 21, 1988

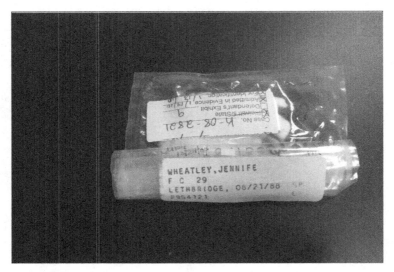

Tampon
Evidence Collected by Dr. Lethbridge
August 21, 1988

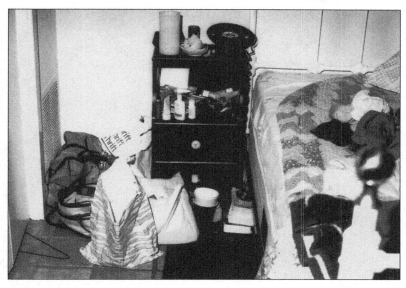

Victim's Bedroom

Crime Scene Photograph, August 21, 1988

"I went into the bathroom and brushed my teeth. I came back out of the bathroom, and when I walked toward my bedroom door, I noticed the light was off. The overhead light was off...I didn't remember turning it off. I hesitated, just for a second and then....And then, when I took that first step into the room, I was grabbed from the right-hand side. And this person was saying to me, "Why did you hang up on me? I told you if you hang up on me I'm going to kill you!"

— Jennifer Wheatley's testimony, January 13, 2010

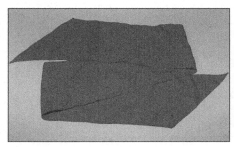

Red Scarf

Collected on August 21, 1988
by Evidence Technician Mary Pat Whiteley

Woven Belt

Collected on August 21, 1988
by Evidence Technician Mary Pat Whiteley

"Red scarf & brown belt found on bottom bed rail. They were intertwined."

— Ms Whiteley's testimony, January 14, 2010

Evidence Bag — Candles
Crime Scene Photographs, August 21, 1988
Evidence bag containing 2 candles.

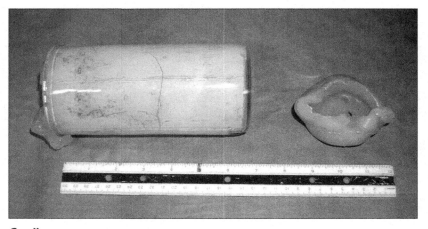

Candles
Crime Scene Photographs, August 21, 1988
The defendant's fingerprints were found on the large candle (left).

Fingerprint Evidence Collected at Crime Scene
August 21, 1988

Photograph of the actual finger-prints lifted from the candle in the victim's bedroom. The prints were positively identified in 2008 as the middle and pinky fingers of the left hand of William Joseph Trice.

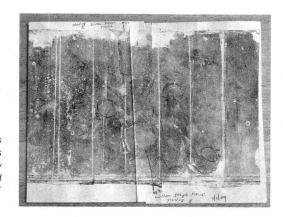

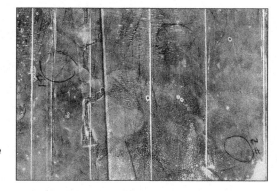

Detail of Fingerprint Evidence Collected at Crime Scene
August 21, 1988

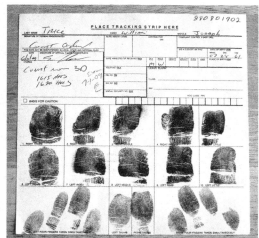

"Known" Fingerprints of William Joseph Trice

**William Joseph Trice Arrest Photograph
November 21, 2008**

I looked at him sitting at the defense table and I wondered, does the face you are born with determine your fate? Or, does the life you lead imprint onto you? Do lines etch and features reposition until you look the part of the role you have chosen for yourself?

— Jennifer Wheatley-Wolf

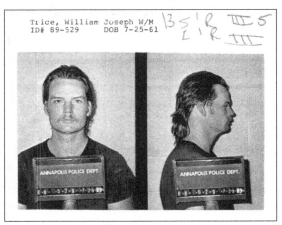

**William Joseph Trice Arrest Photograph
July 23, 1989**

Trice was arrested on a Peeping Tom charge. The girls saw him outside and called police.

— Chief Investigator David Cordle

Investigator William Johns

Tracy Frye Morgan
Sergeant in charge of Sex Offense Unit
and Sex Offender Unit
Anne Arundel County Police
Annapolis, Maryland

Assistant State's Attorney Kathleen E. Rogers (left) and
Victim Witness Specialist Cindy Martin Haworth

**Anne Arundel County State's Attorney
Chief Investigator David H. Cordle, Sr.**

Jennifer Wheatley-Wolf and David H. Cordle, Sr., 2010

79

Petition for Judgment of Acquittal

9:59am

(Jury is not present.)

Mr. Szekely: Your honor, I would at this time make a motion of judgment of acquittal, um, on behalf of, um, I think the State wants, before I did...Your honor, I would enter Nolle Prosequi* to the counts charging assault and assault and battery. I believe it's counts 6 and 7.

Judge Hackner: **Alright, hold on, just...okay, count 6 — assault and battery, and count 7 — assault will be *Nolle Prosequi*.**

Mr. Szekely: And on behalf of Mr. Trice, I would reassert his right to a speedy trial as to those counts.

Judge Hackner: **Okay, very good. Thank you.**

Judge Hackner: **Alright. Thank You. Ms Rogers?**

Ms Rogers: *Your honor, I believe in a light most favorable to the State that [the] testimony of Jennifer Wheatley*

---

*Nolle Prosequi is a legal term that means "we shall no longer prosecute." Under Nolle Prosequi, a declaration is made by the prosecutor in a criminal case or by the plaintiff in a civil lawsuit either before or during trial, to indicate that the case against the defendant is being dropped. The declaration may be made because the charges cannot be proved, the evidence has demonstrated either innocence or a fatal flaw in the prosecution's claim, or the prosecutor no longer thinks the accused is guilty. (USLegal.com)

supports the 2nd degree rape, 1st degree rape, and 2nd degree sex offense, and 1st degree sex offense. With regard to the burglary, the evidence of breaking is the fact that the defendant is in the house at all — it's certainly circumstantial evidence. I don't know if the court has seen the pictures that are in evidence? The defendant was in the victim's car, his shoe prints are on the hood of her car, which is right directly below the door that had been left open to her home. So, based on the circumstantial evidence, it's clear that the defendant did break into the home. He certainly didn't have permission. And I think the State has met its burden on that count.

Mr. Szekely: If I can respond just briefly, your honor. In terms of Mr. Trice being in the car, there's no evidence that Mr. Trice was in the car. Um, in terms of it, there being shoe prints on the car, there are somebody's shoe prints. There hasn't been, and Ms Whiteley was clear that they were not of any identifiable use. And again, there [were] two people in the house and there was not testimony from one of the people in the house, that Mr. Trice had broken into the house, he was not let in. So I think even taken in the light most favorable to the State, there's not enough evidence to submit the charge of burglary to the jury. As to the other ones, I would just submit on my previous argument.

Judge Hackner: **Alright. Well, with respect to the burglary charge, there isn't any specific evidence about the shoe prints belonging to Mr. Trice. But there is evidence that the document[s] that were inside of the car were then later** produced inside the house after the rape. And certainly reasonable inference could be that somebody went into the car. But that's sort of a side issue.

I think there's plenty of evidence from which the jury could conclude that the defendant entered the dwelling house of another at night by moving an opening. Either the cracked door or the slider or some other means. At 2:30 in the morning, the inference is that the place was secured, but for that opened door that the victim's mother had left. And that the entry would have been by the movement of a door or a window. And that it was without authorization. And that would be, with the other elements, would be sufficient for a burglary finding.

And the court finds that there is in a light most favorable to the State, sufficient evidence to submit the 1st degree rape, 2nd degree rape, 1st degree sexual offense, and 2nd degree sexual offense to the jury. Each of the elements of those offenses has been borne out at least by some evidence that they could conclude they find believable and would support a verdict in those counts. So the motion for judgment of acquittal will be denied. Would you like to advise your client?

Mr. Szekely: I would. Mr. Trice, could you stand up? Mr. Trice, the State has, or I guess will when the jury comes back, and the court will rest and it will be the defense case. You and I have discussed this matter as to whether you would like to testify, I believe, on a number of occasions. And you have an absolute right to testify in this case and you may get on the stand and, ah, testify.

And then the State would then be able to cross-examine you. I don't believe, and Ms Rogers can correct me if I'm wrong, no convictions of the appropriate age or nature to impeach while, Mr. Trice, is that right?

Ms Rogers: *I believe that is correct.*

Mr. Szekely: So in terms of any prior record you may have, the State would not be able to introduce that. However, they could introduce any testimony in a prior proceeding in this matter to impeach you, and I believe there was a recorded telephone call along the way that they could also use to impeach you, if they so chose.

However, you could, of course, tell your version of events. If you don't wish to testify, you don't have to and you have an absolute right to remain silent. We don't have to. The burden is on the State. We don't have to put forward any evidence in this case. If you choose not to testify, Judge Hackner will instruct the jury that you have the right not to testify and they may not even take that into consideration or mention it during their deliberations. In other words, they can't say, "Well, Mr. Trice didn't testify. He must be guilty." They are going to be instructed specifically they can't discuss this matter at all. Based on our last conversation when [we] arrived at this matter, you indicated to me that you did not wish to testify. Is that still your wish?

Mr. Trice: *That's correct.*

Judge Hackner: **Alright. Now if you change your mind between now and the time the jury comes back, I'm going to ask your** attorney, on the record, is he intending to produce any evidence? If he calls you to the stand and you come to the stand, I'm assuming you waive your right to remain silent. And if he says, "No further evidence," or, "No evidence," then I assume that you're exercising your right to remain silent. Okay?

Mr. Trice: *Yes, sir.*

Judge Hackner: Okay, very good. Thanks. You can have a seat. And do you intend to call any other evidence? Any other witnesses?

Mr. Szekely: No, your honor. Maybe right after Ms Rogers rests on the record, I'd rest on the record.

Judge Hackner: I need to take a few minutes to go over the verdict sheet and jury instructions. Would this be a good occasion for me to do that, and then would you be prepared to have me instruct right after that?

Ms Rogers: *Yes, your honor.*

Mr. Szekely: Yes, and we can move right into closings right after the instructions.

Judge Hackner: Alright. Then let me go ahead and recess another few minutes and then I'll...

Mr. Szekely: Is the court going to take care of Mr. Terrace's plea in the interim, or, just so I know how long the recess is going to be?

Judge Hackner: Um, that's a good question. Maybe I should do that. Can you see if you can drum up Mr. Case in this?

Mr. Szekely: Yes.

Judge Hackner: **Okay, I'll do that.**

Bailiff: *All rise.*

80

Brief Recess

$\mathcal{A}$s soon as I got into the courtroom, Judge Hackner called a recess. The judge had to go to another courtroom to do some other legal stuff with another case, and then he had to get papers together for the jury instruction. So I went back out into the hall again.

My group hung around outside the courtroom trying not to talk about the case. There were lots of conversations going on, but I wasn't following them. I was feeling anxious about being in the courtroom with the creep and Marcus at the same time. I knew Marcus had heard details of the rape during the opening statements, and I was pretty sure he was going to hear even more this time. However, I wasn't sure how he would react. I remembered something Marcus had said to my brother-in-law at dinner on Monday night when he had asked, "If Jennifer said it was okay for you to be in the courtroom when she testified, would you have been in there?"

Marcus' response actually made me cry, although I'm not sure if he knew that.

"No. I wouldn't want her worrying about my reactions to what she was saying. She had an important job to do and she didn't need me distracting her while she did it."

I was glad Marcus would be sitting next to me on the bench. I wanted the defendant to know I had a whole world outside the courtroom that did not include him. I have a husband who, even though he had known of all of this for only a little over a year, was happy to sit with me to see this through to the end. And I had my friends who would be sitting on the benches with me.

I also thought about how sad I was that neither of my sisters was going to be here. Mollie had left for a long weekend in Ireland with some friends the day after I testified. Although she was on her way back home, her plane wasn't scheduled to land in New York until early afternoon. No way she could get here in time. And my sister Deborah was stuck at home waiting for some repairmen who had arranged to show up to fix the furnace, "sometime between noon and 4:00." I really wished they were with me to see this for themselves. Debbie had been following the story through my e-mails and the online newspaper articles, but as far as I knew, Mollie was out of the loop. I had promised to call both of them as soon as the verdicts were announced.

What I was really looking forward to the most was finally being able to discuss the case. Too many days had passed since I'd testified and I really needed to talk about the whole experience. Once the judge gave the case to the jury, we would be free to talk about everything and anything. I wasn't the only one looking forward to being able to share details. Scott and Sherry had listened to all the testimony and I was eager to hear their take on what the witnesses had said and what questions the defense lawyer had asked them. All of us were eager to discuss what had happened that night and compare it to the testimony and evidence presented in court.

With all these thoughts swirling around in my head, I couldn't help but wonder what must be going through the defendant's mind. I wondered what his lawyer had told him. Did Mr. Szekely actually believe he was going to get his client cleared of these charges? Had he told the defendant as much? Had he given the defendant false hope? And, even if the impossible were to happen and he actually did win this case, there was still another victim and another court date awaiting him.

But the defendant *had* gotten away with his crimes for all these years, and I felt he thought this was a testament to how good he was at what he did. The very fact that he was free to wreak havoc in the lives of women for the past twenty-plus years had undoubtedly bolstered his ego. I honestly believed he thought, *No way am I going to be brought down by this woman. How dare she?*

But he didn't know me. He had no idea that all those years ago, I knew he had to be stopped and I had decided I was going to have something to do with making that happen. He chose the wrong woman when he chose me as his victim. He didn't realize that night that I was paying attention, and although I couldn't tell the detectives much about the person who had raped me, it turned out that what I did provide was just enough evidence to figure out who he was; enough to convict. Although there was an unforeseen twenty-year wait for science and technology to catch up in order to make the evidence useful, I knew, once my attacker was arrested, I would be there in the courtroom to witness the end of his reign of terror. It was time for him to realize how life, as he had come to know it, was about to change drastically.

Finally, it was time to go back inside. Marcus and I sat side by side on the front bench holding hands. I checked twice to make sure I had turned my cell phone off. Imagine how that would look if I got a call in the middle of the judge's instructions to the jury or during closing arguments!

The jury filed in and took their seats. Many of them noticed me sitting on the bench and made eye contact with me as they waited for the proceedings to start. This time, I didn't look away. I didn't think meeting their glances was going to influence them one way or another. There was no more testimony to be heard; they had the facts and soon they would be deliberating.

The door to the left of the judge's bench opened and the defendant entered. He was dressed in a suit. He walked slowly, closely and deliberately, down the entire length of the jury box. His eyes were locked on mine the entire time. I could only assume this was a display suggested by his lawyer in an effort to sway the opinions of the jury members. But like his bad hair dye job, I doubted it would have much chance of working.

I watched him take each step closer and closer, and I thought it was fortunate for him the jury could not see how his attempted expression — of shame? remorse? sorrow? — did not touch his icy-cold eyes. They were filled with what I can only call smug sarcasm. It struck me that he was going through this display at his lawyers' request only. His eyes told me he believed this was an exercise he didn't feel was necessary. Playing the role of someone filled with remorse or sorrow for his behavior didn't fit him. The defendant looked uncomfortable trying to adopt an emotion that was so foreign to him. Although I couldn't hear from where I was sitting, I could see his mouth moving the whole time he walked. It looked as though he were talking to himself. Maybe he was reminding himself to walk slowly and be sure to look like a victim.

As he got close to the end of the jury box, his expression changed to reveal his true feelings. He was looking directly into my eyes when the veil fell away. I felt a chill run through me and I shivered, but I did not look away. I wanted him to see in my face how, even though years ago he had left me broken and scared, I was not that terrified girl. I wanted him to realize his days of victimizing were over, and I wanted him to remember the face of the woman who was finally able to stop him. He turned his eyes away from me when he reached the end of the jury box and then turned toward the defense table. I watched as the policemen unshackled his hands and ankles. He chatted animatedly with them the entire time.

81

Instructions to the Jury

10:44am
(Case is recalled)

Ms Rogers: *Kathleen Rogers representing the State.*

Mr. Szekely: *Andrew Szekely representing Mr. Trice, who is present to my right.*

Ms Waters: *And Gwendolyn Waters, on behalf of Mr. Trice.*

Mr. Trice: Forgive me, your honor.

I heard the defendant say this to the judge and thought, *You are asking forgiveness of the wrong person.* It wasn't toward the judge he should be directing *that* statement.

Judge Hackner: **Please have a seat.**

Judge Hackner: **Ms Rogers, does the State wish to present any additional evidence?**

Ms Rogers: *No, you honor. At this time, the State would rest.*

Judge Hackner: **And the court having ruled on the issues at the bench previously, does the defense wish to present any evidence?**

Mr. Szekely: *Your honor, the defense would rest. But may we approach briefly?*

Judge Hackner: **Yes.**

(White noise.)

Judge Hackner: Okay, ladies and gentlemen. I'm going to do a little talking now, and then the attorneys are going to make their closing arguments. I'm going to ask Ms Vanderhook if, when the jury goes to deliberate, would you speak up on behalf of the jury as a foreperson? Ms Vanderhook?"

Ms Vanderhook: *Okee-dokee.*

Judge Hackner: **Yeah?**

Ms Vanderhook: *Sure.*

Judge Hackner: **There's no extra pay or anything like that. But, if you don't mind, I usually just pick whoever is the first seat. So if you will be the foreperson of the jury for us, we would appreciate that.**

Judge Hackner then began to give his instructions to the jury.

Judge Hackner:

Now the time has come for me to explain to you the law that applies to this case and I ask for your forgiveness in advance because I'm going to be reading most of this to be sure I am reciting the jury instructions to you accurately. You're going to get the written jury instructions, just as I read them to you. So you don't have to write down everything I say. Listen and certainly make notes if you feel it's appropriate, but you're going to have — once you get into the jury room — I'm going to have these things printed up for you, so you can have them for your convenience. You'll notice there are titles and numbers — don't worry about that. I cut and pasted them from another source. There will be seven pages, but they will not be sequential. Just ignore that.

The instructions I give you about the law are binding upon you. In other words, you must apply the law as I explain it to you in arriving at your verdict. On the other hand, any comments I make to you other than the law are not binding upon you and are advisory only.

It is your duty to decide the facts and apply the law to those facts. The verdict must be the considered judgment of each of you. In order for you to reach a verdict, all of you must agree. Your verdict must be unanimous. You must consult with one another and deliberate in a view to reaching an agreement and do so without violence to your individual judgment. Each of you must decide the case for yourself, but do so only after an impartial consideration of the evidence with your fellow jurors.

During deliberations, do not hesitate to reexamine your own views. You can change your opinion if convinced you are wrong. But do not surrender your honest belief as to the weight or effect of the evidence only because [of] the opinion of your fellow jurors. Or, for the mere purpose of reaching a verdict.

The defendant is presumed to be innocent of the charges and this presumption remains with the defendant throughout every stage of the trial and is not overcome unless you are convinced beyond a reasonable doubt that the defendant is guilty. The State has the burden of proving guilt of the defendant beyond a reasonable doubt. This burden remains on the State throughout the trial. The defendant is not required to prove his innocence. However, the State is not required to prove guilt beyond all possible doubt or to a mathematical certainty. Nor is the State required to negate every conceivable circumstance of innocence.

A "reasonable doubt" is a doubt founded upon reason. "Proof beyond a reasonable doubt" requires such proof as would convince you of the truth of a fact to the extent that you would be willing to act upon such belief without reservation in an important matter in your own business or personal affairs. However, if you are not satisfied as to the defendant's guilt to that extent, then reasonable doubt exists and the defendant must be found "Not Guilty."

Your verdict must represent the considered judgment of each juror and must be unanimous. In other words, all twelve jurors must agree. You must consider and decide this case fairly and impartially. You are to perform this duty without bias or prejudice as to any party. You should not be swayed by sympathy, prejudice, or public opinion. In making your decision, you must consider the evidence in this case. That is the testimony from the witness stand, physical evidence or exhibits admitted into evidence, and stipulations. In evaluating the evidence, you should consider it in the light of your own experiences. You may draw any reasonable inferences or conclusions from the evidence that you believe to be justified by common sense or your own experiences.

The following things are not evidence and you should not give them any weight or consideration: the charging document, any inadmissible or stricken evidence, or the questions and objections of the counsel. The charging document in this case is a formal method of accusing the defendant of a crime and it is not evidence against the defendant and must not create any inference of guilt. Inadmissible or stricken evidence must not be considered or used by you. You must disregard questions that I did not permit the witness to answer. And you must not speculate as to the possible answers. After I have ruled that an answer must be stricken, you must disregard both the question and the answer in your deliberations.

During the trial, if I have commented on the evidence or asked a question of the witness, you should not draw any inferences or conclusions from my comments or questions, either as to the merits of the case or as [to] my views regarding the witness.

The opening statements and closing arguments of lawyers are not evidence in this case. They are intended only to help you understand the evidence and to apply the law. Therefore, if your memory of the evidence differs from anything the lawyers or I may say, you must rely on your own memory of the evidence.

The physical evidence in this case will be available for you to look at in the jury room during deliberations. You are asked not to open the sealed envelopes that contain biological evidence. The other matters, the documents and photographs, you are welcome to look at, if you wish.

There are two types of evidence: direct and circumstantial. And the law makes no distinction as to the weight to be given to either direct or circumstantial evidence. No greater degree of certainty is required of circumstantial evidence than of direct evidence. In reaching a verdict, you should weigh all of the evidence presented, whether direct or circumstantial. And you may not convict the defendant unless you find that the evidence, when considered as a whole, establishes guilt beyond a reasonable doubt. The State and defense have entered into stipulation as to some of the evidence. That evidence is not in dispute and should be considered proven.

The defendant is charged with 1st degree rape, 2nd degree rape, 1st degree sexual offense, 2nd degree sexual offense, and burglary. You must consider each charge separately and return a separate verdict as to each charge. And you will be given a verdict sheet, which I will discuss with you in a few minutes, to explain to you the process that you might choose to go through that analysis. You are the sole judge as to whether a witness should be believed. In making this decision, you may apply your own common sense and everyday experiences.

In determining whether a witness should be believed, you should carefully judge all the testimony and evidence, and the circumstances under which the witness testified. You should consider such factors as the witness's behavior on the stand and the manner of testifying. Did the witness appear to be telling the truth? Did the witness [have] opportunity to see or hear the things about which testimony was given, the accuracy of the witness' memory? Does the witness have a motive not to tell the truth? Does the witness have an interest in the outcome of the case? Was the witness' testimony consistent? Was the witness' testimony supported or contradicted by evidence that you believe? And whether, and the extent to which, the witness' testimony in court differed from statements made by the witness on any previous occasion. You need not believe any witness even if the testimony is uncontradicted. You may believe all, part, or none of the testimony of any witness.

An expert is a witness who has special training or experience in a given field, and you should give expert testimony the weight and value you believe it should have. You are not required to accept any expert witness' opinion. You should consider an expert's opinion together with all of the other evidence. In weighing the opinion of an expert, you should consider the expert's experience, training, and skills, as well as the expert's knowledge of the subject matter about which the expert is expressing an opinion.

The weight of the evidence does not depend on the number of witnesses on either side. You may find that the testimony of a smaller number of witnesses for one side is more believable than the testimony of a greater number of witnesses for the other side.

The defendant has an absolute constitutional right not to testify. The fact that the defendant did not testify must not be held against the defendant. It must not be considered by you in any way or even discussed by you. Evidence has been introduced that the defendant made a statement to the police about the crime charged. The State must prove beyond a reasonable doubt that the statement was freely and voluntarily made. A voluntary statement is one that under all the circumstances was given freely. To be voluntarily, it must not have been compelled or obtained as a result of any force, promises, threats, inducements, or offers of reward. In deciding whether a statement was voluntary, consider all the circumstances surrounding the statement, including the conversations, if any, between the police and the defendant, whether the defendant was warned of his rights, the length of time the defendant was questioned, who was present, the mental and physical condition of the defendant, whether the defendant was subject to force or threat, or forced by the police, the age, background, experience, education, intelligence, and character of the defendant. Or any other circumstances surrounding the taking of the statement.

If you find beyond a reasonable doubt that the statement was voluntary, give it such weight as you believe it deserves. If you do not find beyond a reasonable doubt that the statement was voluntarily, you must disregard it.

The defendant is charged with the crime of 2nd degree rape. "Rape" is unlawful vaginal intercourse with a female by force or threat of force and without her consent. In order to convict the defendant of 2nd degree rape, the State must prove that the defendant had vaginal intercourse with Jennifer Wheatley, that the act was committed by force or threat of force, and that the act was committed without the consent of Jennifer Wheatley.

"Vaginal intercourse" means the penetration of the penis into the vagina. The slightest penetration is sufficient and emission of semen is not required. The amount of force necessary depends on the circumstances. No particular amount of force is required, but it must be sufficient to overcome resistance or the will to resist. You must be satisfied that Jennifer Wheatley resisted and that her resistance was overcome by force or threat of force. Or that her will to resist was overcome by the defendant's actions under the circumstances. If Jennifer Wheatley submitted to sexual intercourse, and if you find that her submission was induced by force or by threats that put her in reasonable fear of bodily harm, then her submission was without consent. Her fear was reasonable if you find that under the circumstances a reasonable woman would fear for her safety. "Consent" means actually agreeing to the act of intercourse rather than merely submitting as a result of force or threat of force.

The defendant is also charged with the crime of 1st degree rape. In order to convict the defendant, the State must prove all the forcible elements of 2nd degree rape, and must also prove one or more of the following circumstances:

1. That the defendant inflicted suffocation, strangulation, disfigurement, or serious physical injury against Jennifer Wheatley in the course of committing the offense, or

2. That the defendant threatened or placed Jennifer Wheatley in reasonable fear that she would be imminently subjected to death, suffocation, strangulation, disfigurement, serious physical injury, or kidnapping, or

3. That the defendant committed the offense in connection with a burglary. And the definition of burglary will be provided later in these instructions.

The defendant is charged with the crime of 2nd degree sexual offense. In order to convict the defendant of 2nd degree sexual offense, the State must prove:

1. That the defendant committed fellatio with Jennifer Wheatley.
2. That the act was committed by force or threat of force.
3. That the act was committed without the consent of Jennifer Wheatley.

"Fellatio" means that the defendant caused Jennifer Wheatley to apply her mouth to the defendant's penis. The amount of force necessary depends on the circumstances. No particular amount of force is required, but it must be sufficient to overcome resistance or the will to resist. You must be satisfied that Jennifer Wheatley resisted and that her resistance was overcome by force or threat of force, or that her will to resist was overcome by the defendant's actions under the circumstances. If Jennifer Wheatley submitted to fellatio, and if you find that her submission was induced by force or by threats that put her in reasonable fear of bodily harm, then her submission was without consent. Her fear was reasonable if you find that, under the circumstances, a reasonable woman would fear for her safety. "Consent" means actually agreeing to the act of fellatio rather than merely submitting as a result of force or threat of force.

The defendant is also charged with the crime of 1st degree sexual offense. In order to convict the defendant, the State must prove all the forcible elements of 2nd degree sexual offense and must also prove one or both of the following circumstances:

1. That the defendant inflicted suffocation, strangulation, disfigurement, or serious physical injury against Jennifer Wheatley in the course of committing the offense, or
2. That the defendant threatened or placed Jennifer Wheatley in reasonable fear that she would be imminently subjected to death, suffocation, strangulation, disfigurement, serious physical injury, or kidnapping.

The defendant is charged with burglary. Burglary is the breaking and entering of someone else's dwelling in the nighttime with the intent to commit certain crimes. In order to convict the defendant of burglary, the State must prove that there was a breaking, that there was an entry, that the breaking and entry was into someone else's dwelling, that it occurred during the nighttime. That it was done with the intention to commit rape or sexual offenses therein and that the defendant was a person who committed the act. Now, "breaking" means the creation of an opening. Such as breaking or opening a window or pushing open a door. And "entry" occurs when any part of the defendant's body is inside the house. A "dwelling" is a structure where someone regularly sleeps.

Judge Hackner: **Counsel, will you approach please?**

(White Noise.)

Judge Hackner continues:

Okay, ladies and gentlemen, the court has completed instructions, and as I mentioned to you, I'll have those available later for you. There's one thing I mentioned briefly, but I'm going to mention again, but I'm going to say it at this point, as well. You're going to be given a verdict sheet that lists the questions that you need to answer as a jury unanimously. And the verdict sheet will ask you to reach a verdict as [to] each of the charges that are pending in this case. You can discuss the charges in any order you want, and you can come to any conclusions you want, in any order you'd like to, but when you go through the verdict sheet, you are going to be asked, "Do you, the jury, find the defendant "Guilty" or "Not Guilty" of 2nd degree rape?" and then "Do you, the jury, find the defendant "Guilty" or "Not Guilty"of 1st degree rape by the circumstances that the defendant inflicted suffocation, etc. against Jennifer Wheatley, or by the circumstance that the defendant threatened or placed Jennifer Wheatley in reasonable fear, etc., or by the circumstances that the defendant committed the offense in connection with a burglary." And as to each circumstance you're going to be asked to indicate "Not Guilty" or "Guilty."

The three circumstances are the same ones in the jury instructions. The reason we start with 2nd degree and then go to 1st degree instead of the other way around is because, you might recall from my jury instructions, because the offense of 1st degree rape or 1st degree sex offense builds upon the 2nd degree offense. So, in order for there to be a 1st degree rape, you have a 2nd degree rape plus certain circumstances that have to be found by the jury unanimously. And those are spelled out for you exactly the way they are in the jury instructions.

So, as to each of those circumstances, you can — you have to go through each of [them] and agree unanimously as to each circumstance. You may find that one circumstance exists, another one may not, or two or three or none exists. And so they are not mutually exclusive, you have to go through each one of those. And, at the end of the case, I'm going to talk to you a little bit more in the way in which you're going to deal with this verdict sheet. But I want you to be aware of it. Because it is something that may be mentioned by counsel.

82

Closing Arguments: Kathleen Rogers

10:47am

Ladies and gentlemen of the jury, when Jennifer Wheatley testified in this courtroom last week, you could have heard a pin drop. And I think that's because, as Jennifer Wheatley sat on the edge of her bed after that attack and thought, *This can't be real,* everyone in this courtroom, as you heard her testify, realized the true horror of what had happened to her on August 21, 1988. On behalf of the State and Jennifer Wheatley and her family, I would like to thank each and every one of you for being here and serving on a jury. I'm sure it couldn't have been easy when you received that notice in the mailbox and said, "Oh!" and maybe you did say, "I don't have time — I've got important things going on in my life," and I know that each and every one of you do. But, if people like you were not willing to serve, our system of justice would fail. So, on behalf of Ms Wheatley, the State of Maryland, and I'm sure Mr. Szekely will join me, I thank you for your service.

I noticed that a lot of you were taking notes during this trial. And also, I noticed that every one of you was paying attention to everything that each witness said. I know that you listened very, very closely, but I still need to take a few minutes to talk about the evidence that you heard and to talk about the law that Judge Hackner has instructed you [on] how to apply that law to what you have heard in this courtroom.

I believe that the facts in this case are undisputed. Jennifer Wheatley told you what happened on August 21 of 1988. She is completely uncontradicted in what she has told you. She got home from work at about 2:30 in the morning. She entered her home on the level of where her bedroom was, the bottom level. She changed her clothes. She'd had a long night at work. She was hungry. She went into her kitchen and she made herself something to eat. She then went back to her bedroom. She even remembers what book she was reading that night. She told you it was a Stephen King novel. Probably not a very good choice, but who could have ever known?

She begins reading her book and eating her food. Did the defendant follow her? What brought him to Chesapeake Landing that night? Those are questions we will never have the answer to. All we do know is that the defendant went into Jennifer's car, that he found a piece of paper with her name and a date of birth on it. And we know that he made a decision to terrorize that young lady that evening. It wasn't going to be enough for him to break into her home and to rape her. He wanted to scare her and he wanted to terrorize her.

Her phone rings as she [lies] in bed in the safety of her home, 3:00 am. She picks it up: *"Jennifer, you have a beautiful body."* She hangs up, she doesn't respond. So he calls back, because he wants to scare her. He needs to terrorize her. He calls back and says, *"You were born to live in 1958."* She hangs up again. He then calls two more times! And she doesn't listen. She puts the phone under her pillow. She hangs it up.

Is this a game for him? A game of terror? Clearly, it is. We know he is calling from the phone just steps away. And we know that because he's gone into her car and gotten her information. So we know he's there, right there outside of her home. Jennifer goes into the bathroom to brush her teeth. She's spooked and she's decided she's putting her book down. She's finished eating and she's just going to go to sleep. This must be when the defendant climbs onto the hood of her car and enters her home through the balcony.

He knows where she lives. He knows her name. He's picked his victim. She's not listening on the phone to what he's saying to her, so he must now enter her home and complete his plan. He's only been able to terrorize her so much because she wouldn't answer his last two calls.

So, it's time for him to attack. Jennifer hears the step crack. He's in her house. He's in her home.

While she's brushing her teeth, he hides in her bedroom. He turns out the overhead light. When she starts walking back to her bedroom, she notices that the light's out and she thinks, she pauses and she thinks, *I left that light on. I know I left that light on.* But the light's off. She's in the safety of her own home. It's okay, it's okay. She walks into her bedroom — her sense of safety, at that moment, is shattered forever.

The defendant grabs her from behind. He's waiting. She's struggling. She screams out once before he is able to gag her, to suffocate her. She can hardly breathe. She begins to get lightheaded, and he says, *"You are alone."* At that moment, she believes that her mother, who was several floors up, must be dead. There's no other explanation for that statement, "You are alone." He's already killed her mother. And she told you she screamed out and she couldn't understand why her mother didn't hear. She must be dead.

He takes her clothes off. She is sure that she is going to die, too. He's told her he'll kill her. He's holding her around her neck and she can hardly breathe. He makes her touch her own vagina. He then touches her vagina — all the while, holding her tightly. He tells her to take her tampon out. He forces her to the bed, he forces his penis into her mouth. She's gagging. She throws up onto her own hand. She's sure she's going to die. She's sure her mom is already dead. He's not done. He's not done. He forces her to the bed, places her on her stomach, penetrates her vagina with his penis from behind. He rapes her. He ejaculates very quickly.

He then asks her for drugs or money. And when she tries to give him money, do you remember what he said? He said, *"No. I don't want this to look like a robbery."* He was there to terrorize and rape that young woman, and he didn't want it to look like anything else. Because he was proud of what he was doing. He's also proud [of] how he found her information — he can't wait to tell her. *"Do you want to know how I know who you are?*

I'm your DMV man." And he puts the papers from her car on her bed. This is all a game. It's a game to him. A game of terror, a game of rape.

Ladies and gentlemen, those are the facts. That is what you heard from Jennifer Wheatley. Those facts are uncontradicted. So what does that mean for your deliberations? In a short time, when you walk back to that jury room to make your decision, what must you do? Well, ladies and gentlemen, in every criminal case, jurors must answer two questions. And the first question that you must answer: What, if any, crime was committed? And that is why the judge gave you those instructions, and you will be able to take them back with you, which will make it very easy for you. Answering that question in this case is very, very simple. The State, by the way of testimony by Jennifer Wheatley, has proven each and every one of the five charges that the defendant faces today.

The first count that he is charged with is burglary. The judge told you what the State must prove in order to convict the defendant with the charge of burglary. Let's take a look at the evidence that you've heard and relate it to the law the judge has provide to you. Jennifer Wheatley's sliding glass door had been left open a little bit. Her car was parked, right there, below. I'm going to show you that picture. It's in evidence and you'll take it back with you. You can see where her car was parked. You can see the sliding glass door that was left open. And that is the car, ladies and gentlemen, the car that we know the defendant was in, the car that he took the papers out of, and it's the car that had the shoe impressions on the hood — right up here where he could climb up to the balcony to make his entry through the sliding glass door which had been left open a little bit. Because it was a nice night and the screen was there and the air was coming in. Breaking and entering? *Yes.*

The judge told you also in one of the instructions about the difference between direct and circumstantial evidence. And what he told you about that is there are two types of evidence: direct and circumstantial. The law makes no distinction between the weight to be given to either direct or circumstantial evidence. No greater degree of certainty is required of circumstantial evidence than of direct evidence. This, ladies and gentlemen, is an example of what circumstantial evidence is. We know the defendant got into Jennifer Wheatley's home. Do we have any direct evidence of how that occurred? Did anyone see him enter the home? The answer is "No." But we have circumstantial evidence. We know he was in the home, so we know he got in there somehow. We know that the one door that was left open and unlocked was the sliding glass door. We know that he was in this car and there are shoe prints on the hood of that car. The inference that you can make from that is the same as if it was direct evidence and someone had seen him enter the home.

We know that he "broke" and "entered" the home — and remember, you'll have the instruction with you — but the breaking can be anything as simple as opening a door. It's not what we might think of in terms of breaking, like breaking down a door. All someone has to do is open a door and enter that home, and that's what he did.

This has to occur in the nighttime. Well, ladies and gentlemen, nighttime has the normal meaning that you and I would all think nighttime has. It's dark outside, you're sleeping. It's [a] time when you are in your home and you should feel safe. The other element is that the State has to prove that the defendant had the intent to commit rape or another sex offense. Again, ladies and gentlemen, the best way to prove intent is by what one's actions are. What did he intend to do? I told you he intended to terrorize her. But he also intended to rape her and force her to perform a sex act upon him. And remember his statement when you think about that, too: "I don't want this to look like a robbery." Because that wasn't his intent, ladies and gentlemen. The defendant is guilty of burglary.

Now, let's look at 2nd degree rape. The State must prove, as the judge has told you, that there was vaginal intercourse, that there was a force or threat of force and that it was without the consent of Jennifer Wheatley.

Very simple, ladies and gentlemen. The State has proven each and every one of those elements.

Second degree sex offense is very similar. The State must prove that fellatio occurred, that Jennifer Wheatley was forced to put her mouth on the defendant's penis, that it was by force or by threat of force, and that it was without Jennifer Wheatley's consent. Again, very simple. The State has proven each and every one of those elements.

So ladies and gentlemen, once you determine that both of these crimes — 2nd degree rape and 2nd degree sex offense — have occurred, you then move on and look at the 1st degree rape and 1st degree sexual offense. The State has to prove one additional thing for each of those crimes. The State does not have to prove each and every one of those things.

But let's look at 1st degree sexual offense first. Of course, we have the vaginal intercourse, force or threat of force, without consent — all the things that go with the 2nd degree sexual offense. And then you have to find one of two things — either one of these two things — that the defendant threatened or placed Jennifer Wheatley in reasonable fear that she would be imminently subjected to death, suffocation, strangulation, disfigurement, serious physical injury, or kidnapping. Ladies and gentlemen, that's a no-brainer. How scared was Jennifer Wheatley that night, and did she believe, and was her fear reasonable, that the defendant was going to kill her? Absolutely 100%. And, in fact, she was strangled at some point when something was wrapped around her neck, and clearly the defendant inflicted suffocation when he placed that object in her mouth and she could not breathe.

The other way of proving this is that the defendant actually inflicted the suffocation, which he did in this case. It wasn't just the threat. Strangulation, disfigurement, or serious physical injury in the course of committing this offense. Again, ladies and gentlemen, it's a no-brainer; the defendant did, in fact, commit that offense.

Now with regard to 1st degree rape, which is the final charge that I would suggest you look at, the State has to prove all the elements of 2nd degree rape and then the State must prove one of three things: the defendant inflicted suffocation, strangulation, disfigurement, or serious physical injury against Jennifer Wheatley in the course of committing this offense — the same as for the 1st degree sexual offense. Again, of course the defendant did those things. The second one is that the defendant threatened or placed Jennifer Wheatley in reasonable fear that she would be imminently subjected to death, suffocation, strangulation, disfigurement, serious physical injury, or kidnapping. And the third way that the defendant can be found guilty of a 1st degree rape is that he committed the offense in connection with a burglary. And, obviously, the State has proven each and every one of the elements of burglary, so that would automatically mean that the defendant would be guilty of the 1st degree rape.

The evidence showed all of these things. All of the elements the State is required to prove have been proven. And therefore, the defendant is guilty for each and every one of these crimes.

But what I said to you is, you are determining first if the crimes occurred. And then your next question is, who committed these crimes? I said that the defendant did them, but you need to look at the evidence and answer these questions separately. And if you look at the evidence, the answer is, again, abundantly clear. Who committed these crimes? Well, we have the testimony that there were two latent fingerprints lifted from the candle that was touched by Jennifer Wheatley's attacker in her bedroom. You heard the testimony of Mr. Lowman, who the court accepted as an expert in fingerprint comparison. He rolled this defendant's, William Trice's, known prints. And then he compared them with the latents, the two fingerprints that had been lifted from the candle. And in his expert opinion, the fingerprints on the candle matched the defendant's. "Fingerprints are unique." That is what he told you. Those two fingerprints on the candle in Jennifer Wheatley's bedroom belong to that man.

(Ms Rogers points to Trice.)

We could stop there, we know who did it. But we have more. Jennifer Wheatley's attacker ejaculated, he left his DNA behind. Jennifer put a tampon in after the attack. She told you she went into the bathroom after she sat on her bed for a while. When she got to the hospital, not only vaginal swabs were done, but that tampon was taken out and packaged and turned over to the police to be used later in testing.

You heard from two more experts with regard to the DNA. You heard from Courtney McCoppin and you heard from Annette Box. Judge Hackner, again, told you that each of those two witnesses were qualified as experts in the field of DNA analysis and testing. When Ms McCoppin did her testing, she was the first witness, she did her testing in the year 2004, I believe. She told you that there were no suspects at that point in time, but that she was testing the evidence to develop a profile. To develop the DNA profile of Jennifer Wheatley's attacker, to determine the sperm fraction and to [map] out that profile from the tampon and the vaginal swabs. So that one day, if ever there were a suspect, we would be able to compare that evidence and find out if that person, that suspect was, in fact, the person who had left that profile there. There were two different items of evidence that she looked at. She kept them separate. They were never put together, they were never mixed. And she tested them. Two pieces of evidence, one attacker. One profile.

Detective Morgan was the next witness you heard from. She told you she got the defendant's DNA in 2008. She told you she was trained in how to swab his mouth for DNA. She took that DNA to the Anne Arundel County police laboratory where Ms Box, the expert witness in DNA testing and analysis, developed a profile from that swab. Developed a known profile of this defendant.

(Ms Rogers points to Trice.)

So now we had a suspect, we had a person to compare the DNA that had been collected in 1988, the DNA that had been profiled in 2004, to our suspect. Ms Box told you that she did that comparison. She compared the defendant's profile to the DNA of Jennifer Wheatley's attacker — the DNA that was on her vaginal swabs and the DNA that was on her tampon. And Ms Box told you that these are her results.

(Ms Rogers shows the jury the chart of DNA fractions — all matching.)

She told you that if there was a match at all sixteen sites, then she would be able to conclude to a reasonable degree of scientific certainty that the DNA on the vaginal swabs and the DNA on the tampon, the DNA of Jennifer Wheatley's attacker is the DNA of that man.

(Ms Rogers points to Trice)

The defendant made two huge mistakes in this case. He left his identification in two different ways, but they are both equally conclusive. But, ladies and gentlemen, there's even more! The defendant was questioned in New York, and he admitted that he lived in this area in 1988. He told the detectives he worked as a courier making deliveries to various places in the area. He was shown two pictures of Jennifer Wheatley, and what did he say? "Never seen her. I've dated a lot of women and if I dated her, I would remember." But then he's told that his fingerprints and DNA are at the scene. And what is his reaction, ladies and gentlemen? *"No way, that's not me!"* He puts his head down and says, *"I'm worse than I thought I was."* A guilty man.

Ladies and gentlemen, the person who committed each and every one of these crimes sits before you today. Justice may have been delayed in this case. Justice was delayed in this case, and Jennifer Wheatley had to look over her shoulder for twenty years. But when you return your verdict of "Guilty" today, justice will be served, and Jennifer Wheatley will look forward. Thank you.

83

Closing Arguments: Andrew Szekely

11:07am

Good morning. At the beginning of this trial I stood before you, and I told you two things. The first thing I told you is that Mr. Trice is innocent of these charges, and the second thing I told you is that nobody, until now, has asked any tough questions in this case. Judge Hackner gave you jury instructions just before we began our closing arguments. Those instructions dealt with the offense charged, deliberation, duties to deliberate, presumption of innocence, and reasonable doubt. And what I submit to you is the job to deliberate as a jury is to ask those tough questions.

Now, the concept of reasonable doubt is a complicated one and an analogy may be helpful here. Now, this case is drawing to a close and you'll remember at the end of every session and before the long weekend, Judge Hackner instructed you to not discuss the case amongst yourselves or with anybody else. Now, I trust that you have taken that instruction seriously and not discussed this case at all. You will now, shortly, have the opportunity, back in the jury room, to discuss the case amongst yourselves. But when this case is over and you return a verdict, you will be free to discuss this case with whomever you want. And you're going to be talking about this case. It might be with your husbands, wives, friends, coworkers. They're going to ask, *"You were on a jury? What was it like?"* And you're going to tell them about the evidence and you're going to tell them what the witnesses were. And you're going to talk about the case. You're going to talk about coming down here to Church Circle every day and sitting on the jury. And maybe in discussing that case you'll stop and think, *You know, there's something that didn't quite add up*. There were a few things that were brought up, and they didn't quite make sense and they didn't quite add up. And each of those is "reasonable doubt," and the time to ask those questions and to think about what doesn't add up in this case isn't this Saturday when you're getting together with friends for dinner or Friday at work, when you're having your lunch break; the time to think about that is now, when you're together as a jury with eleven other people who just heard all the evidence in this case.

And there's three areas in this case where things just don't add up. That would be the burglary, the attack, and the police work in this case. Now, the burglary is relevant in several different ways in this case. First off, it's a count on the verdict sheet and you're going to be asked whether a burglary occurred. It is also a circumstance that relates to the charge of 1st degree rape. But it's also something by which you can judge the general credibility of the case the State has put forward.

Now, the first area of difficulty is gonna be with the timeline the State has put forward. Now, it's important to remember that Chesapeake Landing is a gated community. So if the State's theory is correct, Mr. Trice jumped over a fence, went and rummaged through a car without leaving a single fingerprint or any trace of himself inside the car, exited the car, went back over the fence, stood outside the fence for approximately half an hour to make several phone calls, and then came back in over the fence. Which just doesn't make a lot of sense. If someone is going to be committing a burglary, they're not gonna stand around and wait for a half an hour in the public exposing themselves. They're gonna go over the fence and they're gonna commit the burglary. So, the timeline, it just doesn't make sense.

The next issue is entry into the apartment. The State has said that Mr. Trice hoisted himself up off the car and went in through a sliding glass door. Now, you heard from Mr. Lowman, who sat in the witness stand right over there and testified that the harder you press on something, the more likely you are to leave a mark. Now, the State's theory is that Mr.

Trice lifted himself up onto the balcony and pulled himself up. And you also heard from Mr. Lowman that your palms leave prints, too. And you can be identified by your palms, and, like your fingertips, your palms are unique. Well, that railing that the State says Mr. Trice used to hoist himself up would have been a great surface for him to have left a palm print on there. And what did Ms Mary Pat Whiteley tell you? That she checked thoroughly, that area, and didn't find any evidence of a palm print.

Now, the State's next step on their theory is that Mr. Trice slid the sliding glass door open. Again, Ms Whiteley testified, "Glass is an excellent surface for recording of fingerprints." Sliding glass door, not a fingerprint to be found. Now, Ms Wheatley testified that later, when her attacker was leaving, that he tried the front door, or the other door — it might be a back door — and couldn't get out that way, and came back the other way. Well, you saw a photo. You're going to have it back in the jury room with you. Well, that door is covered with fingerprint dust from where Ms Whiteley had checked to see if there were any fingerprints. And there's none there. And you heard Ms Whiteley say, "I'm the crime scene technician. It's my job, I go in, when I look at a scene, I think, where could someone have touched something in this room?" And she checked door knobs, doorjambs, sliding glass doors. All those places. Not a trace. The light switches? Well, they were never checked. Even though Ms Wheatley says the lights were turned off.

And the thermostat where, presumably, under the State's theory, Mr. Trice had adjusted the air conditioning before any of this happened, that also wasn't checked for any sort of fingerprints. Wasn't checked. And the third reason as to the burglary is an element of burglary — is not being allowed in the house. If you let somebody in your house, it's not a burglary. And, remember, there's two people home that night. And we only heard from one of those people. We don't know what the other witness, who was in the house that night, would have said. And with the lack of physical evidence of a breaking and improbable timeline and lack of testimony from the other person in that house, it's not enough to convict for burglary. And it's enough to cast significant doubt on Ms Wheatley's account of the entire incident.

Now, the next step is going to be Ms Wheatley's account of being choked and strangled. Now, it's important to remember that everyone — of people's perceptions — and Ms Wheatley had testified that she had had three beers that evening. And we all know that, using your common sense, that alcohol can impair your perception. And the next thing to remember is that Ms Wheatley told the police the man that attacked her was blond. So, think about that, look at Mr. Trice, think about the testimony that she [sic] was a blond man.

And more importantly, you're going to have medical records back with you, and you're going to have a chance to look through them. And you also heard from Ms Knuckles. There was no trauma found on Ms Wheatley's neck. Now, her testimony was, which the State would like you to credit, is her neck was wrapped around by a shirt. Her neck was pulled so far back she couldn't breathe and yet, somehow, there's not a mark, not a mark left on her neck. Now, if someone's squeezing your neck so tightly you can hardly breathe, that's gonna leave a mark. Now, the mark's gonna go away after a few days, certainly, but Ms Wheatley gets to the hospital very shortly after this occurs, and there's not a mark on her neck. There's no physical corroborative evidence of the attack. And when the State says it's uncontradicted, that's not quite true because, not quite correct because, the, ah, contradiction comes in the form of those medical records. Which say no mark of trauma — it's gonna say, let's, then it says "general trauma,"and then it's gonna say, "none."

And the third area here is gonna be the police work and the investigation in this case. Now, this case happened twenty years ago, so in some senses, you can't really fault people for having perhaps diminished recollection of the events. But you heard from Detective Leo, the lead investigator in this case — and he doesn't remember a thing about this case. Ms Wheatley testified that she gave an audio taped statement after the incident. Former Detective

Leo — no recollection of that. The single most accurate statement of what would have happened would have been the statement Ms Wheatley gave immediately after the attack. The incident. And that statement — maybe it wasn't taken, maybe it's been lost to the years, either way, it's not here. We don't know, we don't know what's in that statement.

Now, I will say that Ms Whiteley was very through and she testified and she had her report; if you remember, she referred to her reports during her testimony. And at one point she was asked, "What items did you collect from the house?" And she listed them, and I'm going to list them briefly here — she collected driver's license papers from the front seat of the car, she collected a red shirt from Ms Wheatley's bed, two candles, and if you remember, the candles were collected because someone had asked Ms Wheatley was there anything that was touched? And she said, "Oh, those candles." So the candles were collected on Ms Wheatley's suggestion. And, ultimately, and the State is absolutely correct, Mr. Trice's fingerprints were found on that candle. Ms Wheatley's panties were collected from the bed. Two grayish blue socks were collected, a shirt, a driver's license paper which Ms Wheatley said was laid down next to her, and you'll note, that for all the fingerprint testimony in this case, Mr. Trice's fingerprints — not on that piece of paper. A paper towel, a Kleenex, a quilt, a pillow case, a pillow, another pillow, a mirror, and a scarf and a belt that had been wrapped together. And you know what's not on that list is the nightgown which Ms Wheatley said was torn. Now, if the police had said is there anything that was touched, *"the candle was touched,"* but that nightgown that was torn during the attack would have been a very good piece of evidence to collect, and it wasn't collected. It's not here for you to look at. You don't have the opportunity to look at this physical evidence, which could have helped you determine the truthfulness or the accuracy of Ms Wheatley's testimony. You don't have an opportunity to look at that. And I submit to you as a jury, to you, that you are entitled to have the full picture. The State isn't supposed to, should, you're owed a full picture of what happened that evening. And you don't have that.

Now, there's three area[s] to Ms Wheatley's story, if you break it down. There is the burglary, there is the choking, and there is the intercourse. Now, certainly, Mr. Trice's DNA, his semen was in Ms Wheatley, so there was indisputably intercourse that night. So we have physical corroborative evidence from one out of the three portions of Ms Wheatley's story. We don't have it for two out of those three. Reasonable doubts, now, we can't put enough on it. We can't say it's this percent or that percent for certain, but what I can...but what is certain about reasonable doubt, is that one out of three isn't enough to convict. There's only...if a story has three parts and you only have corroboration for one out of those three parts, that's not enough to convict in this case. And I suggest you go back in your deliberations and consider that and find Mr. Trice not guilty of these charges.

Now one last thing, I'm about to sit down in a second and Ms — the State is going to stand up and the State is going to have a chance to rebuttal argument. And they get to do a rebuttal because the State has the burden, they go first, and they go last. The defense doesn't have a chance to do any rebuttal argument in this case. But you can bet that I'm going to be sitting over there wishing when the State's done that I could get up to do a rebuttal to their rebuttal. And I don't get to do that. And what I would suggest to you is, as jurors, your job is to perhaps think, "*Well, what would the defense say to the State's rebuttal?*" And that's what deliberation means. What would the defense say to that? Think about it, deliberate it, look at the evidence. When you look at the evidence, you'll find that the State has not produced enough evidence in this case, beyond a reasonable doubt, to find Mr. Trice guilty, and I'd ask you to return verdicts of "Not Guilty."

84

Closing Arguments: Rebuttal — Kathleen Rogers

11:42am

Ladies and gentlemen. I know it's almost lunchtime, and I will be brief. But there are just a couple of points I need to discuss with you. I guess I'm a little confused about Mr. Szekely's theory of the case and what he's trying to suggest to you. But I'm going to hit upon a few things he said first.

He said to you the burglary hasn't been proven in this case. He said to you that perhaps Jennifer Wheatley's mom allowed this man into their home. Absurd, ladies and gentlemen! It is 2:30 in the morning. Jennifer Wheatley's mother is sound asleep upstairs. This man broke into their home and attacked Jennifer Wheatley. He was not invited there. He was not allowed to be there. He was an attacker. That is simply absurd.

He's saying there is no "breaking and entering" because we don't know how he got in. And ladies and gentlemen, I'm not going to go over again the "direct vs. circumstantial" evidence — but we know he's in the home. He got in there somehow. So then, when you look and try to figure out how he got in there, and you look at the circumstantial evidence, it becomes clear — because we know he's in there — that he got in there by climbing on top of the car and entering through the door that had been left open a little bit.

The fact that there are no fingerprints found — we heard from Mr. Lowman, we also heard from Mary Pat Whiteley, that numerous things will affect whether you find a fingerprint on a surface. And we all know that from our common sense — from our life experiences. Environment affects it; whether something's dirty affects it. The defense would love for you to get wrapped up about why there's no fingerprint on that balcony or why there's no fingerprint on that door because, ladies and gentlemen, if you do that, then you will ignore the fact that his fingerprints...

(Ms Rogers points to Trice.)

...were on the candle that he picked up in her bedroom. How do you get around that, ladies and gentlemen? You can't. You can't. So the defense would like you to look and talk about other things and not focus on what the evidence is in this case.

He says to you, "The State's theory is that he's out making phone calls and that's not logical, that nobody would be out there for a half hour because they might be seen; they might get caught." Well, ladies and gentlemen, I have my job because people get caught all the time. And they get caught because they leave their identification at scenes, they leave their fingerprints, they leave their DNA, and they do dumb things. And do you know why? Part of Mr. Trice's game, part of the terror he wanted to inflict, involved making those phone calls. It was worth it to him to be out there because he wanted to terrorize Jennifer Wheatley. And he did just that.

None of the things that Mr. Szekely suggests to you should cast any doubt on Jennifer Wheatley's account of what occurred. You heard and saw Jennifer Wheatley testify. You are the judges of her credibility. She was telling you the truth. She didn't tell you that the squeezing of her neck was what caused her not to breathe. She told you the gag in her mouth, which wouldn't cause any injuries, is what stopped her ability to breathe. She didn't complain about her jaw at the hospital. She told you that. She told you that it had been dislocated, but that she put it back in. She told you she was in shock after this attack. There's no right or wrong way for a rape victim to behave. She was happy to be alive when she was at that hospital. She was happy to know and relieved to know that not only that she was alive — that she had survived this attack — but that her mother was alive, also.

Detective Leo. I'm not going to defend Detective Leo, ladies and gentlemen. I believe that his work was sloppy. I believe it was unprofessional for him not to recall this case. Thankfully, he was not responsible for the collection of evidence in this case. So, of course, the defense would like you to focus on Detective Leo because they don't want you to focus on the fact that he didn't collect the evidence in this case. He didn't lift this defendant's fingerprint from the candle.

(Ms Rogers points to Trice.)

He didn't do the DNA testing in this case. Those things were done by qualified professionals — who I would stand behind any day of the week.

Mr Szekely: Objection, your honor — may I approach?

Judge Hackner: **I'll ask the jury to disregard Ms Rogers' personal views of the professionals.**

Ms Rogers continues:
I guess at the end of the day, ladies and gentlemen, Mr. Szekely is suggesting to you that Jennifer Wheatley consented to having intercourse with this defendant.

(Ms Rogers points to Trice.)

That is simply absurd. But he suggests that to you because he can't get around the DNA. His client's DNA is on the vaginal swabs and the tampon of Jennifer Wheatley. Jennifer Wheatley did not know her attacker. She called the police, she reported her attack, she was tearful, she was in shock. And she gave the best description she could of the stranger who had violated her home here in Annapolis.

Ladies and gentlemen, just because a crime is horrible and a case is serious, that doesn't mean that it's complicated. This case is as simple as a first grade math problem. It is as simple as the defendant's statement, plus the defendant's fingerprint, plus the defendant's DNA equals the defendant's guilt. Thank you.

85

The Jury Retires

*O*nce the attorneys had completed their closing statements, Judge Hackner gave the jury further instructions.

Judge Hackner:
Ladies and gentlemen, a few more minutes from me and then I'm to ask you to retire to your verdict. Um, you are going to be given multiple copies of the verdict sheet just for reference. There is going to be one that we need to have, that is the official verdict sheet. And you will see that there are a number of questions on the verdict sheet. You need to address each and every one of those questions. Obviously, what your findings are as to those questions are strictly up to you. But each of those questions needs to be addressed. And at the end of the verdict, when you have all reached a unanimous agreement, I'm going to ask that one of those verdict sheets be signed by the jury foreperson — Mrs. Vanderhook — and be dated. And when you have reached a verdict, you will knock on the door to let the bailiff know that you've got a verdict. You don't tell him what the verdict is because you have to announce the verdict here in the courtroom. And he'll bring everybody back into the courtroom. It may take a few minutes to gather everybody. And the clerk is then going to ask the jury as a group, "Ladies and gentlemen of the jury, have you reached a verdict?" And, presumably the answer is, "Yes we have." Obviously, if any one of you disagrees and you feel that everyone else says we're in agreement, but you don't agree, then that's your chance to speak up and say, "No, I haven't reached a verdict." But presumably, you all will have all reached a verdict, and we ask that you respond out loud so the clerk can record that you have all agreed, that you all have a verdict.

Then she will ask, "Who will speak on your behalf?" and you will say, "Our foreperson." Mrs. Vanderhook will then be asked to stand and hand up the verdict sheet to me. I'm going to look at it, simply to be sure that it's been completed, dated, and signed, and I'll hand it back. And then the clerk is going to ask each of those questions that is listed on the verdict sheet and ask for Mrs. Vanderhook to respond. So, as for each of those points, there will be an option to respond as "Not Guilty," or "Guilty," "Not Guilty," or "Guilty," and so forth.

And then, when that has been done, the clerk is going to ask the jurors by number, each and everyone of you, to indicate that what you have just heard is a correct statement of your verdict. So she'll say, "Juror #2, you have heard the verdict of your foreperson. Is that your verdict?" Juror #3, #4, etc., to make sure that each and every one of you has agreed that what has just been heard is accurate. And at the end of all that, she will ask you collectively, "Ladies and gentlemen, you have heard the verdict of your foreperson. Is that your verdict?" And you will be given the opportunity to say, "Yes, it is," or "No, it isn't."

When you go back into the jury room, the alternates, Mr. Roozen, Ms DeGuardo, and Mr. Paretti, are going to be excused. Now, I don't know whether it's a disappointment to you that you've paid attention so carefully, but you're not going to be able to deliberate, but it is very important that we have twelve jurors because, by the Constitution, each person who's charged with a criminal offense is entitled to a twelve person jury. And sometimes there are emergencies and reasons why a juror has to be excused during the process, and if we didn't have the alternates available, then we would essentially have to have a new trial on another date. So it's very important to have you alternates, and I noticed you all were paying very good attention and I appreciate your efforts. When you go back, you can take your stuff, you can go and talk about it to whoever you want to, or you can choose not to. That's completely up to you.

The other twelve jurors will be the jury that [is] going to deliberate in this case. When you go back, if you want to begin deliberations immediately, you are welcome to. If you want to order lunch, you can place your order. It usually takes a little while for your orders to be made. But you're going to be cooped up in the jury room until you reach a verdict, so you can make that decision.

If you have questions during the time that you are deliberating, chances are that I'm not going to be able to answer them for you. I might as well tell you up front, but if there are any logistical issues that you need to address with the court, or any communications whatsoever you want to communicate to the us, you need to do that in writing and have that signed by the foreperson. We have some nifty little forms that we ask that you use. The clerk will then give it to me and I will call the attorneys. We will get the attorneys and the defendant together. We will discuss the answer, and then I'll give you the answer back. So what I'm telling you is, it's not a give and take dialogue, it's a process we have to go through. Chances are, like I say, if you're asking about evidence or a fact that you don't remember or anything along those lines, I'm not going to be able to give you any additional information. All the evidence you've heard is what you have to rely on, and there's nothing more that I can give you in that regard.

If at some point in the afternoon you are deliberating and you get a note from me asking if you would like to continue deliberating or recess for the day, that is not intended to rush you, because I'm simply, you know, I don't know how long you're going to be deliberating and it's strictly up to you. I don't retire for many years from now and it doesn't matter to me if you take from now till my retirement in deliberations. So I'm not rushing you, I'm not pressuring you, and that's why I tell you up front that I might send you a note. We don't stay here like you see on TV till midnight or three o'clock in the morning to deliberate. At some point near the end of the day, the court staff needs to go home. They have child care issues and so forth, just as you do.

And so that's the only reason I might send you a note of that sort. And, so, that is so you can tell me you'd like to deliberate a little bit longer or let's call it a day and come back tomorrow morning. Um, you are going to be given the exhibits. They're in the courtroom. We still have to sort through them. And in a few minutes you are going to get the jury instructions and the verdict sheets — there are a couple of typos on it I have to correct. And, ah, at this point, I'm going to ask the bailiff to please be sworn.

Judge Hackner: Do you solemnly swear to keep this jury together in some convenient place, allowing no one to speak to them, nor speak to them yourself, unless it is to inquire [if] they have agreed upon a verdict or otherwise ordered by the court?

Bailiff: *I do.*

Judge Hackner: Ladies and gentlemen, if you will retire, please, and we will await your verdict. Counsel, if you could come up when the jury is out to make sure the exhibits are all together and accounted for, please.

Bailiff: *All rise.*

86

Awaiting the Verdict

I looked at my watch. It was 12:30, and now the case was in the hands of the jury. I stood up and watched as the police put the leg irons and handcuffs back on the defendant. Wow, that was really something else. I had cried from the minute Kathleen started talking until she stopped. And then I'd shook my head in disbelief the entire time the defense attorney had been talking.

I felt sorry for the defendant. If, against all odds, he was found not guilty, it would not be because of the lawyer he had. Andrew Szekely seemed unprepared for both cross examination and his closing. I was confused after listening to his closing arguments. Whose side was he representing? I found his repeated focus on damaging evidence *against* his client to be baffling. I realized he didn't have anything to work with, but a clever defense attorney might be able to spin a tale that perhaps could lead to reasonable doubt. Or, short of that, dazzle the jury with a well-prepared, fabricated version of the truth for his closing. Instead, he presented a horribly inarticulate Judgment of Acquittal and a closing that did nothing but underline and highlight all of the evidence needed for a conviction. However, I didn't feel *that* bad for the creep. Not really. But I sure wouldn't want Szekely representing anyone I know.

I was pretty wound up, a bit nervous, and very eager to get out of the courthouse for a while. When I turned around, I was happy to see Marnie had made it from her doctor's office in time to catch the closing arguments.

"You made it — yeah!"

"Oh, you know it!" Marnie said. "I finally told my doctor I just had to go and hopped up. I raced through traffic, but made it here just after your lawyer got started. She was awesome, Jen."

"She was," I agreed. I still had tears in my eyes, but they were now accompanied by a nervous smile on my face.

Shirli had also arrived sometime during the judge's instructions to the jury. I gave them each a hug. I was so grateful to have them there. We all started talking about the final arguments before we even got completely out of the courtroom. And this felt good! All of us were excited and relieved because no one could tell us not to discuss the case. Now I could hear everything Scott and Sherry had heard and tell them all the bits of information that were not spoken about in court. The corridor outside the courtroom was abuzz with the release of pent-up energy. Kathleen and Cindy stood among the group, waiting for me to come out.

"How long do you think it will be before we hear anything?" I asked Cindy.

"It's impossible to say. Every case is different. But I have a good feeling. They may plan to have lunch first, and then they may want to discuss some of the testimony and read some of the submitted material. So, who knows? Just make sure you stay close and can get back here in a reasonable amount of time when I call."

"Okay, no problem. I think we are going to go get something to eat on Main Street somewhere, and I'll keep my phone in my hand. It's okay if we talk about the case now, right?" I said to Cindy as she started down the steps.

"Oh, yeah. The case is in the hands of the jury, so you guys can talk all you want to now."

Dave Cordle was heading back to his office. "I'll be in my office if you want to talk about anything," he offered. I did want to go talk with him for a bit. I was sure he was going through a lot of crazy emotions that day, too. No doubt even seeing this day dawn was high on the list of things he wanted to chat about. But as much as I wanted to share the whole experience with him, I also wanted to hear what Scott and Sherry had taken notes on and answer the dozens of questions that were being asked of me. And I needed to get out and get some air.

"Thanks, Dave. We're going to head out and get something to eat and unwind a bit. I know these guys have been dying to ask me questions, and I can't wait to hear about the testimony I missed. I'll see you when the verdict is in?"

"You bet," Dave said, "I wouldn't miss it. Well, I'm here if you want to talk. Have fun."

Before we left, Cindy again told me to keep my cell phone on and in sight so I could hear it ring.

"Okay, no problem."

We headed down to Fran's and sat down at a big table in a dining room that was virtually empty except for our group. Everyone was talking at once. Sherry told me about what the defendant had said to Tracy Morgan when he was arrested. *"I'm worse than I thought I was."* It struck both Shirli and me that Trice was referring to his criminal prowess rather than the number of victims he'd had. Scott mentioned that Detective Leo had been no help at all. He couldn't even remember the case. In addition to not remembering the case, he'd lost some valuable evidence — my recorded statement and the T-shirt.

"I don't think either was even available when Dave took over the case in 1989," I said.

I told them all about the tape-recorded statement I'd given that Leo had no recollection of and Dave had never found, and then I told them about how I'd been asked by Cindy not to mention the T-shirt because it was a lost piece of evidence. *"If you tell the story of how you found it on the bridge and we can't produce it, you will just look like a crazy lady,"* she had said. But if that had been in one of the evidence bags, it would have gone a long way to explaining many things.

"It's too bad Leo was such a screwup." I told everyone how, on the way back from the police station, I saw the T-shirt in the middle of the Eastport Bridge. Leo dropped me off at home and then went back and picked it up. He then called me from the station to have me identify it."

"Why didn't he just stop and pick it up right then? That was stupid," Sherry said. "What if it wasn't there when he got back?"

"I wonder if he was trying to hide something. Maybe he knew more than he was letting on."

I didn't think Detective Leo knew more than he was letting on, but I agreed it was a stupid idea, although at the time, I was too tired to even give it much thought. But I knew he wasn't any good right from the start — instinct, I guess. I just didn't like him much. He went on vacation right after he was given my case and never really gave it any attention. I knew the T-shirt was never bagged like the rest of the evidence. I told my friends about picking up my blanket from the police department.

"Dave would never have let me do this." I told them how the kid in the evidence room came out of the back room twirling my T-shirt in the air asking me, *"Do you want this, too?"*

"That was the last time I saw it. But it had been in my car. I'm sure the creep took it out and then used it to wipe his prints down throughout the house. He also must have used it to unscrew the light bulbs in the carport, because they were hot. Once he unscrewed the lights, he wouldn't be seen climbing up onto the balcony. He took his shoes off outside on the balcony so he would be quieter while walking across the living room floor." I told them of how I saw a footprint on the wooden floor just inside the house, but that I didn't think it had ever been lifted.

"He turned on the air conditioner to mask any noises he did make when he walked through the house."

"How did he know where the thermostat was?"

"Had he been in the house before?"

I didn't know for sure. Dave had told me Trice had been a courier at the time, so it was possible he had delivered something to Mom. Or maybe he had been in someone else's unit. They mirrored each other, so if he knew the layout of one, he would pretty much know what they all looked like. He had to know the layout one way or another, because it was really dark on the second floor, too dark for him to have just guessed where the thermostat was.

"So the T-shirt was never found with the evidence?"

"Unfortunately, no," I said. "And since I was told not to mention it, the defense lawyer concocted the whole story of me waiting an hour to call the police so I could wipe down all but two fingerprints from the house. This would imply that I had let the creep in, and then, for reasons unknown, decided to frame him. No way a story like that would convince a jury. I would have to know exactly what he touched throughout the entire house. Impossible. I'm sure he used the T-shirt to open the door and turn on the air conditioner. He also used it to strangle and gag me."

"What about the scarf and belt that were collected? The investigator said they were 'entwined,'" Scott asked me.

I was puzzled by his question, not certain what he was referring to.

"No," I said. "I don't know anything about any belt or scarf. I know he used the T-shirt. Leo asked me a dozen times what I thought was used." He had asked me that question several times when we were in my room together with the investigators. Nothing in the room was the right texture. I told him it was something soft. But long enough to be wound around my neck a couple of times and then shoved into my throat. Like a scarf. Only it was August, and I knew I didn't have any scarves out that time of year. When I saw the T-shirt on the bridge, I knew it was what we were looking for.

He took the shirt out with him. He did open the back door when he was leaving, but then he remembered he'd left his shoes on the balcony. He had to go out the same way he came in or else he would have left them behind. He wiped his prints off, or used the shirt over his hand the entire way through the house. The only time he screwed up was when he picked up the candle. And honestly, for years, I figured maybe he hadn't left any prints there, either. It just took a while for them to be noticed again.

"Can you believe how the defense lawyer said your mother let him in the house?"

"Yeah, and she made him climb onto your car and up to the balcony to come in the house!"

"During the trial, his lawyer kept pointing out the obvious, like how glass is a really good surface to leave fingerprints on. You would think he would be trying to take the jury's attention *away* from this."

"Some of the questions he asked witnesses made the prosecutor's case stronger. I wondered if he wanted his client to be found guilty, or if he was just incompetent. Not that I wanted him to better represent his client."

I think it was Mollie who, before the trial, had asked me who was really worse — the rapist or the guy who defends the rapist, trying to get him off? I couldn't believe some of the things the defense attorney had said in his closing: *"If someone is going to be committing a burglary, they're not gonna stand around and wait for a half an hour in the public exposing themselves. They're gonna go over the fence and they're gonna commit the burglary."*

"That had to have been a Freudian slip," I said laughing. "The creep got his fingerprints into the national database when he was picked up for indecent exposure to a minor. I probably would have laughed out loud in the courtroom if I wasn't so appalled by the lawyer telling us what is appropriate criminal behavior. Very sad."

"I thought lawyers were not supposed to attack the victim on the stand. Wasn't that what the cocaine use and drinking was about? Wasn't he trying to make you look bad?"

I tried to explain the night in 1986 with George, and then I said, "I guess the laws are only designed to protect a victim's sexual history. Certainly, this plays a role in why so few rapes are reported. No one wants to be put in a petri dish on the stand. Everything else must be fair game, including, I guess, something that happened years before. He would have had a better chance of discrediting me as an alcoholic, because Lord knows I did drink a lot. But seriously, three beers and I deserve this?"

"Alcohol can impair you perception!" Shirli said as she sipped her wine and giggled.

"I don't think you have to worry about any of that. The jury knew what he was up to. They knew he didn't have anything to work with and all he could do was try to make you look bad."

"The defense lawyer said in his opening that it took you an hour to call the police," Sherry said.

I wasn't sure how he'd come up with this. He had the diary and the timeframe was basically outlined in it. I didn't remember him saying it took an hour in the closing, so, I guess he figured out from my testimony that he was wrong. I wondered if he'd told Trice this supposed discrepancy was going to win the case for him?

I asked if there was a sherrif's deputy standing behind Trice.

"Actually, there were two deputies. They were there the whole time."

"Odd, when I was on the stand I didn't ever see anything past the defendant's table. It was like there was a wall there or something and I couldn't see past it. Oh, I could see you guys, but the other side of the room seemed to fade away. Did he ever have anyone sitting in the courtroom with him? I mean, family, not police?"

"On the first day, there was a woman with blond hair dressed in pink," Sherry said. "She was taking notes or something. She got up and left the courtroom when you started to get into the details of the attack. Perhaps it was his wife. She was there again the next day with a younger male. His son maybe? But that's just a guess."

"Hmmmm," I said, "I don't remember seeing her." But as I'd said, I hadn't noticed anyone sitting on his side. I guessed whoever she was had heard enough. The lady in pink was only seen for a few minutes on the day I testified, and again the next day when the DNA evidence was presented. As far as I know, she never came back to the courthouse.

87

On the Record

2:15pm

Judge Hackner: We're on the record in the case of State of Maryland vs. William Joseph Trice K-08-002821. Counsel, identify yourselves, please.

Ms Rogers: *Kathleen Rogers on behalf of the State.*

Mr. Szekely: Good afternoon, your honor. Andrew Szekely on behalf of Mr. Trice, present on my right.

Ms Waters: And also Gwen Waters on behalf of Mr. Trice.

Judge Hackner: Alright, the defendant is present in the courtroom, the jury is not in the courtroom at the moment. We have a note from the jury that I've discussed briefly with counsel and the note says:

This refers to MPJI-CR3:01. Whole means everything physical and/or circumstantial evidence. Please clarify what "whole" means.

And we have discussed a proposed response. Apparently, there's some confusion in some of the jury's minds as to what "whole" means as it is in the phrase: *"You may not convict the defendant [unless] you find that the evidence when considered as a*

whole establishes guilt beyond a reasonable doubt."
And the answer that I proposed was "whole" means all of the evidence considered together. Is there any other thought or objection from defense on that?"

Mr. Szekely: I think that's a fair response to that question.

Judge Hackner: Okay. Does the State have any different position?

Ms Rogers: *No, your honor.*

Judge Hackner: Alright. So I've taken the liberty of writing that on the bottom of the jury note, and I was going to go ahead and hand that in with the signature and the date. I don't know whether we want to keep — just in case they don't — keep that one and I'll give this one back. I'll give this one to the bailiff so we don't have to collect...

Mr. Szekely: Your honor, if we can approach to just initial the note before it goes back.

Judge Hackner: Yeah, you can.

Ms Rogers: *It's on the record.*

Mr. Szekely: It's on the record regardless, so I guess it's not in the chambers, so I guess we don't have to do that.

Judge Hackner: Well, I guess, you hold a copy and give this back... just want to make sure when they walk away with it, there's no lapse in the record. Okay, thank you. See ya.

88

Another Round and Security Snafus

*T*he waiter had cleared off our lunch dishes and still my phone had not rung, so we ordered another round of drinks, explaining to him that we were waiting for the jury to come back with a verdict.

"Is it okay if we camp out here for a while?" I asked. "I'm kind of sick of sitting in the courthouse."

"No problem. I'll bring a fresh round and just let me know if you get hungry again," he said.

At 2:40, Cindy called.

"The jury is back. They have a verdict," she said.

"Wow, really? Already? Okay. We're on our way," I said. "Don't let the judge start without us. We're at Fran's at the bottom of Main Street, so it will be a few minutes before we can get there."

We walked quickly back up the hill speculating on what the verdict would be. My head and heart were racing.

I wondered if the fact that it only took them just over two hours to reach a verdict meant they'd found him "guilty," or "not guilty." It had to be "guilty." There was no way they could reach any other conclusion, given the DNA and fingerprint evidence.

"I wonder if they started deliberating right away or if they had lunch first?" someone in our group asked.

"Good question." I wondered, *did they spend all this time discussing the various evidence presented, or did they spend some time forcing down the overcooked vegetables of the day?* It was likely they'd had lunch sent in and discussed the case at the same time. I would have loved to have been a fly on the wall. Was it possible for any of them to *not* reach a "guilty" conclusion? I supposed there was a possibility.

I wondered what had been going through the defendant's mind for the past couple of hours. Had he realized yet that his fate was really in the hands of these twelve people? That their decision would likely influence the rest of his and his family's lives? If they found him guilty, as I presumed they would, he would no longer be able to choose what he would eat every day, what he would wear, where he would go, or what he would do. And — I couldn't help but shudder at the thought — he would no longer be able to choose what woman he would like to terrorized next. God, I hoped this was true.

We had to go through the security check-in when we got back to the courthouse. The policemen at the x-ray machine knew me by sight, yet I still had to go through the procedure. Everyone managed to go ahead of me while I struggled to take off my coat and lay it and my purse on the metal table. I was all thumbs and moving too fast to be at all productive. I hadn't realized until just then that I was really nervous.

After handing my belongings to the guard, I walked through the sensor.

"BEEP!"

"Oh, you have got to be kidding me," I said. The guard called me back.

"The only thing that could be making it beep is my watch," I said as I fumbled to take it off and drop it into the blue plastic tub.

"Okay, go back through and see if that did the trick."

This time the machine was quiet. *Thank God.* As I fumbled to retrieve Nana's watch from the tub, I looked up to see the sherrif's deputy who had been in the courtroom the very first time I'd gone in there with Kathleen and Cindy months ago. This same policeman had been in the courtroom guarding the defendant for at least part of the trial.

"Did Cindy call you? The jury's back already? They have a verdict?" he asked.

"Yeah, I just got the call a couple of minutes ago. She told me they jury is back — they're ready."

Damn this watch band, why couldn't I get it rehooked? All the times I had gone through this process and it hadn't caused any problems at all. It figured it would pick this time to set off the alarms.

"Good luck," the deputy said with a smile.

"Thank you!" I answered, still fumbling with my watch.

Just then Dave Cordle approached the security station from inside the courthouse.

"Hurry up, the judge is ready to start without you."

"Oh, he's not starting without me," I answered as we rushed down the hall. "I've been waiting twenty-two years for this. For some reason my grandmother's watch picked this time to set off all the bells and whistles when I went through. Unbelievable!" *Screw the watch,* I thought, and dropped it into the pocket of my purse.

89

The Verdict

We made it to courtroom 3-D before Trice and the judge entered the room. *These folks really like the dramatic,* I thought. Marcus and I took our places on the first bench. Cindy was again sitting to his right. I took my cell phone out of my purse and powered it off. Then I reached into the pocket of my purse and picked up my watch. Now that I was in the courtroom and settled, I had calmed down enough to put it back on my wrist without any problem at all.

I looked up at the sound of the door next to the judge's bench opening. Trice entered the courtroom and began shuffling toward me. Gone was his pretense of any sympathy toward me. As he made his way into the room, he locked his eyes on mine. A shiver ran through me and my blood slowed under the power of his cold stare. I saw pure hatred in his eyes, but I didn't look away.

I didn't put you in this position, I thought. *This is all you. You chose this lifestyle, and you are responsible for everything you have done. You may hate me for standing up to you, but you brought all of this on yourself.*

I wondered again how many women he'd raped. How many times had he heard the screams and felt superior? How many times had he gotten away with his crimes? He hated me, that was certain. He hated me for stopping him. He hated me because I was standing up to him and he could not retaliate. I doubted anyone else had stood up to him before. He was powerless.

I hope you can hear my thoughts. As if on cue, he looked away from my face and shuffled over to his seat.

2:45

Bailiff: *All rise.*

Judge Hackner: **Be seated, please. Check to make sure your cell phones are off, please, and remain quiet in the room. We're going to resume the matter of State of Maryland vs. William Joseph Trice K-08-00281. Counsel, identify yourselves, please.**

Ms Rogers: *Kathleen Rogers on behalf of the State.*

Mr. Szekely: Andrew Szekely on behalf of Mr. Trice, who is present to my right.

Ms Waters: And also Gwendolyn Waters on behalf of Mr. Trice.

Judge Hackner: **Alright, thank you. Counsel, you may have a seat. I understand we have a verdict and I'll ask the jury to come in, please. If you haven't already done so, before you leave, could you see that the jury lists are given back to the clerk, please? Be seated, please. Alright, the jury is now present in the courtroom and the clerk, may you please inquire.**

Clerk of the Court: Ladies and gentlemen of the jury, have you agreed on your verdict?

Jury Foreperson: *Yes, we have.*

Clerk of the Court: Who will speak for you? Madam Foreperson, please stand and pass the verdict sheet to the court.

Bailiff: *I'll give it back to you after the judge looks at it.*

Judge Hackner: **Thank you. Counsel, come here, please.**

(White Noise)

This didn't seem right. I'd never seen a verdict announced like this on TV. This couldn't be the normal way to do things. Something must be wrong. Hung jury? No, they had only been deliberating for two hours. The judge wouldn't accept that conclusion. Mistrial? Maybe one of the jury members realized they knew me or the defendant? No, they wouldn't have been quiet about this for an entire week.

I looked at Cindy, my brows scrunched up in concern. "What's going on?" I asked.

"Not sure," Cindy said. "This doesn't happen very often. Usually it means the jury didn't do something correctly."

When Kathleen came back to her table after talking with the judge, she whispered to Cindy that the verdict sheet had not been filled in correctly.

"That kind of makes me nervous," I said. "Both you and the judge explained how to fill the form out before they went into the jury room. Seemed pretty straightforward to me."

"Yeah, but you never know," Marcus said. "I'm sure they discussed the charges and thought they were filling it in correctly. It's one thing to hear how to do something, and a lot different when you actually have to do it. Think about it — they were just hired to do this job last week. And they had to start right away. They didn't have any training. They were just expected to learn how to do it. And it's a pretty big responsibility. I'm sure they thought they were doing it right."

"That's true," Cindy agreed. "I never really thought of it like that before. The jury doesn't get any training; they get selected and then they are asked to render a verdict." I sighed nervously. This kind of thing only happens to me.

"Yeah, I guess you're right. You guys are used to how things work because you've been doing it for years, but these folks have only been here for a couple of days," I said.

Judge Hackner: Ladies and gentlemen of the jury, I have reviewed the verdict sheet and I'm gonna have to send you back to the jury room. Each line item has to have a response. You have to come to some conclusion, or if you, you know, after a lengthy deliberation, are unable to come to some conclusion, you can let us know. But there can't be any blanks on any line or else we are left wondering whether you have decided the case on that point or not. So, I'm going to excuse you back to the jury room and give back the verdict sheet. And when you have determined those other matters, then please check them in and initial them again, please. Alright, we'll stand in recess.

Bailiff: *All rise.*

And we all exited the courtroom.

The Verdict: Take Two

Once we were out in the hallway, Kathleen came up to me and explained quietly what the problem had been.

"Each of the charges had been broken down into "sub-charges" that had to be marked as "Guilty" or "Not Guilty," and they only filled in part of the form."

She did tell me at this time what the jury had marked for a couple of the charges, but as she was relaying this information to me, Marcus came up and said, "When you're writing your book, you probably should leave this part out. Kind of ruins the ending, if you know what I mean."

We laughed. He was right. I'd hate to give away the ending.

Kathleen suggested we stay close.

"They have to fill in all the charges and it could take them just a few minutes or it could take them a while. And they are free to change any or all of the answers once they go back in there, so we don't really know what the verdict will be. But I don't want to have to track you down when they are ready."

"No problem," I said. "I'm not going anywhere."

Just like the first day of the trial when we waited in the room downstairs during jury selection, I had the feeling that if this group of people were anywhere but here, it would look like we were having a party. Everyone was talking with nervous animation. We were pretty loud, too, but no one was asking us to be quiet. I looked to my right, away from my friends and family, and saw the two defense lawyers standing by themselves talking. The two of them stood in stark contrast to my large group. Mr. Szekely looked in my direction. The expression on his face was solemn.

I heard my name being called: "Jen, come here."

It was Marnie. She was standing with Dave Cordle.

"Yeah, what's up?"

"Did you know Dave has been to my house?" she asked.

"No, why? What did you do?"

"Ha, ha. Very funny. He came to the house on Route 2."

"The yellow one where we had the garden?"

"Yeah. He was there after the funeral for Jim's father." Jim was Marnie's ex-husband.

"Really? Why? Did he think there was foul play or something?"

"No," Dave said. "My best friend is Jim's brother. Russell and I have been friends for years. He was the best man at my wedding. I was there to pay my respects."

"Really? Unbelievable!" I exclaimed. "Did you know this, Marnie?"

"No, I don't really remember who was there that day. Not sure I would have known who Dave was back then, anyway."

"Probably not." I said. How crazy was this? Bill Johns was one of Marcus' best friends growing up and Dave Cordle was best friends with my best friend's ex-husband's brother. The connections just kept getting crazier and crazier.

"Another piece of the puzzle," Dave said.

Both Cindy and Kathleen were standing close by, chatting. I walked over to Kathleen and asked her if she had any idea how much longer the jury might be.

"Impossible to say. They are probably going over the entire form again to be sure they get it filled in right this time. They want to be thorough," she said.

I couldn't understand why checking a few boxes was taking such a long time and I began to feel nervous. We had been standing in the hall for what seemed like forever.

"Did you hear the latest crazy connection?" I asked. Kathleen indicated that she had not, so I explained.

"Well, did you know that I used to have a crush on Jim when we were kids?" Kathleen asked me.

"That I didn't know," I laughed.

"Dave and I hung out together as kids, and Jim and Russ were often a part of our group," she said.

"That's too funny." So many puzzle pieces I didn't even know about kept falling into place.

After about an hour, Cindy and Kathleen went into the courtroom to see if the jury was making any progress. Just a few minutes later, Kathleen called to me.

"They're ready."

I called to everyone gathered around that the jury was back.

"Make sure your cell phones are turned off," I said.

3:51

Judge Hackner:	**Be seated, please. Court resumes with case of State of Maryland vs. William Joseph Trice K-08-002821. Counsel, identify yourselves, please.**
Ms Rogers:	*Kathleen Rogers on behalf of the State.*
Mr. Szekely:	Andrew Szekely on behalf of Mr. Trice, who is present to my right.
Ms Waters:	And also Gwendolyn Waters on behalf of Mr. Trice.
Judge Hackner:	**Okay. Thank you. If you'll have a seat. I understand that the verdict is ready and we'll have the jurors come on in, please. Be seated, please. The jury is**

now present in the courtroom. Madam Clerk, could you inquire, please?

Clerk of the Court: *Ladies and gentlemen of the jury, have you agreed on your verdict?*

Jury: Yes, we have.

Clerk of the Court: *Who will speak for you? Madam Foreperson, please stand and pass the verdict sheet to the court.*

Clerk of the Court: *Madam Foreperson, in case number K-08-002821 State of Maryland vs. William Joseph Trice, do you, the jury, find the defendant "Guilty" or "Not Guilty" of Second Degree Rape?*

Jury Foreperson: Guilty.

Clerk of the Court: *Do you, the jury, find the defendant "Guilty" or "Not Guilty" of First Degree Rape by the circumstances that the defendant inflicted suffocation, strangulation, disfigurement, or serious physical injury against Jennifer Wheatley in the course of committing the offense?*

Jury Foreperson: Guilty.

Clerk of the Court: *Do you, the jury, find the defendant "Guilty" or "Not Guilty" of First Degree Rape by the circumstances that the defendant threatened or placed Jennifer Wheatley [in] reasonable fear that she would be imminently subjected to death, suffocation, strangulation, disfigurement, serious physical injury, or kidnapping?*

Jury Foreperson: Guilty.

Clerk of the Court: *Do you, the jury, find the defendant "Guilty" or "Not Guilty" of First Degree Rape by the circumstances that the defendant committed the offense in connection with [a] burglary?*

Jury Foreperson: Guilty.

Clerk of the Court: *Do you, the jury, find the defendant "Guilty" or "Not Guilty" of Second Degree Sexual Offense?*

Jury Foreperson: Guilty.

Clerk of the Court: *Do you, the jury, find the defendant "Guilty" or "Not Guilty" of First Degree Sexual Offense by the circumstances that the defendant inflicted suffocation, strangulation, disfigurement, or serious physical injury against Jennifer Wheatley in the course of committing the offense?*

Jury Foreperson: Guilty.

Clerk of the Court: *Do you, the jury, find the defendant "Guilty" or "Not Guilty" of First Degree Sexual Offense by the circumstances that the defendant threatened or placed Jennifer Wheatley [in] reasonable fear that she would be imminently subjected to death, suffocation, strangulation, disfigurement, serious physical injury, or kidnapping?*

Jury Foreperson: Guilty.

Clerk of the Court: *Do you, the jury, find the defendant "Guilty or "Not Guilty" of burglary?*

Jury Foreperson: Guilty.

Judge Hackner: **Alright, if you could hand the bailiff the verdict sheet.
You may have a seat.**

(to the clerk)

Judge Hackner: **Alright, please hearken [the] verdict.**

Clerk of the Court: *Ladies and gentlemen of the jury, you have heard the
verdict as the court has recorded it. Your foreperson
says you find the defendant "Guilty" as charged. Do
you all agree on that verdict?*

Jury: Yes.

I did not take my eyes off Trice the entire time these verdicts were being
announced. He stood with his hands clasped behind him. Oddly, his stance
was not unlike the posture he assumed when he was being handcuffed.
As Judge Hackner took the jury form from the bailiff to check that it had
been filled in correctly and completely, Trice stared straight ahead. By the
time the jury announced the third "Guilty," I saw him raise his eyebrows
and suck in a big breath of air, filling his cheeks, then releasing the air
slowly. He bowed his head and shook it from side to side as if to say,
"No, this can't be." I was shocked to witness his surprise and disbelief at
the guilty verdicts. I believe, until he heard the announcements himself, he
truly thought he was going to be freed of the charges he faced.

Through my steady tears of release and happiness, I witnessed Trice
deflate like a spent balloon. His disguise had been stripped away, layer by
layer, with each announced "Guilty" verdict until the weak shell of a man
was revealed. He was no longer cocky, relaxed, and in control. He was
broken, and he appeared to be trembling.

Judge Hackner: **Ladies and gentlemen, thank you very much for your
conscientious effort in this matter. I appreciate your**

time and the attention that you paid to us. And I'm going to excuse you with our thanks. You are welcome to go and talk to no one or talk to anyone you care to talk to. The bailiff is going to hand you your notes, and I thank you again. You may be excused, and you'll go back out this door, please.

Bailiff: *Okay, follow me, please.*

Judge Hackner: **Alright, counsel, it'll be likely that I'll defer sentencing for some period, and if you like, I can order a pre-sentencing investigation.** *

Mr. Szekely: Your honor, I would ask for a pre-sentencing investigation. I don't know the State's feeling on the matter.

Ms Rogers: *That's fine, your honor.*

Mr. Szekely: But as terms of the PSI, your honor, given that I, ah, haven't discussed this with Mr. Trice as, ah, this eventuality we are, we will be filing an appeal, and he does have another pending case of a similar nature by no other members of this bench in the past ordered the...[unintelligible]... Department ask to not discuss the facts of this case with...

---

* *"A pre-sentencing investigation is governed by state and local laws, which vary by jurisdiction. It is designed to provide the sentencing court with succinct and precise information upon which to base a rational sentencing decision. They are typically performed by probation officers.*

Generally, neither courts nor any other agency or organization shall prescribe or proscribe either directly or indirectly the content of the probation officer's analysis and recommendation. However, the court may recommend or order that additional information be included and analyzed in any particular case(s). Similarly, the court may recommend but not order that certain information be omitted from probation reports." http://definitions.uslegal.com/p/pre-sentence-investigation/

Ms Rogers:	*Sure.*
Judge Hackner:	That's fine. Will you please indicate that the Department of Parole and Probation will not ask any questions about this case and that counsel may be present during the interview? And I was going to propose, I don't know what your thoughts are, but I know Mr. Trice has another matter pending. I don't know whether you would find it efficacious to have the sentencing before or after the trial.
Ms Rogers:	*I think it would be in everyone's best interest to do it before.*
Mr. Szekely:	Ms Rogers made a point that if we could, maybe more on the six week range than the eight week range? That way both, maybe, we'll have an idea whether we need to start gearing up for the other trial or not.
Judge Hackner:	Sure. The week of the 15th? Nah, that's...the week of the 8th of March, or do you want to do it sooner?
Ms Rogers:	*That's fine with me.*
Mr. Szekely:	I am available any time that week, I think.
Judge Hackner:	Alright, I'll propose that how about Monday, the 8th or Thursday, the 11th?
Ms Rogers:	*Either one.*
Mr. Szekely:	Either one.
Judge Hackner:	Alright, let's make it Monday, the 8th, at 1:30pm. And I don't know what the defendant's bail status is, but

any bail would be revoked. The defendant is to be held without bond pending sentencing on March the 8th. And if the pre-sentencing investigation is back sooner and you want to advance the date, you are welcome to do that. Now, what happens between now and then, who knows? Alright, thank you very much, counsel.

Ms Rogers: *Thank you, your honor.*

Mr. Szekely: Thank you, your honor.

I could hear whispering between Mr. Szekely and Trice: "We'll talk," Mr. Szekely said.

Judge Hackner: Okay... Hold on a second, counsel? Mr. Trice, let me advise you, sir, that you have ten days from today to file a request for a retrial. If you'd like to exercise that right, you can file it with the clerk in accord of your right.

Bailiff: *All rise.*

Sentencing

Sentencing was set for March 8th and Judge Hackner ordered a "Pre-Sentence Investigation." This is a comprehensive report provided to the Division of Parole and Probation which includes almost every aspect of a person's history. Once completed and received by our office, we send a copy to Trice's attorney. Judge Hackner would determine the harshness of Trice's sentence dependent on the defendant's previous criminal history and the pending rape trial.

Jennifer gave a lot of thought to what she wanted to say to Trice in her Victim Impact Statement during the sentencing hearing. After the trial I, had an opportunity to read her statement. It was, by far, the most compelling I have ever witnessed in my career. I know Jennifer had been really looking forward to confronting her brutal attacker in an environment where she was finally in control. However, Jennifer's final confrontation with Trice would never take place.

92

Celebration

*A*s I listened to the exchanges between the judge, the three lawyers, and Trice, I watched as he was shackled and handcuffed in preparation for his trip back to the Detention Center on Jennifer Road. I could see that most of my group had already filed out into the hallway, wiping tears and smiling at the same time. Marcus held my hand, and he seemed eager to exit the room. I fumbled around in my purse for a tissue to dab my eyes. I really needed to blow my nose, but I wanted to wait until I could get to the bathroom to do that.

"Are you ready?" Marcus asked.

"Yup," I answered.

As I tucked the tissue back into my purse and stood up, I heard someone say, "*You're not going to see him again.*" Who said that? I'd heard the softly spoken words as clear as a bell in my right ear, so I looked in the direction of the voice. There was no one there. I looked toward the defendant's table. Trice was starting to scuff toward the exit with a guard on each side of him. The judge had left the room. Both Kathleen and Cindy were on their way out to the hallway. Marcus and I were the last two from our group to leave the room. *Of course, I was going to see him again,* I thought as I walked out the heavy wooden door. *I'd see him on March 8th.*

As soon as I walked out the door, I was surrounded by my friends, and I quickly forgot about the voice I had just heard. I made sure to thank each one from my group and gave each of them a hug.

"Oh my God, Jen, you did it! The son-of-a-bitch is going to jail. Unbelievable," Marnie sobbed in my ear as we hugged each other tight.

"Couldn't have done it without you," I said. "I'm so glad you were here with me for this; to see it to the end."

"Wouldn't have missed it, babe!" Marnie answered, wiping tears from her eyes.

I looked up and saw Andrea walking toward us.

"Are you just getting here," I asked.

"Oh, no, I've been here for a while. I just couldn't remember what courtroom you were in. I've been wandering around trying to figure it out. I called, but you must have already turned your cell off," she answered.

"Oh, no! 3-D, same as before. So you missed it?"

"Yes, but I was there when I was supposed to be; when you needed me to be," she answered as I gave her a hug.

I turned to Kathleen, who for the first time — maybe the only time since I had known her — was smiling.

"The fucker honestly thought he was going to get off. I can't believe how shocked he looked when the verdicts were read," I said as I hugged her. "Thank you."

Cindy hugged me. "I'll be in touch to go over your Impact Statement with you. But today is a happy day. Now is the time to celebrate!" she said. "You go celebrate, have fun."

"Okay, we're going to do that for sure, but I have my statement finished. Started working on it about a year ago and I took it out and finished it last week."

"You might want to change it or add to it," she said

"Nope, I don't think so. It's finished. I've written just what I want to say to him. I'll e-mail it to you for your approval. You can let me know if it's okay."

"Okay! I'll be in touch. Go have fun," Cindy said. As she hugged me again, I thanked her for all her help, and thought how odd it felt to finally be close to the last lap of this journey.

The group of us decided to have an early dinner at Galway Bay restaurant on Maryland Avenue. It was a beautiful afternoon, so we walked over as a group. Everyone was talking. We met Charlotte from the B&B as we rounded State Circle. She looked at us and knew right away we'd gotten the conviction.

"Guilty on all counts!" I said as she hugged me. "I'll see you later. We are going to go unwind a bit."

"Congratulations! Go have fun with your friends, you deserve it," she said and continued on her way. I felt like someone had taken jumper cables to me — I was full of nervous energy! I had made several phone calls and sent what seemed like dozens of text messages spreading the news, and still my phone was ringing off the hook.

After we arrived at the restaurant and eager to let my mother know the verdict, I walked downstairs to the quiet ladies' room. I knew she was waiting by the phone for a call from me. When she answered the phone, I immediately began to cry tears of relief.

"Hi, Mom," I said. ""Guilty" on all counts!"

"Oh goody," Mom said. "I'm so glad. I knew that SOB was guilty. I don't even know why he made you go through a trial."

"You should have seen his face when the judge was reading the verdicts," I said. "I honestly believe he thought he was going to get off. He was shocked."

"Shocked? I don't know why he would be shocked. They had DNA and a fingerprint. He knew he did it. He knew he was guilty."

I told Mom that sentencing was set for March 8th.

"I hope he rots in jail," Mom said. "He deserves it. Well, I'm glad it's finally over and you can relax now. Oh, I can't wait to call Babs and Betty and tell them that SOB is finally going to get his comeuppance."

Mom was clearly as excited and relieved as I was. She had been waiting years to hear this news, too.

"I guess you can get rid of the bat now," I said, laughing through my tears.

After we said our goodbyes, I returned to our table. Our animated group was chatting nonstop and a bit loudly, but so early in the evening, we were the only people in the dining room.

Art and Hope had to drive back to Pennsylvania, so they were the first to leave.

"We have to check our schedules, but I am pretty sure we will be able to drive back for sentencing on March 8th. I'll let you know for sure," Hope said as she hugged me goodbye.

"Okay. Have a safe trip home. Thanks so much for driving down today. I'm so glad you two were here," I said as they got ready to go.

Gradually our group thinned until just Shirli and Andrea and I remained. Galway Bay runs a trivia contest on Tuesday nights and since we were already there, we decided to play. Unfortunately, the King of Trivia, Marcus, had to drive home because he had to work the next day. We could have really used him on our team because we didn't do so well with our answers. I think we got about half of them correct, but on so many that we got wrong, I said, "Crap, Marcus knows the answer to this one."

Shortly after the trivia contest ended, Shirli headed home for the night, and Andrea and I headed back to her car on State Circle. As we rounded the corner, we heard a familiar voice singing *The Unicorn Song* faintly from a window above us at Harry Browne's.

"Want to stop in and say "hi" to Seamus Kennedy?" Andrea asked me.

"Is that him singing? I haven't seen him for, hell, nineteen or twenty years. Yes, I would love to stop in for a few songs," I said.

As we climbed the steps to the small bar, I mentioned to Andrea that I doubted if Seamus ever really knew who I was. "I remember singing with him and Tim King at The Drummer's Lot a couple of times, but I don't think he'll know who I am." His set was ending just as we sat down at the bar, and Seamus walked over to say hello to Andrea. "You remember Jennifer, don't you? She's a friend of Tim's from the old days at the Maryland Inn." I wasn't convinced that he did remember me, but Seamus was gracious and said hello, and then stayed and chatted with us for a while.

"What brings you two ladies into town this evening?" he asked us. Andrea mentioned that we were catching up after finding each other on Facebook. "And I'm hanging out with Jen while she's in town for a few days."

I explained to Seamus that I was "playing tourist" for a week and that I'd testified for the State in the rape trial that had been going on. We told him how the rapist had been caught after twenty years, and was linked to at least one other victim by DNA evidence, and that I had been a key witness. I didn't get into a lot of details about the crime and tried to keep my description short. He wasn't satisfied.

"In what capacity did you testify?" Seamus asked. "As a scientist or police officer or...?"

"No," I said. "As one of his victims."

I'd heard of the expression, "watching someone's face melt." I witnessed just this phenomenon as the words I spoke sunk in. He'd known me back then and had had no idea that I had been raped. He was visibly moved by what I'd said. I could detect the anger in his voice and see it in his eyes for just a second, but he regained his composure quickly, telling me how proud he was of me for what I had done. He then took a step toward me, embraced me, and in my ear he said, "Thank you."

As Seamus walked back to the microphone and picked up his guitar, Andrea and I moved to a table closer to the stage, where we sang along to his last few songs. I thought about how different I felt, having triumphed over my fears, and how incredible hearing the "guilty" verdicts announced made me feel. In many ways, everything was unfamiliar and new and not unlike moving into a new home. All your belongings are there, but they all look different because they are arranged in a new way. And yet, sitting at Harry Browne's with Andrea and listening to Seamus sing transported me back, yet again, to the familiar, comfortable evenings spent similarly more than twenty years ago.

After Seamus' last song, we got up to leave. As we said good night, Seamus hugged me and thanked me again for what I had done. I told him to keep an eye on the papers.

"Even though I have not seen them myself, I hear it's been big news and has been in the Annapolis and Baltimore papers," I said. "The reporters were in the courtroom today, and I would guess the story will be in tomorrow's *Capital*. It was wonderful to see you again, Seamus."

Andrea dropped me off at the Flag House Inn. "Thank you so much for everything," I said as I got out of the car. I'll be in touch. Hopefully, I will see you before March 8th, but if not, I will "see" you on Facebook!"

Once back in my room alone, I could feel my energy begin to fade. What a day! I turned on my computer and opened the Text document, *Impact Statement* and added a few sentences. Then I e-mailed it to Cindy for her approval. I sent off a few thank-you e-mails, packed up most of my clothes, and then went to bed. I think I was asleep before my head hit the pillow.

Wednesday was another sunny day. Before I headed out, I checked my computer for any new messages. I wanted to be sure to send Susan an update because I couldn't remember if I had sent her a text message after court the day before. After typing my e-mail, I headed out of the B&B in search of food and a newspaper. I was early for the latest edition of the *Capital*, so I had a sandwich and a cup of coffee in Hard Beans Coffee & Booksellers. While I sat eating, I wondered if I would have the courage to read my statement out loud in the courtroom. I really wanted to. I needed to. But I didn't want stagefright to win. *Crap*, I thought, *I'd just done one of the toughest things in my life.* If I could go into that courtroom and see that creep eye-to-eye and then testify, I could get through my statement. I'd gotten through Karaoke the other night without a missed note, hadn't I? I could do it!

After I finished my sandwich, I walked back to the newsstand and bought a paper. I sat on a cold bench nearby and read the article, "Rapist Found Guilty," and then headed back to the Flag House Inn. I knocked on the door to Charlotte and Bill's apartment.

When Charlotte opened her door, I said, "Just wanted you to know Marcus is on his way, and I'll be out of your hair pretty soon."

"Oh, no problem. It's been great having you," Charlotte said.

I handed her my credit card and asked if I could have a separate statement for the days of the trial.

"Dave Cordle told me I would be reimbursed for some of the cost if I send him a copy." After we settled the bill, we sat in the parlor and chatted about how we'd passed the day. Pretty soon, Charlotte's husband, Bill, joined us and we started talking about the closing arguments. The two of them had sat in for the closing, and I hadn't gotten a chance to hear what they'd thought about what they'd heard.

"I think, given the evidence against him, the defense lawyer did a pretty good job. There wasn't much he could argue with DNA and fingerprint evidence against him," Bill said. Neither of them had heard any of the testimony, and they had only listened to what Mr. Szekely and Kathleen had covered in their closing statements.

"It's interesting to hear that," I said. "I think one thing that is really crazy is what *wasn't* mentioned in the courtroom — missing evidence and how the defense attorney had a lot of wrong information." I went on to tell them the story about the T-shirt and how, in his opening statement, Szekely had said it took me an hour to call the police — implying a setup or suggesting I was lying about knowing the defendant. The three of us sat and talked for an hour about the juggling acts and theatrics that go on in courtrooms all the time. Marcus arrived, and after we packed the car, we said our goodbyes and headed home.

It was nice to be home. The trial had been quite an experience and I'd had a great time hanging out with my friends, but I was happy to have some "alone time" to get back to my normal routine. The cat was definitely happy to see me. She doesn't get along with anyone and is afraid of everyone except me, so she was glad to have me back.

I started writing this book right away while the events of the trial were fresh in my memory. The words came quickly. It took only a few days to get fifty pages finished, and it felt good.

A couple of days after I got home, I got an e-mail from Cindy:

Wow, your impact statement is one of the most powerful I have ever read. Let me talk to Kathleen to see how we can present this in court. It's different than most, but great!

Really? I thought. I wondered what made it so different. Eventually, my statement made its way around the office, and I also got an e-mail from Dave:

Wow, your impact statement is one of strongest, profound statements I've ever seen. Bet you felt good writing it, but I'll be there with you when you read it, and it will be so much better. Have a great weekend!

I guess I didn't have to worry about rewriting it. Debbie sent me an online link to the latest newspaper story, and I noticed that one of the jury members had added a comment. I couldn't help but wonder if this was the woman I had mouthed, "Thank you!" to just a couple days ago.

William Trice Rape Trial – Hometown Annapolis-online-2010-01-21 15:29:14

As a member of the jury on this trial, it was with great satisfaction that I saw Mr. Trice finally get the convictions he deserved for his heinous crimes. I pray that the "victim" gets some relief and feeling of justice, finally. And, after learning about his past history of indecent exposure and upcoming 2nd rape trial in April (which was not allowed in during the course of the trial), it just solidifies my belief that we, as a jury, without a doubt came to the right conclusion.

I would like to thank all the police officers from multiple agencies and states who worked on the cold case and secured the evidence necessary to bring Mr. Trice to justice. To Detective Tracy Morgan in particular — fantastic job! And, also, to State's Attorney, Kathleen Rogers, thanks for your hard work and dedication — great job!

~ Nancy B — Jessup, MD

SENTENCE

You could live with knowing what you had done,
but you couldn't live with the world knowing what you had done.
~ J. A. W. ~

January 25, 2010

I awoke early this morning to a gray sky that was spitting rain, and a cold wind blew. Before noon, though, the clouds began to break up, revealing a crisp blue sky. I stepped out to the front porch with my camera in hand. The breeze was warm on my face and it smelled of a premature promise of spring. Crazy breaks in the clouds, a tangle of bare branches, and a mourning dove caught my eye. I snapped a few photos, enjoying the false spring.

It was just six days since the verdict and a few weeks until the sentencing date. *I might just have my book written by then,* I thought as I reluctantly returned to my computer and took up with my story where I had left off.

After just a few minutes, the phone rang.

"Hello, Jennifer." I recognized Cindy's voice. "This is Cindy Haworth at the State's Attorney's Office." I couldn't imagine what she wanted; maybe she was calling to set up a meeting to go over what would happen at sentencing. It seemed kind of early for that.

"Hi, Cindy, what's up?"

"I wanted to tell you before anyone else did or before you see it in the paper — Trice killed himself."

"Holy mother of God," I said. I felt a chill run through me. Every nerve in my body vibrated and I felt blanketed with cold.

94

Unexpected Outcome

On January 25, 2010, at 10:00 a.m., I received a call on my cell phone from Cindy Haworth. The Anne Arundel County Detention Center had called to inform her that Trice had committed suicide by hanging earlier that morning — just six days after his conviction.

Trice had taken the coward's way out. Perhaps I should not make that judgment, but, for whatever reason, Trice could not accept his past, nor endure his future. Perhaps he realized that he really was bad and could not live with the knowledge of the crimes he had committed.

I immediately called Jennifer who seemed to be in a quandary about how she felt about what had just happened. We both had mixed emotions about Trice's suicide. In my opinion, Trice chose to be an animal, yet he was still human. I'd known he would not survive too well in jail, but by taking his own life, Trice only created more victims of his actions — Jennifer, once again, would not get the final closure of seeing him sentenced for his crimes. The family Trice left behind — his mother and wife* in New York, and his father and brother in Maryland — would have to live with the pain and shame of how Trice had led his life. And the other rape victim, who is now in her sixties and living overseas, will never have her "day in court."

---

* *During a conversation with Trice at the jail in New York, Trice's wife told him she was leaving him.*

"Final Chapter"

I was overcome by a mix of emotions — astonishment, guilt, disappointment, anger, and relief.

I was astonished because this end had never occurred to me. I never considered he would take his own life. I'd supposed because he had spent the previous fifteen months in jail, he would continue there for the duration of his sentence. I have no way of knowing what a life behind the bars of a jail cell is like. I believed the emotional prison he'd put me in for so many years was still a life worth living. I assumed he would think being alive in jail was far better than being dead. I can only surmise that he knew his past had truly defined him and he couldn't live with the daily reminder of the person he was.

I felt guilt because, no matter what Trice had done to me, I did not want to be the cause of his decision to take his own life. I realize *he* made the choice to end his life rather than spend the rest of his days behind bars. I did not force his hand. But I felt that my victory in the courtroom certainly played a role in his decision.

I felt disappointment. Even if I could forgive him for what he had done to me, I could never forgive him for what he'd done to his other victims. It wasn't up to me to forgive him for them. When he met my gaze in the courtroom just before the closing arguments, he was clearly putting on a show for the jury, but I did not look away. I will have to be satisfied that the times the defendant and I made eye contact were enough for him to see that the pain he had caused me all those years ago had been replaced by a conviction of purpose and determination to stop him. I was disappointed, though, because I had realized the power gained by testifying against this man, and I knew his other victims would never have this opportunity. I hoped what he saw in my eyes that day spoke for all of his victims.

I was angry because serving fifteen months in jail did not seem like a fair sentence to me. When my counsel and I were discussing a plea, they had asked me what I felt was a fair deal.

"I want him to have to spend as many years in prison as he has walked a free man after he raped me. Twenty-one years."

He was facing a life sentence. Serving only six days since his conviction did not seem at all long enough.

I was angry because his final selfish act in life denied me the opportunity to speak to him. I had begun to write my thoughts over a year before the trial took place. Reading my statement to him publicly was to be my final triumph over the power he'd reined over me. Testifying in the courtroom had been empowering for me, and I was able to take back what he had stolen all those years ago. But I wanted him to hear my voice telling him so in my own words, while he looked into my eyes.

I was angry because I wanted him to know what it felt like to have everything I had ever believed in, everything I believed to be true in life, ripped to shreds. I wanted him to be aware of the repercussions of his actions. I wanted him to know what an emotional struggle it is to pull yourself back up on your feet and begin to live again. I felt cheated because, after he raped me, I had to rebuild my life one struggle at a time, and he took the easy way out. I wanted him to struggle.

I suppose in the end, he did realize just this. The words of an old friend explained it:

Geez — just read the paper — I am in awe...he faced the music against a strong soldier — you — and then he simply quit. I am glad you had the last word my dear.
Luv you, Janis

I was relieved, because so many of my family and friends had been in the courtroom with me. They were able to free themselves from any grip this man had had on them over the years.

And finally, I was also relieved because the monster was gone. He had taken the coward's way out, but he would not be able to hurt anyone again. This one final act of taking his own life was, to me, a declaration of his guilt — an admission of guilt for what he had done to me, what he had done to the other victim he was to face in trial, guilt for the crimes he had been charged with over the past two decades and guilt for all the other crimes he had committed and had yet to be charged with.

A couple of days after Trice killed himself, Cindy called to tell me the newspapers had been calling her with questions concerning his death. Apparently, this was the third rape case that she and Kathleen had tried in court, had succeeded in getting a conviction, and had ended with the defendant committing suicide. Although Cindy didn't care to comment about this latest development, remembering that I was working on a book about the case, she thought I might be interested in speaking to a reporter.

"Eric Hartley from the *Capital* is interested in talking to you. Is it okay to give him your phone number?"

"Okay, sure. Maybe it would be easiest to send him my last chapter and "Victim's Impact Statement." I'm not sure I really have much more than that to say."

"I still can't believe he did this. Is it selfish of me to say I'm pissed?" Cindy said. "I'm really disappointed, because your Impact Statement was the best I have ever read. I was really looking forward to hearing you read it in court."

"No, it's not selfish at all. I am really pissed that he won't get to hear it," I said.

It wasn't too long after I hung up that Eric called and got his story for the paper.

96

"Decades after rape, not defined as a victim"

By Eric Hartley, Staff Writer
The Capital — 01/31/10

Jennifer Wheatley needed to tell the man who raped her 21 years ago that his act, while it has changed her, does not define her. She is who she is in spite of him, but also because of him. After all, who knows how her life would have gone had the attack never happened?

"This is apparently where my life was meant to go," she told me.

Jennifer was a victim, but that is not who she is. He had to know that — know what he had done to her and what he hadn't. At the end of the remarks she planned to deliver directly to him during a March sentencing hearing, she wrote, in language as devastating as it is simple:

"I am an artist.

"That is my legacy."

"You are a rapist. That is how the world will remember you."

She never got to say those words to their intended audience. The rapist, a 48-year-old who'd gone on to drive a tow truck in New York state, hanged himself in the Jennifer Road Detention Center in Parole last week.

He took the easy way out, a final act of cowardice. A prosecutor once asked Jennifer how long she wanted him to go to prison, and she decided that 21 years — the amount of time between crime and conviction — was about right. It had a certain ring of poetic justice. Instead, he spent 15 months in jail.

Jennifer's emotions, still raw late last week when we talked, are a jumble. There is guilt that she in some way was involved in a person's death, anger that he never had to face justice, and disappointment that she and another woman he was accused of raping never got to speak to him directly in court.

Usually, in news stories on sexual assaults, the attacker is named but not the victim, for obvious reasons. But Jennifer agreed to be identified by her maiden name, saying, "It's something that should be talked about more."

So why name the attacker here? For once, he will be the anonymous one, and the victim will have a human face.

Jennifer, now 51, was 29 years old and single in 1988, working as a waitress at the Chart House restaurant in Eastport, the neighborhood where she also lived.

After getting home from a late shift Aug. 21, Jennifer got a series of strange calls from a man who knew her name and age — because, as it turned out, he had stolen papers from her car. Later, the 27-year-old man broke into the apartment she shared with her mother, surprised her and raped her.

With the perspective of time, Jennifer called her reaction in the aftermath "textbook." She slept in her clothes with the lights on, afraid to undress, afraid of the dark, afraid to be alone, afraid to live.

"When somebody attacks you in your house, you don't feel safe anywhere," she said.

Even as the immediate shock slowly faded, she remained angry at God and unable to trust for a long time. For more than a year, she drank heavily. It's been nearly 20 years since she stopped after a realization with the help of friends.

"I was worth saving," she recalled. "I was just giving him too much power, and he had destroyed so much of my life already. ... I had to discover who I really was."

She learned picture framing and worked for years in shops around Annapolis. Her art, a hobby from childhood, became a calling. She painted watercolors and has sold more than 300 works. Now, using colored fabrics and paint, she creates quilts so intricately detailed they look like paintings. (View her work at www.artgiftsetc.com.)

About 10 years after the rape, she told herself it would never be solved. He had gotten away with it.

Then came the calls from investigators. The case broke, little by little. First a DNA match to another rape case, then a fingerprint match between a candle from her apartment and a suspect, and finally, a conclusive DNA match to that suspect.

After a jury convicted him Jan. 19, she started writing a book. She hopes that story will help other women see the hope that's there, but hard to see. "This is a story that I had known for a long time," she said. "I just didn't know how to write the ending."

"I didn't see it for years, and I wouldn't have believed it then," Jennifer said. "But I think maybe if I had heard from someone who had walked in that path and had done all the things that I had to do, maybe it would have been easier to hold a little hope."

Jennifer, who was born and raised in Annapolis, no longer lives here. She preferred that her current residence not be printed.

He does not get to win. She has bravely made a life and created art that brings light to the world and joy to people. And she has let hope and trust return to her life. At her 20-year high school reunion, she asked a classmate to dance. They'd shared a homeroom class, but [had] never been close.

Six years ago, they married.

Eric Hartley's editorial about my case won him 1st place and "Best of Show" honors in the 2010 MD/DC/DE Press Association contest.

97

News Travels Quickly

$\mathcal{A}$s soon as the newspaper broke the story and I was allowed to tell everyone the news, I sent an e-mail out to everyone, along with a link to the online story. Responses in the form of phone calls and e-mails started coming. I was still in a state of shock and feeling like I had been denied "the last word." A couple of months passed before I worked through much of my anger at the creep's suicide. I am not sure how long it will take for me to let go of the feeling of being in a sort of limbo.

Not getting to read my "Impact Statement" to Trice in the courtroom was a mixed blessing. On the one hand, I felt as if he had pulled the rug out from under me. On the other, having the story by Eric Hartley and my words to the defendant published in the paper and online for everyone to see allowed me to speak to a much larger audience. By having more people read my thoughts, perhaps my words to Trice would help a stranger to realize that hope is found at the most unexpected time and place.

Once again, I find myself saying that receiving so much support has made this whole crazy journey much easier. Through the e-mails I received, I was truly amazed to discover how many people had learned of the trial. Family and friends had spread the word, and apparently the ripple had grown.

Watching you get up there and testify — Words can't express it. You mentioned that the three times you made eye contact with him and that the pain he saw in your eyes would have to be enough to realize the pain he had caused you. I have to tell you — my perception was something different... you got up there, and you shed some tears. But as you told your story, it seemed more to me that you were shedding this weight, this incredible burden, that you had been carrying for years. What I saw as I looked in your eyes as your testimony went on was strength — not pain, but determination and what I think I would have to describe as a certain fierceness.

You weren't broken. I realize that your life was irrevocably changed, but you lived your life and found your peace and your happiness. You survived all these years of not having answers. You made it through not knowing if you would ever get your justice. You have made this world a better place and have inspired.

Now, it seems that any time I've said how amazing or strong you are, how absolutely inspiring it is to have witnessed your journey, your initial reaction is that you didn't do it alone. You mention everyone else who was affected by this and helped you through, which is a beautiful and gracious sentiment. And I know that without friends and family that your struggle and burden would have been incredibly difficult, if not impossible. I sat with your sisters during your testimony, and there is no denying that they have carried your pain with them (what a loving family you have — you truly are blessed). But please do not diminish the steps that YOU have taken — the steps that nobody could take for you.

This last chapter you've written — who would have thought? Such an unexpected ending. It made me sad that you would have had a moment of guilt, even if you realized that it was not rational. You didn't start this story, and you didn't write this chapter. The beautiful part is that you do get to write how it ends.

Your life is so much more than the events of one night, and it is more than the days since. Your story is one of hope and justice. It's friendships and finding love and creating a life with Marcus. It's your family and friends and your beautiful art and the beauty you find in the everyday things. Your spirit is beautiful.

I hope that you have some sense of peace. I feel the same mixed emotions that you do. How unfair that you didn't get to say those words you waited all of these years to say. But how unbelievably wonderful that you got to hear that word "guilty." And I don't know what your belief system, but I believe that, while he avoided a lifetime in prison, he's now serving a much worse sentence for eternity.

I am proud to be your friend. I am proud to have been with you then, and I'm proud to be with you now. Thank you for allowing me to be part of your journey.

Now we need to get everyone together and celebrate! We need to celebrate the end of this, but I want to celebrate you! We need to plan that...
~ Jackie

The following e-mail was sent to my sister, and she forwarded it to me.

My dearest Mollie,
You think you can empathize with someone who has gone through what Jen went through, but after reading this, I don't think you can. It makes me so sad that she had to go through this all her adult life. And I thank God that she found her peace in her art and, of course, in her family and friends. I didn't realize how strong she is and, well, I'm so proud of her and pray that God always keeps her safe and sound. Her writing is very powerful and she is so talented.

The only thought I had when I saw that the bastard killed himself was, "Good, he deserved it." I didn't think of the impact on Jen and her need to say what she wanted to say. Thank you for sending me the article even

though it made me cry. I was glad to be able to read what Jen said.
God Bless you and your family.
Love, Lisa

Hi Jennifer,
Did you read the Capital article on Sunday? I thought it was fantastic..........
I love how it wasn't about him and they didn't even use his name!

I am really "proud" of you for all the strength you have shown (not to
sound like your Mom or anything) but I think you are great!
best,
Cindy

I want to thank everyone who came to Annapolis to support Jennifer.
It's a shame that sometimes it is the tragedies in life that bring us
together; friends and family. But there everyone was, enjoying each
others' company and having fun, despite the gravity of the trial. Trice
didn't have that. As far as I'm concerned, that's punishment in itself.
We will see you all again many times and continue to have great times
together. As much anger as I have for him, I also pity him. He doesn't
have what we have, and it's extraordinarily valuable!
~ Marcus

I am speechless. I just tried to call you on your cell phone, but I don't even
know what to say. I'm just stunned. And so sorry that you won't get to speak
to him. A tidy and definitive end to the story. By the way, you are a great
writer. Wow — I never saw this coming. Stunned! Why do I want to cry?

That was a great article in the paper on Sunday. You really did get to
have your say in front of him, though, in a way, just by going on the
stand and telling your story with such grace and dignity. He got the
message that you would have given him in your statement, even if it
wasn't in so many words.

I really am so proud of you and I hope you have some peace now.

Have you ever thought about doing rape counseling? Don't women's groups have women with your experience who are on call to help at hospitals when the victims come in?

I would think talking to you would be an inspiration to them at a terrible time in their lives.

I can't help being curious about him, though. I know he was a monster and did terrible things, but he was a person who at one time was a little baby that (hopefully) his mother loved. What made him like he was?

Why [were] there no family or friends there? No character witnesses? I heard him talking to the guard about how he learned to tie a tie.

He bought a clip-on and took it apart and kept practicing until he learned how to do it. Was he trying to improve himself?

Didn't he have a father who could teach him? Was he abused? Was he bullied in school? Why was he angry at women?

Good real-life crime books delve into the psyche of the criminal, but I like that your writing is about you and your journey.

I liked that the newspaper article didn't give him a name and focused on you. Too many books, movies, and TV shows, and even news stories focus on the evil criminal and make them the star and the victim is a nameless, helpless woman.

Your story certainly changes that stereotype.

I don't get onto FB very much, but I have things come to my e-mail. What you wrote, Marcus, was very sweet and oh, so true. I really did feel sorry for him (on top of anger, disgust, etc.) that he was alone. No one there to even wave and let him know he's not alone. And then he died alone. And I

was having a great time! I hate to tell people that I went to a rape trial and had a great time being with family and friends, making new friends, going out to eat, staying at the inn with Art. No mother, no children, no job. I'm just sorry that Jennifer had to suffer for it, but it was also a thrill to see her do so well on the witness stand and represent rape victims everywhere and see the correct verdict come in, and to see all the behind the scenes stuff and hear the fingerprint expert. I was really looking forward to the sentencing — had Art talked into making a long weekend of it — and then the guy goes and ruins all my plans!
~ Hope

Yeah... I'm glad this was published. It's brave of you to put yourself out there this way, but it's also good for ANY victims to read. It's also the best way for you to have your say, to have the last word, since now there won't be a sentencing hearing.

And I like that they included the link to your website in the article! Hopefully people will take a look. I know Marilyn did...she told me she couldn't believe how stunning your quilts are.
Good job!!
Deb

Brilliant! Too bad you cannot copy this statement and have it buried with him.
~ Mollie

To My Favorite Niece,
Ain't life a bitch, just when you think you've figured it out, it smacks you right between the eyes. I certainly agree with your mixed emotions and initially thought that the coward took the easy way out. In reality he did, but he also put himself in a place where no one else can be hurt. I am sorry you didn't get to have the closure of making your very

powerful statement to him and the court. I am very proud of you and love you very much.
~ Your Favorite Uncle

Jennifer
I am just numb after reading this.

His choices are over and, oh, how yours have blossomed.

Thank you for sharing your words — they are very powerful, Jennifer. They riveted through me. You are such a blessing.
Love and big hugs from Nancy

My friend Kathie sent an e-mail to a mutual friend, Barbara, and then forwarded her letter and Barbara's response to me:

I mentioned to Kim recently that I was going to Annapolis for a friend's rape trial. I thought you might want to know that that friend is Jennifer Wheatley-Wolf. She has been amazingly brave through the trial ordeal. The jury found Jen's rapist guilty on all counts. He then committed suicide 6 days later. He raped at least one other woman and apparently was arrested many times and at least once for indecent exposure. "Home Town Annapolis" published an article about Jen and the rape. She wrote an amazing impact statement and she is writing a book about her experiences.
~ Kathie

I just finished reading your e-mail and the article Jennifer wrote. I am sitting here writing and crying. I hurt so bad for her. The saving grace is that she decided to take charge of her life...and a wonderful life it is. She drips of talent. Tell her I am extremely proud of her. First, for realizing that no one has power over you unless you give it to them, and second, for the lovely and talented human being that she is. I love her.
~ Barbara

Hi Jen,

WOW, that is quite a tough story. You've been going through a long and difficult time. Yeah, you're an artist: also in writing.I hardly can find words to express my feelings. I'm very glad that you came out so strong. Thank you for sharing your story.
Take care.
Love, Els

Jennifer ...
I am at a loss for words. Yet another almost unbelievable twist to this road. Truth IS stranger than fiction. I am glad that you are putting pen to paper and telling your story. Your artistry is flowing to paper in a different way through the telling of your journey. You are amazing, and I am so fortunate to know you and call you my friend.
~ Andrea

Jennifer:
I guess you know I have only heard about your horrible experience a few days ago and was not sure what to say to you until today when Marcus said that you were talking about it and it was (my words) cathartic. Sometimes people want to go back to forgetting the whole thing, I agree it is better now to talk about it.

I do not understand what makes people so evil. I sort of can almost accept stealing a loaf of bread when you are starving, but to attack innocent people over and over is beyond horror. You must be a very strong and brave person to have come through that attack. I am glad it is over for you, thrilled that such a monster will never hurt anyone else again. Sorry it happened to such a good person. Our thoughts are with you. I am getting an even better picture of your experience. I think the book would be great. You are right it could be helpful to others. So sorry you had to go through all of that. So glad you met Marcus.
~ Enid

Whew! Very powerful! I believe in Quantum Physics—that EVERYTHING is energy. Even though you were unable to read this to him, there is no doubt that he felt the energy of your words in a cosmic way as you were putting [them] on paper. I have no doubt that he got your message and probably in a more clear way than if he were physically reading it. The universe delivers emotions in a very immediate and direct way.

What a journey this has been for you! I'm glad that it's over (as much as it is able to be over) for you. And the gift that you take away is your amazing artistry that has more depth to it than anyone could possibly know, but they sense it (feel it) in your art. How cool.
~ Shirli

Jennifer,
My heart goes out to you. What a sad end to a long saga. I hope you're okay. You will get the last word, in the form of your book. And I do believe he knew what you were going to say to him on March 8th. Just remember, he chose all of this. His end is solely on his shoulders. Either one, life in prison or an end of suicide, was a direct result of his actions all those years ago. Keep writing. That is going to be your catharsis.
Lots of love,
Sherry

21 years ago...and I thought my life was a mess at that time...I was floored when I read the "Capital" today. Your words, so true. So very deep. I am sorry you weren't allowed to tell the bastard who hurt you. Just know he is in hell right where he belongs and none of it is your fault. Never feel guilty for making him pay for his brutality! You always were a wonderful person, and have made a wonderful life for yourself! Definitely something to proud of.
((hugs)) Susan C.

Dear Jennifer,

I applaud your courage and compassion for the other victim(s). Your writing is heart-felt, penetrating, deeply revealing, and beautiful. Thank you for sharing this most painful chapter of your life with me. I empathize in ways I could never disclose.

Much love, much much love,

Beatrice

Hi Jennifer,

I just finished reading your thoughts online and I was, to say the least, deeply moved. You are not only a visual artist, but also a literary artist as well. I was so moved throughout the reading of your thoughts as of Jan 25. Your pain, your progress, and your circle of family and friends was obvious as I read your statement. For all of the comfort that has surrounded you throughout this long ordeal I am eternally grateful for you sake. I know that has helped to sustain you each step of the way.

Now look forward to spring and more creativity in your artistic pursuits and in your life.

With much affection to you and to Marcus,

~ Charlotte

My dear friend Jennifer,

What I have to say to you can only be done face to face. Text on a page cannot ever convey my abject admiration of your courage, determination, and strength. All qualities which just pile on to the many others which make our friendship one that I, what's the right word, treasure? Probably not strong enough but it will have to do for now.

The world is free of a blight, and it has you to thank.

Until I can thank you in person, I remain, most proudly, your amigo.

~ Jon

It was our honor to work on this case with you! The good guys won!!!!!!
Hooray!
Best,
Cindy

Jennifer —
What a powerful story!! It wasn't until a day or two before the trial that I found out from Art about this horrible crime committed against you. Until then, I had no idea that this was part of your life, and the personal struggles and triumphs you have faced over time.

Thank you so much for sharing this story with me. You are such an amazing, strong, focused, and determined person, and in the end, chose not to be a victim. I would like to think that I could be all of those things if faced with a horrifying and life changing event, but to be honest, I'm just not sure. You are without a doubt, a hero. And, you have probably helped spare many others the same fate you were put through.

Words cannot express how very proud I am of you, and I'm very proud to call you a close friend and to call you "family"!
Much love,
Michael

Thanks everyone! It was a terrible end to a horrible life. I count my blessings to have such supportive and loving family and friends. It was a crucial part of this whole process for me to have everyone close and to share the experience with them. I could have gone in the courtroom alone and told the jury what happened, but that wasn't enough for me. The whole process was all about celebrating life and the bonds that tie us together. That part became really clear as the days went on and the crazy connections between people became known.

It's sad to think someone can screw up so badly in life that everyone abandons him and he has no one. I have to assume the trial wasn't the only time in the defendant's life when he found himself without a friend, but it may have been the most obvious. No doubt he realized his choices in life affected more than just me — as evidenced by the number of supporters I had. Everyone there had their own reasons for seeing justice done. And, in the end, it was.

He chose his own sentence.
~ Jennifer

How ironic that the guy who raped Jennifer died in a prison on a street named Jennifer Road. Did this coincidence occur to anyone? How karmic.
~ Victoria

Case Closed

In closing this chapter of my involvement in Jennifer's life and on one of my longest-lasting investigations, I have to say the journey has been a road well worth traveling. Jennifer's case was the third oldest of the cold cases I have investigated. I am still working a rape/murder from 1973 and a murder from 1988.

Jennifer was my first survivor, and as I came to know her over the years, I was impressed with her strength and resilience. The good thing about Jennifer is that she is capable of pretty much anything. I remember telling Kathleen Rogers, "This is going to be your best witness ever," and during the trial, Jennifer proved me correct.

This case was fraught with frustrations: the poorly handled initial investigation, the lost evidence, my failure to link the three cases that I thought were connected. However, I am overly optimistic and stubborn. I never see a closed door. The grant money that allowed us to recheck the DNA from Jennifer's case was the break we needed; the time that had passed had allowed technology to catch up with the crime. The excellence of Sergeant Lykken's handling of early portions of the investigation, especially her dealings with Jennifer, and the professionalism of the New York State Police Department gave us the evidence we needed to gain our conviction. I now review every element of every case and reread every report to make sure nothing is missed. I'm sure that Jennifer was not Trice's first victim — he was too calm, too confident — and I fully expected to find more cases. So far I have not, but I continue to look.

I take every case personally. I see myself, especially in cases that also involve murder, as the last voice for the victim. Every case has a significant impact on me. The job is challenging and sometimes dangerous. The compassion I hold for the victims makes it easier to continue. It was with great satisfaction that I saw this case come to fruition. I have the watercolor Jennifer gave me hanging in my family room. Her gift was a simple gesture, but it is a constant reminder of her case and of the others that are out there. I know I can't continue forever. I wish I could. The thought that I will soon be leaving this job, and leaving cases behind, fills me with regret. These are cold cases. I'm afraid no one will pick them up. The thought that haunts me is that I am going to let these victims, these families, down.

99

March 8, 2010

$\mathcal{W}$hat a beautiful day! Crocuses are blooming and birds are nesting. The sky is a deep blue and the temperature hovers just around sixty degrees. After a winter of record-breaking snowfall, it is a true pleasure to feel spring in the air. Rejuvenating — alive!

This is the day we were to assemble in Annapolis for sentencing. It was the day I was supposed to be able to address you in court. But, you will not see this day because you chose to end your life. Although we will not be in court today, there will be a gathering; a celebration. Rather than spending time with my friends tonight rehashing the fearful tale, I have decided we will raise a glass instead to thank Dave Cordle for his determination in making good on his promise to me that, *"I'll get him."* And we will thank you for making the impossible possible. I let the assault and all of my fear, anger, and shame draw me away from my old friends, and ironically, it is because of you that we are now back together again.

You chose to end your life and take all your secrets with you. How frustrated and angry I was when I heard the news of your suicide. I wrote what I thought would be the final chapter of this book on that day after hearing the news. But, I see now how your death marked the beginning of a new chapter in my book and in my life.

Just as I took the stand in court and spoke out against what you did to me, this book speaks out against all rapists. It is your story as much as it is mine. I have no doubt that your decision to choose me as a victim was not a random act — in the grand scheme of things, it was in no way random. I had to write this story and you made it possible. It is because of your death that I am able to do this at all.

Our lives have been tangled together for twenty-two years now. I have been constantly aware of your presence as I write these words. As I have made my way through each page, I see how I let you influence so much of my life. Even though for years I hated and feared you and had nightmares about you, now I feel only sadness and pity for you. And what a waste your life appears to have been. No one but you will know what led you to make the terrible choices you made. No one but you will know how many women you terrorized. No one but you will know what your last thoughts were. You had no friends or family to support of you. You were alone.

Our lives stood in stark contrast to one another. Throughout all the years and during my time in that courtroom with you, I had my family, my friends, and my creative spirit to give me hope when I needed it. No doubt my feelings of courage, strength, and release, along with the show of support from my family and friends, was not lost on you.

Your end has given me the ability to tell a story that does not stop with you or me. My story is more than the events of that night. My story is one of hope and justice. Knowing the value of hope and learning the reward of justice may give those who read our story the tools to regroup and rebuild after a devastating spiritual trauma. Maybe somewhere in these pages I have helped another to realize it is possible to find her inner strength. Maybe she will understand by facing her own demon she can and will reclaim her spirit, her life. Eventually she will see that the monster hiding in the dark does have a face.

100

— Thoughts —

Why is a rape victim never identified by name?

In the article published in the *Capital* about this case, there was a line that really confused me:

Usually, in news stories on sexual assaults, the attacker is named, but not the victim, for obvious reasons.

I have been told that handling a sexual assault case "is complicated," and that the first concern is to "protect the victim." As a victim, I understand this. But shouldn't these positions be true for every crime? Why are only rape victims shrouded in a veil of anonymity? Anonymity by definition strips the identity; in news stories, rape victims lack individuality, distinction, or recognizability.

I believe rape is handled differently from other crimes because of the introduction of the sexual element. The sexual aspect moves this crime into the realm of social taboo, imbuing it with negative associations beyond the criminal act itself. I realize many rape victims have been brutally beaten, and are paralyzed by fear and the possibility of continued harassment and retaliation. These are very real concerns. I can understand why it makes sense not to reveal the names of these victims. In our technological world, where personal information is at everyone's fingertips, safety should be a priority and certainly has to be taken into consideration.

I can also see where the argument could be made that exposing the name of the victim could also pose problems when the case is brought to trial. The more information and misinformation released to the public, the more the crime becomes general knowledge. This has the potential to make guilt more difficult to prove or disprove because of prejudice toward either the victim or the attacker. In consideration of this concern, shouldn't the defendant's name also be shielded? And wouldn't this be true of every crime committed and every criminal trial? There has to be a way to keep victims safe while removing the stigma of shame that is attributed to victims of sexual assault crimes.

Throughout history we have secreted away the old, sick, and diseased — the unwanted, the impure. Within my lifetime, when young girls got pregnant but were not married, they were hidden away until the baby was either born or aborted. The girl would re-enter her world with a story about "visiting relatives" or "traveling" — anything but the truth. To reveal the truth to anyone outside a small circle of trusted relatives would reveal the girl's deficit of character, causing embarrassment for the family and the girl.

It seems that the practice of withholding a rape victim's identity was born during this same era. The desire to insulate the rape victim from embarrassment is understandable. But current policy must be revisited. Old practices must be revised. The stigma associated with pregnancy out of wedlock has all but disappeared. Why then do we as a society continue to isolate the rape victim in the name of sheltering her? The crime is hardly about a woman's sexual behavior. Rape is about violence.

We hear about violence in a million different ways on the daily news, but when we introduce the element of sex to the violence, it becomes taboo. Protection of a victim is important, but maybe some of what is thought of as protection actually causes unnecessary harm.

The rape victim, in many ways, feels the same isolation that we assign to people we no longer find productive or who are somehow "different." Regaining your footing and rebuilding your life after an assault is difficult enough. Toss isolation from every level in on top of that struggle and it is nearly impossible to know where to start to regroup. Nobody talks about rape. Nobody feels comfortable talking about rape. When we fail to speak freely with the victims of rape, when we are unable to feel comfortable enough to let the victims speak freely about what has happened to them, the victims' feelings of isolation are magnified.

I have experienced how awkward the discussion of rape is on every social level. An assault may physically happen to one person, but it touches everyone who is dear to that person. None of my family or friends knew how to enter into a conversation or discuss their thoughts and feelings with me. Even law enforcement officers and my own rape crisis therapist had difficulty speaking openly about my attack. Don't get me wrong, I was given advice and was treated with kindness and respect, but there was no one who felt comfortable hearing what I had to say or discussing the rape itself. I believe there is a huge amount of healing to be garnered from open discussion. Giving the victim her identity back may go a long way in helping to remove the stigma surrounding this crime.

It is true the incidence of reporting sexual assault and abuse has gone up since legal reforms have given rape victims more leverage in the courtroom. But socially, the uncomfortable mishandling of victims has not changed at all. No doubt, the awkwardness surrounding the crime has prevented many incidences from being reported. I have three friends, whom I know of, who did not report sexual abuse crimes — not because they feared their attackers, but because they did not want to be treated as outcasts by friends, family, and the public in general.

It is hard to overcome the fears an attack creates. Withholding the identity of a victim elevates the status and inflates the power of the assailant. This is exactly what the assailant wants. The act of rape is all about the attacker dominating and overpowering his victim, then stripping the victim of her dignity. The violence demonstrated by the crime is rooted in aggression and self-importance. Committing the crime is the source of enjoyment for the perpetrator. The eventual acknowledgment of the crime usually only offers a vague (and in my case, inaccurate) newspaper account of what happened. By directing all of the focus on the perpetrator and keeping the identity of the victim secret, we inadvertently extend the enjoyment of the crime for the criminal.

By shielding the victim's identity, we also imply that it's not okay to talk about the crime. We, in effect, tell the woman that she should not show her face, that she should be ashamed about what was done to her, that she shoulders some responsibility. It's no wonder women don't report being raped or run to the police if they have useful information that could lead to an arrest. The very practice of withholding information about the victim perpetuates the *"mum's-the-word"* climate. When we suppress information about the victim by withholding the name in every case, we, in effect, are also guilty of suppressing each victim. And when we suppress the victim, we extend the control of the sexual predator over his victim.

I believe that once you declare a thing with your voice, once you have set your mind to a goal and announced it to the world, you have set your plan in motion. Everything you do after this vocal declaration will lead you inexorably to your goal. When we give the victim an identity, we also give her a voice. By giving her a voice, we also give her power. The very act of empowering a person who has suffered a sexual assault removes the social isolation felt by this person.

Each sexual assault case is different. With this in mind, shouldn't each case be treated differently? Each person should be given the opportunity to direct the shame and social stigma associated with rape in the appropriate direction — toward the rapist. The misdirection of shame is a real problem. It should not be directed intentionally or unintentionally toward the victim. It is the rapist who should be made to feel shameful. I believe this can be achieved by increasing the chances of catching the criminal through the reporting of the crime, and by offering strong support and encouragement to the victim through open discussion of the crime.

After I was raped, I felt my identity had been stolen by my attacker. I did not recognize myself or anything I held dear. Everything I thought true about my world was shattered. The last thing I needed was to feel isolated. Isolation creates a feeling of blame in the victim: Did I do something to cause this attack?

I needed a strong leader, not hushed voices. I needed people to talk to me and to listen to me. I needed to trust again. By failing to speak openly, we send the message that no one should talk about this terrible crime. The victim finds the people she *needs* to talk to the most, the people who love her, are reluctant to bring up the topic. "It's too painful," they claim.

Family and friends feel awkward and unsure of how to proceed when they learn someone they love has been raped. The veil of uncertainty, isolation, anonymity, and uneasiness spreads out to include all the people who could potentially help the victim the most. The healing power that could potentially be gained through just talking to the victim about her experiences and fears is stifled.

I believed what I feared most was the violence and the threat to my life that night. I was one of the lucky ones. I was not cut or killed. I survived. But, my wounds ran deep. They were compounded by Stephen's death less than a year later. When I was at my worst, people could talk freely to me about his death. But to speak about how Trice tried to kill me and then forced me to act upon his will was taboo.

My attacker already knew where I lived; he found my name easily, and I believe he returned to the scene of the crime a couple of months later. So what was the point in withholding my name? I believe the press would have done me and the investigators a great service by telling the world this man had committed a crime against me. I believe if my name had been released, a broader range of people would have been aware of the crime. Through greater awareness, we increase the chances of catching the perpetrators. Perhaps by making the incidence of rape headline news in the daily paper instead of a poorly written and overlooked article in the "Police Beat," we could begin the process of vocalization. I, myself, was vocal about the attack right from the start. My family and friends were the first to know. Unfortunately, this is a small number when trying to find one man in thousands, perhaps millions.

I have no doubt that *he* spoke of his crimes. He probably bragged about them. I believe there was probably an exchange at some point in his life about the *date* he had with this girl. I doubt that someone who commits a crime like this likes to keep it to himself, although his telling of the story would, undoubtedly, be a much different version than what actually happened.

Someone must have heard him tell the tale. It's possible *he* remembered my name for a while and used it when he bragged about his conquests. If the newpaper had declared "Jennifer" was a victim of a crime, perhaps his listener might have realized "Jennifer" wasn't a date at all. It's a long shot, to be sure, but printing my name in the police column or on the front page might have nagged at the conscience of the recipient of the story, and maybe that person would have offered the authorities information that would have helped solve the crime. Maybe the crime would not have gone unsolved for over twenty years.

Even if printing the victim's name, when possible, doesn't lead to an arrest, it may eliminate one of the unnecessary emotional moguls a victim has to navigate during the healing process. The courts have slowly started to change how a rape victim is treated on the stand. But it is not enough. Defense attorneys may not attack a victim's sexual history, but they still have almost free rein to explore every other aspect of a victim's life in order to discredit her. The victim has been attacked once when the crime was committed, and is attacked again in the courtroom. Current defense practices seem designed to shame the victim rather than reveal any truth that would acquit the defendant. The victim's name is linked to every twisted allegation a defense attorney asserts in court, whether it has anything to do with the crime or not. Enduring this shameful practice, as well as facing their attackers in court, is more than many rape victims can endure. They remain silent.

We need to empower the women who have suffered this offense. Changes must be made to our treatment of rape cases. We must give the victim her dignity back, and strip away the veil of anonymity. By doing so, we send a message to the world that a faultless individual has been harmed, and we send a message to the perpetrators that they cannot get away with their crimes.

Take sexual assault out of the Dark Ages and give rape victims a voice. If you are a victim, I say, scream your name. Let the world hear you. You are not anonymous. Do not shroud yourself in the archaic, antiquated cloak of suppression, anger, and fear by staying quiet about what has happened to you.

Feeling shame for a crime that was not your fault should be a thing of the past. Report the crime, face the perpetrator in a court of law, and regain control of your life by taking back your spirit. Empower yourself and make the punishment of these criminals front page news.

It is only through talking about this crime that the offenders can be stopped. And by stopping them, one by one, we spread the word to our assailants that what they did to us is *not okay*. By publicly announcing that this person is a terror to women, the shame assigned to this crime moves away from the victim and toward the perpetrator where it belongs.

101

My Victim's Impact Statement

We are all responsible for our own actions. No matter what our environment growing up, no matter what our life's circumstances, there comes a time in our lives when we are considered adults and we begin to make choices and decisions for ourselves. These decisions and choices make us each unique. Through these decisions, we define ourselves. Through the repercussions and ramifications of our choices, we are remembered. Our lives are defined and we are remembered by the influence we have on others.

I am an Artist.

I recently said that I am who I am because of you and in spite of you.

I spent a few years after you raped me letting my fear of you rule my life. I was bent on self-destruction. I felt afraid and angry because of what you had done to me, and what you would do to other women if you were not stopped. Some simple words from a friend made me realize that my self-destruction was empowering you and destroying the very things that made me *me*. I made the decision to change.

Eventually, I chose to try to take back what you stole from me. I chose to live without looking over my shoulder. Although it was difficult to work through and let go of my fear, I did it the best I could. I made the decision to surround myself with supportive friends and family, and I started to focus my attention on my talents. I used my talent to re-create worlds where my fear of you did not exist.

Over the past twenty-two years, I have created a world of light, color, and texture through watercolor painting, photography, and fabric art.

I made the decision in spite of you — in spite of what you did to me — and because of you — because of what you did to me — to focus on things in life that brought light to the dark and frightening memories.

My obsession with painting, quilting, and photography is my way of keeping my life in the light, despite the fact that you made me afraid of the dark. It is through my artwork that I have been able to dispel many of the fears you had instilled in me. And, although I painted beautiful gardens, I have been told that many of my paintings give the impression that something unexpected is about to happen or has just happened. Some have gone so far as to say they are unsettling. This was not intentional, but I was not surprised to hear these remarks. I looked at my painting as a kind of therapy, a way to displace my fears. No doubt the very fear I was working through made its way into my paintings. But, little by little, they were less about you and more about me.

In spite of any good you may have done in your life, it is by the horrible choices that you will be remembered.

Because it is true that we are responsible for our actions, it is also true that we are responsible for the repercussions of our actions. It is impossible to know how many people have been affected by what you have done. The ramifications of your behavior are still echoing, and this time they have begun to rip through your family and friends. You are now making them painfully aware of the evil and dark side of your life. Everyone here today and previous days, has been affected by your actions, and who knows when or if the rippling effects will stop.

Some have taken from this the awareness that their safety may be more vulnerable than they imagined. Others have been moved to tears and angry frustration. But, none has been more affected than me. You made me brutally aware of the evil in this world and of the darkness that dwells within you and others like you. And, even though I have spent the past two decades re-creating my world through my artwork, I was given a daily reminder of you. I surmise it was a Higher Power's way of letting me know that the strength of my creative power is equal to the terror I felt that night. It won't be too long now before the rest of my hair turns completely gray and I will no longer be reminded of you every time I pass a mirror.

Somehow, that night, I knew that I would be a key player in stopping you. Unfortunately, I was unable to do this before you raped again. I told the events of that night in this courtroom in front of family, friends, counsel, judge, and jury in honor of those who were not in the courtroom with me. And I relived the nightmare for those who walked with me every step of the way so that they, too, could heal from the hurt you have caused.

It is because of me that you are here today. You probably hate me, and I wouldn't be surprised if you blamed me for your fate. But you are responsible for that. One word at a time, I gave back the evil you left with me that night and filled that space with the combined strength, love, and empowering courage given by my friends and family.

Remember, it was you who chose to stalk me and spy on me. It was your decision to climb onto my car and onto the balcony, and make your way into my house. It was your decision to hide on the stairs until you could sneak into my bedroom and attack from the shadows. It was you who decided to try and suffocate me. And it was your decision to rape me. It was also your choice to continue to terrorize other women and children. You are responsible for the choices you made. You are responsible for your actions. At any given time you could have made different choices. You could have chosen not to do any of this.

In spite of any good you may have done in your life, it is by these horrible choices you have made that you will be remembered.

I use to have nightmares of a faceless monster that pursued me in the dark.

You.

But not anymore. Although I like to have doors wide open so I know no one is hiding behind them, and I continue to turn on lights when I walk into a room and keep nightlights on around the house — that is all you get. You are no longer a larger than life monster who springs unaware from shadows. You are small, sad, and pathetic. You are a monster to be sure, but you are no longer able to terrorize.

I am an artist who will continue to invent worlds full of color and light. My life as an artist has been rewarding to myself and influential to others. I hope to continue to inspire others. I suppose, in some way, I have you to thank, because my success as an artist and the strength of my creative power are equal to the terror you made me feel that night.

I am an Artist.
That is my legacy.

You are a rapist. That is how the world will remember you.

102

An End, A Beginning

We may never come to know how all the choices we make, the things we do, the places we go, and the people we encounter each day will affect our lives. We may never realize how these choices and events connects us each to another.

Many of the events of our lives make us scratch our heads and wonder — *What was that all about?* Filled with disbelief or confusion, we may not realize that an inexplicable event, no matter how big or small, may have just provided someone else with the missing piece that will close a circle in his or her life.

For me, having the opportunity to reconnect with old friends and take a stand against the man who raped me has shown me that I am blessed. I witnessed the convergence of so many pieces of my life, and I had the opportunity to see how clearly interconnected they have been; and now, I believe, they are yet pieces of an even bigger picture.

Upon his arrest for the August 21, 1988 rape of Jennifer Wheatley, the defendant asked the detectives:

"Are there more victims?"

At that point, the detectives explained the CODIS system to him. As he stood to leave the room, the defendant said:

"Everything is now over. My life is over."

His life is over.

My life has begun again.

Acknowledgments

I would like to acknowledge Assistant State's Attorney Kathleen E. Rogers and Victim Witness Specialist Cindy Martin Haworth for their tireless pursuit of justice for all victims, and a special thanks to both for helping me through this "Made for TV" trial. Thanks to Kathie Kneff, who had the uncanny ability of finding every shortcut I tried to take in the writing of this book. It was because of her eagle eye that I went back and filled in the blanks, leaving nothing out. Special thanks to Sherry Audette Morrow for doing an excellent job of making this book a reality. I couldn't have done it without her help.

For years, I have known most of this story and have carried it with me unwritten. As I went about living, I had questions I believed could never be answered. This tale, unwritten, was like an old book that someone had torn the last few chapters from and kept hidden in a drawer undiscovered for two decades. I never expected to learn how it would end. If not for the dogged determination of Dave Cordle, the Chief Investigator for the State's Attorney's Office of Maryland, who worked my case for twenty years, this book could not have been written. He, in effect, found missing pages for me, answered many of my questions, and made it possible for me to tell this story with the ending intact. I can now turn the last page on this chapter of my life and close the book. For this, I thank him.

~ *Jennifer Wheatley-Wolf*

While pacing the halls of justice awaiting the jury's verdict, I mentioned to Jennifer that I hoped to retire one day soon and write a book about not only this case, but hopefully two others as well, which as of this writing remained unresolved. Jennifer stated she, too, wanted to write about her case, and that's where this all began.

So here we are, and now is the time I need to acknowledge *all* of the people who have contributed in so many ways to the resolution if this case.

First, Detective Sergeant Zora Lykken, who imparted so much knowledge in not only this case, but the field of criminal investigation in general in my early years.

Evidence Technician Mary Pat Whiteley, for her professional work at the crime scene.

Maryland State Police DNA Scientists Melissa Stangroom and Pam Marshall.

Detective Bill Johns of the Annapolis Police Department, my partner, who broke this case open in a matter of hours. Teamwork works!

Expert Fingerprint Technician Ernie Lowman of the Anne Arundel County Police Department, who confirmed the match of Trice's known fingerprints to those recovered at the scene.

Detective Tracy Morgan, for teaming up for the closure. A true professional, may her career go far.

Senior Investigator Dave Madden and Detective Mike Student of the New York State Police. These guys gave all, plus. This was not their case, they would close none of theirs, but at every stage of our New York State experience, these guys were there — at all hours.

The Anne Arundel County Police Lab Scientists, for their timely turnaround on Jennifer's case in relation to the county case of Tracy's.

The prosecution team of Assistant State's Attorney Kathy Rogers and Witness Advocate Cindy Haworth, for their belief in Jennifer and their zeal for the case.

Lastly, my boss, State's Attorney Frank Weathersbee, for his trust, understanding, and support since 1985 when I embarked on my first cold case investigation.

~ David H. Cordle

ABOUT THE AUTHORS

JENNIFER WHEATLEY-WOLF

Jennifer Wheatley-Wolf is an artist who loves to work in fabric, photography, and occasionally, words. No matter where life takes her, she seems to always have a camera in hand. Inspired by color, texture, and the unexpected discoveries in the world around her, Jennifer brings her vision of the world to life through her art. Jennifer and her husband, Marcus, reside in Virginia.

DAVID H. CORDLE, SR.

David H. Cordle, Sr. began his career in 1980 as the Chief Investigator for Anne Arundel County State's Attorney's Office in Annapolis, Maryland. He solved his first cold case, a homicide, in 1985. In addition to investigating cold cases, he also does domestic violence lethality assessment and danger assessment, as well as running the Witness Security Program. Mr. Cordle teaches forensics classes at the Anne Arundel Community College and lives in Annapolis, Maryland, with his wife and four children.

Index

NOTES

Made in the
USA
Middletown, DE